SAP Fiori® Certification Guide

SAP PRESS is a joint initiative of SAP and Rheinwerk Publishing. The know-how offered by SAP specialists combined with the expertise of Rheinwerk Publishing offers the reader expert books in the field. SAP PRESS features first-hand information and expert advice, and provides useful skills for professional decision-making.

SAP PRESS offers a variety of books on technical and business-related topics for the SAP user. For further information, please visit our website: *www.sap-press.com*.

Anil Bavaraju
SAP Fiori Implementation and Development (2nd Edition)
2017, 615 pages, hardcover and e-book
www.sap-press.com/4401

Goebels, Nepraunig, Seidel
SAPUI5: The Comprehensive Guide
2016, 672 pages, hardcover and e-book
www.sap-press.com/3980

Bönnen, Drees, Fischer, Heinz, Strothmann
SAP Gateway and OData (2nd Edition)
2016, 785 pages, hardcover and e-book
www.sap-press.com/3904

Gahm, Schneider, Swanepoel, Westenberger
ABAP Development for SAP HANA (2nd Edition)
2016, 641 pages, hardcover and e-book
www.sap-press.com/3973

Krishna Kishor Kammaje

SAP Fiori® Certification Guide

Development Associate Exam

Editor Will Jobst
Acquisitions Editor Hareem Shafi
Copyeditor Julie McNamee
Cover Design Graham Geary
Photo Credit Shutterstock.com/51207601/© antishock
Layout Design Vera Brauner
Production Graham Geary
Typesetting SatzPro, Krefeld (Germany)
Printed and bound in the United States of America, on paper from sustainable sources

ISBN 978-1-4932-1604-8
© 2018 by Rheinwerk Publishing, Inc., Boston (MA)
1st edition 2018

Library of Congress Cataloging-in-Publication Data
Names: Kammaje, Krishna Kishor, author.
Title: SAP Fiori certification guide : SAP certified development associate exam / Krishna Kishor Kammaje.
Description: 1st edition. | Bonn : Rheinwerk Publishing, 2018. | Includes index.
Identifiers: LCCN 2017052869 (print) | LCCN 2018000518 (ebook) | ISBN 9781493216055 (ebook) | ISBN 9781493216048 (alk. paper)
Subjects: LCSH: SAP Fiori--Examinations--Study guides. | Enterprise application integration (Computer systems)--Examinations--Study guides. | Cross-platform software development--Examinations--Study guides. | User interfaces (Computer systems)--Examinations--Study guides. | Business enterprises--Data processing--Examinations--Study guides.
Classification: LCC QA76.76.A65 (ebook) | LCC QA76.76.A65 K35 2018 (print) | DDC 005.1--dc23
LC record available at https://lccn.loc.gov/2017052869

Contents at a Glance

Dear Reader,

Practice makes perfect. This is something that developers learn early on. Developers learn from their mistakes, as every bug in your code is a teaching moment. The feeling of clean code is hard to beat, much like the feeling of acing an exam.

This certification guide, combined with a developer's lived experience with SAP Fiori, is the practice to make perfect on your upcoming certification exam. SAP PRESS has teamed up with SAP Mentor Krishna Kishor Kammaje to create the ideal resource for C_FIORDEV_20 certification exam takers. And, when you're answering the practice questions provided at the end of each chapter, use pencil. We learn from our mistakes.

What did you think about *SAP Fiori Certification Guide: Development Associate Exam*? Your comments and suggestions are the most useful tools to help us make our books the best they can be. Please feel free to contact me and share any praise or criticism you may have.

Thank you for purchasing a book from SAP PRESS!

Will Jobst
Editor, SAP PRESS

willj@rheinwerk-publishing.com
www.sap-press.com
Rheinwerk Publishing · Boston, MA

Contents

1 SAP Fiori Strategy, Standards, and Guidelines 31

2 SAP Fiori Architecture Overview 79

3   SAPUI5 Foundations   125

4   SAP Cloud Platform and SAP Web IDE Basics   185

5   OData and Advanced Data Handling   231

6   Extensibility in SAPUI5

7   Deployment

333

8   SAP Hybrid App Toolkit

363

9   Testing

Foreword

Experience is so central to our very being, to the way we see, and how we will see life as we travel through it. In the enterprise, your customers, vendors, and employees will all have some kind of experience when they use the applications you build, so I implore you to do your very best to apply everything in this excellent book to ensure the experience is thought through, well designed, and well built. You're embarking on a journey to become a developer in a technology that has such potential to create positive and effective user experiences, to free the SAP user community from the chains of confusing transaction codes that need significant training to operate, and to simplify and streamline the enterprise user experience.

The value of a great user experience is tremendous to the enterprise in the speed with which change can be implemented, new systems and processes can be rolled out, and staff can move between job functions with minimal training on the system, focusing instead on the business objectives and being guided to success by the tools and applications they use. Always remember to be guided by a consistent language, the SAP Fiori design guidelines, in how you craft your applications to ensure they can be adopted quickly and easily. A great SAP Fiori experience will be guided toward a specific business goal, a task, or an objective that should be simplified beyond the traditional transaction codes to the very essence of what the business needs to achieve.

Let's pause for a moment to think of a very specific example before and after SAP Fiori by looking to the Sales Order Fulfillment Issues app in which previously more than a dozen reports and transactions needed to be completed to get the basic information before action could be taken in following transactions. Now with SAP Fiori, the issues are summarized with a simple button to resolve them. Beautifully simple by comparison, this is a tremendous improvement in user experience that demonstrates thinking and design beyond the transaction, focusing on the desired business outcome of smoothly flowing customer sales orders. This level of simplification is likely only possible with an in-memory processing engine, so as with all your apps, think about how you too can help ask a better question and present the context and options for user decisions more effectively than the legacy spinning disk databases could allow. The responsiveness and depth of question is a key component of the user experience, and the opportunities to delight your end users with simplicity like this app are many.

This book will help you guide and provide feedback on designs, to share the art of the intended and the possible, to help reinforce the coherence of the SAP Fiori user experience, and then to craft excellent applications using the technology as it was intended. You'll be able to confidently articulate how the criticality of investing in good application user experience design and how design research and iterations of the prototype application with input from real end users is critical to success. It's a sad reality that many enterprise applications miss the mark so widely, often because of a lack of good design and lack of input from real end users. However, you'll be a certified expert to defend your applications from failure due to lack of real end-user input. Don't let your app be "that app" that no one uses; advocate for and defend good user experience design and be proud of how much more successful your applications will be when they are well designed.

You'll quickly find, if you haven't already, that the SAP Fiori user experience is much like Microsoft PowerPoint. The tool is very powerful, and the range of flexibility is immense, whereas the experience of those consuming the end product can be intuitive and easy or frustrating and unengaging. Take what you learn in this book and the associated reading to help your apps be the engaging successful apps your end users deserve, giving them a well-designed and effective experience for the type of environment and device they will need to be successful.

By helping you understand the foundations of the SAP Fiori technology stack, this book will enable you select and apply the most appropriate parts of the SAP Fiori toolkit to bring great design to life. You'll see tips to help make sure your application is upgradable, that it takes full advantage of in-memory processing capabilities, and that it aligns with the intended technical functioning of SAP Fiori apps. Extensibility, net-new custom applications, and, very importantly, testing, are covered in depth. These sections will again help make sure you avoid building "that app" that needs your attention after go live or an upgrade to make corrections or fixes. Take extra care in thinking about data modeling and the exchange of information to and from the backend OData service as this is often a departure from traditional ABAP development.

I hope you'll seize this opportunity to become more than an SAP Fiori developer; instead, become an SAP Fiori application and user experience developer, bringing more value to your enterprise than ever before.

Shaun Syvertsen
Managing partner and CEO of Convergent IS

Preface

The SAP PRESS certification series is designed to provide anyone who is preparing to take an SAP certified exam with all of the review, insight, and practice they need to pass the exam. The series is written in practical, easy-to-follow language that provides targeted content that is focused just on what you need to know to successfully take your exam.

This book is specifically written for those preparing to take the C_FIORDEV_20 – SAP Certified Development Associate – SAP Fiori Application Developer exam, so if you've purchased this book, you're obviously interested in learning how to successfully pass the certification exam. You've come to the right place.

This book will help you become an SAP Certified Development Associate – SAP Fiori Application Developer. It is your first step to propel your career by setting yourself apart from your peers. The certification exam verifies your knowledge of the fundamentals of SAP Fiori 2.0 and SAPUI5 release 1.38.

This includes knowledge obtained from attending SAP training courses in the SAP Fiori curriculum and project experience. To help prepare you to pass the exam, we'll cover the facts and applications of each topic discussed in this book.

You'll find all of the practical, real-world information you need to get a clear understanding of the topics that will be covered on the exam, insightful tips about the types of questions you'll encounter, and strategies to use to answer them correctly. The book is closely aligned with the course syllabus and the exam structure, so all of the information provided is relevant and applicable to what you need to know to prepare for the

SAP Certified Development Associate – SAP Fiori Application Developer. We explain the SAP products and features using practical examples and straightforward language, so you can prepare for the exam and improve your skills in your day-to-day work as an SAP Fiori developer.

Each book in the series has been structured and designed to highlight what you really need to know. The chapters begin with a clear list of the learning objectives for the chapter, such as this example:

What You'll Learn:

- How to prepare for the exam
- Understanding the general exam structure
- Practice questions and preparation

From there, you'll dive into the chapter and get right into the test objective coverage. So let's take a look at how the book is structured.

Structure of This Book

Let's discuss how you can use this book to prepare for the exam. This book is divided into nine chapters:

- **Chapter 1**
  This chapter begins with a discussion about the evolution of UI and the idea behind SAP Fiori. Readers will learn about the SAP Fiori Design Guidelines and the various types of SAP Fiori apps.

- **Chapter 2**
  This chapter discusses the architecture of SAP Fiori apps, the SAP Fiori Launchpad, and how to change the look and feel of SAP Fiori, based on a customer's corporate theme.

- **Chapter 3**
  This chapter introduces readers to SAPUI5 and discusses the various foundational concepts of SAPUI5 that are essential to SAP Fiori.

- **Chapter 4**
  This chapter will begin with an introduction to SAP Cloud Platform, explaining its capabilities. It then focuses on the SAP Web IDE and its uses in SAP Fiori, including for developing, extending, and packaging SAPUI5 apps.

- **Chapter 5**
  This chapter explores OData and the various data manipulation techniques that are needed for an SAP Fiori app.

- **Chapter 6**
  This chapter discusses how to extend SAPUI5 applications, which allows users to adapt standard applications to specific requirements.

- **Chapter 7**
  This chapter describes how to deploy an SAPUI5 application to various target environments.

- **Chapter 8**

  This chapter describes the SAP Hybrid App Toolkit (HAT) and how it helps mobilize SAP Fiori apps.

- **Chapter 9**

  This chapter explores unit and integration testing and discusses its benefits. Readers will create a QUnit test and an OPA5 scenario to better understand these types of testing.

Throughout the book, we have also provided elements that will help you access useful information:

- *Notes* will provide other resources to explore or special tools or services from SAP that will help you with the topic under discussion. The following boxes are examples of these elements:

> **Note**
>
> The content provided in each chapter and subtopic does not exhaustively cover everything that appears on the exam. In other words, the certification guide does not cover every exam question, but it acts as a refresher to highlight the major points for each topic. In addition, it points out areas where further review is needed.

- *Tips* call out useful information about related ideas and provide practical suggestions for how to use a particular function.

> **Tip**
>
> This book contains screenshots and diagrams to help your understanding of the many SAP Fiori concepts.

- *Warnings* will indicate possible problems, issues, or pitfalls regarding certain topic areas.

> **Warning**
>
> Remember to get a full night of sleep before your exam. Sometimes the mental clarity of eight hours of sleep is more beneficial than a sleepless night of studying.

Each chapter that covers an exam topic is organized in a similar fashion so you can become familiar with the structure and easily find the information you need. Here's an example of a typical chapter structure:

- **Introductory bullets**

  The beginning of each chapter discusses the techniques you must master to be considered proficient in the topic for the certification examination.

- **Topic introduction**

  This section provides you with a general idea of the topic at hand to frame future sections. It also includes objectives for the exam topic covered.

- **Real-world scenarios**

  This part shows a scenario that provides you with a case where these skills would be beneficial to you or your company.

- **Objectives**

  This section reviews the material the authors feel provides you with the necessary information to successfully pass this portion of the test.

- **Key concepts refresher**

  This section outlines the major concepts of the chapter. It identifies the tasks you will need to be able to perform properly to answer the questions on the certification examination.

Note

You should pay particular attention to the points raised in the Key Concept Refresher section and those from the Objectives section.

- **Main part**

  The next section of the chapter provides the objectives of this section of the test. This includes identifying major points of this topic that are discussed in the chapter.

- **Important terminology**

  Just prior to the practice examination questions, we provide a section to review important terminology. This may be followed by definitions of various terms from the chapter.

- **Practice questions**

  The chapter then provides a series of practice questions related to the topic of the chapter. The questions are structured in a similar way to the actual questions on the certification examination.

- **Practice question answers and explanations**
  Following the practice exercise are the solutions to the practice exercise questions. As part of the answer, we discuss why an answer is considered correct or incorrect.

  While some of the questions in the practice test reference actual code, you will find that in the actual certification examination there is a slightly higher number of questions related to actual code solving. However, we feel that an understanding of actual processes will allow you to identify and correctly solve these types of questions. As a consequence, we have attempted to explain processes that occur and what we consider the best way of solving issues. These techniques can be useful to you in your normal work in addition to passing the examination.

- **Take away**
  This section provides a take away or reviews the areas you should now understand. The refresher section identifies the key concepts in the chapter. We also provide some tips related to the chapter.

Note

You should be aware that the practice exercise questions are for self-evaluation purposes only and do not appear on the actual certification examination. Answering the practice exercise questions correctly is no guarantee that you will pass the certification exam.

Exam Objective

SAP Certified Development Associate – SAP Fiori Application (C_FIORDEV_20), aims to test the fundamental concept and practical skills in the area of SAP Fiori. The certification test verifies the test takers knowledge both in the UI (frontend) area as well as SAP Gateway (backend) area. It tests the theoretical knowledge as well as practical skills of the test taker in using the right methods and tools for the various challenges in performing daily tasks of an SAP Fiori developer.

This is an associate-level exam, which aims to test the foundation skills of an SAP Fiori consultant role in mind and ensures that the test taker is able to apply those skills under the supervision of an expert consultant in SAP Fiori implementation projects.

Exam Structure

To understand the structure of this certification success guide, it is important to understand the base structure of the exam. The SAP Certified Development Associate - SAP Fiori Application Developer exam consists of the following:

- Question amount: 80 questions
- Cut-off score: 61%
- Duration: 180 minutes
- Language: English

The SAP Certified Development Associate – SAP Fiori Application Developer covers the following topic areas:

- SAP Fiori strategy, standards, and guidelines
- SAPUI5 foundations
- SAP Cloud Platform and SAP Web IDE basics
- OData and Advanced Data Handling
- Extensibility in SAPUI5
- SAP Hybrid App Toolkit
- Deployment
- Testing
- SAP Fiori Architecture Overview

Likewise, this book is also broken down by these same topics to set the focus and align content for exam preparation.

Exam Scoring

Table 1 lists each certification topic and its weightage in the certification exam. There will be 80 questions in all, and you need to score at least 61% to pass and get certified. These are only approximate numbers, so the actual breakdown of questions may differ on the exam.

Topic	Percent of Exam	Approximate no. of questions	Chapter reference
SAP Fiori strategy, standards and guidelines	> 12%	12	1
SAPUI5 foundations	> 12%	12	3
SAP Cloud Platform and Web IDE basics	8%–12%	8	4
OData and Advanced Data Handling	8%–12%	8	5
Extensibility in SAPUI5	8%–12%	8	6
SAP Hybrid App Toolkit	8%–12%	8	7
Deployment	8%–12%	8	8
Testing	8%–12%	8	9
SAP Fiori architecture overview	< 8%	6	2

Table 1 Topic-wise Distribution of Exam Questions and Reference to Chapters in this Guide

Practice Questions

We want to give you some background on the test questions before you encounter the first few in the chapters. Just like the exam, each question has a basic structure:

- **Actual question**
  Read the question carefully and be sure to consider the details from the stimulus because they can impact the question.

- **Answers**
  The answers to select from depend on the question type. The following question types are possible:
  - **Multiple response**
    More than one correct answer is possible.
  - **Multiple choice**
    Only a single answer is correct.
  - **True/false**
    Only a single answer is correct. These should be minimal, especially as you experience the more advanced exams.

- **Fill in the blank**

  This type is of question is rarely found on the associate examination but is found on the professional-level exam. Although capitalization does not matter, only a limited number of answers are considered valid. You should therefore be careful with typing and spelling.

- **Sequence/ranking**

  This type of question will also have a single correct answer. The answers will provide the same options in different order, and you must select the correct sequence.

Test Preparation Resources

For test preparation, we recommend the official reference materials distributed by SAP Training. These training materials can be obtained by attending the following SAP Classroom training courses:

- UX100 – SAP Fiori Foundation
- UX402 – Developing UIs with SAPUI5
- UX410 – Developing SAP Fiori UIs
- UX412 – Mobilizing SAP Fiori Standard Apps

These official training materials can also be accessed by subscribing to SAP Learning Hub – Professional Edition and may be accessed at *https://training.sap.com/course/hub030-sap-learning-hub-professional-edition-public-cloud-version-learninghub-010-in-en/*.

There is a relevant OpenSAP course that covers the SAP Hybrid Application Toolkit, which is free: Build Your Own SAP Fiori App in the Cloud – 2016 Edition available at *https://open.sap.com/courses/fiux2*.

- SAP's easy to follow, illustrated tutorials
  Available at *https://www.sap.com/developer/tutorial-navigator.tutorials.html#tutorials*. SAP and SAP Community keep adding tutorials here. You can look for SAP Fiori related tutorials here.
- SAP Community
  https://www.sap.com/community/topic/fiori.html. You can read many community-authored SAP Fiori-related blogs here, including content from SAP and its employees.

- SAP's official help pages
  This is a great source for every topic in the certification area. SAP's help pages for SAP Fiori can be accessed here: *https://help.sap.com/viewer/p/SAP_FIORI_OVERVIEW.*

> **Tip**
> Both SAP's Classroom Training and SAP Learning Hub need you to pay for the classes or buy the subscription. Whereas OpenSAP courses, SAP Tutorials, SAP Community and SAP's official help pages are all accessible without any cost.

Test-Taking Strategies

Here is a list with some useful tips to use to prepare for the exam:

- Bulleted lists in materials are a great resource for creating questions, especially multiple selection questions, so always keep your eyes open for the bulleted lists.

- Use the assessment questions in the materials and in this book to gauge your understanding of a topic. If you don't understand something, re-read the relevant section, check the correct answer details, and if needed ask a question in an online forum or community.

- There is a lot of content to cover, give yourself the time required to study all of it. You will not be able to review all of it the night before the exam, so better invest in a good nights sleep rather than another review cycle.

- Avoid or at least do not put too much heed in answering "certification" questions outside official SAP resources. These are usually badly written and many times answered incorrectly. The education courses (and this book) give you plenty to work with.

And here is a list with some tips for during the exam:

- Answer all questions and bookmark the questions you are unsure of to revisit them; this allows you to focus in on the specific ones instead of wasting time on selections you made confidently.

- Experience has shown that your initial selection is usually better than a revised one. Be careful with going back over questions and answers too many times.

- Do not worry too much about time. In most cases, you will be able to go over the questions two or three times if you want to.

- You do not have to get it all correct. Don't stress out because you hit two or three questions in a row you are unsure of, try to rationalize and keep your cool.

- Try to read the question a couple times and try to confirm you understand the question by restating it in your own words. Then, move to the answer options and read through all of them thoroughly. Even if it is a multiple choice and you know identify the right answer, always read all answer options.

- Eliminate the answer options that don't make sense or are obviously wrong. Usually one of the wrong answers sticks out as incorrect, the fewer options, the better the chance of selecting the right one.

- In some cases, there might be answer options that are paired. This means that if the one answer is correct, then the other must be wrong. Since both can't be correct, you must select one of the two in any case.

- Questions might look similar, or might cover the same topic. Though we avoid having too many questions that have overlap, it does happen. Watch out for the differentiators in the question and answer options and treat them as new questions.

Summary

With this certification success guide, you'll learn how to approach the content and key concepts highlighted for each exam topic. In addition, you'll have the opportunity to practice with sample test questions in each chapter. After answering the practice questions, you'll be able to review the explanation of the answer, which dissects the question by explaining why the answers are correct or incorrect. The practice questions give you insight into the types of questions you can expect, what the questions look like, and how the answers can relate to the question. Understanding the composition of the questions and seeing how the questions and answers work together is just as important as understanding the content. This book gives you the tools and understanding you need to be successful. Armed with these skills, you'll be well on your way to becoming an SAP Certified Developer in SAP Fiori.

Acknowledgments

I would like to thank my dear wife Divya for her encouragement and understanding throughout writing this book. I am thankful for her and my dear son Abhi's unconditional love and faith in me, which inspires me to achieve more.

I would like to thank my parents Jayalakshmi and Shankaranarayan Bhat and my sister Poornima for their love and instilling values of discipline, perseverance, and hard-work through my childhood, which have helped me throughout my career and even in writing this book.

I would like to thank the SAP Community and many colleagues and friends who kept encouraging me throughout this period.

I would like to thank Shaun Syvertsen and Convergent IS for giving me the permission to make use of screenshots required for writing the book as well as for keeping me busy with numerous SAP Fiori projects to sharpen my SAP Fiori skills.

It has always been one of my cherished dreams to write a book. I would like to thank Will Jobst, Hareem Shafi, the editors, and the reviewers from SAP PRESS for providing this fantastic opportunity and for guiding me through this process.

Chapter 1
SAP Fiori Strategy, Standards, and Guidelines

Techniques You'll Master:

- Principles behind SAP Fiori
- Understand SAP Fiori application types and their goals
- Elements of user experience design
- Role of design thinking in user experience design
- SAP Fiori design guidelines

When you're starting a new user experience (UX) project for your SAP Fiori apps, it's important to accurately identify the current pain points and address them when you design the new UX. You also want to ensure that your apps are easy to use with a consistent experience.

In this chapter, we'll start by discussing SAP's traditional user interface (UI) strategy, its advantages and disadvantages, and the need for SAP Fiori. We'll examine the differences between various types of SAP Fiori apps and their purpose. We'll explore how Design Thinking can be used efficiently for coming up with a UX design by deep diving into the Design Thinking process. Before wrapping up with some practice questions, we'll discuss SAP Fiori design guidelines and how to use them to design consistent and coherent apps.

Objectives of This Portion of the Test

The objectives of this portion of the SAP Fiori Certification Test are to test your fundamentals regarding SAP Fiori and the UX area. The certification test expects SAP Fiori developers to be knowledgeable in the following areas:

- SAP Fiori key principles
- SAP Fiori app types
- Process of Design Thinking
- SAP Fiori design guidelines

Key Concepts Refresher

In this section, we'll explore the importance of user experience and how the need for SAP Fiori arose. We will discuss how SAP Fiori handles user experience by looking at the principles behind the design of SAP Fiori. We will also discuss about Design Services, SAP's consulting service to help customers to identify and implement SAP Fiori use cases.

Next, we will discuss Design Thinking, a methodical approach to problem solving, and how design thinking is used in user experience design. We'll also take a deep dive into SAP's cloud-based tool, SAP Build, which is used for user experience design.

While designing the UI mockups, there are unlimited options available for screen layouts, placement of UI elements like buttons, messages, forms, and so on. In this section, we will discuss SAP Fiori design guidelines, which provides a set of rules which provide an optimum and uniform user experience for end users. Also, we'll discuss important SAP Fiori design guidelines related to layouts, messages, floor plans, and so on.

Importance of User Experience

Before SAP Fiori, SAP's focus had always been on providing a user with as much functionality as possible, and the UX always took a back seat. It was common for SAP's customers to complain about the amount of training required for newly hired SAP end users to become productive. In fact, the complaint of having complex UIs with too many features is common across enterprise applications and not just specific to SAP.

In contrast, successful consumer applications focus on the user, providing a simple and intuitive UI with that delights customers and keeps them engaged. After using these consumer applications, end users of enterprise applications are expecting this UX at work as well, thus setting high expectations for the UX of enterprise applications.

Researchers have found that a great UX also has business value, and it's not only about making the user happy. Some of the direct benefits are as follows:

- Increased user involvement, resulting in increased productivity
- Simple UIs reducing training costs and making new hires productive sooner
- Improved process compliance and efficient processes, resulting in reduced audit costs
- Decreased errors during data entry, resulting in accurate reports that aid in decision-making

SAP's New User Experience Strategy

With an aim to improve the UX while considering the huge number of existing applications and the new ones that are needed, SAP developed a UX strategy called "New, Renew, and Enable" (Figure 1.1):

- **New**

  Any new business application created by SAP going forward will have a consumer-grade UX. This can be seen in the new SAP cloud applications, such as SAP Cloud for Sales and SAP Cloud for Customer, as well as analytics, procurement, and customer engagement tools.

- **Renew**

  New modern UIs will be provided for existing business apps. At TechEd 2013, SAP started this process by introducing 25 prebuilt enterprise apps, branded as SAP Fiori. Top-used employee and manager scenarios were chosen for this. At the time of writing this book, SAP had created more than 1,200 apps using the SAP Fiori design guidelines. SAP continues to develop new apps based on most-used scenarios so that these apps can be used to jumpstart customers' UI transformation projects.

- **Enable**

  Customers are provided with the required tools to adopt and build new UXs themselves. SAPUI5 application development tools, SAP Screen Personas, and SAP theme designer are a few of the tools that enable SAP customers to create the UI experiences they need. A few of these tools enable customers to create a new UI altogether, whereas some, such as SAP Screen Personas, enable customers to adapt their current UIs to make them simple and streamlined.

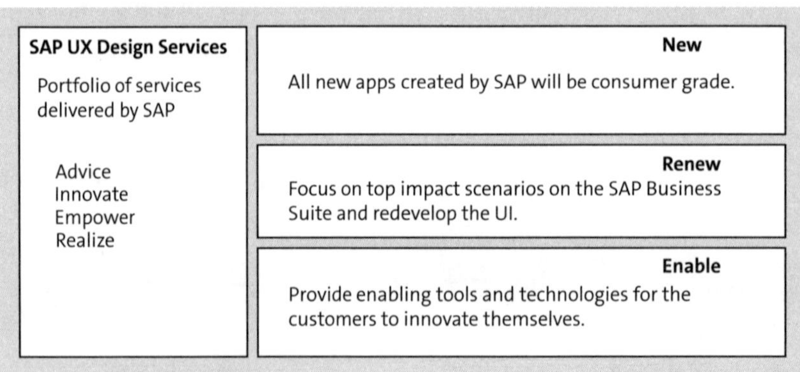

Figure 1.1 SAP UX Strategy

Let's explore different parts of this new user experience strategy in the following section.

Design Services

SAP UX Design Services is a combination of information and services, guiding customers on how to approach UX transformation projects. As part of SAP UX Design Services, customers can avail themselves of SAP services to devise an organization-specific UX strategy and set up a UX roadmap to achieve it.

SAP UX Design Services can be classified into four categories:

- **Advise**
  These services provide advice to customers regarding business value as well as technology so that customers can plan and set up their UX transformation projects.

- **Innovate**
  SAP runs Design Thinking sessions to enable business innovation. SAP can also create proof of concept apps so that customers gain confidence regarding what is possible.

- **Empower**
  These services mainly focus on providing training in the areas of UX and design, such as training on Design Thinking, SAPUI5, SAP Screen Personas, and rapid-deployment solutions.

- **Realize**
  As part of this service, SAP will execute the UX project. Some of the specific services include developing a set of SAP Fiori apps, adapting the existing SAP Fiori apps, and setting up SAP Fiori rapid-deployment solutions and SAP Screen Personas.

SAP Fiori Application Types

Current SAP Fiori apps can be classified into three types based on architecture and design. In this section, we discuss general aspects of these apps. The technical overview and architectural review of each apps are covered in Chapter 2.

The SAP Fiori app types are as follows:

- **Transactional apps**
  These apps are task based and perform business processes (Figure 1.2). They have one or more of the create, read, update, and delete operations and involve data moving bidirectionally between the app and the backend. These apps require significant development efforts compared to the other two types.

Although an SAP HANA database isn't mandatory for these apps, SAP recommends it for optimum performance.

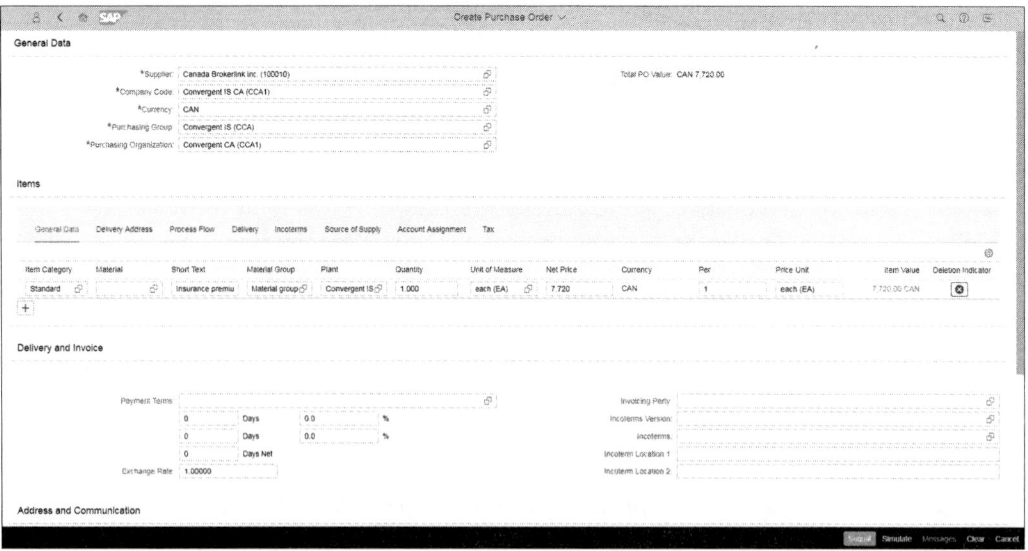

Figure 1.2 Example of a Transactional App

- **Analytical apps**
  These read-only apps typically address the use cases of number crunching, visualizing data, and predicting the future using the power of SAP HANA (Figure 1.3). By using the KPI modeler provided by SAP, you can create key performance indicator (KPI) graphs and charts without programming. In addition to graphs and charts, you also get a tabular format data display by default. Ready-to-use KPIs are also delivered by SAP. These apps require SAP HANA as the database.

- **Fact sheet apps (search and view)**
  These apps display contextual information about a business object or business transaction (Figure 1.4). These apps usually don't have a tile to launch them. Instead, they are launched either by clicking on search results or by clicking on various drilldown links available in other transactional, analytical, or fact sheet apps. Fact sheet apps also provide links to other transactional apps. For example, from a Purchase Order fact sheet app, you may navigate to a transactional app that converts the purchase requisition into a purchase order. These are read-only apps that rely on CDS views for data and annotations for UI rendering. Fact sheet apps require SAP HANA as the database.

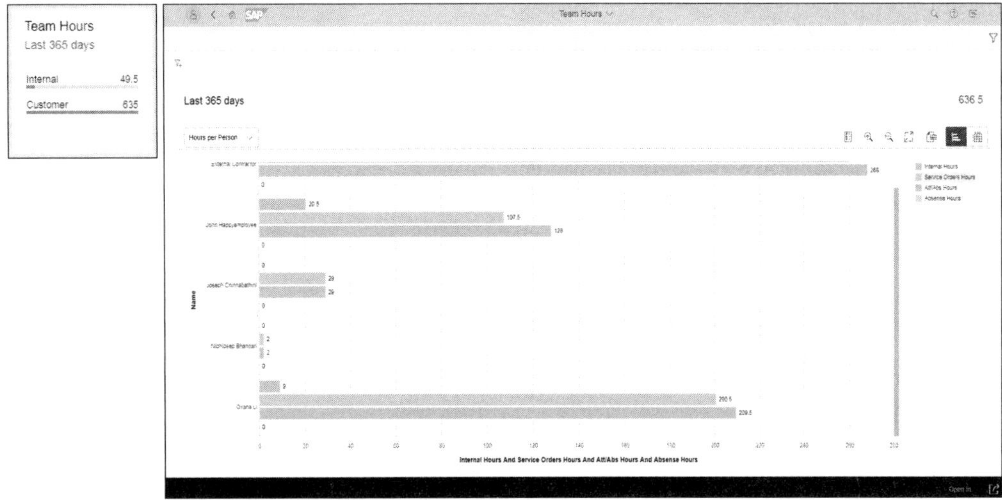

Figure 1.3 Example of a KPI Tile and KPI Chart

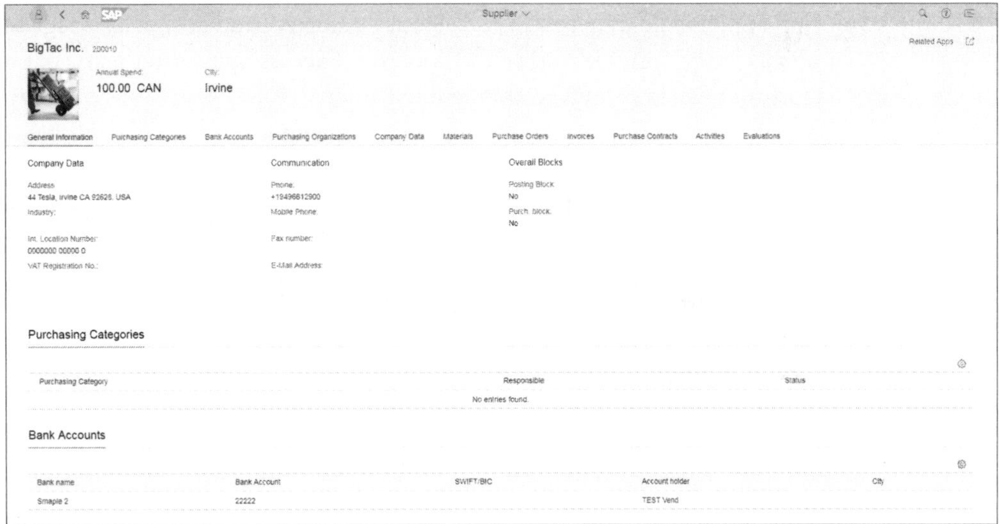

Figure 1.4 Example of a Fact Sheet App

Key Design Principles behind SAP Fiori

SAP Fiori is a big part of SAP's new UX strategy. Most of the apps that will be created in the "New" and "Renew" parts of SAP's new UX strategy will use SAP Fiori principles and technologies.

With this in mind, let's explore the key principles behind SAP Fiori:

- **Role-based apps**
  Each SAP Fiori app needs to focus only on the task of a specific user role, for example, a purchasing clerk or a sales agent. By focusing only on one role, app screens will be clutter free and allow users to focus.

- **Adaptive**
  In today's world, it's common for users to access apps from devices of various sizes. An SAP Fiori app should adapt to various screen sizes of devices, thus reducing the need to develop a new app for each device type.

- **Simple**
  SAP Fiori apps should not be cluttered with too much information or unnecessary buttons. It's common for a new user to get overwhelmed from the various options and data available on a purchase requisition screen or any other classical graphical user interface (GUI) transaction. This is an important design principle to ensure that new users can be onboarded with minimal or no training.

- **Coherent**
  SAP Fiori apps should adhere to a consistent interactive and design language so that app usage becomes intuitive and consistent across apps. After using a few SAP Fiori apps, users should be able to navigate in new SAP Fiori apps comfortably because they adhere to the same interactive language.

- **Delightful**
  Users should get a pleasant feeling working on an SAP Fiori app. The user should experience an emotional connection with the apps that goes beyond the ordinary and amazes the user. This can be done by using better visuals and animations or by offering simple but timely features.

User Experience Design

Here are the elements of UX design:

- **Visual design**
  This element not only focuses on making aesthetically pleasing screens but also on removing distractions and letting the user focus on his tasks, communicating a brand identity, consistent use of color contrasts and typography, and so on.

- **Information architecture**
  This deals with how to organize and structure the content and provide navigation structures so users can use the application efficiently.

- **Interaction Design**

  This element determines how the application behaves when user interaction occurs. It also involves how to arrange the interface components to facilitate intuitive navigation.

- **Usability**

  Usability refers to how easy your application is to use and includes learnability, memorability, efficiency, and user satisfaction.

- **Accessibility**

  This element defines whether the application is accessible to people with a wide range of hearing, vision, and mental abilities.

- **Human-computer interaction**

  This element focuses on interaction between humans and computers and ways to optimize it.

In this section, we'll explore Design Thinking as a tool for user experience design. We will also explore decomposition and recomposition as two approaches of converting existing transactions into SAP Fiori applications.

Design Thinking

Design Thinking is a methodology used to solve complex problems in various areas such as forming new strategies, validating business models, or even starting a business. End user needs and user-oriented innovation are key to the process. An ideal innovative idea is an intersection of desirability, feasibility, and viability, as shown in Figure 1.5.

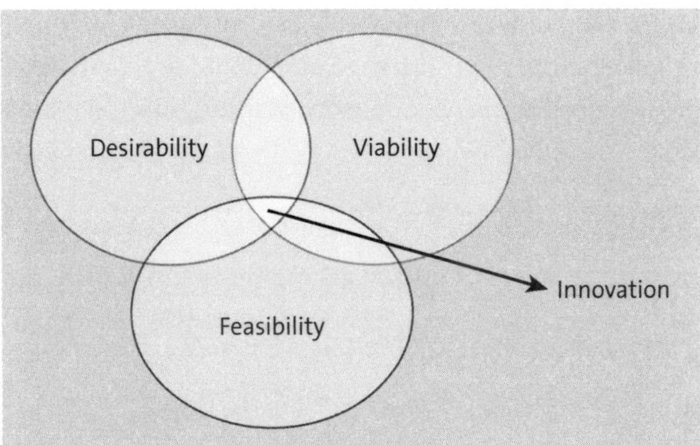

Figure 1.5 Innovation Intersection

Let's take a look at desirability, feasibility, and viability, as follows:

- **Customer desirability**
  Understanding customers' needs and desires is key here. It's important to interview and survey customers to understand problems and determine their real needs.

- **Technical feasibility**
  Even great ideas must be technically feasible. It's important to investigate whether you have the right technology and tools to realize the idea.

- **Financial viability**
  An idea must be financially viable and meet the business goals of the organization to get it realized.

A Design Thinking process may not always solve the problem. Team composure along with Design Thinking workshops play an important role in successful Design Thinking. There are three ingredients to making a successful Design Thinking exercise:

- **Multidisciplinary teams**
  Innovations are usually generated when a diverse group of people collaborate. Divergent views from multiple backgrounds can generate new ideas to solve complex problems. Such teams also need to have decision-making ability in their own areas to arrive at various design decisions.

- **Design Thinking workshop**
  A Design Thinking trained coach leads this workshop and keeps the focus and discussions constructive while driving the team through the process.

- **Creative and collaborative space**
  Design Thinking workshops require a collaborative space, unlike a traditional workspace. They need tools such as Lego bricks, cards, whiteboards, colored pens, and prototyping materials. Teams usually work standing up to create a dynamic and collaborative atmosphere.

Note

Out of desirability, feasibility, and viability, Design Thinking focuses more on desirability compared to the other areas. This focus requires the feedback of actual users, making them part of the Design Thinking workshops and increasing the up-front costs.

The Design Thinking process is an iterative process, and the tasks involved can be classified into two types (as shown in Figure 1.6):

- **Problem space**

  Steps under this category try to understand the problem or the challenge better. This category can be broken up into multiple stages:

  - Understand: At this stage, participants get introduced to the problem and attempt to understand it better. This is called a diverging step because participants are encouraged to explore all variant ideas and ask lots of questions.

  - Observe: At this phase, participants observe the problems firsthand, maybe by observing the actual users, scenarios, or business cases. Participants also might get a chance to move into actual user's shoes and get a realistic feeling for the problem.

  - Point of view: At this stage, participants sit together and articulate their understanding of the problem and various related observations. This is called a converging step because participants are agreeing on various points about the problem and documenting them.

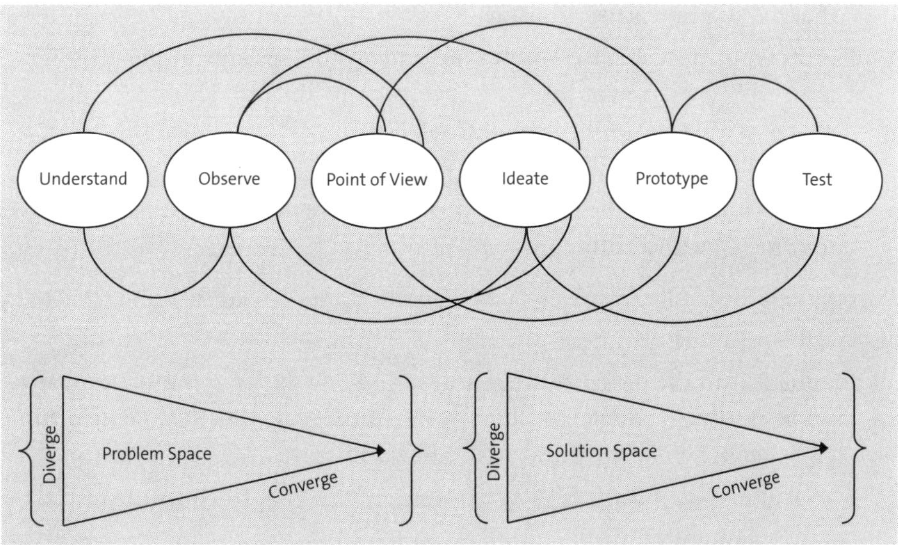

Figure 1.6 Iterative Design Thinking Processes

Throughout the problem space, participants try to identify reliable and realistic representations of the actual users of the application and document them as *personas*. Personas document real users' goals, needs, job responsibilities, and pain points in performing their roles. Creating a persona helps to keep the discussions focused around the end users and can help in making decisions as well.

It's important to validate the persona with the actual stakeholders of the application.

Tip

While designing an SAP Fiori app, it's recommended to have only one persona because SAP Fiori is role based and aims to solve the problem of only one user segment, role, or persona.

- **Solution space**
  Steps under this category aim at formulating a solution or a strategy to overcome the challenge. This category can also be broken up into multiple stages:
  - Ideate: At this stage, participants pour out different ideas to solve the problems. Particiants are encouraged to think of wild and extreme ideas (diverging phase)p. Participants also build on others' ideas to improve them. While coming up with ideas and solutions, the user must be kept in mind to ensure that the solution is user-centric.
  - Prototype: At this phase, wireframes and prototypes are developed. Interactive prototypes can increase user involvement and provide an accurate indication of what the product would look like.
  - Test: At this stage, prototypes and wireframes are sent to actual users for feedback. Based on the feedback, you may move to any of the previous tasks to come up with a better product.

Throughout the Design Thinking process, participants can go back and revisit any tasks if needed.

Although tasks in the problem space are started first, tasks in the solution space can also be started in parallel and iteratively. In addition, these are flexible, iterative steps that don't need to be taken in a linear fashion.

In this chapter, you'll learn how to use Design Thinking to come up with a UX design for a new SAP Fiori app.

Decomposition and Recomposition

Current SAP transactions (e.g., Transactions IW31 and ME21) were designed from a utility perspective which aims to provide more functionality to the user. Multiple options are available to achieve the same functionality, which often confuses new users rather than empowering them. Various functionalities are hidden in buttons and deep menus that are complex for users to discover.

At the same time, some SAP transactions only partially correspond to an actual business transactions, forcing users to navigate through multiple SAP transactions to perform a single business transaction. SAP Fiori aims to solve these anomalies.

An SAP Fiori application might end up breaking down the functionality of one big, complex, SAP transaction into multiple Fiori apps. This approach is called *decomposition*. Another approach is to create an SAP Fiori application which performs a complete business transaction by combining the functionality of multiple SAP transactions, called *recomposition*.

While solving the previously-mentioned issues, an SAP Fiori application might end up breaking down the functionality of one big, complex, SAP Transaction into multiple SAP Fiori apps in an approach called *decomposition*. Another approach is to create an SAP Fiori application that performs a complete business transaction by combining the functionality of multiple SAP Transactions, called *recomposition*.

- **Recomposition**

  While designing an SAP Fiori app, the system is rarely a consideration; rather, the user is at the center point. As we saw in the Design Thinking of UX design, the process starts with the discovery phase, where end-user feedback is given the utmost priority. Using an SAP Fiori app, you can build functionality by combining the capability of multiple GUI transactions. This increases user productivity significantly by reducing the navigation that users need to go through and simplifying screen interactions. This recomposition process is shown in Figure 1.7.

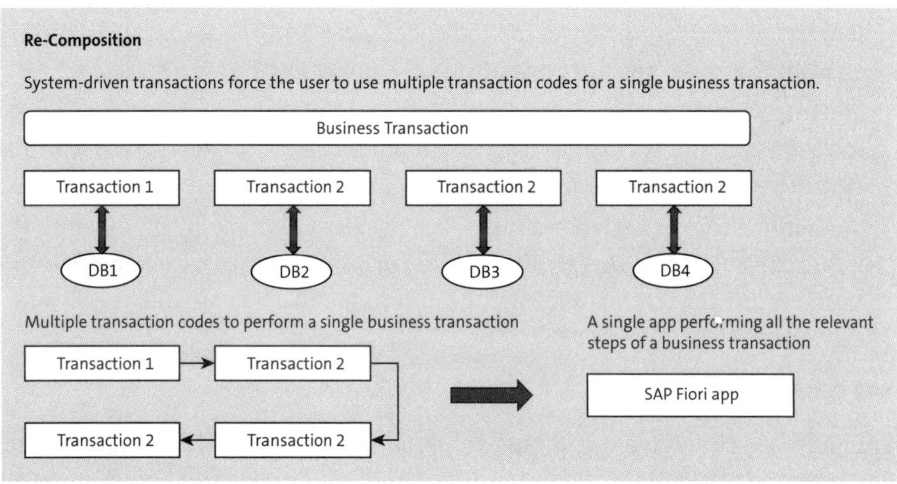

Figure 1.7 Recomposition

- **Decomposition**

  A generic transaction code used by multiple roles can be broken into multiple apps for each role, which is called the decomposition process (see Figure 1.8).

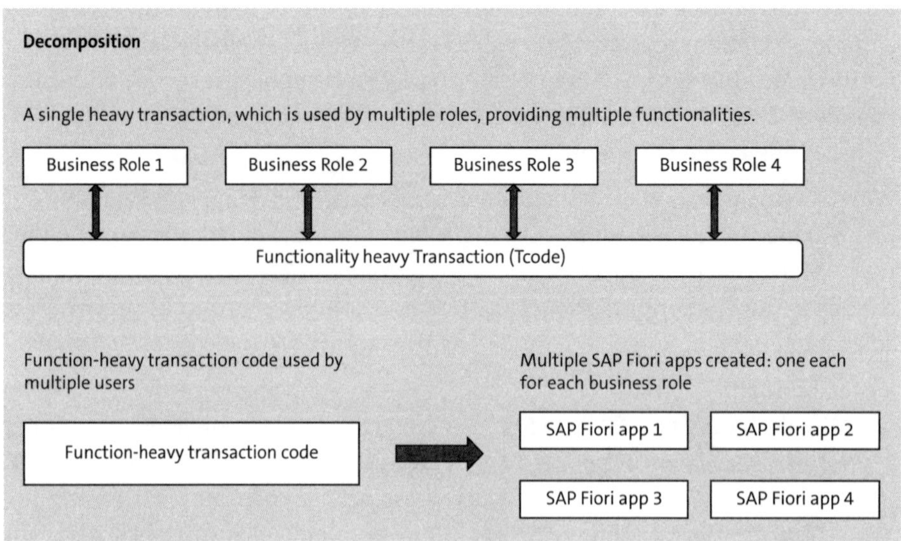

Figure 1.8 Decomposition

Most transactions in SAP have too many buttons and menu options that provide a lot of functionality not directly related to the business transaction at hand. Transaction screens aren't specific to a role; that is, many users with different roles use the same transaction code. Some buttons are set up to display an error if the user clicking the button isn't authorized based on his role.

Too many functions and options are confusing and make it difficult for users to focus on the task. This complexity is a hindrance that creates a steep learning curve for new users to become productive.

SAP Fiori is role based, so it aims to keep the apps simple by giving only the required screen elements for the user to perform his tasks based on the user's business and needs, thus allowing the user to maintain focus and be efficient.

SAP Build

SAP Build is a cloud-based tool built for designing and prototyping your custom SAP Fiori apps. With SAP Build, you can easily collect feedback on your prototypes from multiple stakeholders and build better designs by collaborating with other team members. You can also speed up the design process by using example prototypes as templates.

Tip

Developers can generate code from SAP Build prototypes and use it as a starting point for application development.

Note

SAP Build provides a free trial, which allows you to create a limited number of active projects.

Let's explore features of SAP Build by building a simple prototype.

Inviting a Team

Inviting a team to the project is the first step because you'll be collaborating with other users during the entire design process. This team can be your fellow designers, end users, and any other key stakeholders in the application. The team can build the design with you by collaborating and providing feedback on the persona and prototype.

To invite members, click on **INVITE TEAM** from within the SAP Build project and then enter email addresses for the prospective team members as shown in Figure 1.9.

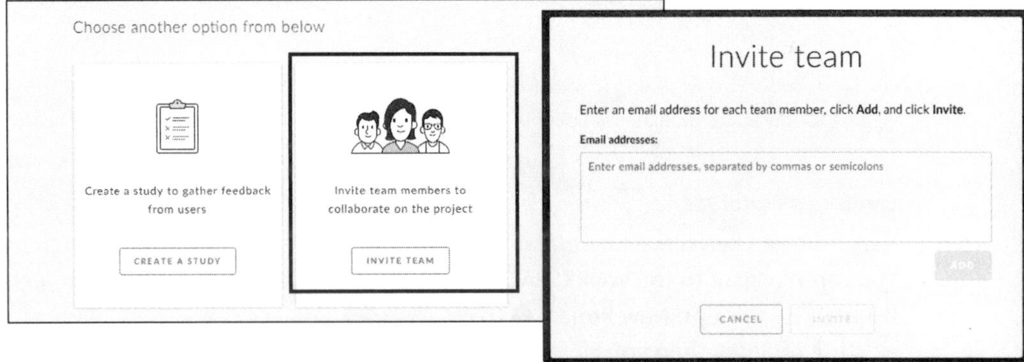

Figure 1.9 Inviting Team Members to the SAP Build Project

Creating a Persona

One of the important outcomes of the problem space is having a persona. SAP Build helps document a persona by providing a template. The persona is part of the SAP Build project, and having it along with the prototype can reinforce persona's goals, pain points, and needs while reviewing the prototype. Figure 1.10 shows a persona template within SAP Build.

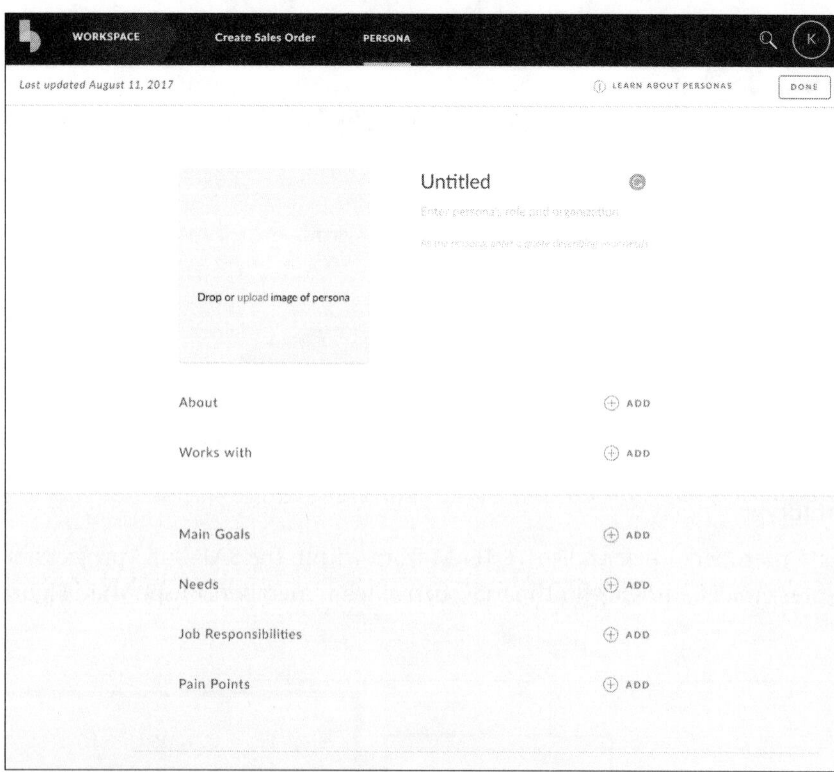

Figure 1.10 SAP Build Template for Documenting a Persona

Creating a Prototype

SAP Build can be accessed at *https://www.build.me*. After you sign up and sign in, you can navigate to the **WORKSPACE** tab ❶, which will list your existing projects (Figure 1.11). Click on **New Project** ❷ to create a new project. If you don't have any existing projects, then you click on the **Create New Project** button to create a new project.

You can start with a freestyle project from scratch or use any of the predefined templates from the gallery (Figure 1.12). After selecting a template from the gallery, click on **Clone** under the template to get the template copied and a new project created.

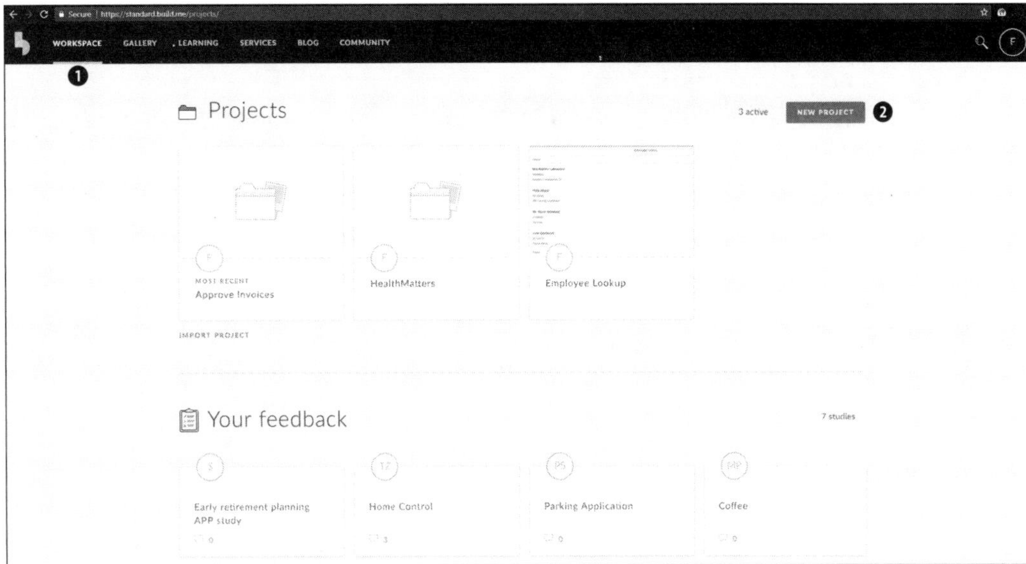

Figure 1.11 List of Existing Projects and Option to Create a New Project

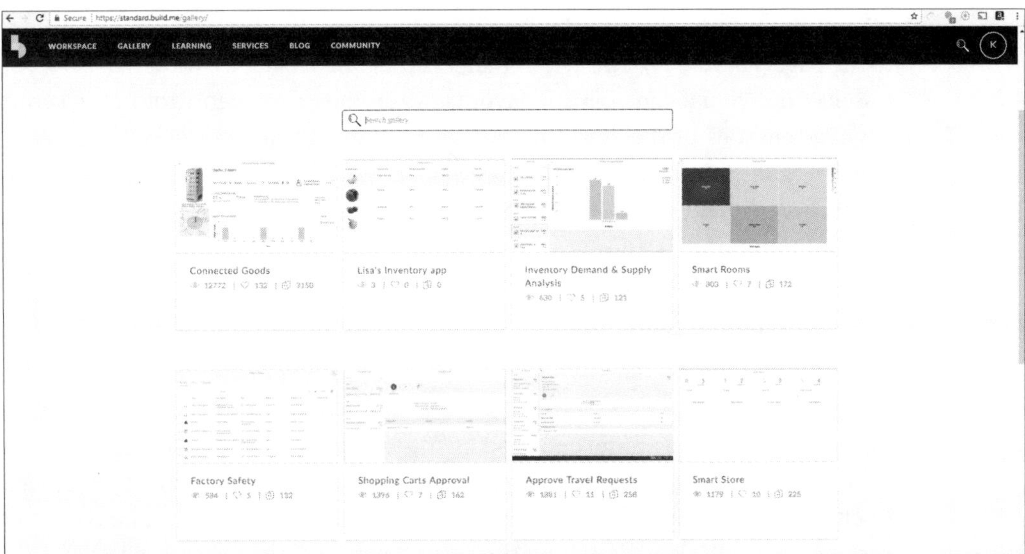

Figure 1.12 Few of the Available Templates in the Gallery

In this example, the **Create Sales Order** template is selected as shown in Figure 1.13. Click on **GO TO PAGE MAP** to see all the pages that are part of the prototype. As you see in Figure 1.13, there are five pages in the prototype and an option to add a page by pressing the plus icon in the top left menu. You can also click on any page to focus on that page and modify the page manually.

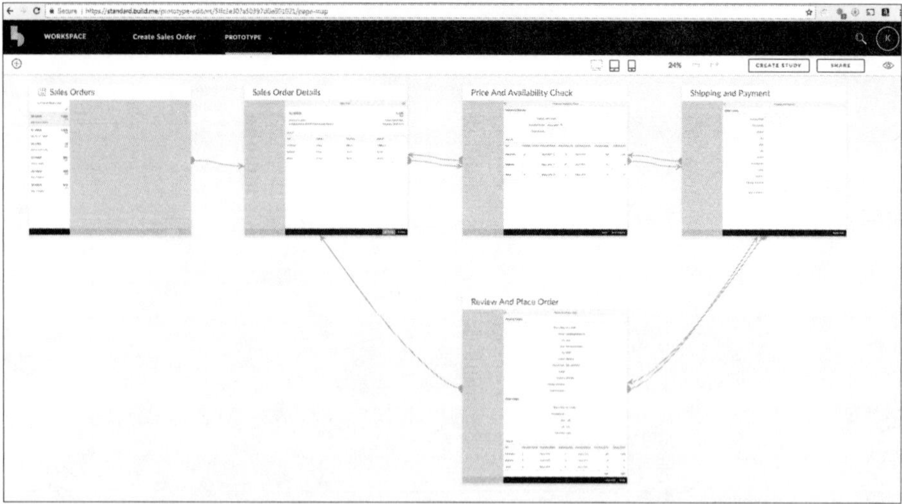

Figure 1.13 Page Map of the Create Sales Order Template

When you open the page, the left panel contains a list of controls that you can add to the page (Figure 1.14). The center panel shows one view at a time and allows you to select individual controls and layouts. After you select a control in the center panel, properties of the selected control or layout are available in the leftmost pane and can be edited. The **DISCUSSION** tab is available to record your comments as well as for collaboration scenarios.

You can see that the prototype shows some data records in the master and detail pages. These are dummy records that can be maintained by the user. SAP Build allows you to maintain your own data set or edit the dummy data that came with the template. To edit the data, click on the **DATA** tab on the first panel and then click on **Data Editor**.

Now you see the data model expected by the template. As shown in Figure 1.15, the data model contains a **SalesOrders** object that is connected to other objects **LineItems**, **ItemsAvailabiltiy**, and **OrderDetails**. This data model can be edited by clicking on the **RELATIONS** tab on the second panel to add and remove relations. You can also specify the cardinality of the relationships here.

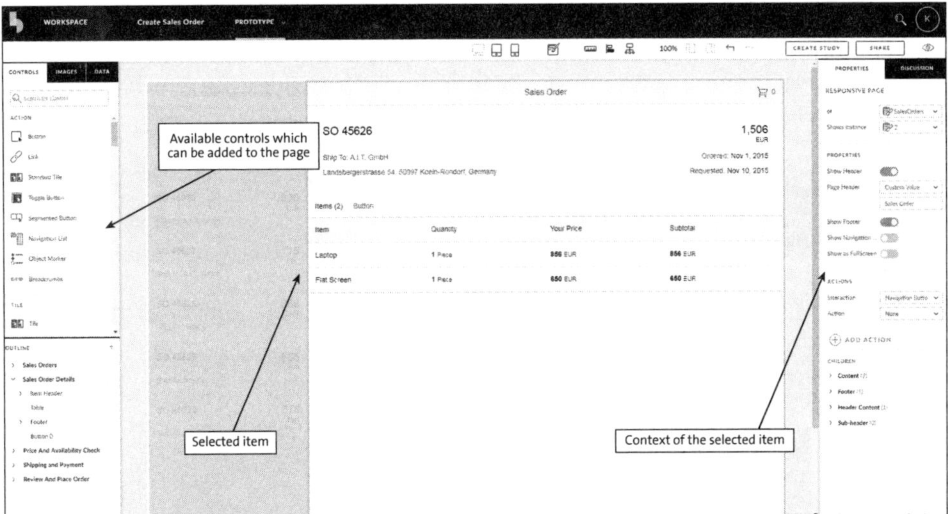

Figure 1.14 Editing a Page

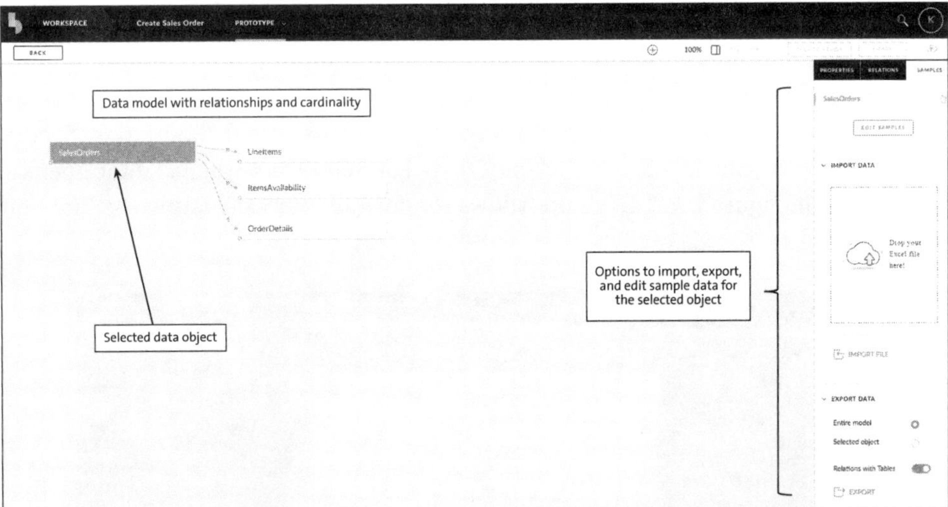

Figure 1.15 Data Model and Options to Edit Sample Data

You can maintain data for each of the model objects by selecting the object and then clicking on **SAMPLES** on the second pane. As you see in Figure 1.15, there are options to import the data from an Excel file, and you can export the current sample data into an Excel file to edit and import it again.

You can also manually edit the sample data by clicking on **Edit Samples**. As shown in Figure 1.16, you can edit each cell by clicking on it and entering a new value. Some of the columns will be calculated fields, such as **SubTotal**, which is indicated by an icon on the column header. You can't edit those cells.

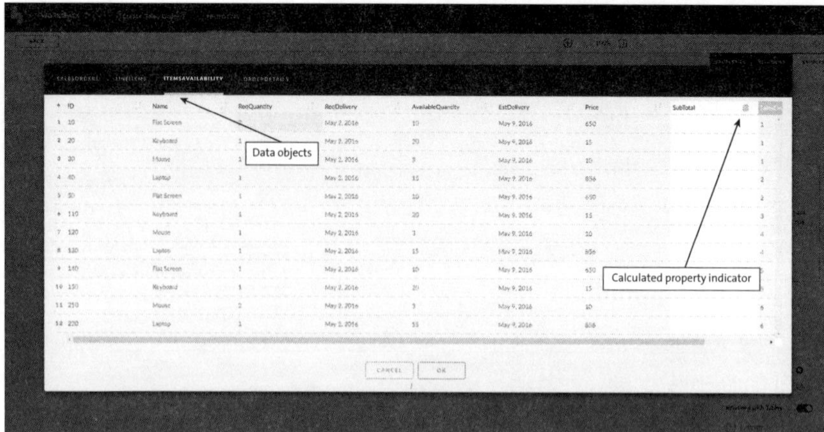

Figure 1.16 Options to Edit Data

You can maintain formulas for calculated properties by selecting the **PROPERTIES** tab on the second panel of the **Data Editor** screen. Next you choose the property that is to be calculated and click on **Create Formula**. The **Formula Editor** opens as shown in Figure 1.17. This figure shows the formula for calculating the line item **Total**.

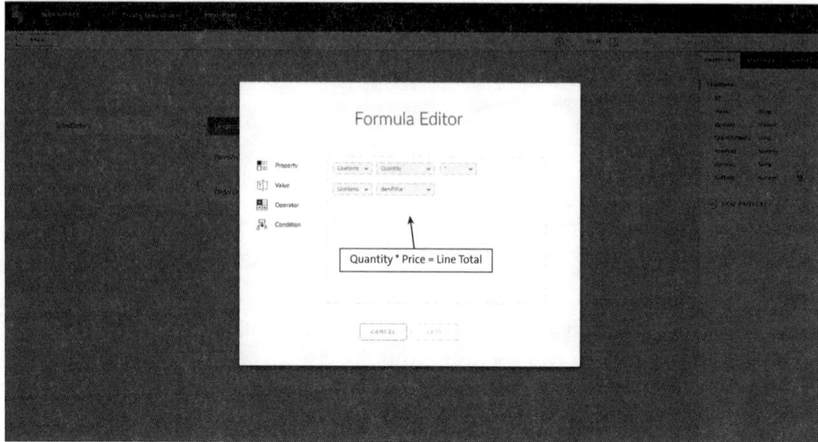

Figure 1.17 Formula Editor Showing Formula for Line Item Total

You can create complex calculations to include If-Else conditions, arithmetic, and logical operations as well.

Creating a Study

As you create the prototype, you can ask for user feedback whenever you think it's ready. To get the user feedback, you need to create a study within SAP Build. Study lets you select your prototype (or any images) and lets you ask questions and receive feedback from the users.

Figure 1.18 shows the following steps that are involved in creating a study:

1. Click **CREATE NEW STUDY** ❶.
2. Enter a **NAME** and **DESCRIPTION** for the study and click on **Create Study** ❷.
3. Choose the prototype for which you want to give feedback and then click **SELECT** ❸.

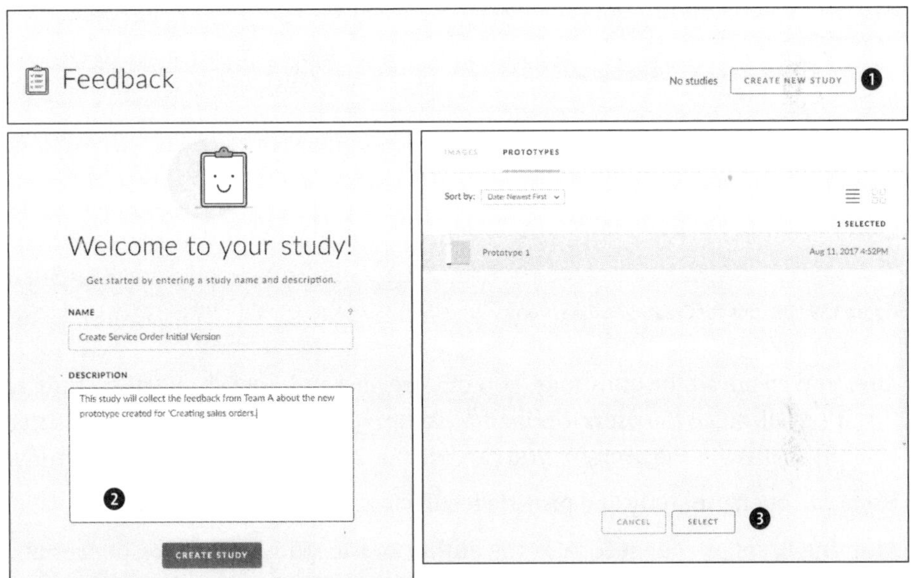

Figure 1.18 Steps to Create a New Study

To get feedback from users, you can create multiple questions. Responses from users can be in any of the following forms:

- **Annotations**
  Users can annotate on the prototype to indicate their feedback.

- **Text**

  Users can enter free text as feedback.

- **Multiple choices**

  You can provide predefined answers and let users choose one of them.

- **Perform action**

  You can ask users to start at a view of the prototype, click through the process, and end at another view.

You can also specify the device display format that users will see while providing feedback. Figure 1.19 shows the options for editing a question.

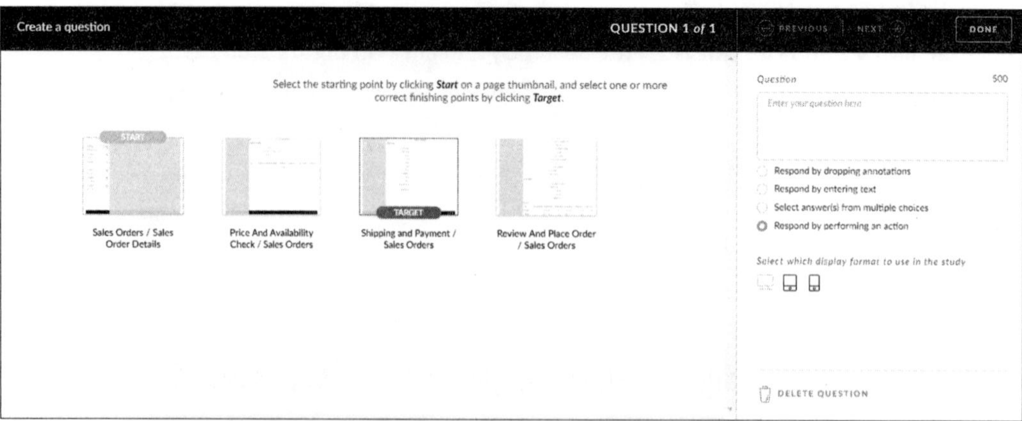

Figure 1.19 Options for Creating a Question

After you create all the questions, you can preview and publish the user study so that it's available to the users. Upon publishing, you'll be provided with a URL that you can share with the users, or you can add participants from a published study.

Users can open the study and provide feedback as shown in Figure 1.20.

After the users provide feedback, the author of the study can see responses and analytics regarding responses. In the **OVERVIEW** section, the author can see the number of participants, number of answers, number of comments, reactions by users, and time invested by users for providing the feedback. In the **QUESTIONS** section, the summary of responses to each question of the study is shown. Each response to the question can be seen by clicking on the question. In the **PARTICI-PANTS** section, the name of each participant is shown unless the user preferred to give his responses anonymously while providing the feedback. In the **SETTINGS** section, you have options to deactivate, archive, and delete the study.

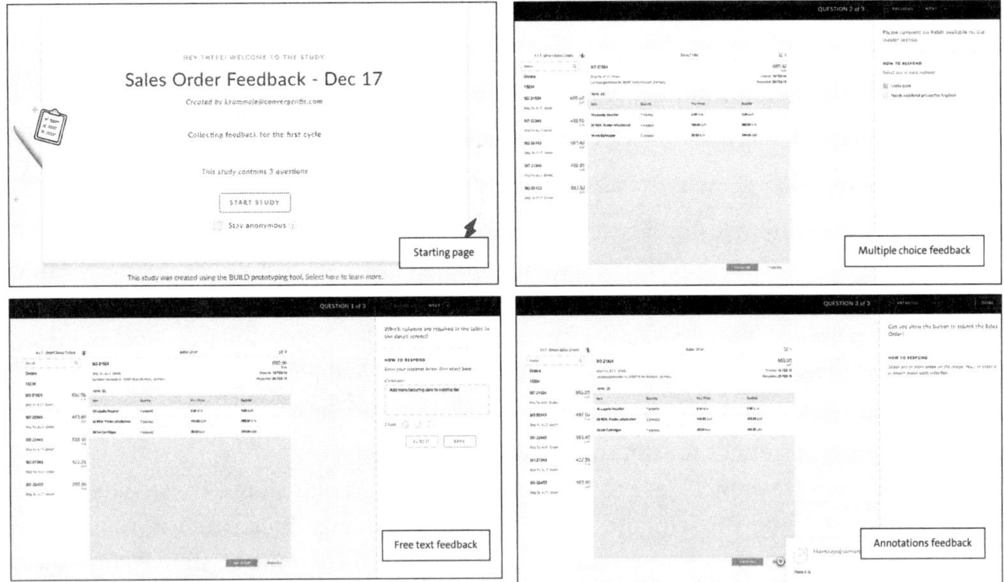

Figure 1.20 Feedback by Users

Figure 1.21 shows the author's view of the feedback received.

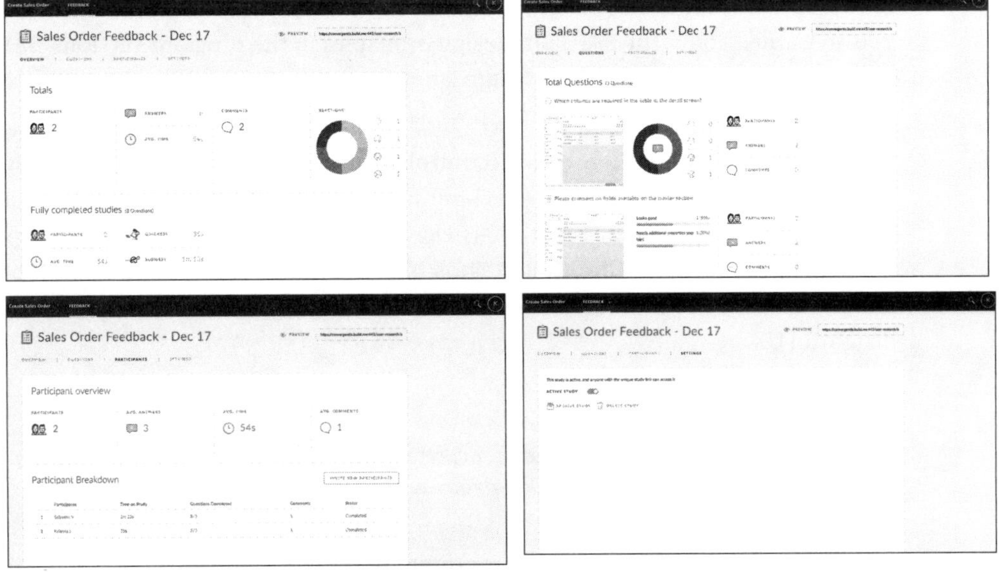

Figure 1.21 Author's View of Received Feedback

SAP Fiori Stencils

Design stencils allow you to quickly design wireframes for your application. Wireframes and prototypes built with these stencils aren't as elaborative as those built with SAP Build, but they can meet the need for quick prototypes.

SAP provides stencils in two flavors:

- **Design stencils for Axure RP**
  Axure RP is a powerful tool for building interactive prototypes. Axure provides its own UI elements to build the prototype. However, if you want the prototype to have an SAP Fiori flavor, then you need to load the stencils provided by SAP into the Axure tool and use the UI elements provided by SAP to build your prototype.

- **Design stencils for Microsoft PowerPoint**
  These are draft slides provided by SAP as PowerPoint slides. These slides can be edited, and UI elements can be moved to achieve the desired mock-ups. SAP provides only a limited number of controls and layouts as stencils for PowerPoint. Mock-ups created with these stencils don't represent the SAP Fiori visual design exactly.

SAP Fiori Design Guidelines

You've learned about the SAP Fiori design principles in the previous sections. SAP Fiori design guidelines act as the design language of SAP Fiori and guide the developer on how to create an SAP Fiori app while adhering to the design principles.

SAPUI5 provides more than 100 UI controls and layouts for building SAP Fiori apps. Although the SAP Fiori design is built-in to this library, there can be multiple designs to achieve the same functional behavior. By following the SAP Fiori design guidelines, apps built by multiple teams of SAP Fiori developers can still look coherent, behave similarly, follow a consistent design pattern, and provide a delightful UX.

Tip
The SAP Fiori design guidelines for creating a web application can be accessed at *https://experience.sap.com/fiori-design-web/*.

In this section, we'll discuss several important design guidelines.

Message Handling

This section discusses the best way to show various messages in the following categories to users in an SAP Fiori app:

- Error
- Warning
- Information
- Success
- Confirmation

Messages can be shown in multiple ways using different controls in an SAPUI5 application, as follows:

- **Message popover**
  The message popover control (`sap.m.MessagePopover`) is the most preferred way of showing messages upon validating a form. It can automatically show server-side messages by linking to a message manager. Message popover is usually triggered by a button on the page's footer (Figure 1.22).

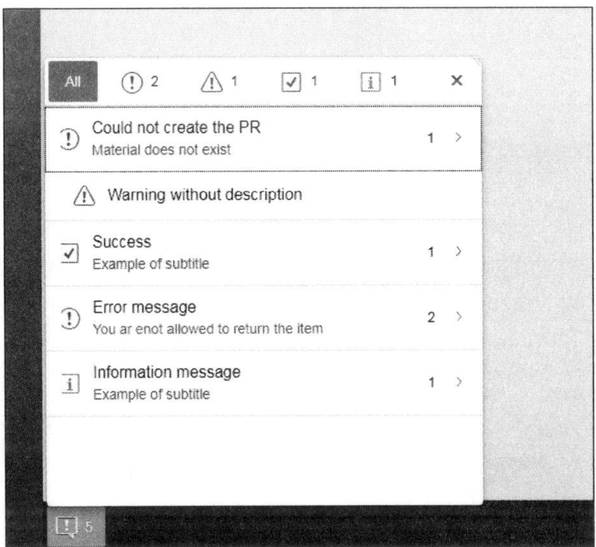

Figure 1.22 Message Popover Showing Messages in a Page

- **Message box**
  When there are errors that aren't directly related to a form field, such as a generic error or a technical error, then a message box (`sap.m.MessageBox`) can be

used (Figure 1.23). It interrupts the user in his action, and the user should explicitly acknowledge the error/information/warning message before continuing.

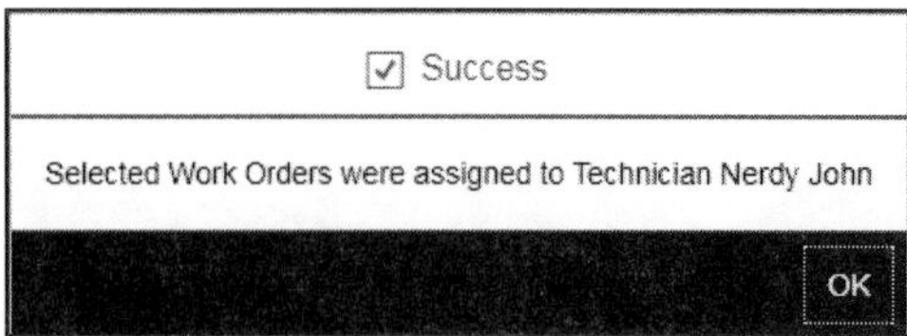

Figure 1.23 Message Box

Another use case for a message box is for confirmation messages (Figure 1.24). Whenever a user performs an important action that must be confirmed by the user before performing the actual action, then a message box can be used. It can also capture additional information such as comments or rejection reason.

Figure 1.24 Confirmation Dialog

Often more information is available for which there may not be enough real estate to show in its entirety. In such a case, a **Show Details** link can be used to show more information (Figure 1.25).

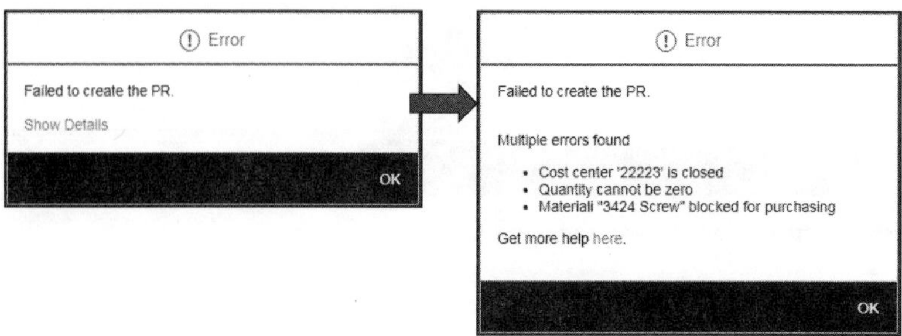

Figure 1.25 Additional Details in a Message Box

- **Message strip**

  A message strip (`sap.m.MessageStrip`) can be used to show object-related information (e.g., for a material) in a detail page (Figure 1.26). The message strip should be placed in the detail area of the object rather than the object header. A message strip can be closed by the user.

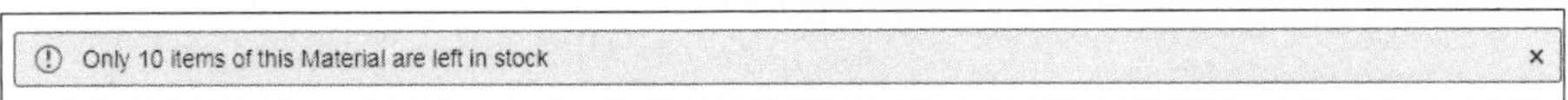

Figure 1.26 A Message Strip Showing a Warning Message

- **Message toast**

  Message toast (`sap.m.MessageToast`) can be used to show a short success message (Figure 1.27). Because it disappears automatically after a specified time, the message toast is nondisruptive and doesn't require explicit action by the user to close the popup.

Figure 1.27 Message Toast

- **Message page**

  When a user navigates to a nonexisting page (by an earlier bookmarked page or a by an unexpected navigation), or if there is nothing to show in the app (due to filtering or search), then a message page can be shown indicating that there is nothing to show (Figure 1.28). You can use control `sap.m.MessagePage` to create such a page.

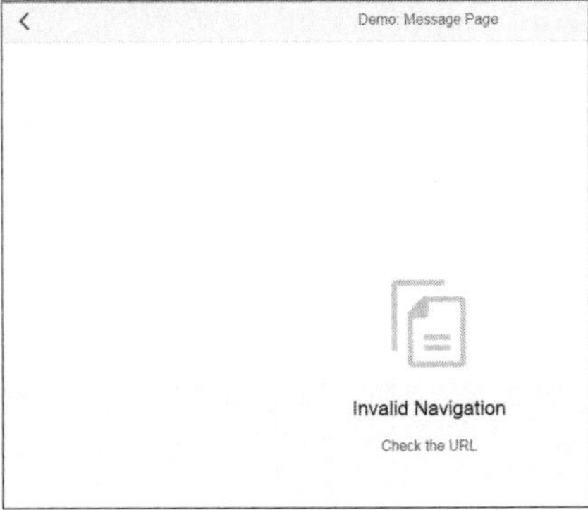

Figure 1.28 Message Page

SAP Fiori Elements

SAP Fiori elements provide a framework for creating a UI without writing the frontend code by interpreting the annotations supplied with the service data. An *annotation* is additional piece of information which describes how to interpret the various information returned by the service. SAP Fiori elements modify their behaviors automatically by understanding the supplied UI Annotations. Some examples include:

- Deciding which action buttons to be shown on a page
- Deciding which are editable fields in a table
- Deciding default displayed columns in a table

SAP Fiori elements fulfill the following objectives:

- Design consistency
- Auto update of the apps per the latest design guidelines
- Minimal or no frontend coding

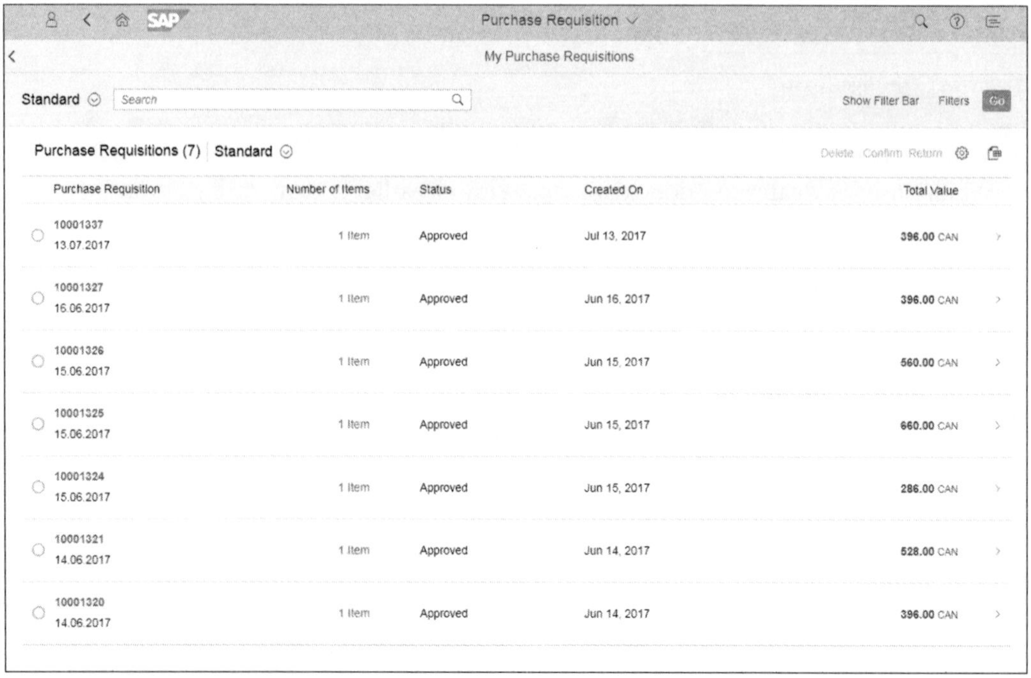

Figure 1.29 SAP Fiori Elements Using a List Report Floorplan

The following floorplans are currently able to be generated from backend annotations:

- List report
- Object page
- Overview page

Figure 1.29 shows an example of an SAP Fiori elements list page, where the number of columns, default displayed columns, column position, and column header are determined by the OData annotations. All SAP Fiori elements using list report floorplans look like the one shown here, that is, with a **Search** field, ability to have variants, a snapping filter bar, and options for the list.

Layouts

SAP Fiori apps are made up of pages, and each page uses an SAPUI5 layout control to organize data within itself. Let's discuss each page, as follows:

- **Dynamic page**
  Dynamic page layout (`sap.f.DynamicPage`) is a layout control introduced with SAPUI5 version 1.42. This layout contains a title, header part with dynamic behavior, content area, and optional footer bar (Figure 1.30). This is a responsive layout, but responsiveness can depend on the content shown in the content area of the layout.

  The header content of the dynamic page layout can be snapped, and its footer can be hidden if not required. Dynamic page layout can be used with various floorplans, and the content of the header and content area of the layout depend on the chosen floorplan.

  You should not use dynamic page layout if you're using SAP Fiori elements because SAP Fiori elements already incorporate dynamic page layout.

- **Full screen**
  Full screen layout is designed to make full use of the screen's width. It can be used to display a wide variety of content, especially tables with a large number of columns, charts, and graphs.

  Full screen layout contains an app header that can contain back navigation, a title, and an action. The content part of the layout is a long scrollable section that is open for freestyle design. A footer can also be added based on the requirement.

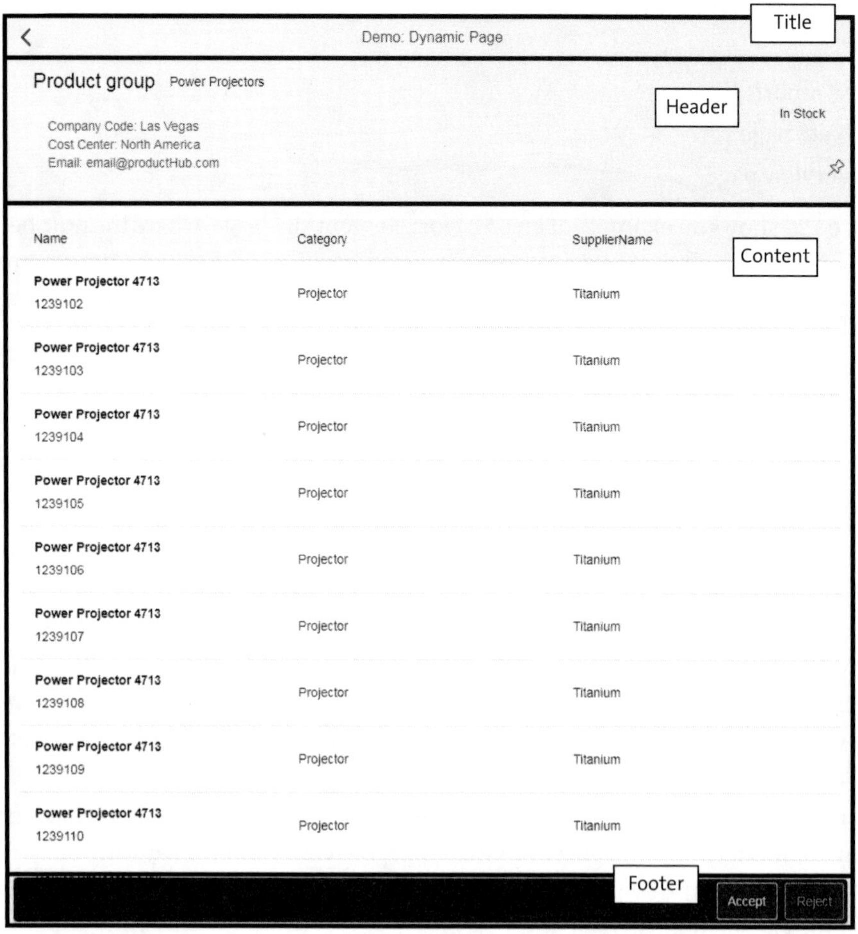

Figure 1.30 Dynamic Page Layout

Warning

Full screen layout is deprecated per SAPUI5 1.44, and dynamic page layout is its successor.

- **Flexible column**

  Flexible column layout can position the content in up to three columns (Figure 1.31). Each of these columns can grow wider when the user focuses on it. Each of these columns can use different floorplans for information display. The third column can be displayed full screen if the user chooses to.

This layout was designed to depict a master-detail scenario (two column) or a master-detail-detail scenario. The way these columns behave in a tablet or a smartphone is on the assumption that it's used in a master-detail-detail scenario.

On a tablet, only two columns are shown at a time. Options are to show the first and second columns, second and third columns, or third column alone.

On a smartphone, only one column is shown at a time.

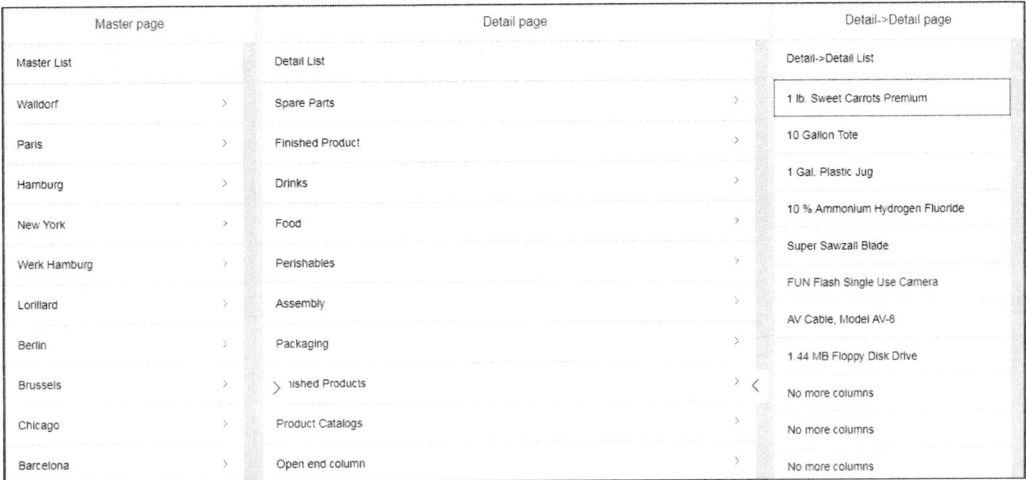

Figure 1.31 Flexible Column Layout with Three Columns

Tip

If you want a dashboard layout or to show additional information to the main content, use the dynamic side content (`sap.ui.layout.DynamicSideContent`) control.

- **Split-screen**

  This is a very popular layout designed to show a master-detail scenario. It provides a two-column layout. On the left, there is a master list of items the user wants to process. Upon selecting an item from the master list, more information about this item is displayed in the second column, called the detail area (Figure 1.32). The detail area can have multiple floorplans to show the required information. Both master and detail areas have separate header and footer areas.

Items on the master list can be configured to allow selecting multiple items or a single item. This layout supports a hierarchical master list (master-master-detail pattern).

Master list can contain options to filter, sort, and group items. If the app supports creating a new instance of a master list item, then an icon can be placed here to trigger the process.

On narrow-width devices, only one of the areas is shown at a time, and users can navigate between them.

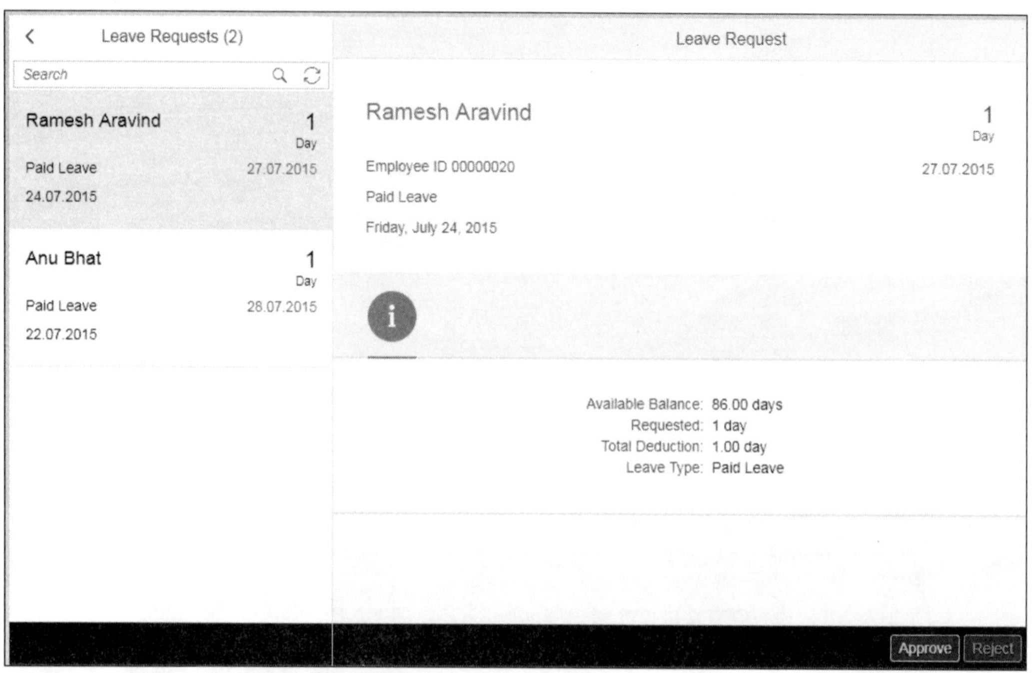

Figure 1.32 Split-Screen Layout Showing Master and Details Screens

- **Dynamic side content**

  You use the dynamic side content layout to show additional content related to a business object or a transaction, which can be shown or hidden on demand and flexibly adapts to different device sizes. The additional content can be a set of filters for a list, a chat on the main content, or settings for charts and graphs. The side content can be shown on the left, right, top, or bottom of the main content. In Figure 1.33, dynamic content is on the right, which can be closed as well.

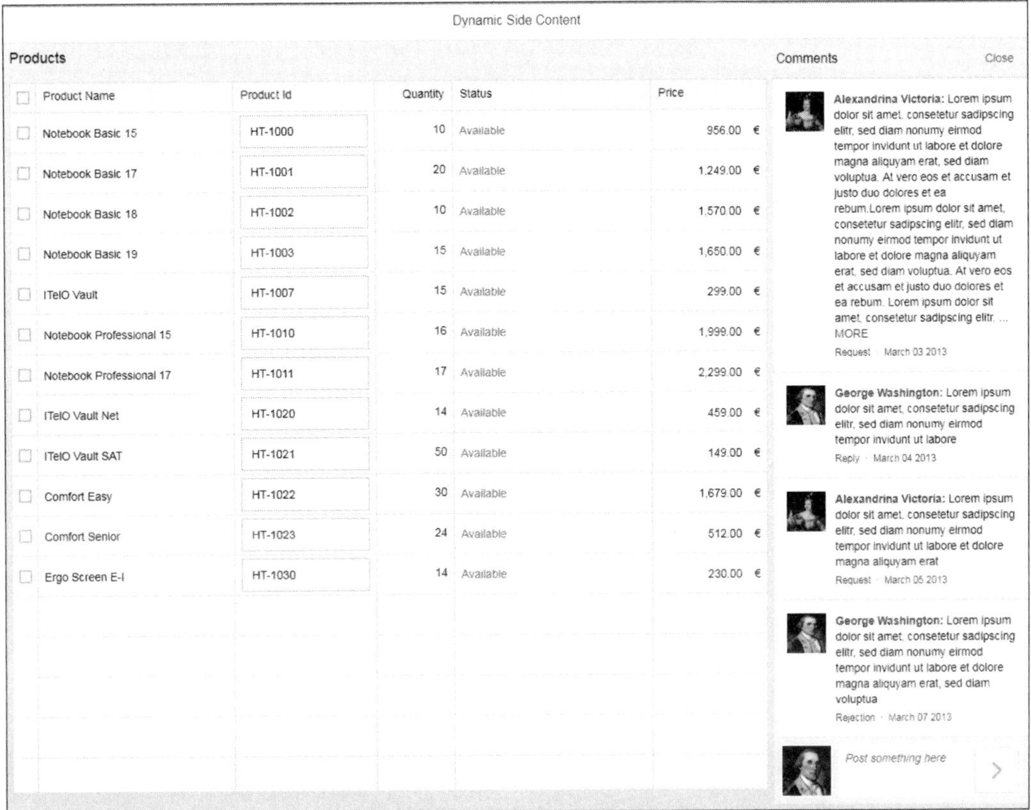

Figure 1.33 Dynamic Side Content Layout

Floorplans

We discussed multiple page layouts in the previous section. These page layouts can be used with multiple floorplans. The following are several important floorplans:

- **Create/edit page**
  The create page floorplan is used when a new business object needs to be created in a full screen layout or split-screen layout (Figure 1.34). The edit page floorplan use cases also use the same floorplan because the requirements for screen real estate and screen interactions are similar.

  The floorplan contains a header title, indicating the type of object being created (e.g., "New Purchase Requisition"). The main content of the floorplan is one of the SAPUI5 forms, namely form (`sap.ui.layout.form.Form`), simple form (`sap.ui.layout.form.SimpleForm`) or smart form (`sap.ui.comp.smartform.SmartForm`). The create floorplan usually has a footer containing buttons to perform actions such as **Save** and **Cancel**.

Responsiveness (the ability to adjust to smaller screen sizes) of the create floorplan depends on the controls used in the main content of the page.

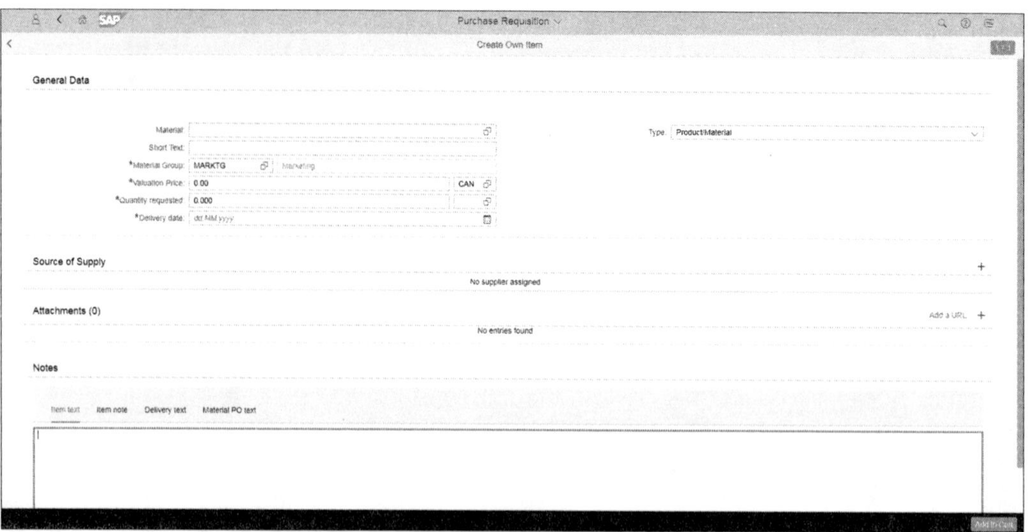

Figure 1.34 A Create Page Floorplan Used in the Create PR App

- **List report**

  List report shows large numbers business object or business transaction instances as rows and lets the user click on these instances to view the details (Figure 1.35). Fields are provided to filter the records, and options are provided to sort and group the records.

  List report is shown in a full screen layout (now deprecated) or in a dynamic page layout.

  For creating a list, any of SAPUI5 controls, such as grid table, analytical table, responsive table, tree table, and smart table, can be used. Responsiveness of the list report depends on which control was chosen for the report.

- **Object page**

  The object page floorplan is a popular floorplan that is recommended for display, create, and edit scenarios. Object Page comes with a flexible header and the main content page, which can be navigated via tab or anchor (Figure 1.36).

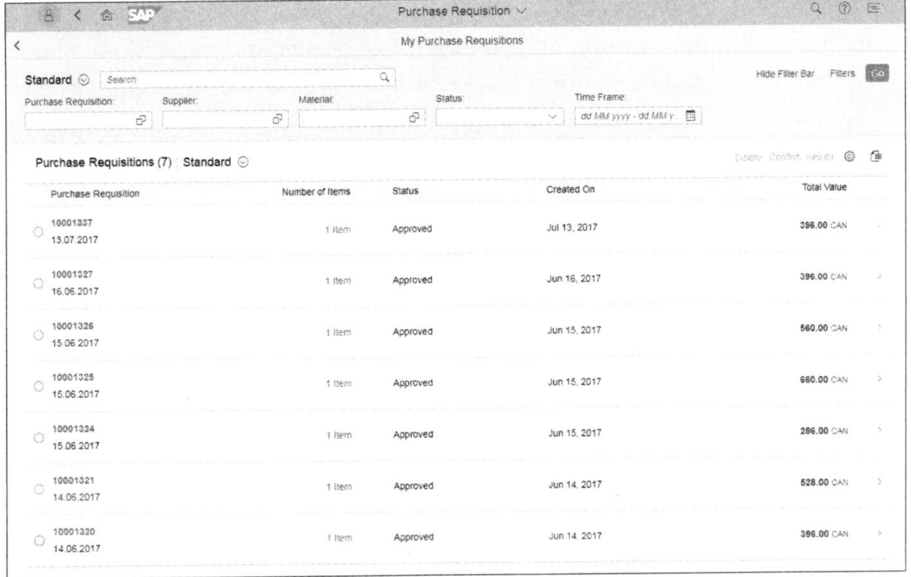

Figure 1.35 A List Report Floorplan

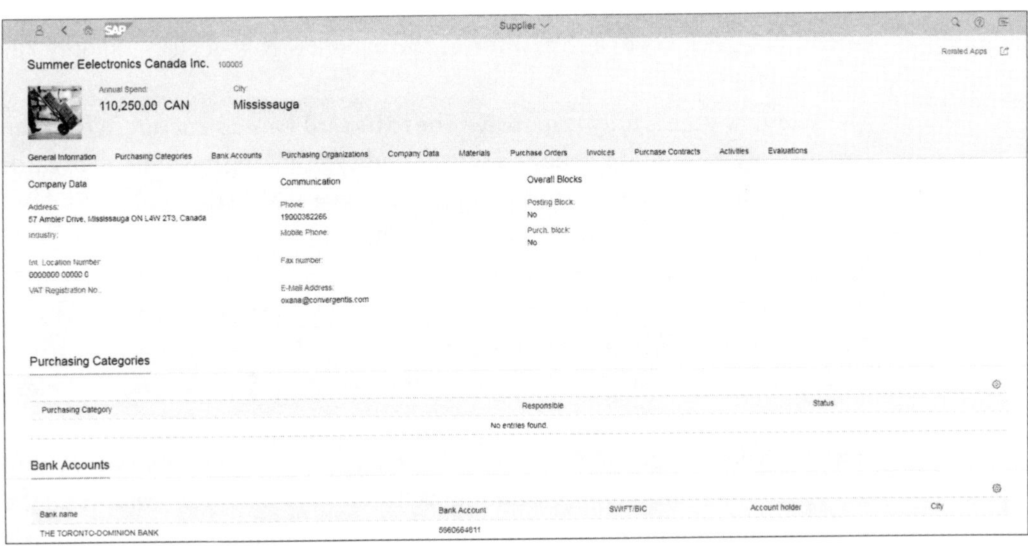

Figure 1.36 Object Page Showing Vendor Details

The object page layout can be realized either using SAP Fiori elements or using individual SAPUI5 controls. Due to its flexible header and navigation-enabled content, object page is responsive and can be used across all three device types.

Dynamic page layout is recommended for showing an object page floorplan.

- **Overview page**

  The overview page floorplan, as the name suggests, gives various information related to a specific role of a user. Its main use case is to enable the user to focus on important tasks while allowing the user to view and take required actions quickly.

  An overview page is made up of multiple cards, where each card represents a group of information. The content of each card can be a chart, list, table, or any other control and can be chosen according to the type of data and user preferences. The overview page supports providing filters in the header content. Selecting a filter will immediately filter out data in all the relevant cards within the overview page.

  Clicking on an overview page card navigates to other SAP Fiori apps just like clicking on a tile in SAP Fiori launchpad. The key difference between an SAP Fiori launchpad and an overview page is that SAP Fiori launchpad contains tiles to perform all the tasks of a role, whereas the overview page focuses on only key tasks of a role.

  The overview page is fully responsive due to its card-based structure. A card can comfortably scale inside a phone's screen, and by adjusting the number of cards shown on different devices, responsiveness can be achieved.

- **Wizard**

  A wizard can be used for both creating and editing business objects (Figure 1.37). Wizards guide users through a complex data entry process, focusing on one step at a time. Wizards move to the next step only after completing the current step. A wizard can have a minimum of three steps and a maximum of eight steps.

  A wizard has two types of screens. A *walkthrough screen* represents a step within a wizard and usually has one view for each step. A *summary screen* lists all the data entered in the walkthrough screens into a display-only page. It acts as a review page the user can read before deciding to click **Save** or **Submit**.

  The wizard's tile stays the same throughout its various steps. The wizard's floorplan has a header part, which shows the various steps involved and highlights the current step the user is in.

Wizards use the dynamic page layout. The header part can't be minimized unlike other dynamic page layouts because the header of a wizard is a crucial part of the wizard.

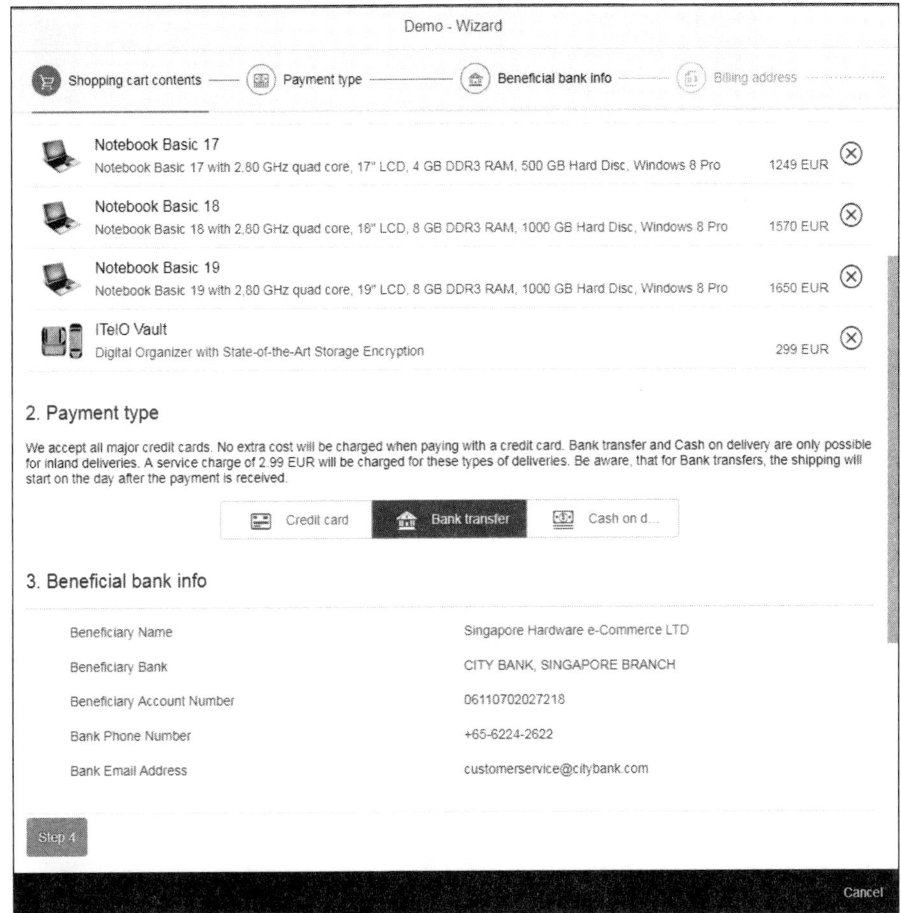

Figure 1.37 Wizard Floorplan

- **Worklist**

  Worklist, as the name suggests, is a floorplan where the user sees a list of items waiting for action (Figure 1.38). The focus in this layout is on processing the list items. In a list report floorplan, the focus is on filtering and listing the items.

  This floorplan usually uses the full screen layout. If the list is very simple, you can use a split-screen layout as well. You can also use the dynamic page layout if you need variant settings, which can be accommodated in the header section.

Products (14)				Search
Product Name	Supplier	Price	Units Ordered	Units in Stock
Alice Mutton	Exotic Liquids	75.00 EUR	20 PC	90 PC >
Aniseed Syrup	Grandma Kelly's Homestead	3.00 EUR	6 PC	100 PC >
Carnarvon Tigers	Grandma Kelly's Homestead	56.00 EUR	40 PC	36 PC >
Chai	New Orleans Cajun Delights	8.00 EUR	10 PC	39 PC >
Chang	New Orleans Cajun Delights	6.00 EUR	7 PC	0 PC >
Chef Anton's Cajun Seasoning	Grandma Kelly's Homestead	108.00 EUR	9 PC	0 PC >
Chef Anton's Gumbo Mix	Forêts d'érables	18.00 EUR	0 PC	21 PC >
Grandma's Boysenberry Spread	Plutzer Lebensmittelgroßmärkte AG	18.00 EUR	25 PC	25 PC >
Ikura	Forêts d'érables	13.00 EUR	10 PC	4 PC >
Mishi Kobe Niku	Plutzer Lebensmittelgroßmärkte AG	130.00 EUR	0 PC	40 PC >
Northwoods Cranberry Sauce	Lyngbysild	35.00 EUR	32 PC	4 PC >
Schwarzwälder Kirschtorte	Grandma Kelly's Homestead	19.00 EUR	3 PC	2 PC >
Teatime Chocolate Biscuits	Exotic Liquids	7.00 EUR	40 PC	0 PC >
Uncle Bob's Organic Dried Pears	Lyngbysild	35.00 EUR	7 PC	29 PC >

Figure 1.38 A Worklist Floorplan with an Option to Navigate to Details

Draft Handling and Lock Concept

A draft document is an intermediate version of a business object or a transaction that isn't yet active in the system. Usually, drafts are automatically saved as the user makes changes without the user needing to perform the save action.

In SAP Fiori, drafts are used for fulfilling the following objectives:

- Allow the user to stop working on an object anytime and continue later.
- Prevent data loss if the application or the network terminates unexpectedly.
- Lock the document; that is, stop users from simultaneously editing the same business document.

When a user starts editing a document, a draft indicator appears when the document is getting saved (Figure 1.39).

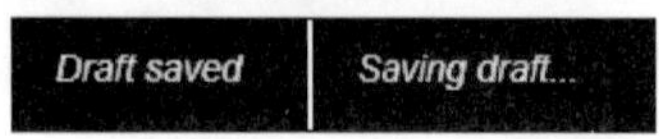

Figure 1.39 Draft Indicator Messages

Usually, business applications want only one user to have edit access to a single business object or a transaction at any time (the lock concept). Handling such a requirement in a stateful application (e.g., ABAP module pool) can be easier, but it can be complex in SAP Fiori apps because they use HTTP, which is a stateless protocol. SAP Fiori design guidelines use the draft concept to achieve this objective.

To stop users from editing simultaneously, only one draft is allowed for a business object instance at any time. The moment a user makes a change, the change is saved as a draft. Unless the user merges his draft in to the original document (thus discarding the draft), or an explicit lock expires, no other user will be able to open the document in the edit sate nor create a draft for the same business object.

Important Terminology

The following important terminology was covered in this chapter:

- **Design Thinking**
  Design Thinking is a process used by designers to solve various design problems. It focuses on innovative solutions that are desirable by users, technically feasible, and economically viable.

- **SAP Build**
  This cloud-based tool can be used to build interactive, responsive prototypes and get and analyze user feedback. It can also generate startup code from the prototype to jump-start the development.

- **Persona**
  This is a reliable and realistic representation of a user who is going to use the application that you are designing. Documenting a persona allows you to refer to it throughout the UX design process to remain focused on the end user.

- **Prototype**
  A prototype is an early model of an application that is used to represent the UI elements, page layout, and user interactions. Prototypes provide end users and other stakeholders with a feel of how the finished product (application) will work and an opportunity to give their feedback to improve the design.

- **SAP Fiori design stencils**
  These ready-to-use tools can be used to build a prototype quickly. SAP provides stencils based on Axure as well as PowerPoint.

- **SAP Fiori design guidelines**
  This set of guidelines from SAP focuses on how to use the page layouts, floorplans, and various SAPUI5 controls in designing and building an SAP Fiori app.

- **SAP Fiori launchpad**
  SAP Fiori launchpad is the entry point to all the SAP Fiori apps on all devices.
- **Fiori Elements**
  This framework allows you to generate the application's UI from the OData service's metadata annotations. The main goals here is to speed up the UI coding while standardizing the UI screens.

Practice Questions

These practice questions will help you evaluate your understanding of the topics covered in this chapter. The questions shown are similar in nature to those found on the certification examination. Although none of these questions will be found on the exam itself, they will allow you to review your knowledge of the subject. Select the correct answers, and then check the completeness of your answers in the "Practice Question Answers and Explanations" section. Remember, on the exam, you must select *all* correct answers and *only* correct answers to receive credit for the question.

1. Which of the following attributes can't be associated with SAP Build?

   ☐   A. Cloud-based tool

   ☐   B. Used to build complete responsive prototypes

   ☐   C. Enables writing JavaScript code for data binding in advanced mode

   ☐   D. Generates SAPUI5 starter code for the finalized prototype

2. This floorplan can be used to guide the user through the data entry process, one step at a time.

   ☐   A. Overview page

   ☐   B. Object page

   ☐   C. Worklist

   ☐   D. Wizard

3. Which control is recommended to show multiple messages from the server on a form?

□   A. `sap.m.Dialog`

□   B. `sap.m.MessageStrip`

□   C. `sap.m.MessageBox`

□   D. `sap.m.MessagePopover`

4. In SAP Build, you need to create the following object for getting feedback on the prototype from users.

□   A. Feedback

□   B. Study

□   C. Team

□   D. Dialog

5. Which of the following is *not* an objective of the draft feature within SAP Fiori.

□   A. Enable the lock feature.

□   B. Allow the user to continue data entry at a later point in time.

□   C. Prevent loss of data due to network failure.

□   D. Allow data review by peers.

6. Which application type provides information about a business object or a transaction?

□   A. Transaction apps

□   B. Analytical apps

□   C. Fact sheet apps

7. The process of combining the functionality of multiple GUI transactions into one SAP Fiori app is called decomposition.

□   A. True

□   B. False

8. An overview page is made up of

☐ A. Tiles

☐ B. Cards

☐ C. Charts

☐ D. Tables

9. SAP-provided SAP Fiori apps represent which part of SAP's UX strategy?

☐ A. New

☐ B. Renew

☐ C. Enable

☐ D. Empower

10. Which of these services are *not* part of SAP UX Design Services?

☐ A. Design Thinking workshops

☐ B. Advice on technologies

☐ C. Train the developers on Design Thinking

☐ D. Train the end users on the application

11. Which of these key design principle talks about having a single UI language?

☐ A. Simple

☐ B. Coherent

☐ C. Adaptive

☐ D. Delightful

12. Which apps are usually opened from search results or by clicking drilldown links within other SAP Fiori apps?

☐ A. Fact sheet apps

☐ B. Analytical apps

☐ C. KPI apps

☐ D. Transactional apps

13. In a Design Thinking process, which of the following tasks belong to the problem space?

 ☐ A. Understand

 ☐ B. Observe

 ☐ C. Ideate

 ☐ D. Test

14. Which of the following is the final converging step in the solution space of Design Thinking process?

 ☐ A. Test

 ☐ B. Point-of-view

 ☐ C. Prototype

 ☐ D. Ideate

15. In SAP Build, by using the **Invite Team** option, you send the study to users for feedback on the prototype.

 ☐ A. True

 ☐ B. False

16. What is the limitation of the SAP Build free trial?

 ☐ A. Limited time trial

 ☐ B. Limited number of team members

 ☐ C. Limited number of users

 ☐ D. Limited number of active projects

17. In SAP Build, which of the following is *not* a valid feedback response?

 ☐ A. Free text

 ☐ B. Multiple-choice options

 ☐ C. Editing the prototype

 ☐ D. Annotation on the prototype

18. Which of the following tools does *not* allow you to create responsive proto-
    types?

    ☐   A. Microsoft PowerPoint stencils

    ☐   B. Axure stencils

    ☐   C. SAP Build

19. A message toast can be used in which of the following scenarios?

    ☐   A. A message indicating a successful update

    ☐   B. A message asking the user to confirm an action

    ☐   C. A message warning the user

    ☐   D. A message informing the user that an action failed

20. Overview page can be displayed on the SAP Fiori launchpad.

    ☐   A. True

    ☐   B. False

Practice Answers and Explanations

1. Correct answer: **C**
   You can't use SAP Build to write code, as its primary focus is on building proto-
   types. SAP Build can generate startup code that you can import into SAP Web
   IDE and use to jump-start your development.

2. Correct answer: **D**
   The wizard floorplan/control can be used from SAPUI5 version 1.30. Whenever
   there is a complex data entry task, it can be broken into three to eight steps
   using a wizard control to ease the data entry process.

3. Correct answer: **D**
   `sap.m.MessagePopover` is recommended for showing messages related to data
   entered in a form. It can show messages of multiple types such as information,
   warning, and error.

4. Correct answer: **B**
   A study needs to be created within SAP Build, which is basically a set of questions and instructions for the users. Users can respond by dropping annota-

tions, entering text, answering multiple-choice questions, or performing an action on the prototype.

5. Correct answer: **D**

   The draft functionality isn't intended for data review by peers. A draft created by a user will not be visible to others, but will stop others from editing the same object. Draft achieves all other objectives.

6. Correct answer: **C**

   Fact sheet apps provide contextual information about a business document. Transactional apps perform a business transaction, while analytical apps provide business insights based on data.

7. Correct answer: **A**

   True. The process of combining the functionality of multiple GUI transactions into one SAP Fiori app is called recomposition. The process of breaking down a single SAP GUI transaction's functionality into multiple SAP Fiori apps is called decomposition.

8. Correct answer: **B**

   In an overview page, data is visualized in a card format. Different cards are available for different content types.

9. Correct answer: **B**

   Renew stands for providing an improved UX for existing business applications. SAP Fiori apps are new UIs for widely used business scenarios.

10. Correct answer: **D**

    Advice on technologies is provided by Advisory Services, Training is provided by Empowerment Services, and Design Thinking workshops are provided by Innovation Services. End-user training isn't part of any of the services.

11. Correct answer: **B**

    The coherent design principle underscores the need to have a single, consistent interaction and visual language across SAP Fiori apps to minimize end-user training requirements, making the experience comfortable and familiar.

12. Correct answer: **A**

    Factsheet apps provide all around information about a business object or a transaction. So, these apps are usually opened from other applications by clicking on contextual links.

13. Correct answers: **A, B**

    A problem space contains the following tasks: understand, observe, and point-of-view. The main goal of the problem space is to understand the problem better by listening to end users, to observe them and then discuss and agree on an understanding of the problem.

14. Correct answer: **A**

    Design Thinking is an interactive process of divergence and convergence. As a last step in the solution space, the solution (prototype) needs to be tested (by getting user feedback) to ensure that it solves the identified problems.

15. Correct answer: **B**

    False. The **Invite Team** option is for inviting fellow colleagues to collaborate as project team members, not as users to give feedback. Users are invited to give feedback from within the study feature.

16. Correct answer: **D**

    The SAP Build trial limits you on the number of active projects you can have at a time. It is available for unlimited period of time and does not limit on number of users you can collaborate with.

17. Correct answer: **C**

    The user can't edit the prototype while proving feedback on the prototype. Users can provide answer to multiple choice questions, provide a text answer, or drop annotations on the prototype.

18. Correct answer: **A**

    You can't create responsive prototypes using Microsoft PowerPoint stencils. SAP Build is the recommended tool for prototyping, however you can create prototypes using Axure stencils as well.

19. Correct answer: **A**

    A message toast automatically disappears after a specified amount of time. Therefore, it's suitable for a message indicating a successful update. In case of an error or warning messages, the message should be available for the user for long time as user might need to review the error message and understand the message.

20. Correct answer: **B**

    False. Overview page can be launched from the SAP Fiori launchpad, but it can't be displayed on the SAP Fiori launchpad.

Take Away

In this chapter, we started with discussing SAP's UX strategy and how SAP Fiori fits into it. Then you learned the key design principles behind SAP Fiori and the reasons behind each of them. Next, we focused on the process of UX design and how to achieve it using Design Thinking. We covered how customers can benefit from SAP's expertise by using the SAP UX Design Services. We also explored scenarios where an SAP Fiori app is a result of decomposition or a recomposition of SAP Transactions. As we discussed Design Thinking, we recognized the importance of creating prototypes and user feedback and how the SAP Build tool can be used to achieve them. We also saw the utility of SAP Fiori stencils for PowerPoint and Axure in creating quick prototypes. Next, we considered SAP Fiori design guidelines and started with how messages are displayed on an SAP Fiori app. Then we saw recommended page layouts and floorplans within these layouts. We also saw how drafts can be handled and how the concept can be used for locking documents.

Summary

SAP Fiori is the result of SAP listening to its customers and is a huge step forward from classical SAP screens. SAP Fiori apps are designed using the Design Thinking process, which keeps the user in mind while designing the UXs. SAP provides extensive tools, guidelines, and services to make customers successful in their UX transformation journey.

In the next chapter, we'll go through each SAP Fiori app type to discuss their architecture and technical details.

Chapter 2

SAP Fiori Architecture Overview

Techniques You'll Master:

- Understand the architecture of SAP Fiori
- Explain the data flow in SAP Fiori app types
- Choose the right deployment option for SAP Gateway
- Configure SAP Fiori launchpad
- Brand SAP Fiori with your corporate theme

In this chapter, we'll start by discussing the architectures of various types of SAP Fiori apps. We'll deep dive into these architectures by exploring the data flow in each of these types. Next, we'll see how to choose the right deployment option for your landscape by discussing possible options and the advantages of each option. We'll explore how tiles are configured within SAP Fiori launchpad while covering catalogs, groups, and roles. We'll end the chapter by showing you how to change colors and logos and come up with a custom theme for your SAP Fiori launchpad that represents your enterprise's corporate theme.

Real-World Scenarios

You want to debug an issue in your SAP Fiori app. To pinpoint the issue, you need to find the data flow in various parts of the app so that you can set breakpoints and verify that it behaves as expected.

You're setting up an SAP Fiori landscape in your company. You want to know the possible options and compare them so that you can come up with an optimal configuration for the SAP Gateway.

You have a set of corporate colors and logos that represents your brand and company and is used by all internal and external tools. You want to use these in a theme from SAP Fiori so that SAP Fiori is also consistent with rest of the applications in your enterprise.

Objectives of This Portion of the Test

The objectives of this portion of the SAP Fiori Certification Test are as follows:

- Understand SAP Fiori architecture and data flow for all three application types.
- Understand deployment options for SAP Gateway and your skills in choosing the right deployment option.
- Demonstrate skills in creating a custom theme per your corporate standards and how to apply it to SAP Fiori launchpad.

Key Concepts Refresher

In this section, we'll cover the architecture of SAP Fiori apps for various application types discussed in Chapter 1. A typical SAP Fiori landscape has many components, which results in multiple deployment options. We'll discuss the common options and architectures here.

Generic Architecture

Figure 2.1 shows general architecture components involved with SAP Fiori.

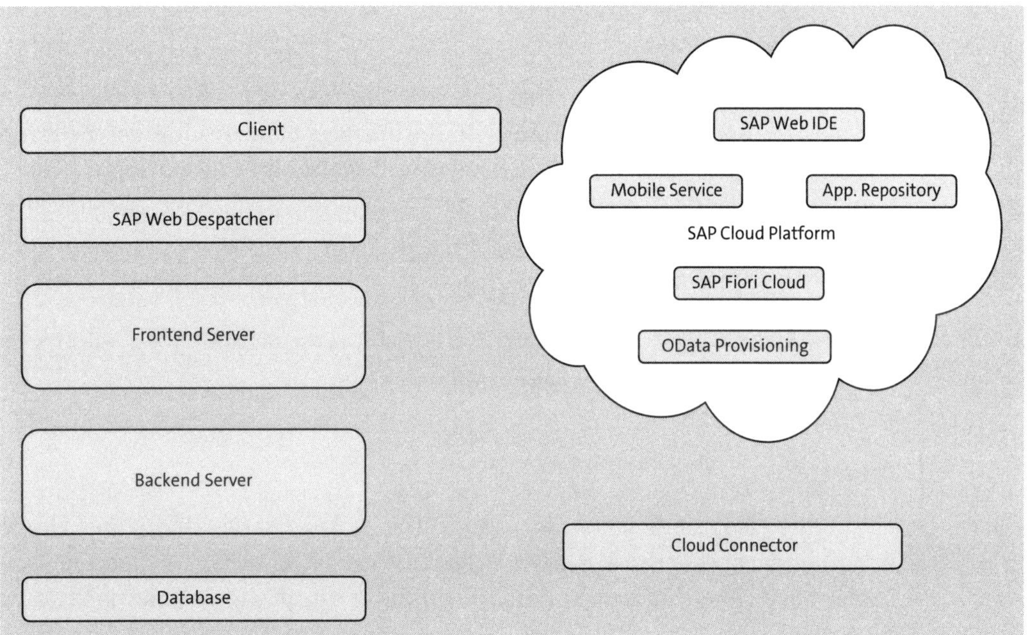

Figure 2.1 Components in the SAP Fiori Architecture

Client

The client here represents a desktop browser, a mobile browser, or an SAP Fiori Client. In an on-premise scenario, clients access SAP Fiori using SAP Fiori launchpad by clicking the link pointing to an SAP Web Dispatcher or to a frontend server.

SAP Web Dispatcher

SAP Web Dispatcher is a reverse proxy product, but it provides more features than a simple reverse proxy. It helps SAP Fiori apps fetch data from more than one source. Without a reverse proxy, such calls from the browser would get blocked due to the Same Origin Policy security concept implemented by browsers. In addition, it can also be a switch that blocks or enables accesses to internal resources.

Another important feature of SAP Web Dispatcher is load balancing in a web scenario. If there are more than one SAP NetWeaver server (ABAP or Java), SAP Web Dispatcher can act as an effective load balancer. Due to these features, SAP recommends SAP Web Dispatcher for all web scenarios.

Frontend Server

This is the SAP Gateway server that hosts the OData service, which is required for the SAP Fiori apps to communicate with the business data. In addition, the frontend server hosts the SAP Fiori launchpad as well as all of the SAP Fiori apps as Business Server Pages (BSP) applications.

Backend Server

This is the main system where the business data and business logic lies. This is also the server where an OData service is implemented.

Database

This is the database that is connected to the backend server and stores all the important business-critical data. This database can be any of SAP-supported databases or even SAP HANA. In SAP HANA, this layer can also work as an application server.

SAP Cloud Platform

SAP Cloud Platform is SAP's Platform-as-a-Service (PaaS) offering providing tools and technologies to fast-track application development.

SAP Fiori Cloud

This is a service that allows you to host your SAP Fiori launchpad and applications on the cloud. For business data, it connects to your on-premise backend system. Along with OData provisioning, this can replace the frontend server from your SAP Fiori architecture.

OData Provisioning

This is one of the services of SAP Cloud Platform, where you can register and expose OData services which were developed on your backend system.

SAP Mobile Service

This is a cloud version of the SAP Mobile Platform on-premise solution.

SAP Web IDE

This is a cloud-based (SAP Cloud Platform) development environment for developing and extending the SAP Fiori apps. Chapter 4 provides a deep dive into SAP Web IDE.

App Repository

This is a repository available on the SAP Cloud Platform that stores the user interface (UI) resources of each SAP Fiori app that is exposed on SAP Fiori Cloud.

SAP Cloud Platform Cloud Connector

This is a lightweight server that is part of the on-premise server infrastructure and exposes the on-premise system to SAP Cloud Platform.

SAP Fiori On-Premise

SAP Fiori was initially released as an on-premise product on the SAP Business Suite to improve the user experience of selected scenarios by creating targeted SAP Fiori apps. As discussed in Chapter 1, there are three types of SAP Fiori apps, and each of them slightly differs in architecture. This architecture gradually evolved in SAP S/4HANA and follows a single architecture for all three types of SAP Fiori apps. Let's review these scenarios.

SAP Business Suite

The three types of SAP Fiori apps, namely transactional apps, fact sheet apps, and analytical apps. Transactional apps run on any database, whereas fact sheet and analytical apps require SAP HANA as the database.

Transactional Applications

Let's consider the architecture of transactional apps as shown in Figure 2.2 shows architecture of transactional app.

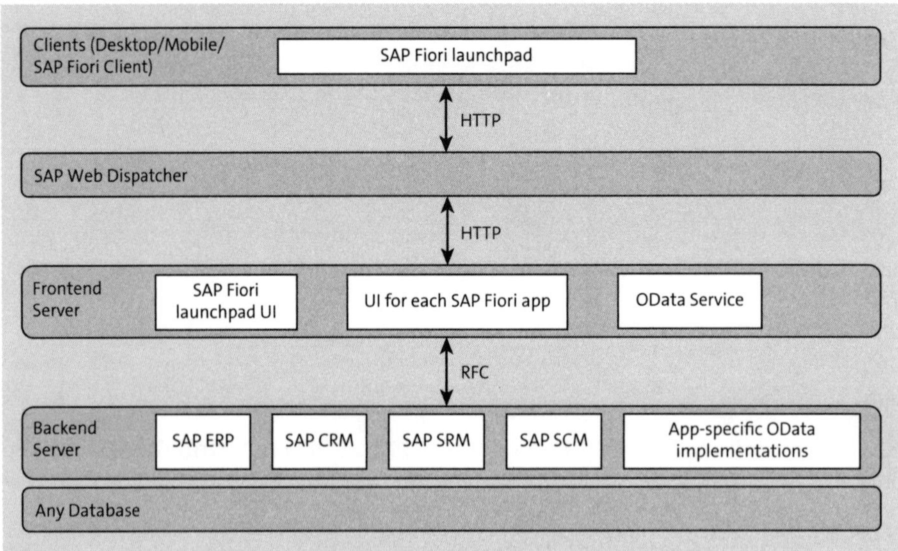

Figure 2.2 Architecture of an SAP Fiori Transactional App

At the top level there is a box representing clients. These clients can be a browser on a desktop and mobile phone or an SAP Fiori Client app. These clients will open the SAP Fiori launchpad and use it to launch the SAP Fiori apps.

The next level from the top is for the SAP Web Dispatcher. For a transactional app, all the calls will end up at the frontend server. Because of this, SAP Web Dispatcher isn't a necessity, but SAP recommends you use one for the security and load balancing features.

In the next level, we have frontend server. The SAP Fiori launchpad and the UI resources for all the SAP Fiori apps are hosted in this server. The SAP Fiori launchpad administration requires data related to catalogs, groups, and roles to be stored here as well. SAP Fiori launchpad doesn't store any data in the backend. All the communication to load and perform administrative operations for SAP Fiori launchpad will end at the frontend server.

UI resources for each SAP Fiori app are packaged as BSP applications. These app-specific BSPs are hosted on the frontend server as well. When a tile pointing to an SAP Fiori app is clicked on in the SAP Fiori launchpad, it will start loading the app by contacting the frontend server.

The frontend server also exposes the OData services for consumption. Even though services are implemented in the backend servers, service exposure occurs through the frontend server. The frontend server can also connect to more than one backend server for fetching the data.

Next, we have the backend server, which is nothing but the application server where all the business logic resides. This can be an SAP ERP, SAP Customer Relationship Management (SAP CRM), SAP Supplier Relationship Management (SAP SRM), or SAP Supply Chain Management (SAP SCM) systems. OData service implementations also reside here.

The last layer is the database layer. For transactional apps, this can be any of the SAP-supported databases.

Fact Sheet Applications

Fact sheets are read-only applications that give information about a business object or a transaction. They are usually opened from search results on SAP Fiori launchpad or by clicking on links on other fact sheet and transactional apps.

Configuring SAP Fiori Search is a prerequisite for fact sheet apps. SAP Fiori Search can be configured to work against multiple backend systems as well. In such cases, you can also configure fact sheet apps to open data from multiple systems. However, when opened, each fact sheet app will provide data from only one backend system.

Figure 2.3 shows the architecture of SAP Fiori fact sheet apps. One big difference when compared with transactional apps is that there is direct communication from SAP Web Dispatcher to the backend server for fetching search results. The UIs for fact sheets are still hosted in the frontend server. Upon receiving search requests, SAP Web Dispatcher routes the calls directly to the backend server. Routing rules to affect these routing changes are required in the SAP Web Dispatcher. This communication uses the SAP proprietary InA search protocol to access the search models built in the backend system using the SAP HANA database. This is the reason for fact sheets having SAP HANA as the database prerequisite.

Note

Because fact sheet apps must connect to two different hosts (frontend server as well as backend server), SAP Web Dispatcher is a mandatory component in the architecture.

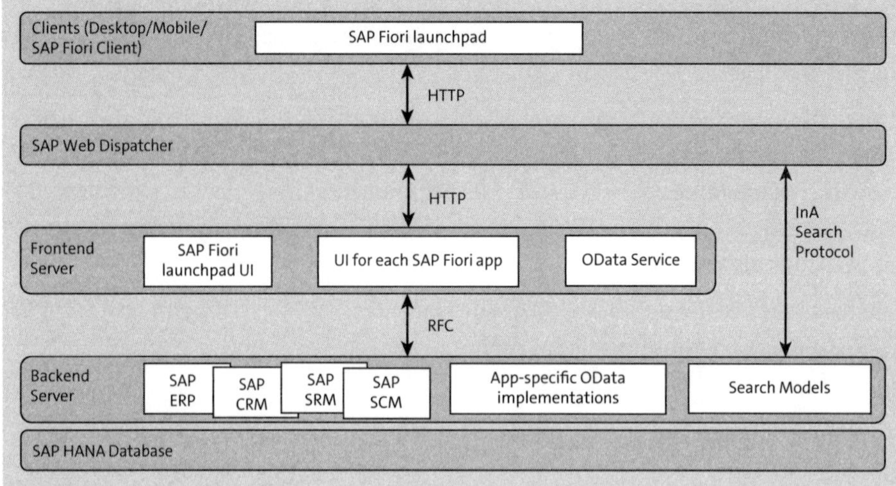

Figure 2.3 Architecture of an SAP Fiori Fact Sheet App

Analytical Applications

As we saw in Chapter 1, analytical apps provide capabilities to report by slicing and dicing the business data in the SAP HANA system. Because of this, it makes use of the application server available in the SAP HANA system instead of using the backend server. OData services for analytics are exposed using the SAP HANA XS engine and provide data for charts and figures in analytical apps. The backend server is bypassed because the business logic in the backend server is of little significance to the analytical apps, and directly contacting the SAP HANA layer will improve performance.

However, for the UI, analytical apps still use the frontend server to host the required UI resources. Because of this, SAP Web Dispatcher is a mandatory requirement for analytical apps as well. Figure 2.4 shows the architecture of an SAP Fiori analytical app.

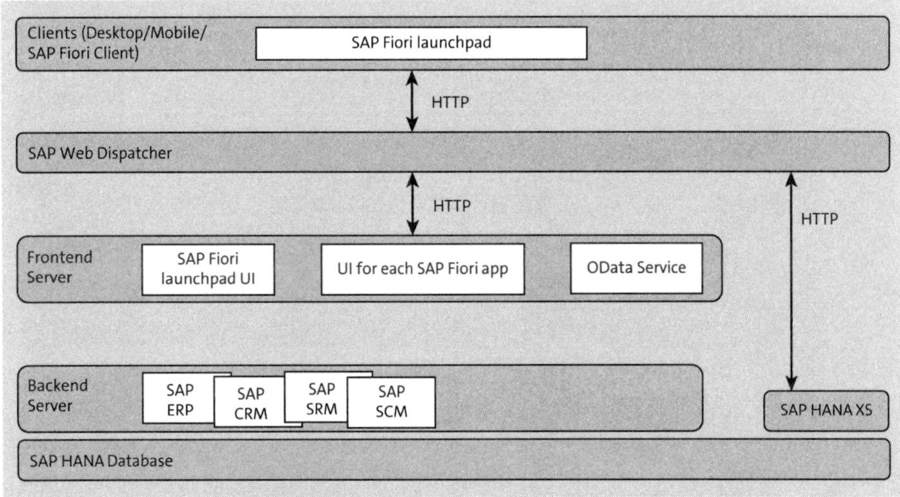

Figure 2.4 Architecture of an SAP Fiori Analytical App

SAP S/4HANA

Because simplification is one of the focuses in SAP S/4HANA, SAP Fiori architecture also aims for simplification at various levels. Now, let's explore various simplifications achieved by SAP S/4HANA in regards to architecture, authorization management, business object models, and technical levels.

- **One Archetype**
  The SAP Fiori architecture for SAP S/4HANA provides only one archetype across all three application types (transactional, analytical, and object view/search), unlike three archetypes that existed with SAP Fiori for SAP Business Suite.

  Figure 2.5 shows the one-archetype architecture of SAP Fiori in SAP S/4HANA.

- **One user/authorization management**
  In the earlier architecture for SAP Business Suite for analytical apps, there was a direct connection to the SAP HANA XS layer. This required maintaining users and their authorizations separately. However, in the current architecture as shown in Figure 2.5, all the connections to SAP HANA occur through the ABAP layer (i.e., through the SAP S/4HANA layer), and there is no direct access to the SAP HANA system. Thus, there is no need to maintain a separate list of users and handle their authorizations.

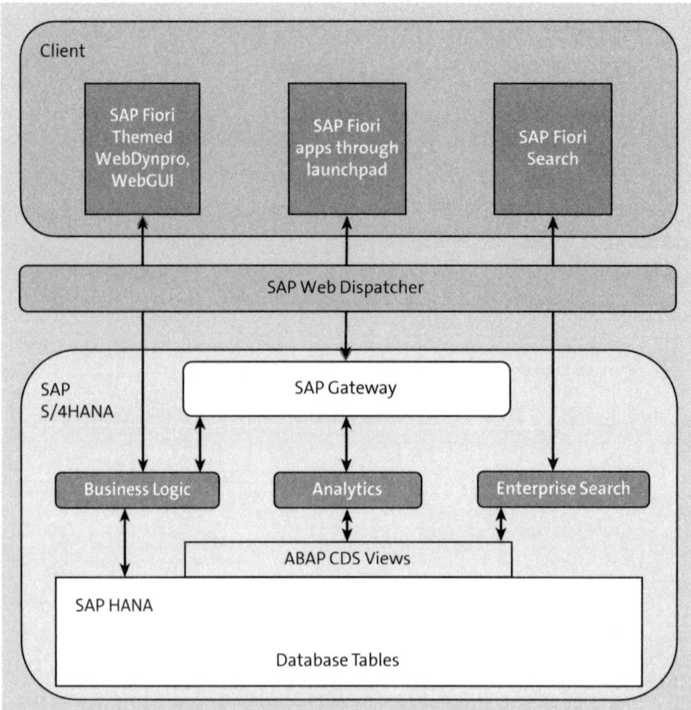

Figure 2.5 SAP Fiori for SAP S/4 HANA's Single Archetype Architecture

- **One business model**

  In the SAP Fiori architecture for SAP Business Suite, data modeling was done on the ABAP layer for transactional apps, whereas modeling was done on the SAP HANA XS layer as well with calculation/analytical views. With the current architecture, ABAP Core Data Services (CDS) views are considered as the central part for all data modeling needs. This is true for all the query scenarios in transactional apps as well as for analytical apps, which will need CDS views with analytical annotations.

- **One lifecycle to manage**

  In the earlier architectures, development artifacts were present both in the ABAP layer and the SAP HANA layer. Thus, their lifecycles needed to be handled separately, increasing the effort involved as well as the possibility of mismatches and failures. But in the SAP Fiori for SAP S/4HANA architecture, all the objects, including CDS views, are created in the ABAP layer, thus providing the ability to maintain all the artifacts together and hugely reducing the efforts involved.

- **One protocol (OData) and one implementation layer (SAP Gateway)**
  Both transactional and analytical apps use the OData protocol for required data. However, in analytical apps for SAP Business Suite, OData services were delivered by the SAP HANA XS layer. But in the current architecture, all the required OData services are delivered through SAP Gateway.

Data Flow in SAP Fiori for SAP S/4HANA Transactional Applications

SAP Fiori transactional apps contain two types of data interactions (as seen in Figure 2.6):

- **Data query**
  ABAP CDS views are modeled for all the required data from the business objects. These CDS views will be annotated as well, so that they can be used in controls belonging to SAP Fiori elements. CDS views allow you to make use of code push down technique to improve query performance. All queries go through CDS views.

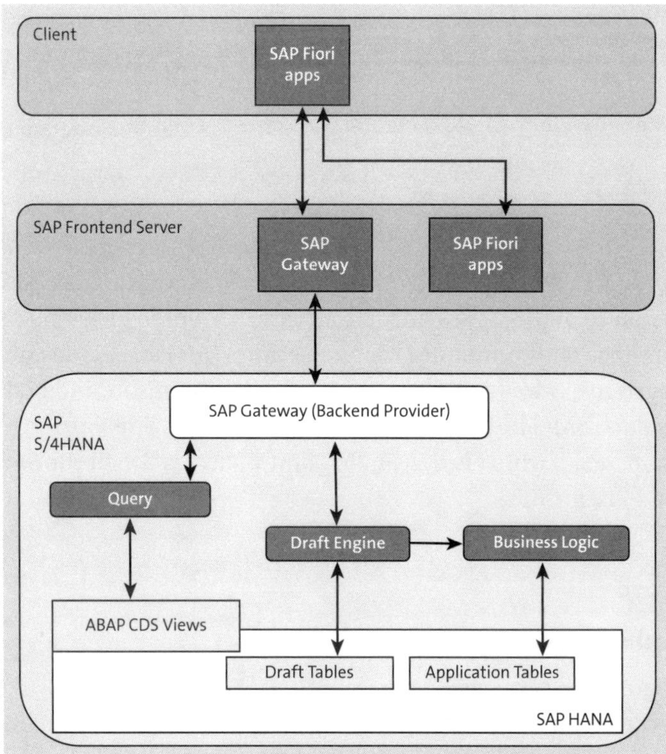

Figure 2.6 Data Flow in an SAP S/4HANA Transactional App

- **Draft handling**
  While making changes to business objects, many times users need to save the business document/object halfway through and then continue at a later time. To facilitate this, a draft handling feature is available.

The Business Object Processing Framework (BOPF) is used to model the business objects and provide all aspects of application development, including draft handling. The moment a business document is edited or created, the draft version gets created. The changes only get saved to the actual business object only when saved explicitly.

Draft handling is also used for concurrency handling for a single business object. Only one draft of an existing business object is allowed at a time. When a user opens an object in edit mode, a draft version of that object gets created and assigned to the user. The changes in the draft get copied to the original object and the draft gets destroyed when the user saves all the changes. Unless the user explicitly saves the changes, no other user will be able to create a new draft and won't be able to edit the same object.

Note

For draft handling capabilities, AS ABAP 7.51 SP02 or higher is required.

SAP Fiori Cloud

SAP Cloud Platform provides the SAP Fiori Cloud for quickly mobilizing applications in SAP Business Suite and SAP S/4HANA. SAP Fiori Cloud enables you to renew your user experience with minimum cost and effort. SAP Fiori Cloud connects to on-premise systems as well as SAP S/4HANA Cloud systems for integrating with the business data. SAP Fiori Cloud allows users to access SAP Fiori apps using the SAP Fiori launchpad, which is the single point of access for all the SAP Fiori apps on SAP Cloud Platform.

Content of SAP Fiori Cloud

SAP Fiori Cloud offers three types of services.

- **Runtime and configuration services**
  This is a set of services required to configure and run SAP Fiori apps and SAP Fiori launchpad. These services allow you to define catalogs, groups, and roles

and assign SAP Fiori apps to catalogs and groups. You can also create multiple SAP Fiori launchpads using these services. These services enable navigation and personalization as well.

- **Lifecycle management services**
  As the name suggests, these services provide ways to package, upgrade, and transport cloud-ready SAP Fiori content.

- **Development services**
  These services allow developers to build and extend SAP Fiori apps. SAP Web IDE is the most important tool as part of these services.

Note

Not all SAP Fiori apps are cloud ready and available on SAP Fiori Cloud. SAP releases standard SAP Fiori apps selectively based on demand and technical feasibility. However, you can push any of your custom SAP Fiori apps on SAP Fiori Cloud.

Architecture and Landscape

In this chapter, we'll go through various architectural options while using a cloud/on-premise hybrid option for SAP Fiori Cloud. The two important architectural styles can be classified based on how the user accesses the SAP Fiori launchpad: from inside the network or from the Internet.

Based on this, the architectural types are as follows:

- Internal access point
- External access point

Let's consider each of these types with more detail.

Internal Access Point

Many customers are apprehensive about exposing their business data to the cloud but are keen to reap the benefits of a cloud-based SAP Fiori infrastructure. This architectural pattern takes care of these requirements by ensuring that data never reaches the cloud, while SAP Fiori launchpad and other SAP Fiori resources are accessed from the SAP Fiori Cloud.

Figure 2.7 gives a high-level overview of the internal access point architecture.

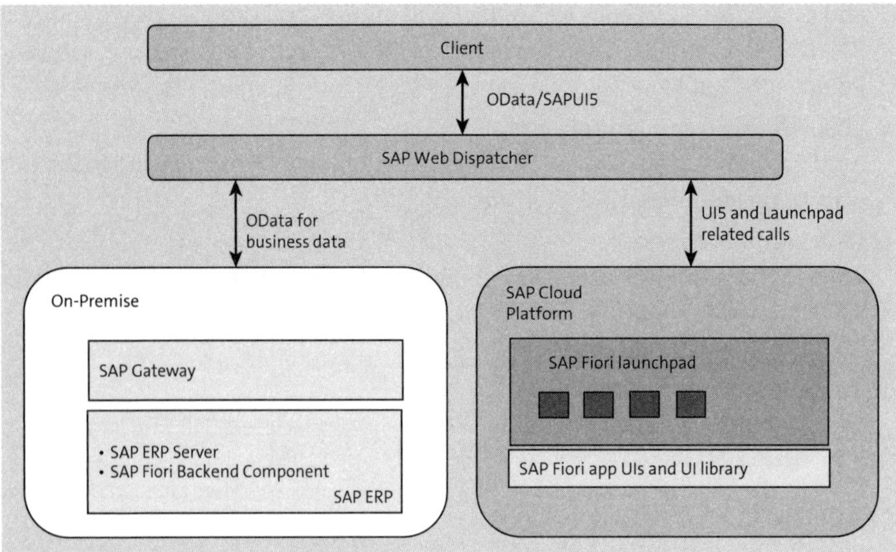

Figure 2.7 SAP Fiori Cloud Architectural Option: Internal Access Point

SAP Web Dispatcher is a very important component of this architecture style because it determines where each call from the client should be routed. When the user/client makes an initial call to SAP Fiori launchpad, SAP Web Dispatcher sees that it's a call to SAP Fiori launchpad-related sources and delegates the call to SAP Cloud Platform. All the calls to load the SAPUI5 library and to load each SAP Fiori app-related resource are also directed to SAP Cloud Platform.

When these resources run on the user's browser, they need business data to be displayed and thus make calls to OData services. These calls will be delegated to the on-premise SAP Gateway system. Upon data retrieval, the data will be shown on the user's browser. So far the data has never entered SAP Cloud Platform and is retained within the customer's network. This architecture style can be used from mobile phones as well; however, this will work if the mobile phone is connected to the internal network.

This is a unique scenario where a customer makes use of SAP Fiori Cloud, and still none of the business data passes through the cloud, thus meeting complex data flow requirements.

Next, we'll see access from the external access point, which can be from anywhere on the Internet.

External Access Point

As the name suggests, this architectural style exposes both the business data and the SAP Fiori apps to the Internet. Both internal and external users access the SAP Fiori launchpad by connecting to the SAP Cloud Platform. The SAP Fiori launchpad, the SAPUI5 library, and the accessed UI content of SAP Fiori apps are all fetched from the SAP Fiori app repository.

OData services are also routed through SAP Cloud Platform, thus there is no requirement for an SAP Web Dispatcher. SAP Cloud Platform connects to on-premise systems via the Cloud Connector, which is a small server hosted and part of the on-premise network. OData service calls are fetched to the SAP Gateway system through Cloud Connector, and data is fetched or updated.

Figure 2.8 shows the external access point architecture.

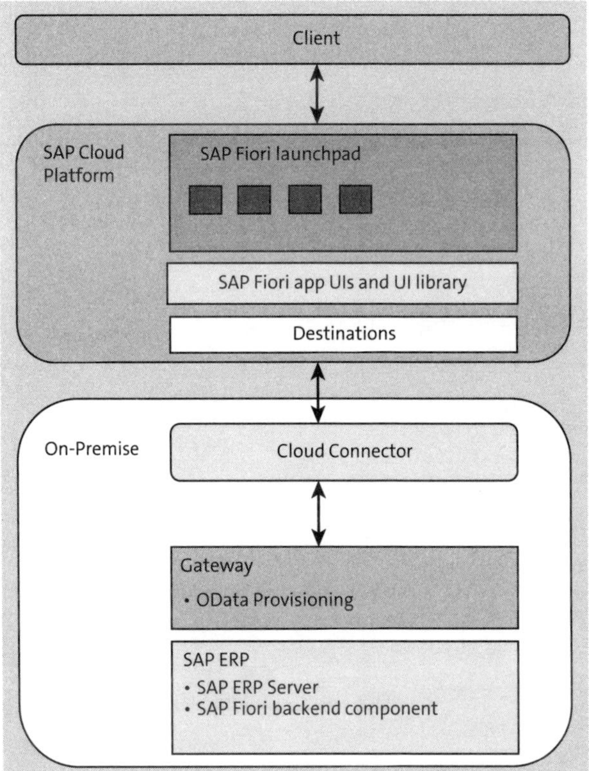

Figure 2.8 SAP Fiori Cloud Architecture: External Access Point

Authentication to SAP Cloud Platform is based on Security Assertion Markup Language (SAML) 2.0 for browser-based single sign-on (SSO), which is a standard feature of SAP Cloud Platform. For connecting to backend systems such as SAP Gateway, SAP Cloud Platform creates a token based on the logged-in user's identity and passes it along with the connection. The backend server may confirm the identity using a SAML 2.0-compliant identity provider.

Using the OData Provisioning Service

As you've seen in the previous architectures, the landscape involves having an SAP Gateway server for provisioning the OData services. However, SAP Cloud Platform provides an additional service for OData provisioning, which can be used to replace the SAP Gateway server.

Figure 2.9 shows such an architecture, where the SAP Gateway server has been replaced by the SAP Cloud Platform OData provisioning service.

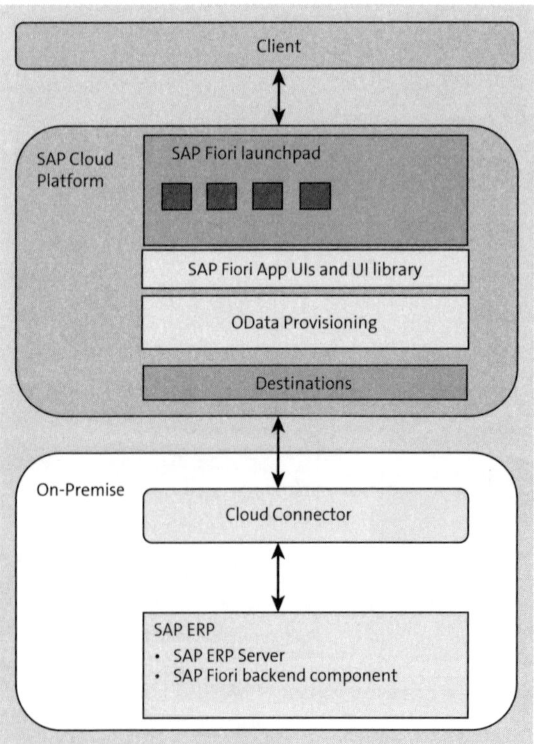

Figure 2.9 SAP Fiori Cloud Architecture: External Access Point with SAP Cloud Platform OData Provisioning Service

The data flow is like the previous architecture with the SAP Gateway server; the only difference is that data is extracted by the OData provisioning service, which connects to the backend again using the Cloud Connector.

SAP Gateway Deployment Options

In this section, we'll consider the various deployment options of SAP Gateway and their advantages. The SAP Gateway product is made up of two functional components: a server component and a backend component. The server component is made up of the GW_CORE and IW_FND add-ons, while the backend component is made up of the IW_BEP software component. You register and expose OData services on the server with the IW_FND component. You implement (code) an OData service on the server with the IW_BEP component. The deployment options determine how these components are installed along with the SAP backend system.

However, starting from SAP NetWeaver version 7.40, all these components have been added to a new software component called SAP_GWFND. So, you no longer need to decide which software component is installed in which system; instead, you just need to choose which functionality is used from which system.

SAP Fiori supports two deployment options for on-premise installation: hub deployment and embedded deployment. Let's consider each of these options in detail.

Hub Deployment Option

In the hub deployment option, there is a dedicated SAP NetWeaver server available for SAP Gateway server functionalities. This server will be either an SAP NetWeaver 7.31 or lower version with GW_CORE and IW_FND component or an SAP NetWeaver 7.40 or higher system leveraging component SAP_GWFND.

Figure 2.10 displays the hub architecture in which the service is registered on the SAP Gateway server (using Transaction /IWFND/MAINT_SERVICE).

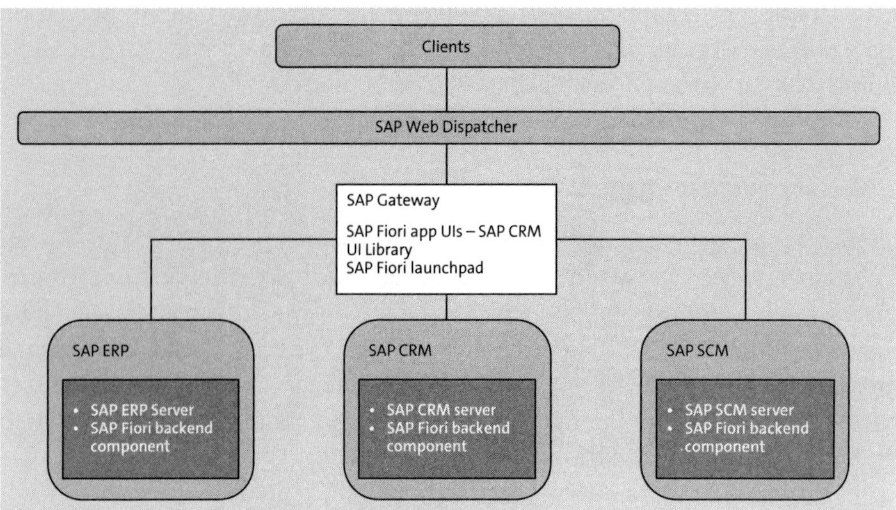

Figure 2.10 SAP Gateway Hub Deployment Architecture

Multiple Routings

In a hub architecture, as shown in Figure 2.10, a hub system (SAP Gateway) can be connected to multiple backend systems. These backend systems can be business systems such as SAP ERP, SAP CRM, or SAP SCM. Each backend systems will have corresponding SAP Fiori app-specific backend software components installed. However, the frontend components of all these diverse SAP Fiori apps are installed on the hub system. SAP Fiori launchpad hosted on the hub system not only shows SAP Fiori apps based on SAP ERP but also other systems such as SAP CRM and SAP SRM. Thus, one of the main advantage of the hub architecture is the ability to provide a single starting point to diverse applications by providing a single integration point.

Tip

In an on-premise SAP Fiori architecture, the dedicated SAP Gateway system in the hub architecture is called the SAP Fiori frontend server. This is because this server also contains the central UI, that is, SAP Fiori launchpad, SAPUI5 library, and a repository for holding all SAP Fiori app-specific UI parts.

Other advantages of the hub deployment option are discussed in the following subsections.

Separating the User Interface Lifecycle

By having a separate server, the lifecycle of UI components, UI library, and SAP Fiori launchpad are separated from that of the backend business systems. Usually backend business systems are upgraded less frequently considering the huge regression testing requirements upon any changes. However, UI components such as the SAPUI5 library get upgrades as often as every quarter. Having a separate SAP Gateway system allows customers to upgrade the SAP Gateway systems much faster than the business systems.

Better Security and Authentication

In a hub architecture, HTTP connections always end at the SAP Gateway system, protecting business systems from any direct attacks. In addition, because there is a separate system for SAP Gateway, this system can be deployed on the demilitarized zone (DMZ) for external Internet access.

Because the hub system can be based on a newer release, it can support a wide variety of authentication options such as Kerberos, SAML, or OAuth. However, the main disadvantage of the hub architecture is maintenance of an additional server for SAP Gateway.

Embedded Deployment Option

In an embedded deployment option, both the server component (GW_CORE and IW_FND) and backend component (IW_BEP) are installed on the business systems for SAP NetWeaver 7.31 or earlier. On an SAP NetWeaver 7.40 business system, no additional add-on or server is required. Both service development and registration are done on the backend business system.

Figure 2.11 shows an embedded system architecture.

As you see in Figure 2.11, in an embedded deployment option, in addition to SAP Fiori app-specific backend components, frontend components are also installed on the backend business system. Unlike the hub architecture, you can't have a single SAP Fiori launchpad to represent all the backend business systems. Each backend system will have an SAP Fiori launchpad of its own.

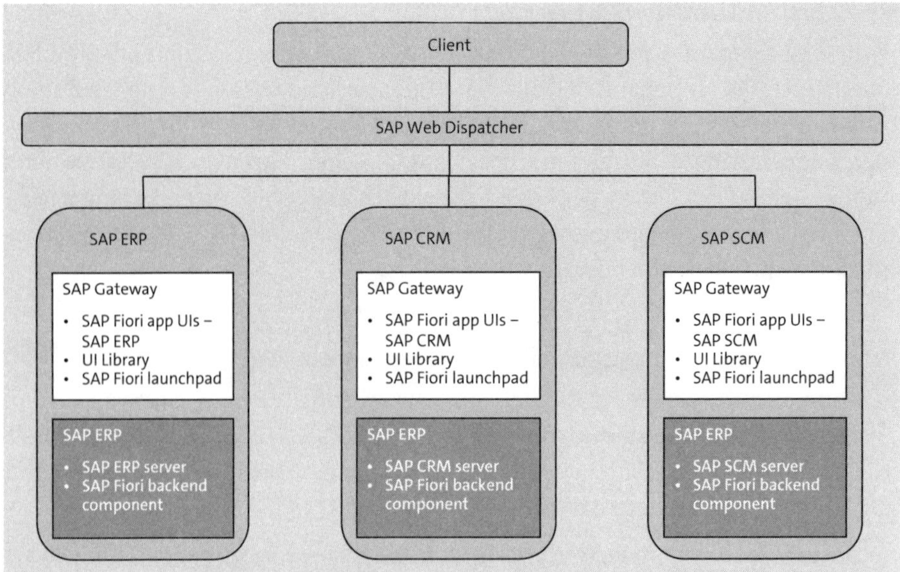

Figure 2.11 SAP Gateway: Embedded Deployment Option

Less Runtime Overhead

Because there is only one system to traverse, data latency is reduced. In addition, from SAP NetWeaver 7.50 SP4, there are enhancements specific to embedded deployment that take advantage of co-deployment of SAP Gateway and business systems to further improve the performance.

No Extra System to Maintain

Because there is no additional Gateway system involved, there is one less system to maintain, thus reducing costs.

Disadvantages

The embedded deployment option has the following disadvantages:

- Because the embedded system should not be used as a hub system for other business systems, you can no longer have a single integrated SAP Fiori launchpad for all your business systems.
- You can't get frequent innovations to the SAP Gateway system because SAP backend business systems can't be upgraded as frequently.

- You need to ensure additional security measures in the network because HTTP connections end at the business systems, thus exposing them to external Internet attacks.

SAP Cloud Platform OData Provisioning

In this deployment option, SAP Cloud Platform's OData provisioning service is used. SAP Cloud Platform's OData provisioning serving replaces the SAP Gateway system in the hub deployment option. Thus, the advantages of this deployment option are like that of the hub deployment option, and this is one of the preferred deployment options by customers. Figure 2.12 illustrates the SAP Cloud Platform OData provisioning deployment option.

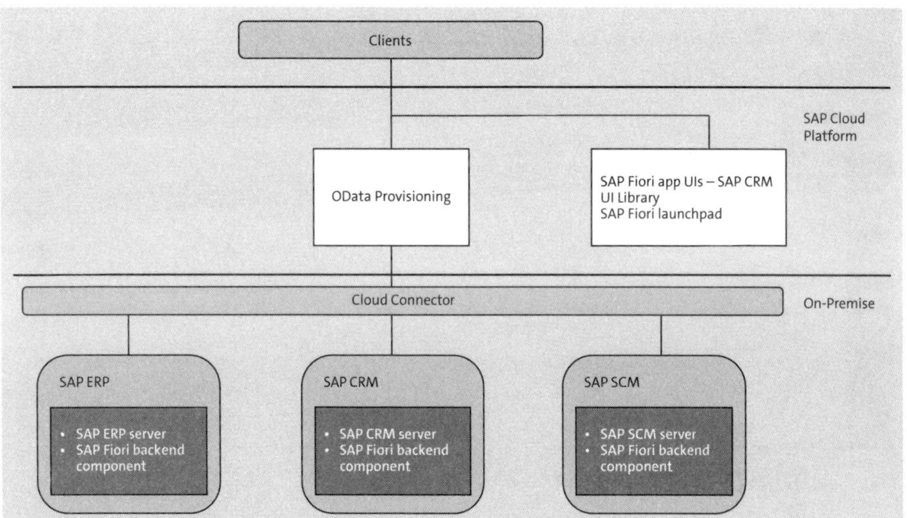

Figure 2.12 SAP Gateway Deployment: OData Provisioning

The advantages of this deployment are as follows:

- Lower total cost of ownership (TCO) compared with SAP Gateway
- Frequent software updates on the cloud
- Automated system monitoring and administration tasks
- Being part of the cloud brings in the quality of elasticity when required

When used in an SAP Fiori Cloud landscape, OData provisioning takes care of OData service registration and exposure capabilities of the SAP Gateway server.

The remaining capabilities of acting as an SAP Fiori UI repository are handled by SAP Cloud Platform as shown in Figure 2.12.

Tip

The OData provisioning service is under active development, and you can expect this service to cover many more related use cases.

The OData provisioning service can be found and activated easily on SAP Cloud Platform, as shown in Figure 2.13.

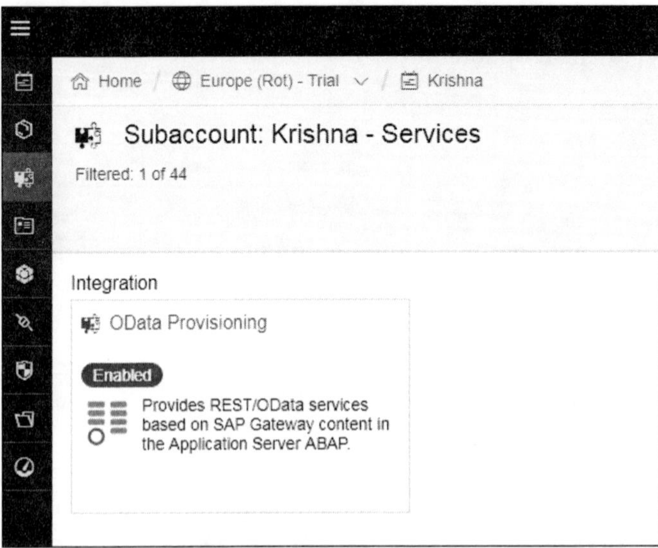

Figure 2.13 OData Provisioning Service

To enable service registrations, each business system needs to be configured as a destination within the service configuration of the OData provisioning service. To go to destination maintenance, click on the service tile as shown in Figure 2.13, and then click on **Configure Service**. Click on **New Destination**, and maintain the details of a backend business system. Figure 2.14 shows the connection details for an SAP-provided ES4 demo system.

Now you can go to the OData provisioning service. Click on **Register**, and choose the destination **ES4**. Upon searching, all the services from the ES4 system will be shown. Select one of the services, and click the Register button shown in Figure 2.15 ❶. Upon successful registration, this service will be listed in the catalog of services as shown in Figure 2.15 ❷.

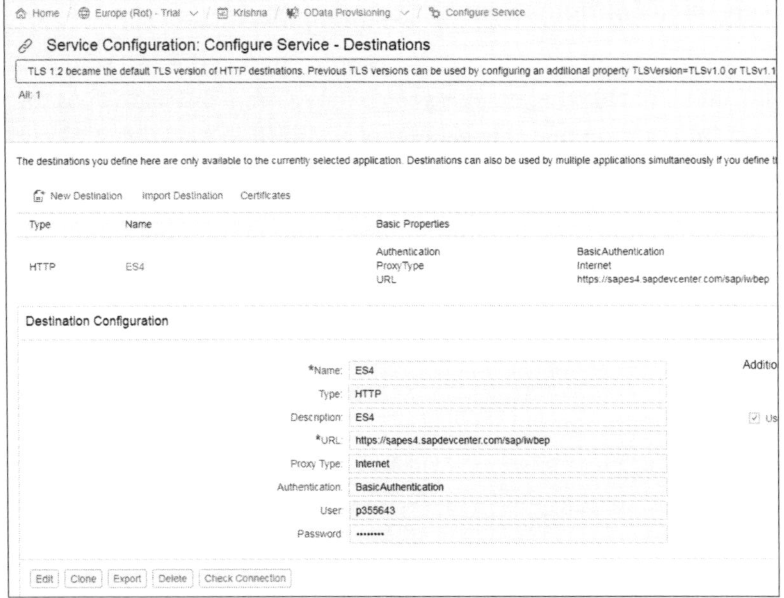

Figure 2.14 Destination for ES4 System for OData Provisioning

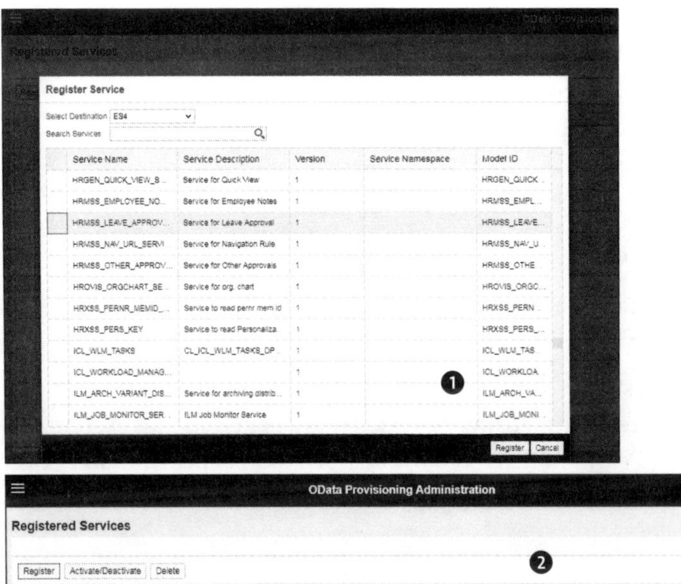

Figure 2.15 Service Registration in the OData Provisioning Service

SAP Fiori Launchpad Configuration

As you've seen so far, SAP Fiori launchpad is a central point to the SAP Fiori strategy, and it provides a single point of access to all the relevant SAP Fiori apps for a user. In this section, we'll discuss the techniques involved in assigning SAP Fiori apps to users by using the SAP Fiori catalog, SAP Fiori group, and Transaction PFCG roles.

SAP Fiori launchpad designer is a browser-based tool used to administer and configure SAP Fiori launchpad. It's recommended to use the SAP Fiori launchpad designer on a desktop screen.

SAP Fiori launchpad designer allows you to do the following:

- Configure static, dynamic, and news tiles
- Create catalogs and groups and assign tiles to them
- Assign these artifacts to transport requests for transporting

Launching SAP Fiori Launchpad Designer

SAP Fiori launchpad designer can be launched with the following URL:

https://<server>:<port>/sap/bc/ui5_ui5/sap/arsrvc_upb_admn/main.html? sap-client=<client>&scope = <CONF/CUST>

<server>:<port> should point to the SAP Gateway server in a hub architecture system, while it will be pointing to the backend business system in an embedded system.

Scope for Content Adaption

As you can see, the SAP Fiori launchpad designer URL has two types of scopes, and a third scope is available as well:

- **CONF-configuration scope**
  Configuration scope refers to settings that are cross-client and thus system specific. All the standard content delivered by SAP is in this scope. You can use the URL parameter *scope=CONF* for opening the SAP Fiori launchpad designer in configuration mode.

- **CUST-customization scope**
  Customization scope is specific to a client. This is also the default scope for all SAP Fiori launchpad designer content if no URL parameter scope is specified. You can use the URL parameter *scope=CUST* to specify this scope, however.

Changes made with the CUST scope take precedence when compared to those made with the CONF scope.

- **PERS-personalization scope**
  Although this scope isn't allowed from the SAP Fiori launchpad designer, whenever a user performs personalization on the SAP Fiori launchpad, the PERS scope is used. The personalization scope has the top precedence when compared to CONF and CUST scopes.

Figure 2.16 shows a screen of the SAP Fiori launchpad designer. On the master list on the left hand side pane, you can select either **Catalogs** (default) or **Groups**. The resulting screen shows details of either a catalog or a group.

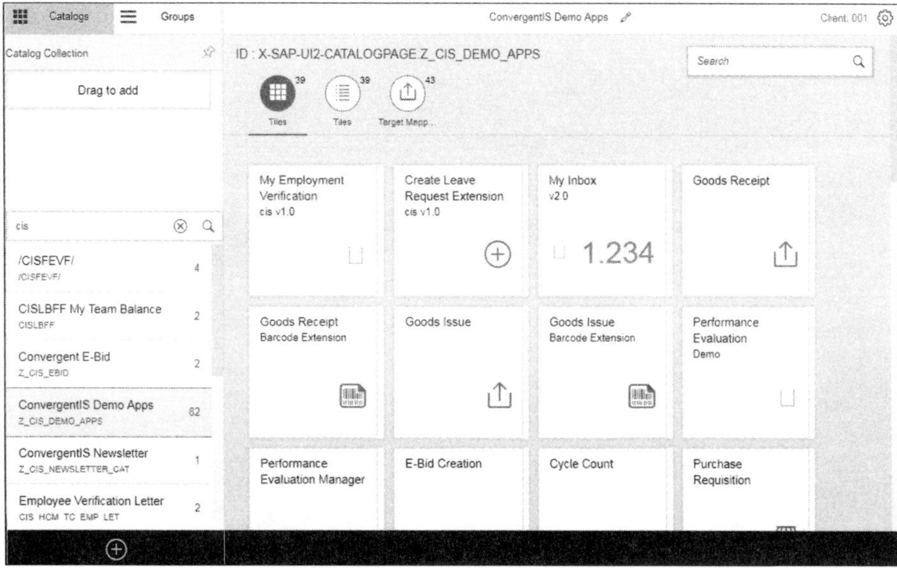

Figure 2.16 SAP Fiori Launchpad Admin Tool

SAP Fiori Catalogs

An SAP Fiori catalog is a set of applications that will be assigned to a role. Unless an application is part of a catalog and assigned to a user's role, the user won't be authorized to access the application.

However, all the applications assigned to a user using the catalog won't be available in the user's SAP Fiori launchpad entry page. The user needs to browse through his catalogs and choose applications to be available in the entry page.

SAP Fiori Groups

An SAP Fiori group, as the name suggests is a semantic group of all the SAP Fiori apps authorized to a user. When an SAP Fiori group is assigned to a user via a role, all these SAP Fiori apps will appear in the entry page of the user's SAP Fiori launchpad with the group title.

Figure 2.17 illustrates how the combination of catalogs/groups and roles affect the authorization and display of applications on the home screen.

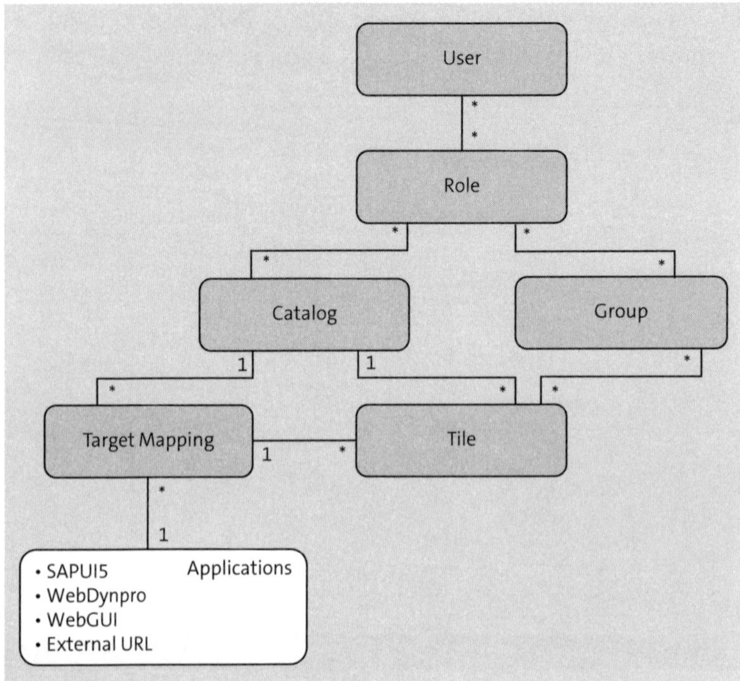

Figure 2.17 SAP Fiori Catalog, Group and Role relations

Let's do a small exercise of assigning an SAP Fiori app to a user using these concepts.

1. Navigate to the SAP Fiori launchpad designer.

2. Before making any changes, it's important to link a Customizing transport with the SAP Fiori launchpad designer, so that all further changes will get captured

within that Transport. To do so, Click on the gear icon (Figure 2.18, ❶) on the top right of the SAP Fiori launchpad designer, and choose an available Customizing transport from the **Customizing Request** dropdown ❷ as shown in Figure 2.18.

3. Click **OK** ❸.

> **Note**
> If there are no transports available, create a new Customizing transport in Transaction SE09.

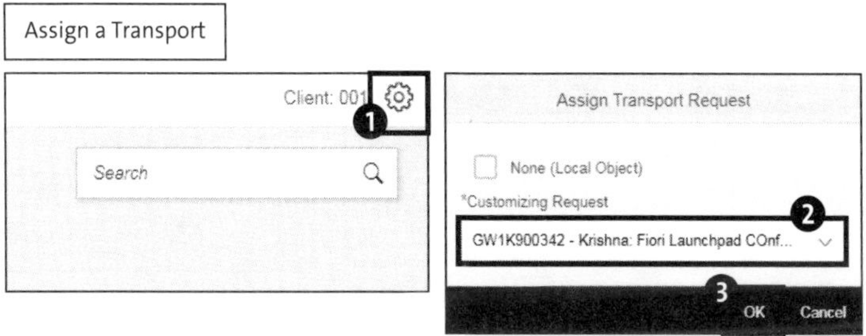

Figure 2.18 Assigning a Transport to SAP Fiori Launchpad Designer

4. Next, create a new catalog by clicking on the **+** button at the bottom of the master list.

5. Provide a **Tile** and an **ID** in the customer's namespace, and click **Save** as shown in Figure 2.19 ❶.

6. Navigate to the **Target Mapping** tab, and click on **Create Target Mapping** ❷.

7. In the form that opens, in the **Intent** section, enter a **Semantic Object** and an **Action** ❸. A target mapping defines supported device types and application details for an intent. If the required semantic object isn't present, you can easily create one in Transaction /UI2/SEMOBJ.)

8. Choose from several options in the **Application Type** list as shown in Figure 2.19 ❹. These are the various types of applications that can be opened from an SAP Fiori tile. You can create a target mapping for an SAP Fiori app, a transaction, an external URL, and a Web Dynpro application.

9. There are two options to create a target mapping for an SAP Fiori app. The first one, **SAP Fiori App using LPD_CUST**, is a legacy option that required the application details to be mentioned in Transaction LPD_CUST. For this exercise, choose

the second option, **SAPUI5 Fiori App**, which will allow you to enter application details (URL and component name) on the screen as shown in Figure 2.19 ❺. Click on **Save** to save the target mapping.

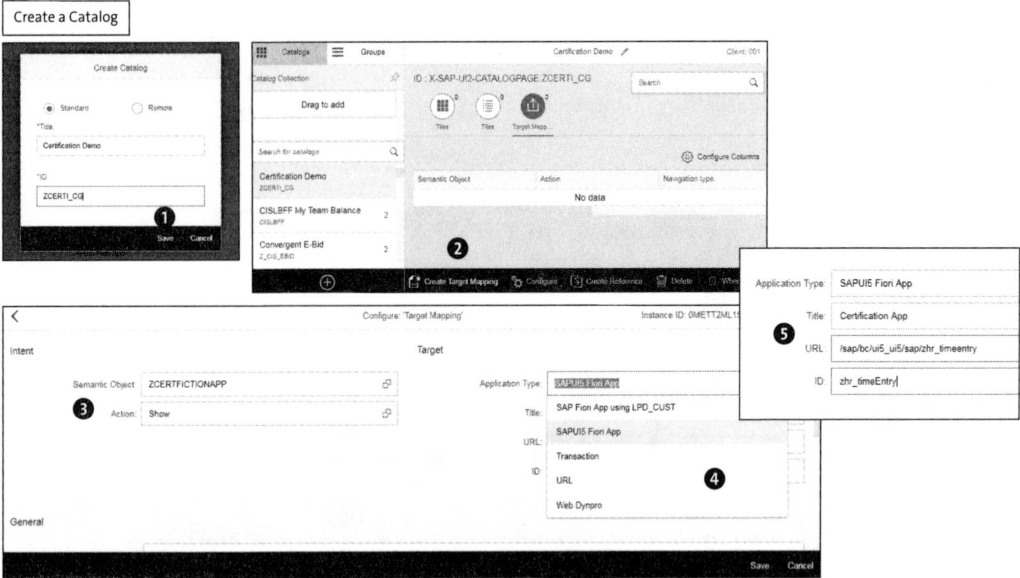

Figure 2.19 Creating a Catalog and a Target Mapping

Now we need to create a tile referring to the target mapping. Follow these steps:

1. Navigate to **Tiles**, and click on the **+** button (Figure 2.20, ❶) to create a new tile.
2. You have three options to choose from for tile templates:

    App Launcher – Dynamic will have a tile with a number and some dynamic text on it. This can be useful if you want to give a numeric summery of some process on the tile itself.

    News Tile will show a feed of news from a specific source.

    App Launcher – Static will show a tile with only static content on it.
3. Choose **App Launcher – Static** for the tile as shown in Figure 2.20 ❷.
4. In the form that opens, provide a **Title** and a **Subtitle** for the tile.
5. Under **Navigation**, choose the **Semantic Object** and **Action** ❸ you provided while creating the target mapping. This is how the tile is linked to the target mapping.

6. Click on **Save** to save the tile. You've now completed all the steps to create a catalog and add a tile to it.

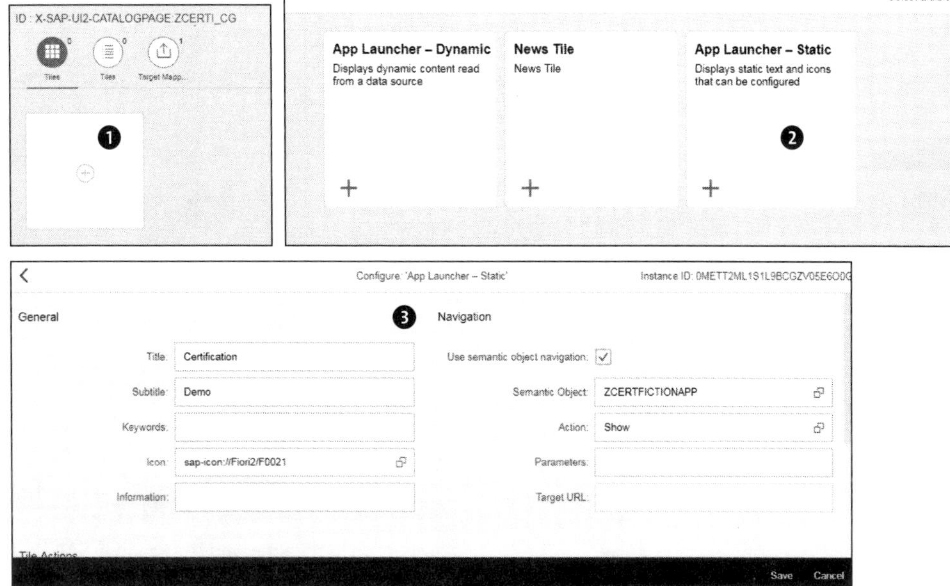

Figure 2.20 Creating a New Tile

Now let's create an SAP Fiori group for this tile by following these steps:

1. Click on **Groups** in the master list, and then click on the **+** icon on the master list to initiate creating a new group.

2. Provide a **Title** and an **ID** (Figure 2.21, ❶) as you did when creating a catalog. The title mentioned here will be used as the group heading in the SAP Fiori launchpad.

3. To add a tile to the group, select the **Catalog** ❷ that contains the tile, and then click on the + button below the tile to add it to the group ❸ as shown in Figure 2.21.

Now that we've created a catalog and a group, both of these need to be assigned to a Transaction PFCG role, so that all users having this role will see the new tile in their SAP Fiori launchpad shown in Figure 2.21.

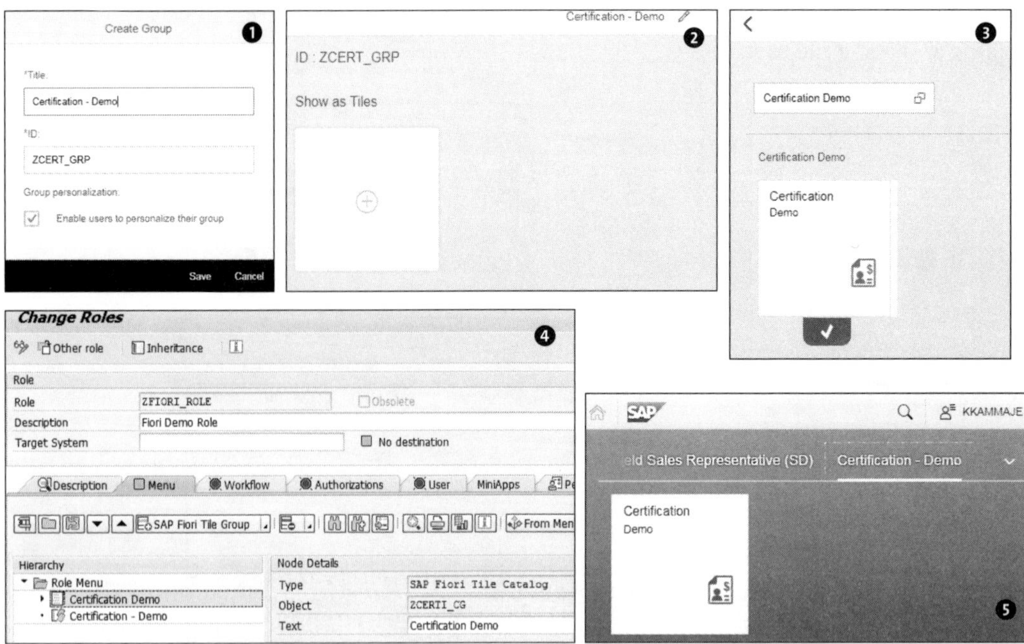

Figure 2.21 Creating a Group, Assigning the Catalog and Group to the Role, and the Result in SAP Fiori Launchpad

SAP Fiori Theming

A common requirement is to modify the SAP Fiori launchpad and the SAP Fiori apps with the corporate theme of the customers, for example:

- Replacing the SAP logo with the customer's logo
- Replacing the standard color combinations with the customer's corporate preferences
- Providing a corporate background image to the SAP Fiori launchpad

Although these requirements can be met by directly writing and including custom CSS, it can be very tough to maintain these CSS files, thus increasing the TCO.

SAP provides the UI theme designer tool to make it easy to create and maintain custom themes. The UI theme designer is not only specific to SAPUI5 and SAP Fiori apps but also available to other SAP UI technologies such as Web Dynpro, BSP, HTMLB, SAP Enterprise Portal, SAP GUI for HTML, SAP NetWeaver Business Client (NWBC), and the Web UI Framework in SAP CRM.

Overview

UI theme designer is available as part of the central UI of the frontend server infrastructure. When working with SAP Fiori apps, we'll be using the UI theme designer hosted on the SAP Gateway server. However, the tool is also available in SAP Cloud Platform as a service and as part of the SAP Enterprise Portal.

UI theme designer can be launched via Transaction /UI5/THEME_DESIGNER in your SAP Gateway/frontend system. You can also go to the following URL to open the tool:

https://<host:port of your Gateway System>/sap/bc/theming/theme-designer

The **UI Theme Designer** screen is shown in Figure 2.22. On the left, you can see a list of custom **Themes** created within this server so far. You can elect any of these custom themes and perform various actions, including **Edit**, **Rebuild**, **Delete**, **Duplicate**, or **Rename**.

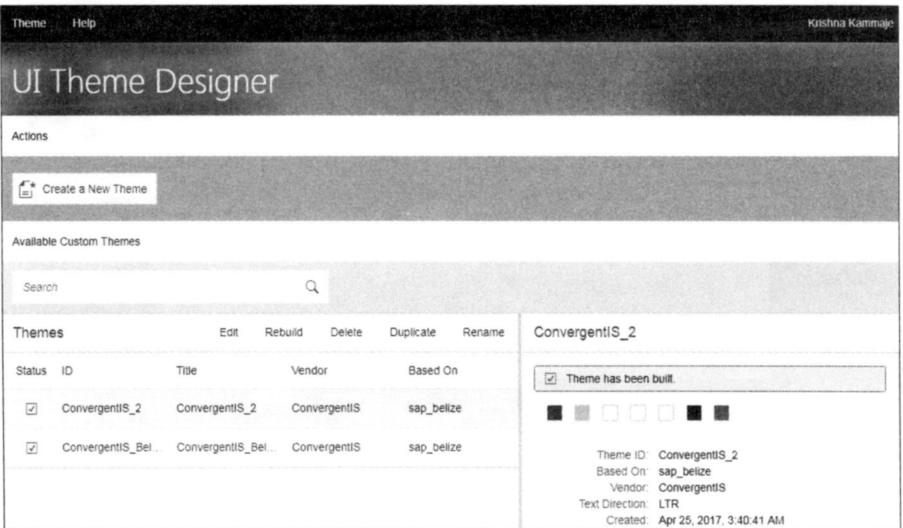

Figure 2.22 Home Screen of the UI Theme Designer

The **Create a New Theme** button is used for creating a brand-new theme based on one of the existing themes. The box on the right side of the screen displays the details about the selected theme.

Creating a Theme

Let's create a new custom theme based on the SAP-delivered Belize theme by following these steps:

1. Click on **Create a New Theme** button. This opens a three-step wizard pop-up as shown in Figure 2.23.

2. In the first step, you need to choose a base theme to start from because a theme contains numerous properties and attributes that are difficult for customers to create from scratch. By basing the theme on an existing theme instead, all those parameters will be copied, and customers can go about making incremental changes on the copied theme. For this example, choose **SAP Belize**.

3. Click on **Step 2**.

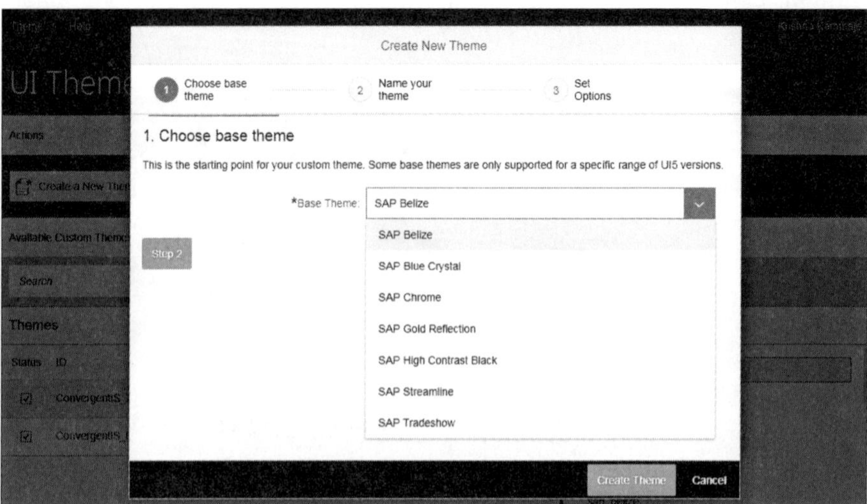

Figure 2.23 Step 1: Choosing a Base Theme

4. Provide a **Theme ID** and a descriptive **Title** for the new theme as shown in Figure 2.24.

5. Click **Step 3**.

6. In the next screen, provide a **Vendor** name, and choose whether the new theme supports **RTL** (right-to-left scripts). Click on **Create Theme**.

7. In the new screen that appears enter the target pages. Target pages are used to preview and test the changes you made to the theme for verifying the results. You can add multiple target pages, so that you can instantly see the effect of your theme on all those pages.

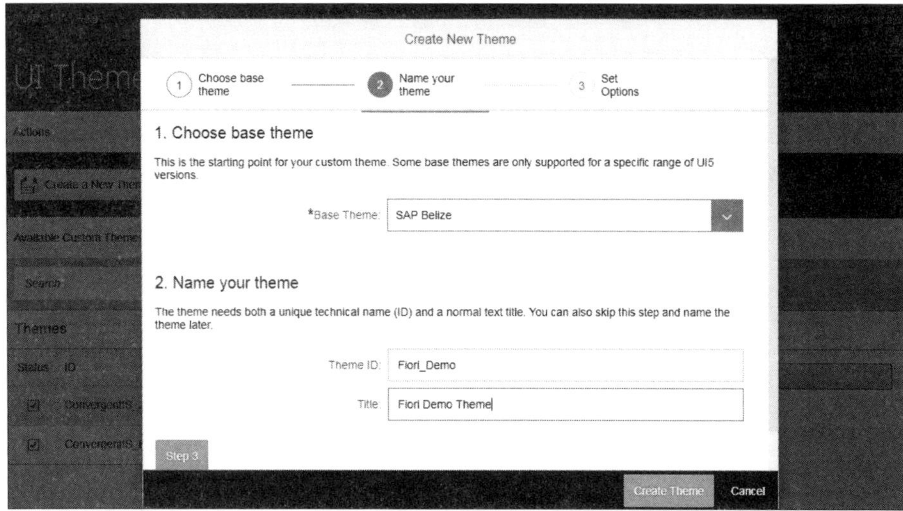

Figure 2.24 Step 2: Providing a Unique ID and a Name for the New Theme

Warning

Adding the target page doesn't assign the theme to the target page permanently.

In the **Link to Application** field, enter the SAP Fiori launchpad URL, and enter a name identifying it in the **Name of Application** field, as shown in Figure 2.25.

8. Click on the **Add** button.

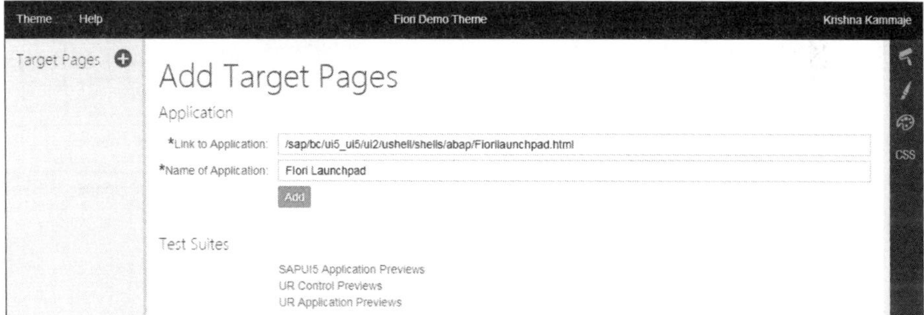

Figure 2.25 Adding Target Pages for the New Theme

This will load the target page within the UI theme designer as shown in Figure 2.26.

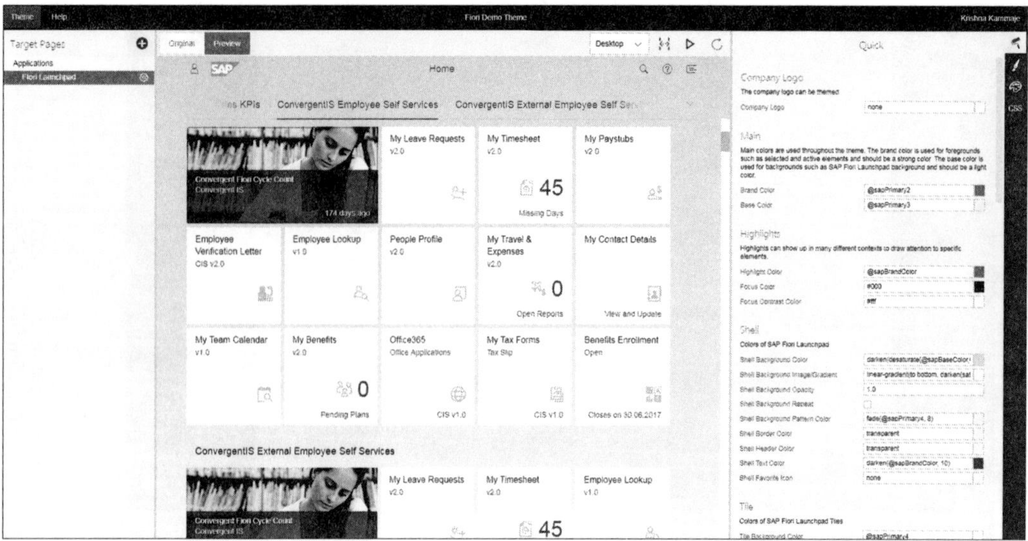

Figure 2.26 Target Page along with the Quick Toolbar

The central area where the target page is loaded is called a canvas, and it has a toolbar providing various options. Figure 2.27 describes the various available options on the canvas area.

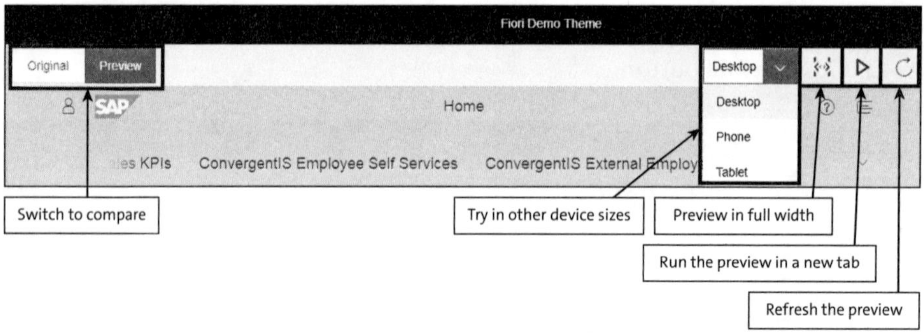

Figure 2.27 Options Available for Previewing

On the right, the **Quick** toolbar opens by default. This toolbar has enough options for beginners as well as for most frequent requirements. You can set the **Company Logo**, **Brand Color**, **Base Color**, and other properties for frequently required items such as **Shell**, **Application Backgrounds**, **Tile**, **Object Header**, and so on, as shown in Figure 2.28.

The second icon (paintbrush) on the right vertical toolbar opens an **Expert'** window that provides advanced options based on theme parameters. These theme parameters are reused in all of SAP Fiori launchpad and its applications.

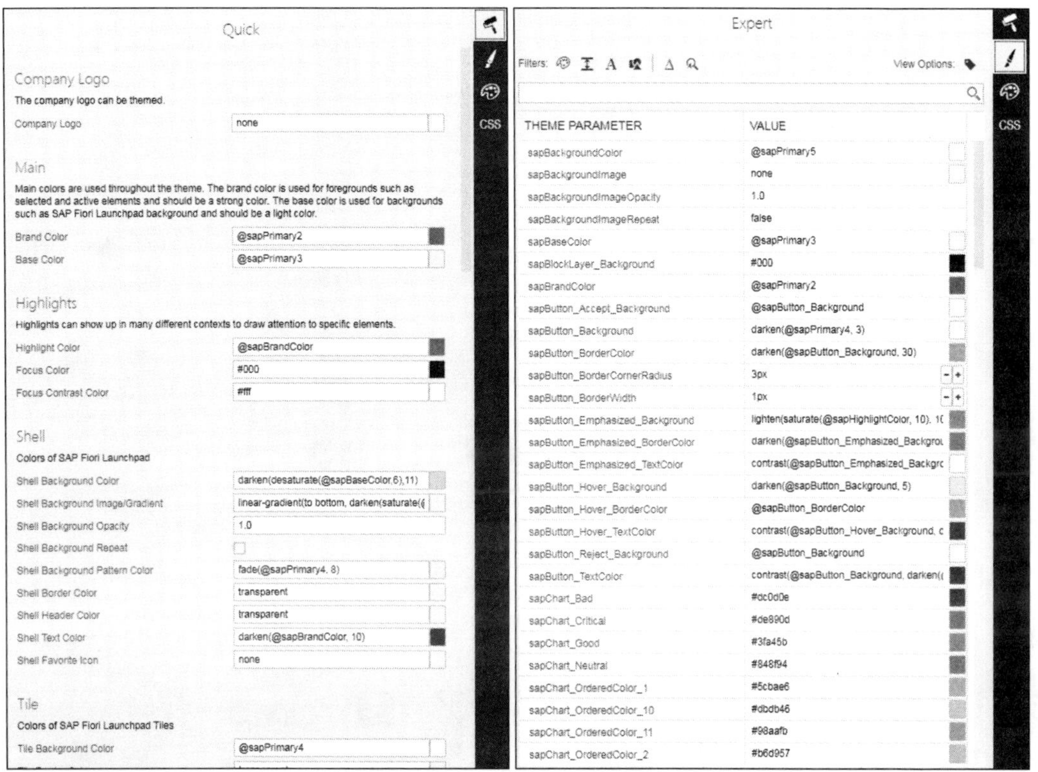

Figure 2.28 Quick and Expert Options

The third icon on the right vertical toolbar is **Palette**, which allows customers to predefine their corporate colors and reuse them in both the **Quick** and **Expert** windows. You can simply enter a parameter name in **New Parameter** and then select the color and its properties such as hue. Click on the + button to add the parameter as shown in Figure 2.29. There are two custom parameters now in total.

Now, go back to either the **Quick** or **Expert** window, choose a parameter, and click on the color picker button. You'll see that new custom parameters are available as shown in Figure 2.30.

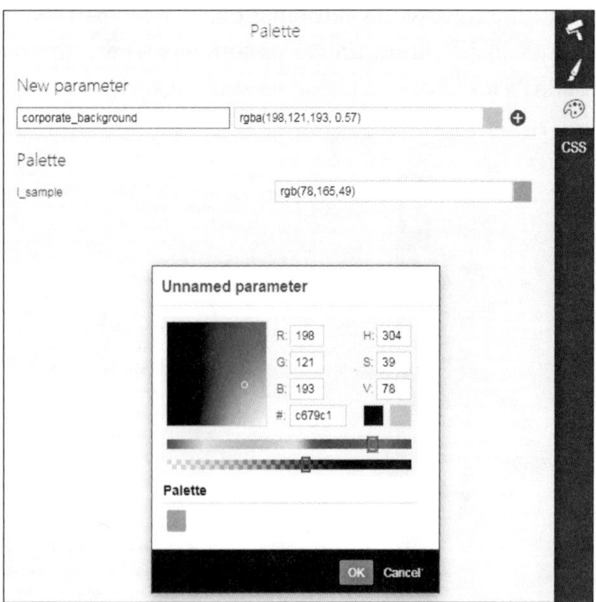

Figure 2.29 Using Palette to Create Custom Parameters with Color Values

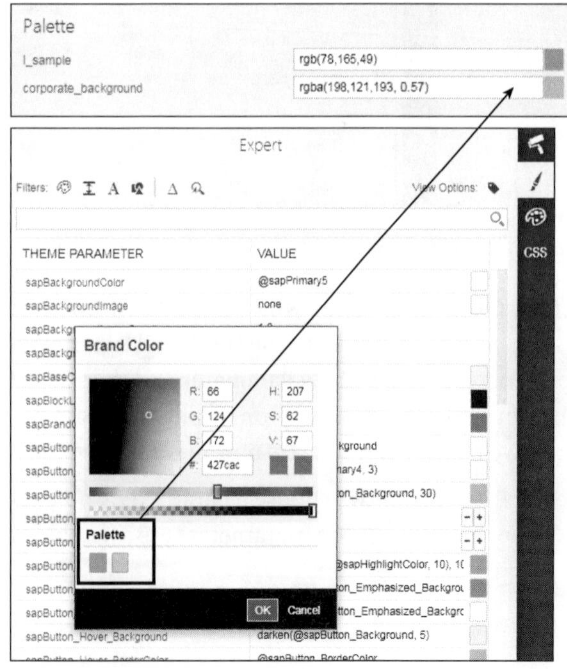

Figure 2.30 Option for Using Custom Palettes/Parameters

The last option on the right toolbar is **CSS**. As the name suggests, this enables customers to influence appearance of apps by inserting their own CSS. However, changes achieved by adding custom CSS can break across upgrades, and SAP provides no guarantee of those changes working. In such cases, customers need to document the expected outcomes well and redo the changes after the upgrade.

Figure 2.31 shows where CSS class names for the status text **No Assignments** were copied, and the color was changed. When you click **Apply**, the changes are reflected on the canvas.

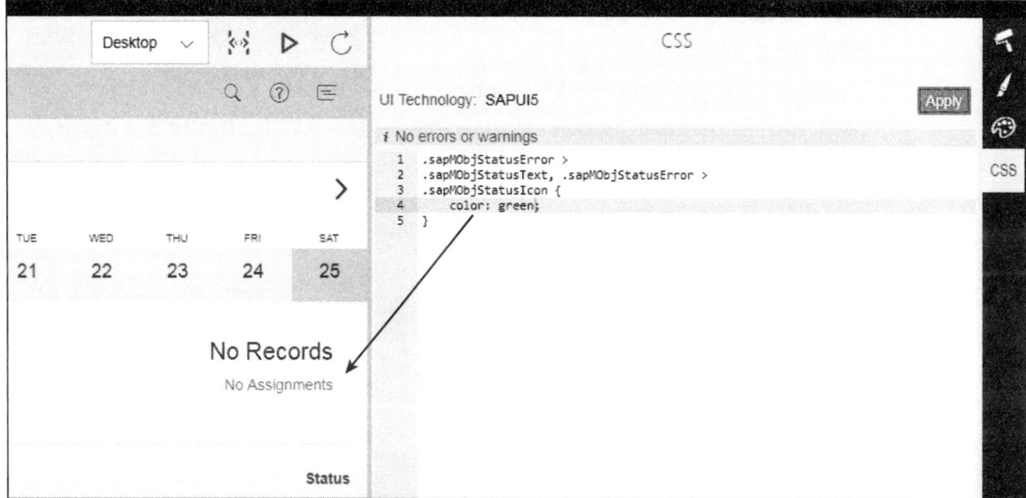


```
1    .sapMObjStatusError >
2    .sapMObjStatusText, .sapMObjStatusError >
3    .sapMObjStatusIcon {
4        color: green;
5    }
```

Figure 2.31 Using Custom CSS

After making changes, the theme can be saved by clicking on **Theme** on the menu bar and selecting **Save**. The theme needs to be built before it can be used. To build it, choose **Theme • Save & Build** from the menu bar.

The new theme is now available in the home screen.

Maintaining Themes

Once a new theme is created in the development system, it needs to be transported to the testing and production systems so that real users can use it. You may also want to set it as a default theme for your users, so that users do not have to explicitly choose it. You can also export the theme from one system and import it into another. Let us explore all these possibilities in this section.

Setting the Default Theme

After a theme is created, it can be set as the default theme for all users so that they need not set the theme from the SAP Fiori menu. To set a default theme, you use Transaction /UI2/NWBC_CFG_CUST in the following steps:

1. Navigate to **Change mode ❶**, and then click on **New Entries ❷** in Transaction /UI2/NWBC_CFG_CUST, as shown in Figure 2.32.

2. In the **New Entries** screen, enter "SAP_FLP" in the **Filter** field, enter "Theme" in the **Parameter Name** field ❸, and press ⌑Enter⌑.

3. This will open the **Value** field for input. Enter the technical name of the new theme that was created.

4. Click **Save** to save the entry. This setting will default the Fiori_Demo as the new theme for all the users. However, users can go to SAP Fiori menu options and choose a different theme to override this setting.

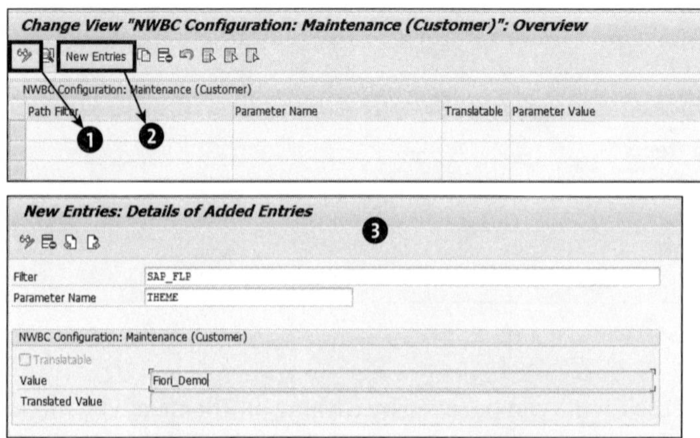

Figure 2.32 Setting the Default Theme

Tip

SAP sets a default theme initially using Transaction /UI2/NWBC_CFG_SAP. However, this should not be changed because further SAP upgrades will overwrite the changes.

Transporting Themes

After completing the development and testing of the theme in the development server, it's a normal requirement to transport the theme to other servers in the landscape. To transport the themes, you need to go to generic Transaction /UI5/ THEME_TOOL. This tool will list each of the custom themes created in the server. Against each theme name, it provides options such as **Info**, **Transport**, **Download**, and **Delete,** as shown in Figure 2.33.

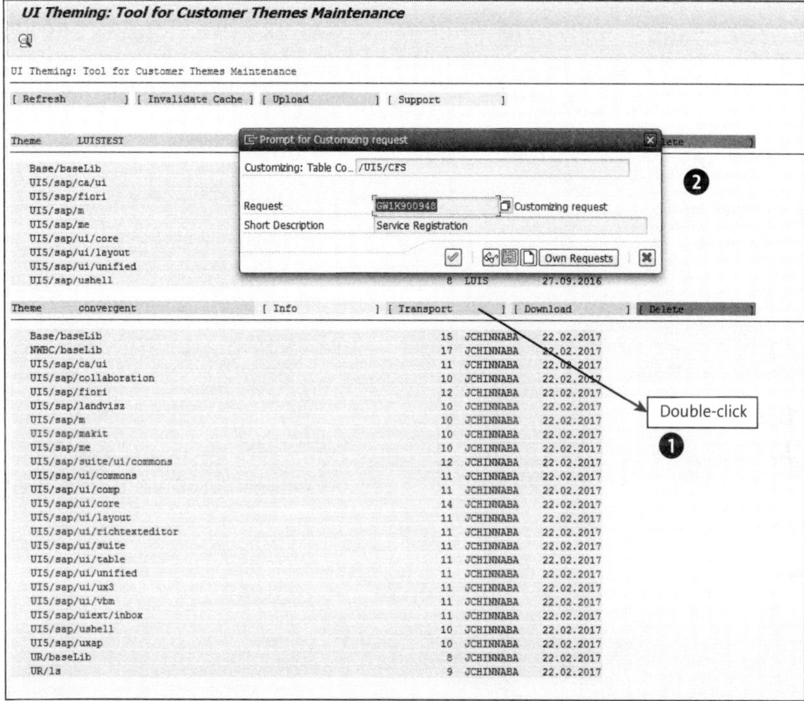

Figure 2.33 Transporting a Theme

To transport a theme, click on the **Transport** button, and then click on the magnifying glass as shown in Figure 2.33. (Or just double-click on the **Transport** button ❶). A standard dialog opens allowing you to choose or create a transport to hold the changes in the theme ❷. After selecting a transport, click on the **OK** button to close the dialog.

Exporting/Importing a Theme

In some scenarios, there are no transport routes between two systems, and you need to manually repeat the theme changes. For such scenarios, SAP provides an export/import (**Download/Upload**) option (refer to Figure 2.33) through which you can achieve the desired changes.

To download a theme, double-click on the **Download** button. SAP will prompt you for a file name and location. Upon providing those details, the entire theme will be written to a file. Transport this file manually to a target system's file system. In the target system, click on the **Upload** button, and choose the previously downloaded file. This will create the new theme in the target system.

When you need details about the theme designer, such as its version and SAPUI5 version, you can use the **Support** button at the top of the screen. Double-click the button to see various related details, including the support component, as shown in Figure 2.34.

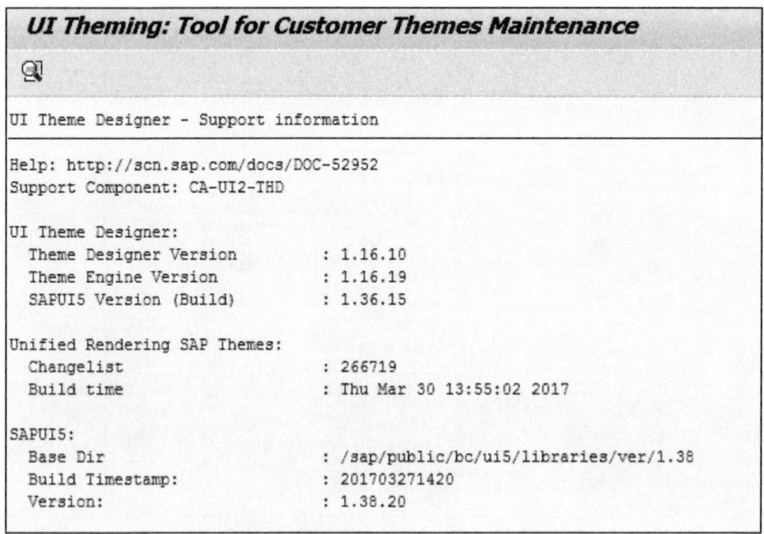

Figure 2.34 UI Theme Designer Support Information

Important Terminology

In this chapter, the following terminology was used:

- **Hub deployment**
  This is one of SAP Gateway's deployment options in which there is a separate system in the landscape for SAP Gateway that connects to the backend by RFC.

- **Embedded deployment**
  This is the other SAP Fiori-supported SAP Gateway deployment option in which SAP Gateway is installed as an add-on on the SAP ERP/backend system itself.

- **ABAP CDS views**

  ABAP CDS views are enhancements to the ABAP Dictionary concept, by which you can create semantically rich data models and use them directly from within ABAP programs.

- **Internal access point**

  This is one of the supported landscape options for SAP Fiori Cloud. In this option, business data always remains within the customer's network, and users will be able to access SAP Fiori only from within the customer's network.

- **External access point**

  This is another important landscape for SAP Fiori Cloud in which users can also access SAP Fiori from external places, that is, outside their corporate network.

- **UI theme designer**

  The UI theme designer is a tool provided by SAP, available on SAP Cloud Platform, on-premise, and SAP Enterprise Portal, which can be used to change the colors, logos, and backgrounds for various SAP UI technologies. It has four important features:

  - Quick mode: In quick mode, you can edit most needed colors, backgrounds, and company logos. This is easy for everyone to use.

  - Expert mode: This allows users to change the properties using semantic parameters. These semantic parameters will be reused throughout the UI; hence, it's important to know and test the side effects.

  - Palette: Palettes let you define your corporate colors and provide a name for reusing it, so that you don't have to define them every time you need them.

  - CSS pane: This lets you override SAP theme colors by inserting custom CSS.

 **Practice Questions**

These practice questions will help you evaluate your understanding of the topics covered in this chapter. The questions shown are similar in nature to those found on the certification examination. Although none of these questions will be found on the exam itself, they will allow you to review your knowledge of the subject. Select the correct answers, and then check the completeness of your answers in the "Practice Question Answers and Explanations" section. Remember, on the exam, you must select all correct answers and only correct answers to receive credit for the question.

1. Which of the following is *not* one of the advantage of SAP Web Dispatcher?

    ☐   A. Acts as a switch to allow or block certain HTTP requests
    ☐   B. Performs load balancing
    ☐   C. Replaces the SAP Gateway server
    ☐   D. Acts as a reverse proxy for SAP Fiori apps

2. What is true about an SAP Gateway server or frontend server in a hub architecture?

    ☐   A. It's the same as the SAP business system server.
    ☐   B. This is where OData implementations are coded.
    ☐   C. The SAP Fiori UI repository is located here.
    ☐   D. It can connect to only one SAP backend server.

3. In SAP Fiori architecture for SAP Business Suite systems, which type of application does *not* require an SAP Web Dispatcher?

    ☐   A. Transactional apps
    ☐   B. KPI apps
    ☐   C. Fact sheet apps
    ☐   D. Smart Business apps

4. Which of the following is *not* one of the advantages of the hub deployment architecture?

    ☐   A. Lower TCO
    ☐   B. Better security
    ☐   C. Routing to multiple backend business systems
    ☐   D. Separation of innovation lifecycles

5. Which of the following describe the OData provisioning service? (2 correct answers)

    ☐   A. Provides an SAP Fiori UI repository to store app-specific UIs
    ☐   B. Provides a way to register and expose OData services
    ☐   C. Lowers TCO of the SAP Gateway landscape
    ☐   D. Used in the internal access point scenario of SAP Fiori Cloud

6.   UI theme designer is available in which platforms? (3 correct answers)

☐   A. SAP Cloud Platform

☐   B. SAP Mobile Platform

☐   C. SAP Enterprise Portal

☐   D. SAP ABAP Server (frontend server)

7.   UI theme designer cannot be used to perform which of the following?

☐   A. Use a CSS editor to change CSS properties to affect an SAPUI5 application

☐   B. Add background images to tiles using **Expert** mode

☐   C. Add a custom logo to SAP Fiori launchpad

☐   D. Change the background color of a button when it is hovered over

8.   Transaction /UI5/THEME_TOOL does *not* offer which of the following capabilities?

☐   A. Upload

☐   B. Download

☐   C. Transport

☐   D. Copy

Practice Answers and Explanations

1.   Correct answer: **C**
SAP Web Dispatcher can't replace SAP Gateway server because it has its own set of functionalities. Other answer options are benefits of using an SAP Web Dispatcher.

2.   Correct answer: **C**
In a hub architecture, SAP Fiori app-specific UIs are stored in the ABAP BSP repository.

3.   Correct answer: **A**
Transactional apps don't require SAP Web Dispatcher because all the HTTP connections required always end up at the SAP Gateway server. Other application types need to contact more than one server.

4.   Correct answer: **A**

Due to additional SAP Gateway systems, TCO is higher in the hub architecture. Thus, "Lower TCO" isn't one of the advantages. The rest of the options are advantages of the hub deployment option.

5.   Correct answers: **B, C**

OData Provisioning service provides a way to register and expose OData services. By moving this feature to SAP Fiori Cloud, it reduces the TCO of the SAP Gateway landscape. In the SAP Fiori Cloud landscape, the SAP Fiori UI repository on SAP Cloud Platform is where app-specific SAP Fiori UIs are stored. In the internal access point scenario, OData provisioning isn't used because one of the aims is to not let the business data pass through SAP Cloud Platform.

6.   Correct answers: **A, C, D**

UI theme designer is currently available only in three platforms. It's not available in SAP Mobile Platform.

7.   Correct answer: **B**

A background image can't be added to a tile using **Expert** mode. Instead, you need to use the CSS section of the UI theme designer, which isn't recommended due to the high TCO involved.

8.   Correct answer: **D**

Transaction /SAPUI5/THEME_TOOL doesn't offer the copy functionality. This can be performed in the UI theme designer tool instead.

Take Away

In this chapter, we explored the SAP Fiori architecture in SAP Business Suite systems. We then saw how the architecture evolved in the SAP S/4HANA landscape and discussed the one archetype concept.

Next, we saw the architecture in hybrid scenarios, including SAP Fiori Cloud. We saw the wide variety of options available such as internal and external access points.

We then discussed the deployment options within SAP Gsateway and the advantages of each option. You learned how the OData provisioning service from SAP Cloud Platform can be used to lessen the TCO.

Next, we covered how SAP Fiori launchpad is configured using catalogs, groups, and roles to determine the assignment of tiles to the user and to the entry page. Finally, we discussed how you can use the UI theme designer to customize SAP Fiori with corporate colors and logos.

Summary

SAP Fiori comes with various architectural options and landscapes, and understanding all the options is very important to zero in on the right approach for your scenario. In the next chapter, you'll learn about SAPUI5 foundations and how generic UIs are built for SAP Fiori apps.

Chapter 3
SAPUI5 Foundations

Techniques You'll Master:

- Fit Model View Controller (MVC) to the application architecture
- Use responsive design controls for development
- Perform data binding to an SAPUI5 control
- Format, filter, sort, and group data
- Visualize business data

In this chapter, we'll start with an introduction to the SAPUI5 framework and why it was created. Next, we'll cover the MVC software architecture design pattern and see how an application built using SAPUI5 implements it. We'll then explore how the data is bound to SAPUI5 controls and how the data interaction occurs between a view and a model. We'll also study how to implement data manipulations such as formatting, filtering, sorting, and grouping. At the end, you'll also learn how to create graphs and charts to visualize business data.

Real-World Scenario

You want to start developing a simple application for employees to update their personal details. To do this, you must understand several important concepts: the basic building blocks of the application (e.g., MVC), how the data flows from the backend to the view and then back to the backend, and how to create the data in various formats on the UI. At the same time, you need to decide which controls to use in building the app so that it's responsive and usable across desktop computers, tablets, and mobile phones.

Objectives of This Portion of the Test

The objective of this portion of the SAP Fiori Certification Test is to test your knowledge on the following:

- MVC architecture
- Data binding techniques
- Data manipulation techniques (formatting, filtering, grouping, sorting)
- Routing and localization
- Component and app descriptors

Key Concepts Refresher

We'll start the introduction to SAPUI5 with concepts of the *component* and *application* descriptors. After that, we'll explore one of the most important concepts of SAPUI5: data binding to the SAPUI5 controls. We will also explore how to navigate to various SAPUI5 views using the *routing* concept. We'll conclude this section by discussing data visualization techniques and responsive design concepts.

MVC Basics

The Model View Controller (MVC) is an architecture used for web application development, and SAPUI5 has adopted it to bring these advantages into programing SAPUI5 applications (Figure 3.1).

Let's go over the responsibilities of each of the following components of this pattern:

- **Model**
  A model is a representation of the data in the database. It also represents the business logic in the backend system and provides methods to update and retrieve information from the backend. Usually, a web application has two parts where a model is implemented. On the client side, it has a class, which represents the data and *provides* methods to fetch and update the data. On the server side, it *implements* the fetch and update methods, validating the data with the business logic.

- **View**
  A view represents the visual part of your application and is usually declarative in nature. View is often a stack of various user interface (UI) controls provided by the choice of your UI library.

- **Controller**
  A controller has multiple responsibilities. It handles the user interaction, directs the model to fetch and update the data, and performs input validation. In a typical MVC application, this component will have the most code because it behaves as a facilitator and has many functions.

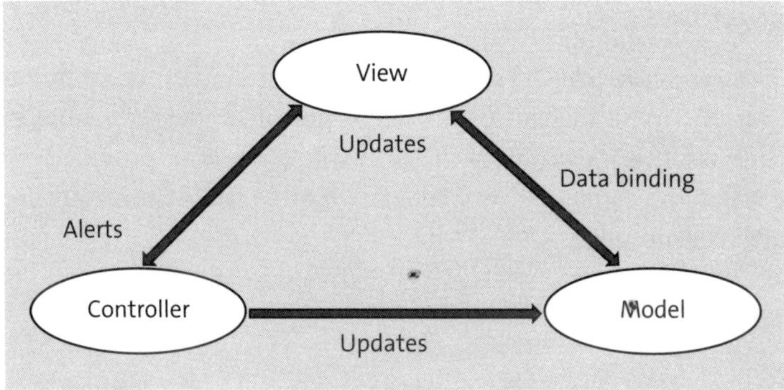

Figure 3.1 MVC Architecture and Components

MVC tries to solve many problems associated with building web applications in the following ways:

- **Modularity**
  By separating components based on their functionality, your web application will be modular in nature, thus improving readability, reusability, and maintenance of your code. For example, you can reuse the model code, and view can be implemented in another flavor or language. Similarly, you can reuse the view code and plug it into a different model code, and no change will be required to the view.

- **Parallel development**
  By separating the application into independent components, this architecture makes it possible to develop each component in parallel, thus increasing the overall speed of application development. Consider a case where a display format needs to be changed in the SAPUI5 app. Just the view can be changed, and the model code can remain untouched. In another case, where an additional business validation is required for the data to be updated, the model code can be enhanced without touching the view code.

The MVC architectural pattern has a few disadvantages as well:

- Breaking down an application into MVC components and defining interaction between them can be difficult.
- Interaction is required between developers developing various components.
- Several components can fail, so debugging can be complex.

MVC Architecture within SAPUI5

In this section, we'll discuss how SAPUI5 supports the MVC architecture for building SAP Fiori applications. We'll disuses of diverse types of models available in SAPUI5. Next, we discuss the View part and the various options provided by SAPUI5 to build the views and compare them. At last, we will discuss the Controller part, and discuss how to structure it.

SAPUI5 Models

As discussed earlier, at the client side, SAPUI5 provides classes (models) that represent the database or data and allow you to perform various operations on data. SAPUI5 provides several such models to represent each type of data source that will be used by the application. We'll explore each of these models in the following sections.

JavaScript Object Notation Model

The JavaScript Object Notation (JSON) model represents data in the JSON format, which is fully available on the client side. This client-side model is supposed to be used for small data sets and is bound to SAPUI5 controls. One common usage of the JSON model is for device properties. Device properties are fetched and stored in a JSON model so that they can be reused across the application for binding controls with this model and influencing various device-specific settings of UI controls. When you perform operations on the model, such as fetching, reading, creating, and modifying, the backend server is never contacted because all the data is already available on the client.

To use the JSON model, follow these steps:

1. Instantiate the JSON model with the following code:

```
var oJSONModel = new sap.ui.model.json.JSONModel();.
```

2. After instantiating the model, you can set data to the model in two ways:

   - You can set data inline in the code as shown below, using the `setData` application programming interface (API):

```
oJSONModel.setData({
    "materialNumber":"3843",
    "materialName":"0.5-inch Screw",
    "unitPrice":"0.55",
    "currency":"INR"
});
```

   - You can load data from a remote URL asynchronously and set it to the model as follows:

```
oJSONModel.loadData("http://datatrove.in/material.json");
```

XML Model

Although the XML model is like the JSON model, one principle difference is that data in the XML format is used as data to be set for the model. This is also a client-side model to be used for small data sets that are completely available on the client side. When compared with the JSON model, XML models are rarely used because most data available at the client side is in the JSON format.

To use the XML model, follow these steps:

1. Instantiate the XML model with the following code: `Var oXMLModel = new sap.ui.model.xml.XMLModel();`.

2. After instantiating the model, you can set data to the model in the following ways:

   You can set XML data inline as a string, as shown in Listing 3.1.

```
oXMLModel.setXML(
"<?xml version=\"1.0\" encoding=\"UTF-8\"?>"+
"<data>"+
"<materialNumber>3843</materialNumber>"+
"<materialName>0.5-inch Screw</materialName >"+
"<unitPrice>0.55</unitPrice >"+
                "<currency>INR</currency>"+
                "</data>"
);
```

Listing 3.1 Setting Data to an XML Model

You can also set XML data from a URL, as in the following code:

```
oXMLModel.loadData("http://datatrove.in/material.xml");
```

OData V2 Model

This is one of the most widely used model types, and it represents the data available on the server. This OData model supports version 2.0 of the OData specifications. Whenever you perform filtering or sorting on a list of data, a request is sent to the server to perform respective operations and send back the data. If the developer has fetched all the corresponding data into the frontend, then he can direct the model to perform these operations on the client side to save the server round trips.

Two versions support OData V2. `sap.ui.model.odata.ODataModel` is an old version and is currently deprecated. `sap.ui.model.odata.v2.ODataModel` is the latest version of the V2 model and comes with improved features as well as many new features. When you build new SAP Fiori apps, it's recommended to use `sap.ui.model.odata.v2.ODataModel`.

The OData model can be instantiated with the piece of code in Listing 3.2.

```
var oModel =
new sap.ui.model.odata.v2.ODataModel("/sap/opu/odata/sap/zpurchaseorder");
```

Listing 3.2 Instantiating the OData Model Class

The service URL is a mandatory parameter when creating a model instance. You can access only one OData service with a single instance of the OData model. If you need to access multiple services, then you need to create multiple instances of the V2 model. When you instantiate an OData model, a request is sent to the service requesting its metadata. For example, the preceding instantiation call would get triggered to `"/sap/opu/odata/sap/zpurchaseorder/$metadata"`.

Warning

Browsers implement the Same Origin Policy security concept, which won't allow you to instantiate OData models that refer to services hosted in a host other than the application itself.

Setting data to the instantiated OData model usually occurs based on bindings assigned to various UI controls (discussed in the "Data Binding" section).

If needed, you can also trigger the following manual operations on the OData instance:

- **Query operations**

  For querying an entity, you need to mention an entity set of the OData service. The success handler method receives the queried data as a parameter. Enter the following code: `oModel.read("/PurchaseRequisitions", {success: successHandler, error: errorHandler});`.

- **Read operation**

  The read operation is used to read a specified entry of the entity. So it's required to pass the entity key in addition to the entity set name. It uses the same API "read" of the V2 model. This triggers an HTTP GET request. Enter the following code: `oModel.read("/PurchaseRequisitions("0003456632")", {success: successHandler, error: errorHandler});`.

- **Create operation**

  For creating a new entry within an entity, you need to mention the entity set name as well as the required properties of the entity. The created entry will be sent back to the success handler upon successful operation. This triggers an HTTP POST request. Enter the code in Listing 3.3.

```
var newEntry = {
    MaterialNumber:"424",
    Quantity: 33,
    Unit: "EA"
};
```

```
oModel.create("/PurchaseRequisitions",
  newEntry, {success: successHandler, error:
  errorHandler});
```

Listing 3.3 Triggering a Create Call from an OData Model

- **Update operation**

  For updating an existing entry, you need to specify the specific entry using its key and the data to be updated. No data is sent back after a successful update. The update operation triggers a PUT or MERGE call based on a setting on the OData model. Enter the code in Listing 3.4.

  ```
  Var updateEntry = {
  PRNumber: "0003456633",
  MaterialNumber:"424",
      Quantity: 35,
      Unit: "EA"
  };
  oModel.update("/PurchaseRequisitions("0003456633")", updateEntry, {success:
  successHandler, error: errorHandler});
  ```

  Listing 3.4 Triggering an Update Call from an OData Model

- **Delete operation**

  For deleting an existing entry, you need to use the Remove method of the OData model with a URL pointing to the specific entry to be deleted by specifying the key in the URL. Remove operation triggers an HTTP DELETE call. Enter the following code:

  ```
  oModel.remove("/PurchaseRequisitions("0003456633")", {success: successHandler,
  error: errorHandler});.
  ```

Resource Model

It's common for the app to contain many string literals for labels, titles, and messages. For translation, these language-dependent texts are stored in files with the extension *.properties*. Using binding techniques, texts in these files are available to the application with the resource model.

SAPUI5 Views

Views in SAPUI5 return a hierarchy of SAPUI5 controls to be rendered on a browser. SAP provides a choice for the developers and allows you to build a view using any of HTML, JavaScript, JSON, and XML formats. Other than the JavaScript flavor, all others are declarative in nature and thus keep the view and the controller logic separate. XML is the preferred way of developing views in standard SAP Fiori apps. It's also a declarative method of building the views. For these reasons, XML is the recommended method of building SAPUI5 views. Now we'll see the syntax of building views in various flavors.

JavaScript Views

A JavaScript view uses suffix `.view.js` for the file name. SAPUI5 provides the following two default methods that can be implemented:

- `createContent()`
  This method creates the UI for the view. This method returns either a single SAPUI5 control or a hierarchy of SAPUI5 controls to be rendered on the screen.

- `getControllerName()`
  This method informs the SAPUI5 framework about the name of the controller for the view.

The code in Listing 3.5 describes how to define a view in JavaScript. The name of the file is *View2.view.js* and will reside in folder *view*.

```javascript
sap.ui.jsview("ViewTypes.view.View2", {
    getControllerName: function() {
        return "ViewTypes.controller.View2";
    },
    createContent: function(oController) {
        var oVBox = new sap.m.VBox({
            width: "50%",
            items: [
                new sap.m.Label({
                    text: "Product Name"
                }),
                new sap.m.Input(),
                new sap.m.Button({
                    text: "Search",
                    press: oController.getProducts
                })
            ]
        }).addStyleClass("sapUiResponsiveMargin");

        var oPage = new sap.m.Page({
            title: "Demo - JS View",
            content: [oVBox]
        });
        var oApp = new sap.m.App({
            pages: [oPage]
        });
```

```
        return oApp;
    }
});
```
Listing 3.5 Example of a JavaScript View

This view returns an app control and has one page inside this app. Method `create-Content` has the controller as the input parameter and can be used to refer to methods, for example, for specifying event handlers.

XML Views

The XML view is created in an XML file with file name suffix *.view.xml*. Each control has a specified XML tag. Most of the SAP Fiori apps delivered by SAP have an XML view. This is the suggested approach when creating an SAPUI5 application. A `controllerName` is specified in the root tag (`<mvc:View>`) of the view file.

Listing 3.6 illustrates how an XML view is defined.

```
<mvc:View xmlns:mvc="sap.ui.core.mvc" xmlns="sap.m" controllerName=
"ViewTypes.controller.View1" height="100%">
    <Page title="Demo - XML View">
        <VBox class="sapUiResponsiveMargin" width="50%">
            <items>
                <Label text="Product Name"/>
                <Input/>
                <Button text="Search" press=".getProducts"/>
            </items>
        </VBox>
    </Page>
</mvc:View>
```
Listing 3.6 Example of an XML View

The root tag lists all the namespaces used in the view. Names of the SAPUI5 control libraries are used as XML namespaces. For example, `xmlns:layout="sap.ui.com-mons.layout"` defines a namespace `layout`, and `sap.ui.commons.layout.MatrixLayout` can be specified as `<layout:MatrixLayout>`. One of the required namespaces (usually the most-used namespace) is defined as a default namespace. No prefixes are required to specify controls from that library. For example, in the preceding code listing, "`sap.m`" is defined as the default namespace. You build a hierarchy of SAPUI5 controls by nesting the corresponding controls within the XML file.

HTML Views

The HTML view type is defined in a file ending with *.view.html*. The name of the
JSON view is derived from the relative position of the file in the folder structure
and the file name of the view. Listing 3.7 shows how HTML views are defined.

```
<template data-controller-name="ViewTypes.controller.View2">
 <div data-sap-ui-type="sap.m.App">
  <div data-sap-ui-type="sap.m.Page" data-title="Demo HTML View">
   <div data-sap-ui-aggregation="content">
    <div data-sap-ui-type="sap.m.VBox" class="sapUiResponsiveMargin"
     data-width="50%">
     <div data-sap-ui-aggregation="items">
      <div data-sap-ui-type="sap.m.Label" data-text="Product"></div>
      <div data-sap-ui-type="sap.m.Input"></div>
      <div data-sap-ui-type="sap.m.Button" data-text="Search"
     data-press=".getProducts"></div>
     </div>
    </div>
   </div>
  </div>
 </div>
</template>
```

Listing 3.7 Example of an HTML View

`template` is the root element of the HTML view and it specifies the controller name.
`data-sap-ui-type` specifies the name of the SAPUI5 control. `data-sap-ui-aggregation`
defines the aggregation of the SAPUI5 control. `id` and `class` are specified without
the `data-` prefix.

JSON Views

The JSON view type is defined in a file name with the suffix *.view.json*. The name of
the view is derived from the folder structure and the file name of the view. JSON
views are defined as shown in Listing 3.8.

```
{
    "Type": "sap.ui.core.mvc.JSONView",
    "controllerName": "ViewTypes.controller.View2",
    "content": [{
        "Type": "sap.m.App",
        "pages": [{
            "Type": "sap.m.Page",
            "title": "Demo - JSON View",
            "content": [{
                "Type": "sap.m.VBox",
                "class": "sapUiResponsiveMargin",
```

```
                "width": "50%",
                "items": [{
                    "Type": "sap.m.Label",
                    "text": "Product Name"
                }, {
                    "Type": "sap.m.Input"
                }, {
                    "Type": "sap.m.Button",
                    "text": "Search",
                    "press": ".getProducts"
                }]
            }]
        }]
    }]
}
```

Listing 3.8 Example of a JSON View

In a JSON view, the `Type` property specifies the SAPUI5 control name. Class `sap.ui.core.mvc.JSONView` is the root control in a JSON view. The `content` property of this class will specify a tree of SAPUI5 controls to be shown as the view's content. Event handlers will be executed with the controller as the context object.

Fragments

Fragments are independent, lightweight, reusable UI parts that can be used to modularize the view part of your app. They are like views, but there is no controller attached to fragments. If they need event handlers, then those event handlers need to be implemented within the controller of the view where the fragment is included.

Fragments are widely used while designing dialogs because dialogs are generally common across screens. Another use case is for designing dynamic screens. You may use different fragments inside the view based on business scenarios (e.g., edit/view, authorization to view limited information).

Listing 3.9 illustrates how to define a JavaScript fragment. As you can see, this is similar to defining a JavaScript view, where the createContent method returns the content of the view as a control. There is no getControllerName method because fragments don't have an associated controller.

```
sap.ui.jsfragment("fragments.view.Body ", {
    createContent: function(oController) {
        var oVBox = new sap.m.VBox({
  items:[
```

```
    ..multiple controls…
new sap.ui.commons.Button({
 text:"Submit",
    press: oController.submit
    })
 ]
      });
      return oVBox;
  }
});
```

Listing 3.9 Example of a JavaScript-based SAPUI5 Fragment

Listing 3.10 shows how to define an XML fragment. As you can see, it's the same as an XML view with the main difference being that there is no <View> tag at the root. The root tag can be any SAPUI5 control. The other difference is that there is no specification of a controller name.

```
<ObjectHeader xmlns="sap.m" title="{/FirstName}"
number="{ parts:[{path:'/SalesRevenue'},{path:'/Currency'}],
type: 'sap.ui.model.type.Currency',formatOptions:{showMeasure:true} }"
numberUnit="{Currency}" titlePress=".titlePressed">
<attributes>
        <ObjectAttribute text="{/LastName}"/>
        <ObjectAttribute text="{path:'/DoB',
type: 'sap.ui.model.type.Date',
formatOptions: { pattern: 'MM/dd/yyyy' }}"/>
    </attributes>
</ObjectHeader>
```

Listing 3.10 Example of an XML-based SAPUI5 Fragment

Note

When instantiating a fragment, the controller instance can be passed so that event handlers for the fragment's controls can be specified within the fragment and defined inside the controller.

Listing 3.11 shows how to include all three types of fragments inside an XML view. Note the value of the type property in the XML element <core:Fragment>.

```
<mvc:View xmlns:core="sap.ui.core" xmlns:mvc="sap.ui.core.mvc" xmlns=
"sap.m" xmlns:commons="sap.ui.commons"
    controllerName="fragments.controller.instantiateFragments">
    <commons:HorizontalDivider/>
    <core:Fragment fragmentName="fragments.view.Header" type="XML"/>
    <commons:HorizontalDivider/>
```

```
    <core:Fragment fragmentName="fragments.view.Body" type="JS"/>
    <commons:HorizontalDivider/>
    <core:Fragment fragmentName="fragments.view.Footer" type="HTML"/>
</mvc:View>
```

Listing 3.11 Using XML JavaScript and HTML Fragments Inside a View

The following code shows how to programmatically instantiate a fragment in a controller for creating a dialog: `var oBody = sap.ui.jsfragment("fragments.view.Body", this);`. Note that the second parameter (`this`) while instantiating a fragment is an object where the event handler for the fragment is implemented. Usually, it's the controller object where the event handler is implemented.

The following code illustrates how to programmatically instantiate an XML view: `var oHeader = sap.ui.xmlfragment("fragments.view.Header", this);`. Here also, you can pass the instance of the controller if the XML fragment refers to any of the controller's methods.

When a fragment is used for showing dialogs, they aren't part of the XML view, so they don't inherit the model and data binding. Dialog is also not part of the view's lifecycle management; that is, the fragment dialog is never destroyed even if the view is destroyed to free its resources. For such scenarios, there is a method called `addDependent` on the view that is used as follows: `oView.addDependent(oFragment);`.

Now, `oFragment` gets added to the dependents aggregation of the `oView`. `oFragment` will inherit the model and binding contexts of the view. `oFragment` will also get destroyed when the `oView` gets destroyed.

SAPUI5 Controllers

Controllers contain methods for handling interactions between the model and view. They also have various event handler methods for the view performing validations and user confirmations.

Within SAPUI5, a view and a controller are usually created together as a pair with similar names. A view specifies the corresponding controller in its definition, and every controller name ends with `.controller.js`.

Lifecycle Hooks

The SAPUI5 framework provides the following four methods that act as event handlers or hooks throughout the lifecycle of a view:

- `onInit()`

  This method is called whenever the view is instantiated, that is, when all its controls are created. But the view isn't yet rendered now, so the Document Object Model (DOM) can't be accessed. But you can refer to the controls by their IDs, perform one-time initializations, bind event handlers, and set models and binding contexts. This is only called the first time when the view is getting instantiated, not when the view is getting rendered every time.

  In a master detail application, for example, consider the master and detail views. `onInit` of the detail view is called only when the first item on the master list is clicked on. This is when the view is getting instantiated. On further selection of different master items, `onInit` of the detail view won't be called because the existing detail view instance is used in this case, and just the binding context is changed.

- `onBeforeRendering()`

  This method is similar to the `onInit()` method but is called every time a view is going to be rendered (or re-rendered). This can be used if you want to perform any data context-specific actions on the view content.

- `onAfterRendering()`

  As the name suggests, this method is triggered when the view is already rendered and the DOM is available. Any post-rendering manipulations of DOM can be done here. This method is called after every rendering of the view.

- `onExit()`

  This method is called whenever the view is destroyed. You can use this to destroy any view-specific resources that are no longer required.

Figure 3.2 gives a visual representation of lifecycle hooks and events.

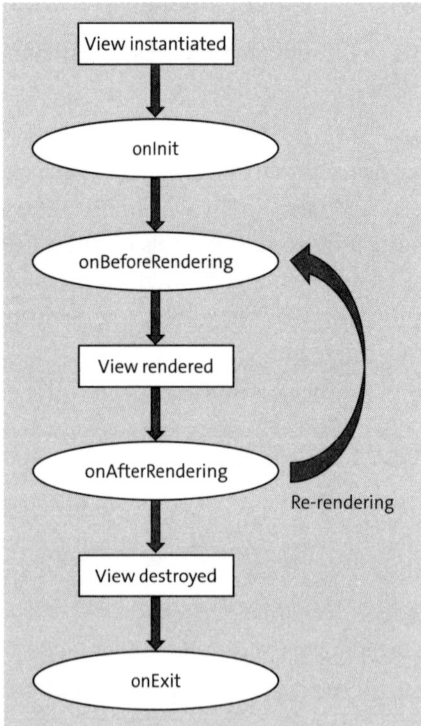

Figure 3.2 Events and Lifecycle Hooks in a Controller

Asynchronous Module Loading

Controllers in SAPUI5 are written in a specific syntax called Asynchronous Module Definition (AMD). AMD is a JavaScript language specification that specifies the definition of modules and dependencies so they can be loaded asynchronously. AMD allows you to define the library in smaller modules with dependencies specified. This approach speeds up library loading by loading only the required parts of the library, thus also speeding up application performance. Synchronous loading also isn't a good user experience for the user because the whole app freezes when a synchronous call is in progress.

At this time, SAPUI5 modules aren't yet ready to be loaded asynchronously. But for future compatibility, SAP recommends using the AMD syntax for the controller definition so that when asynchronous loading of SAPUI5 module becomes available, existing apps will run smoothly.

Let's consider the definition of a controller using AMD syntax, as shown in Listing 3.12.

```javascript
sap.ui.define([
    "sap/ui/core/mvc/Controller",
    "sap/ui/model/json/JSONModel",
    "sap/m/Dialog",
    "sap/m/Button",
    "sap.m.Text"
], function(Controller, JSONModel, Dialog, Button, Text) {
    "use strict";

    return Controller.extend("ViewTypes.controller.View1", {
        onInit: function() {
            var oModel = new JSONModel({
                "FirstName": "Srinivasa",
                "LastName": "Ramanujan"
            });
            this.getView().setModel(oModel);
        },
        onConfirmation: function(oEvent) {
            var dialog = new Dialog({
                title: "Warning",
                type: "Message",
                content: new Text({
                    text: "Are you sure to delete?"
                }),
                beginButton: new Button({
                    text: "OK",
                    press: function() {
                        dialog.close();
                    }
                }),
                afterClose: function() {
                    dialog.destroy();
                }
            });
            dialog.open();
        }
    });
});
```

Listing 3.12 An SAPUI5 Controller using AMD Syntax

`sap.ui.define` allows you to send an array of dependencies and then provides a factory function that gets called when all the dependencies are loaded.

In Listing 3.12, we've sent six modules in an array (first parameter) as dependencies to the controller's definition. Each of these dependencies (their return values) go as parameters to the factory function so that they are further within the controller's methods. The factory function will get executed only after each of the dependencies is loaded.

Component and Application Descriptor

In this section, we'll explore the concept of components in SAPUI5 and how is it used to structure an SAPUI5 app. Then, we'll explore the application descriptor file and learn about the important attributes defined in it.

Component

A component is a self-contained and reusable piece of code in an SAPUI5 application. Components are classified into the following two types:

- **UI components**
  UI components have an associated UI part in addition to the application logic. These components inherit from the `sap.ui.core.UIComponent` class. An SAP Fiori app is an example of a UI component.

- **Faceless components**
  Faceless components are code-only parts without any UI. They inherit from the `sap.ui.core.Component` class. For example, all the attachment-related functionality can be handled by a faceless component and reused across SAP Fiori apps.

SAP Fiori apps are component-based apps, which means that in an SAP Fiori launchpad, an SAP Fiori app is represented by a component. Thus, components are entry points to SAP Fiori apps. Each SAP Fiori app will have one primary component, which will be registered with the SAP Fiori launchpad so that this component gets loaded upon clicking the corresponding SAP Fiori tile in the SAP Fiori launchpad.

- **Metadata**
  Before SAPUI5 version 1.30, a component's metadata property was used to store several app-related settings and properties. From version 1.30, a new application descriptor file called *manifest.json* was introduced, and all app-specific settings were moved to that file. *Component.js* will contain a reference to *manifest.json*, as shown in Listing 3.13, directing the SAPUI5 framework to fetch settings from there.

```
sap.ui.core.Component.extend("certification.fiori.Component", {
    "metadata": {
        "manifest": "json"
    }
});
```

Listing 3.13 A Component Specifying the manifest.json File for the Metadata

- `init`

  This method will be called only once per component instance while the component is getting initialized. This method is rarely called explicitly; rather, it's called automatically by the SAPUI5 framework. You can use this method to perform any one-time operations related to the component or the app.

- `createContent`

  As the method name indicates, this method creates the content of the component. This method should return a hierarchy of SAPUI5 controls, representing the UI part of the component.

Application Descriptor

As the name suggests, an application descriptor is a file with various configurations and properties of an SAPUI5 application. This is inspired by the Web App Manifest, which is a W3C specification. Per the standard, the manifest file should be a JSON-based file, providing developers a central place to control attributes for an application and to store application-related metadata. The *manifest.json* file needs to be created at the root of the SAPUI5 app at the same level as *Component.js*.

Whenever an OData model is instantiated, it first loads the metadata of the model. Using properties in the *manifest.json*, you can preload the metadata to improve the app performance. For JSON and XML models, if their data source is from an external URL, the preload feature will load the entire data in parallel with component loading, thus improving performance. But if the data is located locally within the app, then the data is already available in *component-preload.js*, thus the preload feature doesn't make sense. For the same reason, the preload feature should not be used for resource models.

Table 3.1 lists important (although not exhaustive) application-specific attributes and their uses.

Attribute Name	Attribute Description
`sap.app.id`	Unique identifier of the SAP Fiori app. This should be the same as the component name.
`sap.app.i18n`	Location containing language-dependent text literals of the app. This must be a URL relative to the *manifest.json/Component.js*.

Table 3.1 Application Specific Attributes

Attribute Name	Attribute Description
`sap.app.applicationVersion`	Signifies the version of the app to be maintained by the developer and can be useful in support scenarios.
`sap.app.title`	Title of the app visible at various places within the app. It refers to a property on the *i18n* file so that you can maintain language-dependent titles for the app.
`sap.app.ach`	This is the SAP Support Component which you can use to raise bugs to SAP.
`sap.app.dataSources`	Used to mention details of various data sources such as OData, JSON, and XML. It mentions various properties of the data source and is further referred in attribute `sap.ui5.models`. ■ `uri`: URL of the data source, which can be for OData service, JSON, or XML data. ■ `type`: Type of the data source for OData, XML, JSON, or OData annotation. ■ `settings`: This is a set of attributes specific to the data source type. ■ `odataVersion`: 2.0 (default) or 4.0. ■ `annotations`: URL specifying annotations to the data source. ■ `maxAge`: Cache-specific attribute specifying how long the fetched data can be used from the cache.

`sap.ui.icons`	Specifies the relative path to various icons to be used in the app. Here is an example from a reference app in SAP Web IDE.
	
	`"icons": {`
	`    "icon": "sap-icon://Fiori7/F1373",`
	`    "favIcon": "icon/F1373_Approve_Purchase_Orders.ico",`
	`    "phone": "icon/launchicon/57_iPhone_Desktop_Launch.png",`
	`    "phone@2": "icon/launchicon/114_iPhone-Retina_Web_Clip.png",`
	`    "tablet": "icon/launchicon/72_iPad_Desktop_Launch.png",`
	`    "tablet@2": "icon/launchicon/144_iPad_Retina_Web_Clip.png"`
	`}`

`sap.ui.deviceTypes`	Specifies which of the desktop, tablet, and phone devices are supported by the app.

Table 3.1 Application Specific Attributes (Cont.)

Attribute Name	Attribute Description
`sap.ui.fullWidth`	Defines whether the app uses letterboxing or takes up the full screen.
`sap.ui5.resources`	Used to specify various resources such as JavaScript files and Cascading Style Sheet (CSS) files to be loaded for running the application.
`sap.ui5.dependencies`	Specifies various dependencies for the application to run: ■ `minUI5Version`: Specifies the minimum version of the SAPUI5 library required for the application to run. ■ `libs`: Specifies the various libraries required by the app. ■ `components`: If your application requires other components, you can mention their IDs here.
`sap.ui5.models`	Specifies which models need to be automatically created and destroyed by the SAPUI5 framework. You can create named models by specifying a *key*. ■ `type`: Model class name corresponding to an OData, JSON, or XML model. ■ `uri`: URL for the OData service or data URL for the JSON or XML models. ■ `settings`: Attributes to be passed while instantiating the model. This depends on the model type. ■ `dataSource`: Refers to the `sap.app.dataSources` attribute. The `uri` attribute isn't required if a `dataSource` is mentioned. If this is an OData service, then the OData model V2 version is created automatically. If the V1 version needs to be instantiated, then it needs to be specified using `type`. ■ `preload`: You can specify if the model has to be loaded in parallel to loading the component. This can speed up the performance of the SAP Fiori app.
`sap.ui5.routing`	Specifies the routing-related configuration parameters.
`sap.ui5.contentDensities`	Specifies whether the application supports *compact* and *cozy* content densities.

Table 3.1 Application Specific Attributes (Cont.)

Data Binding

Data binding is one of the most important and useful concepts within SAPUI5. Using data binding, you can automate the movement of data from the view to the model and vice versa. Efficient use of data binding can significantly reduce the amount of code you write in an SAPUI5 application.

As we know, data in an SAPUI5 application always exists in a model. In display scenarios, you need to set this model data to SAPUI5 controls to show the data to the user, for example, when showing a list of purchase orders in an SAPUI5 table.

In update/create scenarios, data from the UI needs to get stored back in the model to further update the database on the server. Instead of explicitly writing code to make these data transfers, data binding provides ways to automate them.

There are three types of binding modes to handle various scenarios:

- **One-way binding**
  In this binding mode, changes to the model are transported to the bound UI controls, but changes made on the UI controls don't affect the values on the model. Figure 3.3 shows how the data gets transported.

- **Two-way binding**
  In this binding mode, values in the model, as well as bound controls, are always in sync. Any changes in either the model or the bound SAPUI5 control are automatically transported to the other. This is a very useful feature in update scenarios. Data is transported as shown in Figure 3.4.

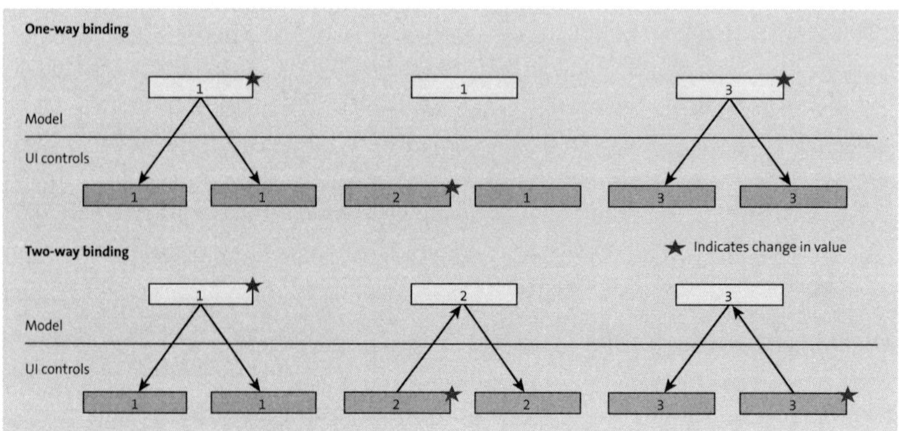

Figure 3.3 One-Way and Two-Way Binding

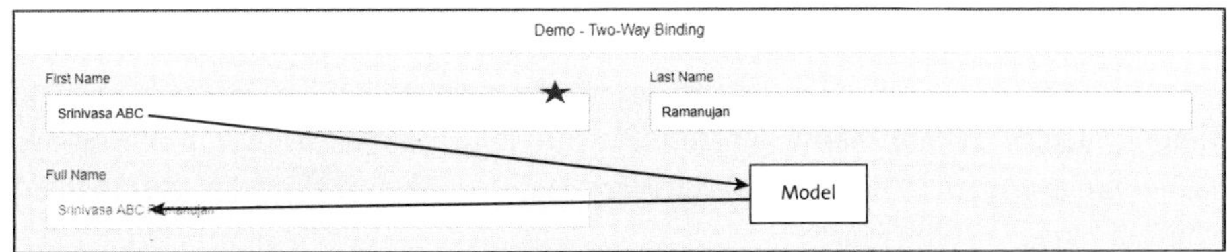

Figure 3.4 Data Transportation in Two-Way Binding

- **One-time binding**

  In this binding mode, values from model to view controls get transferred only once (as seen in Figure 3.5). Further changes to data in neither the model nor the UI controls affect each other. This is suitable to data that seldom changes while running the application. Resource models use this binding mode for setting translatable texts to SAPUI5 controls. Because the model no longer needs to keep a tab on changes and update the UI controls, this is better from a performance point of view when compared to one-way binding.

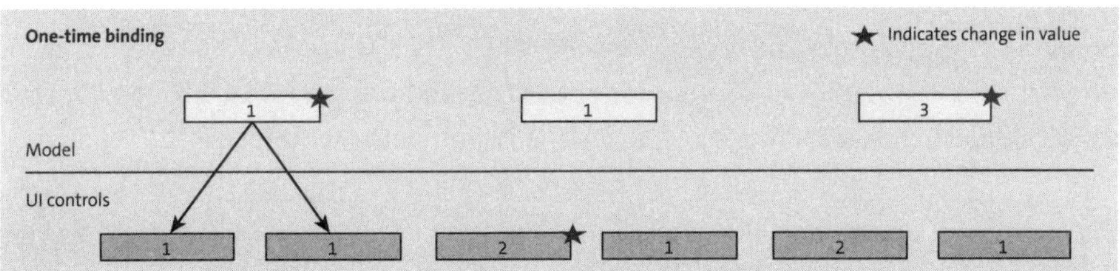

Figure 3.5 One-Time Binding

Table 3.2 displays the default binding and supported binding modes for each model type. The resource model only supports one-time binding because it never changes during application runtime.

Binding Mode Models	One-Way	Two-Way	One-Time	Default
JSON	X	X	X	Two-Way
XML	X	X	X	Two-Way
OData (V2and V4)	X	X	X	One-Way
Resource	–	–	X	One-Time

Table 3.2 Default Binding and Supported Binding Modes for Each Model Type

Now let's explore how to perform these data transfers without using data binding.

Scenario

The UI contains two input fields, one each for **First Name** and **Last Name**, and a text field to display the **Full Name**, which is nothing but the concatenation of first and last name as shown in Figure 3.6. When **First Name** or **Last Name** fields are changed, the **Full Name** is recalculated.

Figure 3.6 No Binding, First and Last Name

There is a JSON model containing first and last names, and the requirement is to show first name, last name, and full name on the screen.

Figure 3.7 shows how the view is coded. Note that there is a change handling method processFullName mentioned for both the **First Name** and **Last Name** controls to recalculate the **Full Name** upon a change in any of these fields.

```
1   <mvc:View xmlns:html="http://www.w3.org/1999/xhtml" xmlns:mvc="sap.ui.core.mvc"
2   xmlns="sap.m" controllerName="DemoWithoutBinding.controller.View1">
3       <App>
4           <pages>
5               <Page title="Demo - No Binding">
6                   <content>
7                       <HBox width="100%" id="__hbox0">
8                           <items>
9                               <VBox class="sapUiResponsiveMargin" width="100%" direction="Column" id="__vbox1">
10                                  <items>
11                                      <Label text="First Name" width="100%" id="__label0"/>
12                                      <Input width="100%" id="__input0" change="processFullName"/>
13                                  </items>
14                              </VBox>
15                              <VBox class="sapUiResponsiveMargin" width="100%" direction="Column" id="__vbox2">
16                                  <items>
17                                      <Label text="Last Name" width="100%" id="__label1"/>
18                                      <Input width="100%" id="__input1" change="processFullName"/>
19                                  </items>
20                              </VBox>
21                          </items>
22                      </HBox>
23                      <VBox class="sapUiResponsiveMargin" width="45%" direction="Column" id="__vbox0">
24                          <items>
25                              <Label text="Full Name" width="100%" id="__label3"/>
26                              <Input width="100%" id="__input3" editable="false" enabled="false"/>
27                          </items>
28                      </VBox>
29                  </content>
30              </Page>
31          </pages>
32      </App>
33  </mvc:View>
```

Figure 3.7 XML View

Figure 3.8 shows how the controller is coded to fetch the values from the model and set them to the view's controls. As a first step, a JSON model is created and supplied with the required data. Next, the required values from the model are fetched and collected in variables. Then, for each of the SAPUI5 controls, the instance is fetched, and the setValue method is used to set the value from the JSON model.

```javascript
1  sap.ui.define([
2      "sap/ui/core/mvc/Controller",
3      "sap/ui/model/json/JSONModel"
4  ], function(Controller, JSONModel) {
5      "use strict";
6      return Controller.extend("DemoWithoutBinding.controller.View1", {
7          onInit: function() {
8              var oModel = new JSONModel({
9                  "FirstName": "Srinivasa",
10                 "LastName": "Ramanujan"
11             });
12
13             //Get values from model
14             var oFirstName = oModel.getProperty("/FirstName");
15             var oLastName = oModel.getProperty("/LastName");
16
17             //Set values to the UI controls
18             this.getView().byId("__input0").setValue(oFirstName);
19             this.getView().byId("__input1").setValue(oLastName);
20             this.getView().byId("__input3").setValue(oFirstName + " " + oLastName);
21         },
22         processFullName: function() {
23             //Get values from UI5 controls
24             var oFirstName = this.getView().byId("__input0").getValue();
25             var oLastName = this.getView().byId("__input1").getValue();
26
27             //Set the Full name to the UI5 control
28             this.getView().byId("__input3").setValue(oFirstName + " " + oLastName);
29         }
30     });
31 });
```

Figure 3.8 Controller Coding without Binding

There is also another method implemented called processFullName, which takes care of updating the **Full Name** upon a change in **First Name** or **Last Name**. In this name, the required values are fetched directly from the SAPUI5 controls, and then they are assigned back to the SAPUI5 control for **Full Name**.

In the following sections, we'll dive into the various binding types.

Property Binding

Using the property binding technique, you can bind the various properties of the SAPUI5 control to the model's data. Property binding involves the following two steps:

1. Set the model to the control (or to any of its parent controls).

2. Associate the property of the SAPUI5 control with a value in the model using a path.

Now, let's code the previous exercise using property binding techniques.

The coding shown in Figure 3.9 demonstrates how a model is instantiated and set to the view. You may notice that we no longer have the steps of fetching data from the model as well as steps to set these values to the SAPUI5 controls.

```
1▼ sap.ui.define([
2        "sap/ui/core/mvc/Controller",
3        "sap/ui/model/json/JSONModel"
4▼ ], function(Controller, JSONModel) {
5        "use strict";
6
7▼      return Controller.extend("DemoWithoutBinding.controller.View1", {
8▼          onInit: function(){
9▼              var oModel = new JSONModel({
10                  "FirstName": "Srinivasa",
11                  "LastName": "Ramanujan"
12              });
13              this.getView().setModel(oModel);
14          }
15      });
16
17  });
```

Figure 3.9 Controller Coding Showing How to Set the Model to the View

The view does the job of associating the value property of Input controls to values from the model. You may notice that the controls on the view no longer have the change handler methods due to the default two-way binding of the JSON model (Figure 3.10).

```
1▼ <mvc:View xmlns:html="http://www.w3.org/1999/xhtml" xmlns:mvc="sap.ui.core.mvc"
2    xmlns="sap.m" controllerName="DemoWithoutBinding.controller.View1">
3▼      <App>
4▼          <pages>
5▼              <Page title="Demo - No Binding">
6▼                  <content>
7▼                      <HBox width="100%" id="__hbox0">
8▼                          <items>
9▼                              <VBox class="sapUiResponsiveMargin" width="100%" direction="Column" id="__vbox1">
10▼                                  <items>
11                                      <Label text="First Name" width="100%" id="__label0"/>
12                                      <Input width="100%" id="__input0" value="{/FirstName}"/>
13                                  </items>
14                              </VBox>
15▼                              <VBox class="sapUiResponsiveMargin" width="100%" direction="Column" id="__vbox2">
16▼                                  <items>
17                                      <Label text="Last Name" width="100%" id="__label1"/>
18                                      <Input width="100%" id="__input1" value="{/LastName}"/>
19                                  </items>
20                              </VBox>
21                          </items>
22                      </HBox>
23▼                      <VBox class="sapUiResponsiveMargin" width="45%" direction="Column" id="__vbox0">
24▼                          <items>
25                              <Label text="Full Name" width="100%" id="__label3"/>
26                              <Input width="100%" id="__input3" editable="false" enabled="false" value="{/FirstName} {/LastName}"/>
27                          </items>
28                      </VBox>
29                  </content>
30              </Page>
31          </pages>
32      </App>
33  </mvc:View>
```

Figure 3.10 XML View Coding Showing Binding to the "value" Property

Aggregation Binding

Aggregation binding is relevant to controls that have several child controls, for example, tables, dropdown fields, and lists. In aggregation binding, an array or a list from the model is bound to an SAPUI5 control, and child controls automatically get created per each entry in the bound array or list of the model.

Templates

In the template-based aggregation binding technique, a static SAPUI5 control tree is provided as a template, in addition to the path where the data is located, and multiple child controls mirroring the template get created for each row of the model data. A sample template for rows of a table in an XML view can be written as shown in Figure 3.11.

```xml
<mvc:View xmlns:html="http://www.w3.org/1999/xhtml" xmlns:mvc="sap.ui.core.mvc" xmlns="sap.m"
    controllerName="DemoWithoutBinding.controller.View1">
    <App>
        <pages>
            <Page title="Aggregation Binding">
                <content>
                    <Table items="{/Products}" class="sapUiResponsiveMargin" width="50%">
                        <columns>
                            <Column width="12em">
                                <Text text="Product"/>
                            </Column>
                            <Column>
                                <Text text="Per Unit"/>
                            </Column>
                            <Column>
                                <Text text="In Stock"/>
                            </Column>
                        </columns>
                        <items>
                            <ColumnListItem>
                                <cells>
                                    <ObjectIdentifier title="{ProductName}" text="{ProductID}"/>
                                    <Text text="{QuantityPerUnit}"/>
                                    <Text text="{UnitsInStock}"/>
                                </cells>
                            </ColumnListItem>
                        </items>
                    </Table>
                </content>
            </Page>
        </pages>
    </App>
</mvc:View>
```


Figure 3.11 Specifying an Aggregation Binding Path and a Binding Template

The result of the aggregation binding is shown in Figure 3.12.

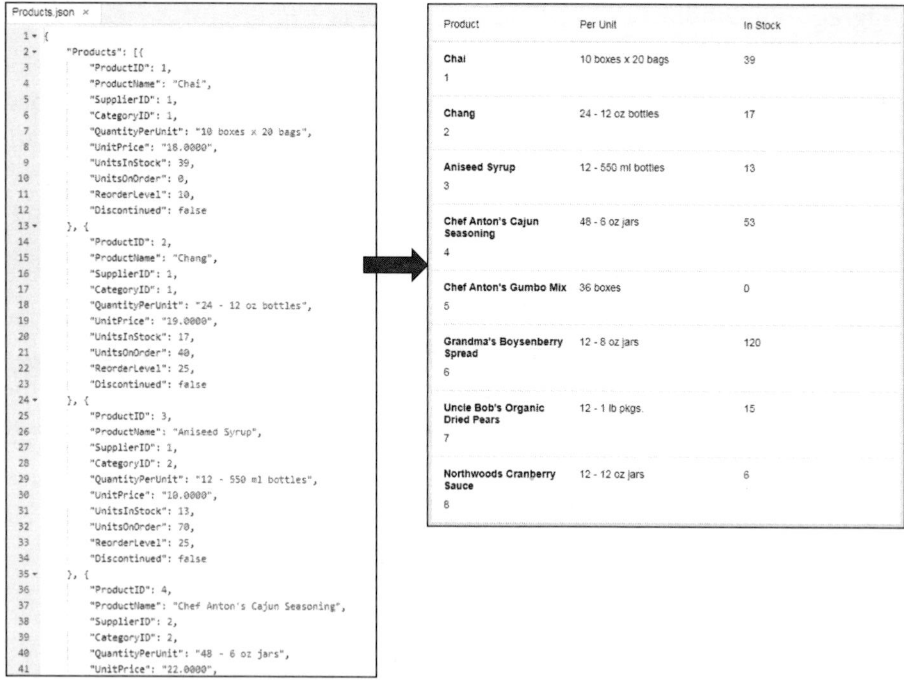

Figure 3.12 Data and the Result of Aggregation Binding

Factory Functions

In this technique, instead of providing a static template, a factory function is provided to the aggregation binding. This function will return a tree of SAPUI5 controls. The factory function will run once per each entry of the bound data, thus creating a list of controls. Because this is a code-based approach, you can design the factory function to return dynamic controls based on the data. Thus, the factory function is useful when you have complex requirements in aggregation binding.

Figure 3.13 shows how to use a factory function and how to add a style class easily to a specific row based on the data that will be bound. You may also decide to use an altogether different control (e.g., error icon) within the row.

In Figure 3.14, the output shows how a row was highlighted.

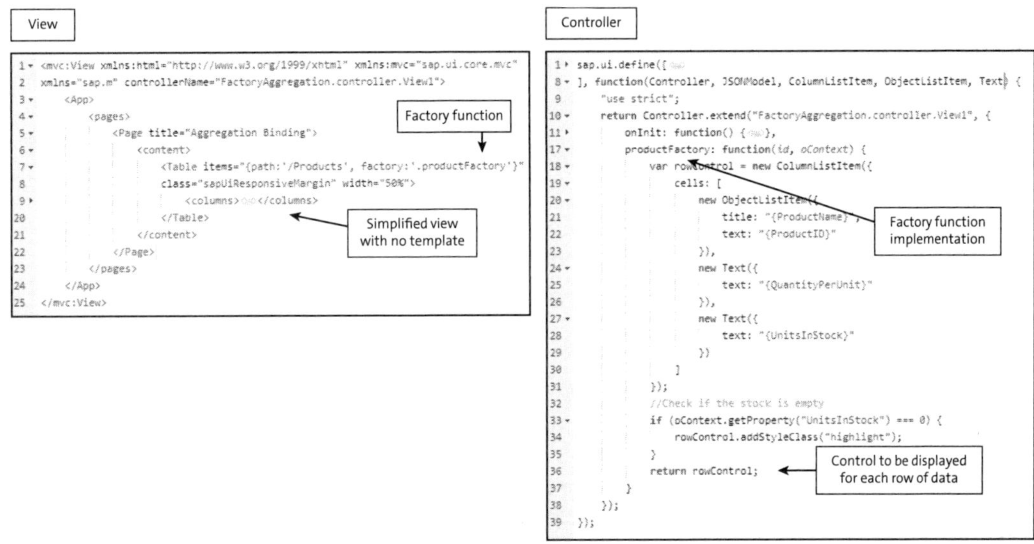

Figure 3.13 View and Controller for Aggregation Binding Based on the Factory Function

Product	Per Unit	In Stock
Chai	10 boxes x 20 bags	39
Chang	24 - 12 oz bottles	17
Aniseed Syrup	12 - 550 ml bottles	13
Chef Anton's Cajun Seasoning	48 - 6 oz jars	53
Chef Anton's Gumbo Mix	36 boxes	0
Grandma's Boysenberry Spread	12 - 8 oz jars	120
Uncle Bob's Organic Dried Pears	12 - 1 lb pkgs.	15
Northwoods Cranberry Sauce	12 - 12 oz jars	6

Figure 3.14 Output of Aggregation Binding Based on the Factory Function

Filtering, Sorting, and Grouping

Now that you know how to perform aggregation binding, let's explore how to do advanced operations like filtering, sorting and grouping. These operations are usually performed in event handler functions, whenever users perform filtering, sorting and grouping on lists.

- **Filtering**

  Whenever the aggregation binding is used to fetch a list of data from the backend, the resulting list can be limited using filters. Class `sap.ui.model.Filter` is used for building filters. `sap.ui.model.FilterOperator` specifies various operators allowed for filtering.

  Filtering code is usually written in the controller as a response to a user entering a filter value and clicking a button.

  Consider an example in which `sap.m.Table` has a list of products that is loaded by aggregation binding path `/Products`. In the event handler of triggering the filter, the code in Listing 3.14 is written to filter the products. This code is for filtering the products belonging to a brand.

```
//Get current binding of the table
var oBinding = oTable.getBinding("items");

//Filtering the products having Brand 'TwoWe'.
var oFilter = new Filter("Brand", "EQ", 'TwoWe');

//Array of filters
var aFilters = [];
aFilters.push(oFilter);

//Filter the aggregation binding
oBinding.filter(aFilters);
```

Listing 3.14 Implementing a Filter

- **Sorting and grouping**

  Sorting helps you to position the allowed columns in ascending or descending order, and `sap.ui.model.Sorter` specifies the attributes of the sorting function. Grouping, as the name suggests, groups the rows per a specified property name. Grouping can be done as part of sorting itself for most scenarios.

The grouping technique shown in Listing 3.15 is an example of when you need to group rows just by the value of a grouping property. For example, if you need to group all the products that have stock from 0 to 10 as low, 11 to 30 as medium, and 31 to 200 as good, you can pass a function in place of Boolean as the third parameter of the Sorter.

```
//Sorter. Sorting by property Brand, ascending order, Grouping enabled.
var oSorter = new Sorter("Brand", false, true);

//Array of Sorters
var aSorters = [];
aSorters.push(oSorter);
oBinding.sort(aSorters);
```

Listing 3.15 Applying Sorting on an Aggregation Building

Note that grouping function in Listing 3.15 is supplied while creating oSorter. The function for satisfying the requirement will look like Listing 3.16.

```
Stock: function(oContext) {
    var stock = oContext.getProperty("UnitsInStock");
    var key, text;
    if (stock <= 10) {
        key = "LE10";
        text = "Low";
    } else if (stock <= 30) {
        key = "LE30_GT10";
        text = "Medium";
    } else if (stock <= 200) {
        key = "LE200_GT30";
        text = "Good";
    }
    return {
        key: key,
        text: text
    };
}
```

Listing 3.16 An Example of a Grouping Function

Figure 3.15 shows the output of such a grouping.

Products				≡
Product	Product Group	Brand	Per Unit	In Stock
Low				
Chef Anton's Gumbo Mix 5	Sourced	TwoWe	36 boxes	0
Northwoods Cranberry Sauce 8	Stocked	TwoWe	12 - 12 oz jars	6
Medium				
Aniseed Syrup 3	Sourced	ToWin	12 - 550 ml bottles	13
Uncle Bob's Organic Dried Pears 7	Sourced	TwoWe	12 - 1 lb pkgs.	15
Chang 2	Sourced	Mehek	24 - 12 oz bottles	17
Good				
Chai 1	Stocked	ToWin	10 boxes x 20 bags	39
Chef Anton's Cajun Seasoning 4	Stocked	Mehek	48 - 6 oz jars	53
Grandma's Boysenberry Spread 6	Stocked	Mehek	12 - 8 oz jars	120

Figure 3.15 Result of Grouping with a Group Function

Element Binding

The element binding technique allows you to bind an SAPUI5 control to a specific data element on a model so that a binding context gets created for the SAPUI5 control and all its children. All the relative binding paths on the SAPUI5 control and its children are resolved relative to this binding context.

Note

Whenever a binding path starts with a /, it's an absolute binding path; that is, the binding path is considered from the root of the model. If there is no / in the beginning, it's a relative binding path, which means that there must be a binding context available on the control itself or for one of its parents (closest parent takes precedence), so that the relative binding path is resolved in relation to this binding context.

Let's consider the concept of binding context first to better understand element binding. Binding context refers to a specific object on a data model. Binding context at the topmost level of your model (i.e., data bound to the model) is called root context. You always require an absolute binding path (beginning with a /) to refer to the root context.

For example, in the "Property Binding" section earlier in this chapter, we referenced the URL path `/FirstName` and `/LastName`, which referenced the root context, so the SAPUI5 framework looked for `FirstName` and `LastName` at the root of the bound data model. Similarly, in the "Aggregation Binding" section, we used the binding path `/Products` to refer to the `Products` element available at the root of the bound data.

Use of Element Binding

Element binding is generally used in a master-detail scenario. The master list is usually bound to a root context, displaying several data entries of this context. When an item on the master list is clicked on, you need to set the context of this selected item to the detail screen so that all bindings within the detail screen are resolved in relation to the selected item.

Element binding is usually performed in the controller part in event handlers to set new binding contexts. For example, in the case of an OData model, if the bound context isn't already available in the model, then a backend call is performed to fetch the required data:

```
oPage.bindElement("/Products/0");
```

You can also perform element binding in the XML view as follows:

```
<Page title="Aggregation Binding" binding="{/Products/0}">
```

Figure 3.16 tries to illustrate the binding context and relative binding path by showing the data in a JSON model and how it's bound to a table in an XML view without element binding. The binding path points to products of the first vendor.

But in practical scenarios, there is rarely a need to directly bind to a specific child element (`Product`, in this case). Rather, it always depends on which parent (`Vendor`, in this case) is in the context. Therefore, let's modify this code to use element binding.

Figure 3.17 shows the controller code where a context of a `Vendor` is set to the view. After the context is set, the XML view will just use a relative path to the bound vendor for aggregation binding to list the products within.

```
{
    "Vendors": [{
        "VendorID": 01,
        "VendorName": "IFB",
        "Address": "No 1, ABC Road, Kolkotta, WB, India",
        "Products": [{
            "ProductID": 22,
            "ProductName": "Chang2",
            "SupplierID": 12,
            "CategoryID": 12,
            "QuantityPerUnit": "2-24 - 12 oz bottles",
            "UnitPrice": "38.0000",
            "UnitsInStock": 27,
            "UnitsOnOrder": 50,
            "ReorderLevel": 45,
            "Discontinued": false
        }, {
            "ProductID": 23,
            "ProductName": "Aniseed Syrup2",
            "SupplierID": 12,
            "CategoryID": 22,
            "QuantityPerUnit": "12 - 550 ml bottles - 2",
            "UnitPrice": "20.0000",
            "UnitsInStock": 13,
            "UnitsOnOrder": 70,
            "ReorderLevel": 25,
            "Discontinued": false
        }]
    }
    ......multiple Vendors-----
    ]
}
```

JSON data showing vendors and products of vendors

```
<Page title="Aggregation Binding">
    <content>
        <Table items="{/Vendors/0/Products}"
        class="sapUiResponsiveMargin" width="50%">
            <columns>
                <Column width="12em">
                    <Text text="Product"/>
                </Column>
                <Column>
                    <Text text="Per Unit"/>
                </Column>
                <Column>
                    <Text text="In Stock"/>
                </Column>
            </columns>
            <items>
                <ColumnListItem>
                    <cells>
                        <ObjectIdentifier title="{ProductName}" text="{ProductID}"/>
                        <Text text="{QuantityPerUnit}"/>
                        <Text text="{UnitsInStock}"/>
                    </cells>
                </ColumnListItem>
            </items>
        </Table>
    </content>
</Page>
```

Binding with absolute path; no element binding used

Figure 3.16 Absolute Binding Path with No Element Binding

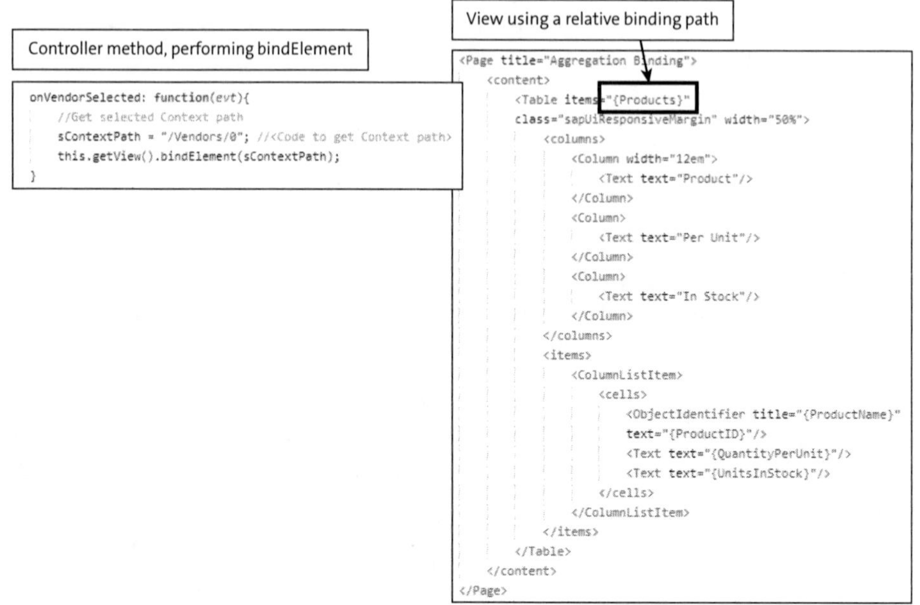

Controller method, performing bindElement

```
onVendorSelected: function(evt){
    //Get selected Context path
    sContextPath = "/Vendors/0"; //<Code to get Context path>
    this.getView().bindElement(sContextPath);
}
```

View using a relative binding path

```
<Page title="Aggregation Binding">
    <content>
        <Table items="{Products}"
        class="sapUiResponsiveMargin" width="50%">
            <columns>
                <Column width="12em">
                    <Text text="Product"/>
                </Column>
                <Column>
                    <Text text="Per Unit"/>
                </Column>
                <Column>
                    <Text text="In Stock"/>
                </Column>
            </columns>
            <items>
                <ColumnListItem>
                    <cells>
                        <ObjectIdentifier title="{ProductName}"
                        text="{ProductID}"/>
                        <Text text="{QuantityPerUnit}"/>
                        <Text text="{UnitsInStock}"/>
                    </cells>
                </ColumnListItem>
            </items>
        </Table>
    </content>
</Page>
```

Figure 3.17 Element Binding

Formatting and Formatters

When you bind a model property to an SAPUI5 control, you might need to format the incoming data in the model and show the property in a different format on the screen. Data formatting can include date formatting and number formatting. However, formatting techniques allow you to link values together (for example, an amount and currency), or show a completely different set of data based on predefined data mapping. In this section, we will discuss formatting the bound data and techniques for implementation.

Formatting Using Data Types

SAPUI5 provides four data types—Date, Float, Currency, and Boolean—that can be used to influence the data format on a screen.

Figure 3.18 shows the formatting of date and currency properties. A date property is formatted to show the date in MM/dd/yyyy format, and the currency value is formatted to contain the currency with thousands separators.

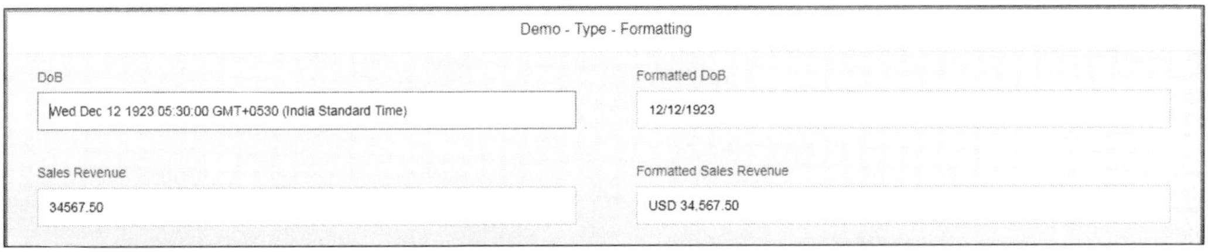

Figure 3.18 Formatting Date and Currency Values

Listing 3.17 shows the controller code that includes the data model.

```
sap.ui.define([
    "sap/ui/core/mvc/Controller",
    "sap/ui/model/json/JSONModel",
    "typeFormatters/util/formatter"
], function(Controller, JSONModel, formatter) {
    "use strict";
    return Controller.extend("typeFormatters.controller.View1", {
        formatter : formatter,
        onInit: function(){
            var date = new Date("1923-12-12");
            var oModel = new JSONModel({
                "FirstName": "Og",
                "LastName": "Mandino",
                "DoB": date,
                "SalesRevenue": "34567.50",
```

```
                "Currency": "USD"
            });
            this.getView().setModel(oModel);
        }
    });
});
```

Listing 3.17 Controller Code Setting a JSON Model to the View, with Date and Amount Fields

Note the DoB and SalesRevenue properties. DoB is a JavaScript date object, and Sales-Revenue contains an amount value.

The following code of the view shows how the DoB is formatted into MM/dd/yyyy. Note that it has been typed as a Date, so that the SAPUI5 framework can interpret it and format it per pattern.

```
<Input value="{path:'/
DoB', type: 'sap.ui.model.type.Date', formatOptions: { pattern: 'MM/dd/yyyy' }}"/>
```

The following code part of the view shows how the SalesRevenue property is formatted to show the currency and thousands separator. Both SalesRevenue and Currency properties are supplied, the value is typed as Currency, and showMeasure is set to true to display the currency with the amount.

```
<Input value="{parts: [{path: '/SalesRevenue'}, {path: '/
Currency'}], type: 'sap.ui.model.type.Currency',
formatOptions: {showMeasure: true }}"/>
```

Custom Formatters

Formatters are techniques used to enhance the utility of binding so that data bound from a model can be shown in different formats on the UI. Formatters are JavaScript functions specified in an SAPUI5 view alongside the binding and implemented either in a controller or a dedicated formatter JavaScript file to store all formatter functions.

Let's consider a simple use case of using a formatter function to calculate age from date of birth.

Specifying a Formatter Function

A formatter function is specified alongside the binding as follows:

```
<Input width="100%" id="__input3" editable="false" enabled="false" value="{path:'/
DoB', formatter:'.formatter.calculateAge'}"/>
```

If the formatter function takes more than one input, then the `path` property is provided as an array:

```
<Input width="100%" id="__input3" editable="false" enabled="false" value="{parts:[
{path: '/FirstName'}, {path:'/LastName'}],
formatter:'.formatter.getFullName'}"/>
```

Implementing Formatter Functions

A typical formatter file returns a JavaScript object containing all the formatter functions inside the `sap.ui.define` call, and it looks like Listing 3.18.

```javascript
sap.ui.define([], function() {
  return {
    calculateAge: function(dob) {
      var now = new Date();
      var birthDate = new Date(dob);
      var age = now.getFullYear() - birthDate.getFullYear();
      var m = now.getMonth() - birthDate.getMonth();
      if (m < 0 || (m === 0 && now.getDate() < birthDate.getDate())) {
        age--;
      }
      return age;
  },
    getFullName: function(firstName, lastName){
      return firstName + " " + lastName;
    }
  };
});
```

Listing 3.18 Definition of Formatter Functions in the Formatter File

The preceding code snippet would return a JavaScript object containing two functions: `calculateAge` and `getFullName`.

Specifying the Formatter Inside the Controller

The formatter file or module is loaded as a dependent module within the controller file. Inside the factory function of `sap.ui.define`, the formatter is returned as a property of the controller object. See Listing 3.19, which shows how the formatter is loaded within the controller.

```javascript
sap.ui.define([
    "sap/ui/core/mvc/Controller",
    "sap/ui/model/json/JSONModel",
    "formatters/util/formatter"
], function(Controller, JSONModel, formatter) {
```

```
    "use strict";
    return Controller.extend("formatters.controller.View1", {
        formatter : formatter,
        onInit: function(){
            var oModel = new JSONModel({
                "FirstName": "Srinivasa",
                "LastName": "Ramanujan",
                "DoB":"1982/05/29"
            });
            this.getView().setModel(oModel);
        }
    });
});
```

Listing 3.19 Loading the Formatter in the SAPUI5 Controller

Expression Binding

Expression binding techniques allow you to write simple logic within the view itself without the need for formatters. Writing formatter functions can be an overhead for simple cases, and expression binding can be used instead.

Tip

Formatter functions are recommended for complex and hard-to-read expressions. Expression binding should only be used for simple scenarios.

Consider a sample scenario in which you want to see different icons based on whether a person is a senior citizen. Figure 3.19 shows how you can achieve this using the formatter function.

You can achieve the same result by using expression binding as follows.

```
<core:Icon class="sapUiTinyMarginBegin" width="100%"
 src="{=${/Age}>60? 'sap-icon://accept':'sap-icon://sys-cancel-2'}"/>
```

As you can see, it's very handy and compact to use expression binding when the controller logic is completely replaced.

Within an XML view, an expression is mentioned using syntax {=<expression>}. A $ symbol is used to refer to a bound variable. You can form complex expressions using binary logical operators, arithmetic operators, comparison operators, regex, and so on. You may refer to the SAPUI5 Demo Kit for the comprehensive list of operations available.

```
<HBox>
    <Label text="Senior Citizen?" width="100%"/>
    <core:Icon class="sapUiTinyMarginBegin" width="100%" src="{path:'/Age',
    formatter:'.SeniorCitizenCheck'}"/>
</HBox>
```



```
onInit: function() {
    var oModel = new JSONModel({
        "Name": "Srinivasa Ramanujan",
        "Age": 32
    });
    this.getView().setModel(oModel);
},
SeniorCitizenCheck: function(sValue) {
    if (sValue > 60) {
        return "sap-icon://accept";
    } else {
        return "sap-icon://sys-cancel-2";
    }
}
```


Figure 3.19 Using the Formatter Function for Simple Logic

Warning

A few mathematical operators, such as "<" and "&" are reserved characters in XML. You need to escape these characters; otherwise, the XML parser will fail to parse the view. For "<", you may reverse the logic and use ">=", which is readable as well.

Model Inheritance

Figure 3.20 shows the model and binding inheritance tree in an SAP Fiori environment. Whenever a model gets set for any of the higher levels of this tree, the model gets inherited by all the levels below. Similarly, a binding context set on a higher level is inherited by all the lower levels, unless overridden by an element binding at lower levels. The UI core (`sap.ui.core`) is the topmost level in the binding tree, and any model assigned to the UI core is automatically inherited by the entire application and available globally. Assigning a model to the core isn't recommended in a production application due to performance reasons.

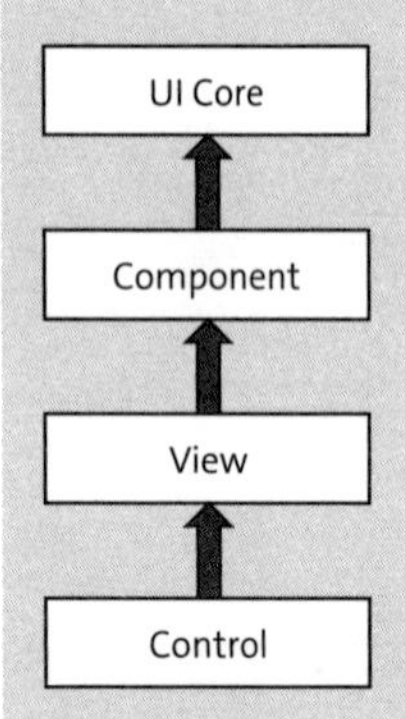

Figure 3.20 SAPUI5 Model and Binding Inheritance Tree

Tip

In an SAP Fiori app, whenever models are specified in *manifest.json*, these models get set on the component so that it's available across all the views of the app.

Named Models

Multiple models can be bound to any of the previously mentioned inheritance tree levels. In such cases, a name can be supplied while setting a model so that this name can be used to specify a model while binding.

The following code specifies how to supply a name while setting a model explicitly:

```
var oView = this.getView();
oView.setModel(oModel, "mainModel");
```

If models are specified in *manifest.json*, a name can be specified there as well, as shown in Listing 3.20.

```
"models": {
    "i18n": {
        "type": "sap.ui.model.resource.ResourceModel",
        "settings": {
```

```
        "bundleName": "ExpressionBinding.i18n.i18n"
        }
    },
    "valueHelpModel":{
        "dataSource": "valueHelpSource"
    },
    "": {
        "dataSource": "mainService"
    }
}
```

Listing 3.20 Defining Models in the Application Descriptor

If the name isn't specified, (as shown in for the data source `mainService`), name `unde-fined` is set for that model. While binding, no name is required to be specified.

Tip

For future compatibility reasons and as a best practice, you should name every model used in the application.

Localization

Every SAPUI5 application will have many text literals that are language dependent. Labels and error messages are a few examples. Whenever an application needs to be used in a different language, these text literals need to be translated. To make this job easier, it's a standard to store all these text literals in a single file, one each for each language supported by the application.

Figure 3.21 shows a typical *i18n* folder containing several language-dependent files.

These *.properties* files contain key-value pairs of language-dependent texts. The key is a uniquely identifiable string, whereas the value is a language-translated text. The file without the language specification is a default file from where the SAPUI5 framework will pick the texts if the right *i18n* file isn't found for the user's locale. Each of these files has a two-character code indicating the language of the file. Applications use the keys to refer to the text literals. Based on the current locale, the SAPUI5 framework chooses the right *i18n* file to read the texts from. These files are also called resource bundles.

Figure 3.22 shows a typical *i18n* file from the SAP Fiori My Timesheet app.

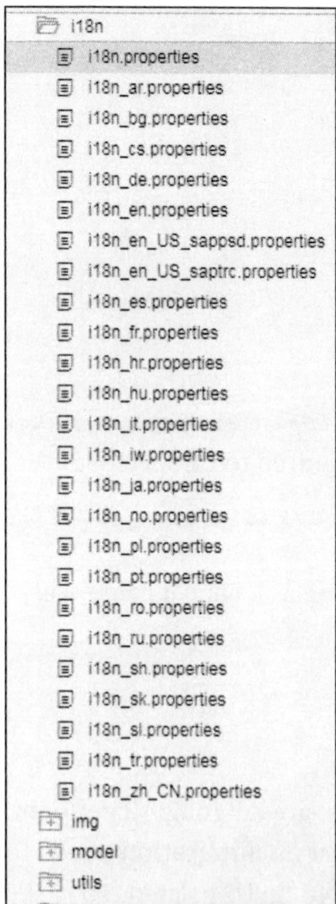

Figure 3.21 i18n Folder with Language-Dependent Files


```
101
102    # XTIT: Legend missing day
103    MISSING_DAY=Action requise de votre part
104    # XTIT: Legend filled day
105    FILLED_DAY=Termin\u00E9
106    # XTIT: Legend filled in process, manager action needed
107    FILLED_MANAGER=Action de l'approbateur requise
108    # XFLD: Rejected by manager - this appears on the legend
109    REJECTED=Refus\u00E9
110    # XFLD: Legend future working day
111    WORKING_DAY=Jour ouvr\u00E9
112    # XFLD: Legend non-working day
113    NON_WORKING_DAY=Jour ch\u00F4m\u00E9
114
115    # XMSG: Footer information about missing hours
116    TOTAL_MISSING=Heures manquantes au total\u00A0\: {0}
117
```

Figure 3.22 A Typical i18n File for the French Language

Resource Model

Resource model is an SAPUI5 class that is used as a utility wrapper around resource bundles (*i18n* files). This resource model is used in the application to bind the *i18n* texts to various controls.

A resource model is instantiated as follows:

```
oResourceModel =
 new sap.ui.model.resource.ResourceModel({bundleName:"localizationDemo.i18n.i18n", l
ocale:"en"});
```

In the preceding code, `localization` refers to the application namespace, the first `i18n` refers to the folder name of the resource bundle, and the last `i18n` refers to the availability of the *18n.properties* file.

This resource model is set to an SAPUI5 control (core, component, view, or to a control) like other models as shown here:

```
oView.setModel(oResourceModel, "i18n");
```

The following code illustrates how *i18n* keys are used within a view:

```
<Label text="{i18n>firstName}"/>
```

Here, `firstname` is the key inside the *i18n* file. The resource model will supply the corresponding value from the *i18n* file as the label's text.

In an SAP Fiori app, *manifest.json* is used to set the *i18n* model to the app:

```
"sap.ui5": {
    "models": {
      "i18n": {
        "type": "sap.ui.model.resource.ResourceModel",
        "settings": {
          "bundleName": "localizationDemo.i18n.i18n"
        }
      }
  }
```

Routing

A typical SAPUI5 application contains several views, and it's normal for a use case to span multiple views. SAPUI5's routing APIs help you navigate into different views and provide features to create bookmarkable URLs so application states can be visited directly later.

Routing in Classical Web Applications

Classical web applications typically contain multiple pages, and routing is handled at the server side. Users request different web pages by explicitly calling different URLs. One of the huge disadvantages here is that the entire web page needs to be reloaded and re-rendered from the server even if the current page differs only slightly from the previous page.

Single-page application frameworks such as SAPUI5 contain just one page as the name suggests. Changes to the screen are handled at the client side by dynamically loading different SAPUI5 controls within the same page. In other words, the user navigates only within a single page. However, it's important to have different URLs for the application's different navigation states so that the corresponding URLs can be bookmarked to revisit later. The navigation is reflected in the hash of the URL instead of the server path or URL parameters.

> **Note**
>
> Consider a business scenario of editing a purchase order. In classical web pages, the following URL would be called:
>
> *http://<host:port>/<server-path-to-the-app>/PurchaseOrder.html?Id='12345'& action='edit'*
>
> In a single-page application, it would look like this:
>
> *http://<host:port>/<server-path-to-the-app>/#PurchaseOrder/12345/edit*
>
> When you navigate from a purchase order to a purchase requisition, the new URL would look like this:
>
> *http://<host:port>/<server-path-to-the-app>/#PurchaseRequisition/23456/display*

In the preceding example, note that whenever the navigation occurred from the purchase order to purchase requisition, the URL content before the hash didn't change; instead, only the content after the hash has changed. For any URL change after the hash, the browser won't reload the page from the server, thus allowing the different navigation states to have their own URLs without reloading the page from the server and providing a better user experience. This change in hash is captured by the application to decide which controls/views to render.

In an SAPUI5 application, the router class captures all changes to the hash and loads different views based on the router configuration. The router also keeps track of the history, which helps in backward and forward navigation. Router also provides ways to perform navigation without updating the hash and without updating the history.

Routing Configuration

Routing configuration is part of SAPUI5 application's *manifest.json*. Here we configure various routes available within the app and instruct the SAPUI5 framework on which views to be instantiated for different routes and related configurations. Although routing configuration can be specified in the applications' component, it's no longer recommended.

At a high level, there are three properties to configure the routing. Table 3.3 explains both these three top-level properties and the important properties they contain.

Property	Description
config	This parameter defines global routing configuration parameters and defines default values for various routes and targets. sap.ui.core.routing.Router is the default routing class for the property routerClass. You can use custom routing classes, which are subclasses of sap.ui.core.routing.Router. By defining custom routing classes, you can define custom parameters and define behaviors regarding how to handle them within routing. Property viewType defines the default view type used throughout the app. viewPath defines the default folder where all views are located. controlId and controlAggregation define the ID of the control and its aggregation, respectively, where the views will be rendered.
routes	This is an array of different valid routes or navigations within an application. The pattern defines a pattern for the hash part of the URL for which the current route is valid. The first route that matches the pattern is selected. Therefore, the sequence of routes is important. The name provides a unique ID for the route so that it can be addressed programmatically by referring to this name. The target can define one or multiple targets to be displayed when the URL hash matches the pattern.
targets	Each target has a name and then specifies a viewName. When a target is chosen, the specified view is instantiated and added to the controlAggregation of the controlId. Multiple routes can use a single target. viewLevel is a property that determines the animation (transition direction) when a view is displayed. A target can be directly shown on the app programmatically without associating with a route. Here is a sample coding for displaying a target with name notFound: this.getRouter().getTargets().display("notFound");

Table 3.3 Routing Configuration

> **Tip**
>
> Before SAPUI5 version 1.30, routing configurations were part of the metadata of component and entered in *Component.js*. Although you can still do that, and SAPUI5 supports this style due to backward compatibility, it's recommended to use an application descriptor file (*manifest.json*) to enter these configurations.

Initialize Routing

Routing needs to be initialized explicitly in the component so that it's available throughout the application. The configurations entered in *manifest.json* are loaded while instantiating the router. Instantiation will happen only once per the app, so it's ideally placed in the init method of *Component.js* as follows:

```
init: function () {
    // call parent's init
    UIComponent.prototype.init.apply(this, arguments);
    // Initialize the router
    this.getRouter().initialize();
}
```

Figure 3.23 shows three different events that trigger navigation and the subsequent steps:

1. When a hash is changed for a URL (1.1) (by typing it or selecting a bookmark), the SAPUI5 framework considers the routing configuration and chooses targets to display in the app (1.2).

2. When the navTo method of the router is called (2.1), the SAPUI5 framework considers router configurations, and updates the URL hash (2.2) as well as navigates to the configured target/s (2.2).

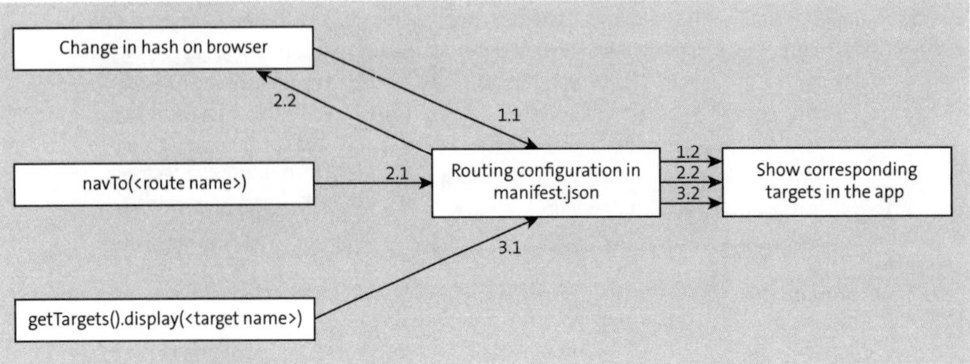

Figure 3.23 Navigations Using Routing

3. When the `getTargets().display` is called (3.1), the SAPUI5 framework considers the router configurations and navigates to the specified target (3.2). The URL hash won't be changed this time.

Visualizing Data

Visualizing data refers to presenting data in terms of charts and graphs. It's easier for the human brain to digest and interpret huge amounts of data in charts and graphs instead of huge spreadsheets. They can be used to highlight key information and identify patterns within data. With interactive charts and graphs, you can take the concept to the next level, multiplying the advantages.

SAPUI5 provides extensive capabilities for data visualization. SAPUI5 provides classes and controls with namespace `sap.suite.ui.commons` and `sap.viz`.

`sap.viz.ui5.controls.VizFrame` is an important SAPUI5 control that takes care of initializing chart visualization, layout of the chart, feeding data to charts, chart customizations, and user interactions.

The typical steps involved in creating a `VizFrame` chart are as follows:

1. Declare `VizFrame` as part of the XML view *or* instantiate `sap.viz.ui5.controls.VizFrame`.

2. Create a dataset of type `sap.viz.ui5.data.FlattenedDataset` specifying dimensions, measures, and the data path where data is available:
   - Set the model containing the data to `VizFrame`.
   - Set the dataset created in the preceding step to `VizFrame`.
   - Set the `VizType`, specifying the type of chart.

3. Specify axes in the chart using `sap.viz.ui5.controls.common.feeds.FeedItem`, and add it to the `VizFrame` using the `addFeed` method.

`sap.suite.ui.commons.ChartContainer` provides a container to hold `VizFrame` with a utility toolbar. The utility toolbar has functions to select between various charts, change dimensions of the chart, zoom the chart, show in full screen mode, and toggle the legend of the chart. You can use the toolbar to add custom buttons to perform additional functionality. Usually a `ChartContainer` will contain multiple `sap.suite.ui.commons.ChartContainerContent` instances, and each `ChartContainerContent` will have a `VizFrame` within it. `VizFrame` doesn't always need to be within a `ChartContainer`, and it can be part of content within other SAPUI5 controls as well.

Figure 3.24 shows an `sap.suite.ui.commons.ChartContainer` containing an `sap.viz.ui5.controls.VizFrame` with a utility toolbar.

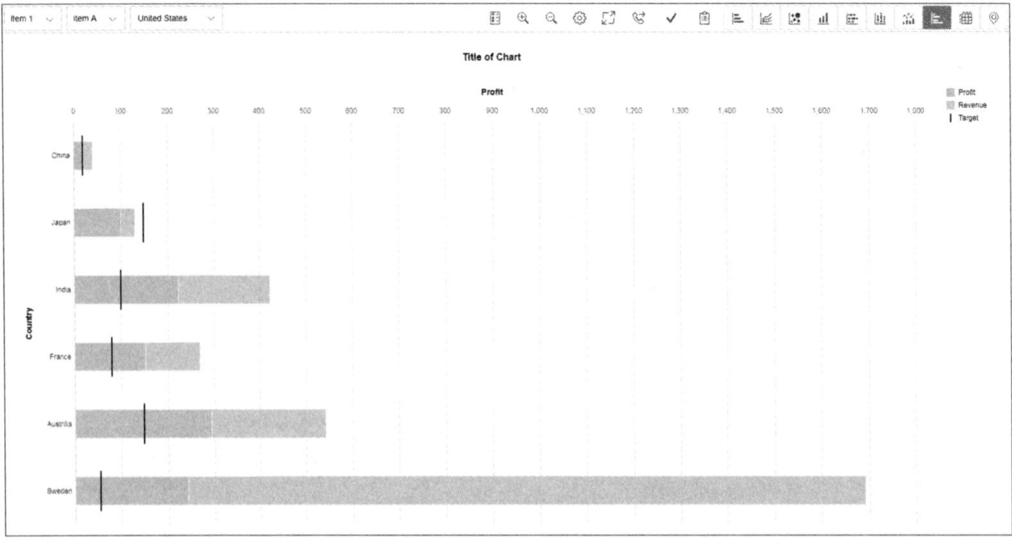

Figure 3.24 ChartContainer and VizFrame with a Utility Toolbar

Responsive Design

Responsive design is about the capability of the web application to work seamlessly across device types, screen widths, resolutions, and pixel densities. SAPUI5 provides you with the tools and technologies to build responsive apps so that you can code once and run across devices. Following the responsive design can save huge costs in development and maintenance of software code in these applications. Figure 3.25 is an example of a responsive web page, which is usable across device types.

There are three areas you need to consider for making an application responsive:

- **Layout**
  This is about having strategies to scale and moving different UI controls to fit well within the available screen width. In addition, there can be strategies to hide less important containers or columns in tables based on the device dimensions and resolution.

- **Responsive media**
  This strategy is about scaling the images and videos so that they fit well across various devices. You may even decide to use smaller fonts on smaller devices.

- **CSS3 media queries**
  Media queries, introduced as part of CSS3, allow you to specify the application to use different CSS rules based on device dimension, device orientation, and display density. You can even specify different CSS files based on devices.

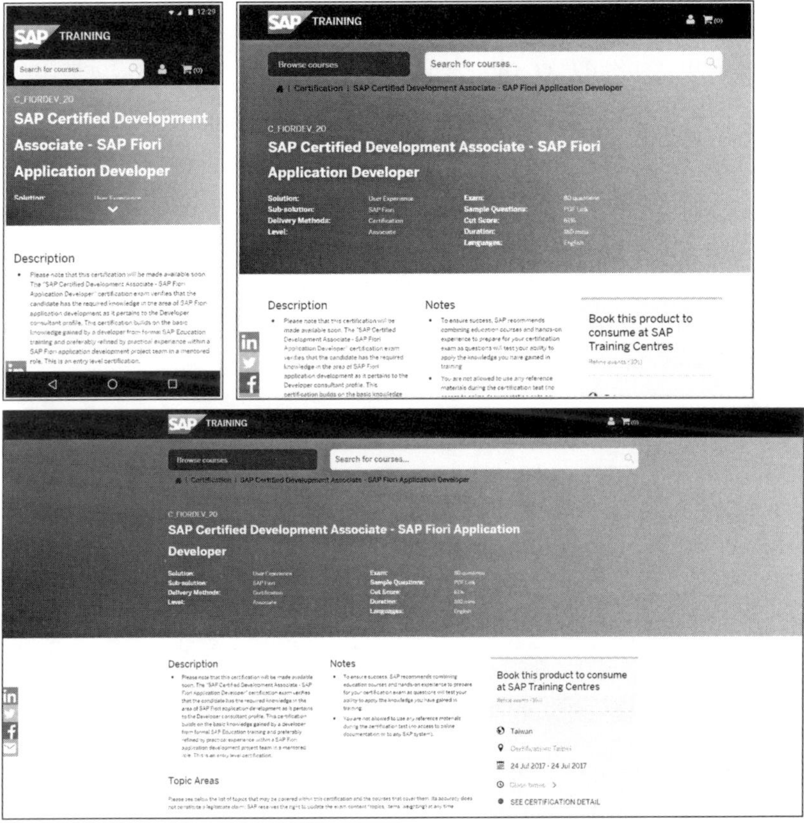

Figure 3.25 A Website Using Responsive Design Principles

Making an application responsive involves development efforts and doesn't come automatically. You need to understand which SAPUI5 controls and layouts to use to make your application responsive. SAPUI5 makes it easier for you to develop responsive applications because of its support of CSS3. Next we'll discuss how you can design responsive applications using SAPUI5.

Layouts

SAPUI5 provides the following responsive layouts:

- ResponsiveFlowLayout

  Using `sap.ui.layout.ResponsiveFlowLayout`, you can stack several SAPUI5 controls into this layout, and the layout will fit them into a row if there is enough width to show them. In a smaller screen, controls are moved into multiple rows and resized again.

- ResposniveSplitter

  sap.ui.layout.ResponsiveSplitter can be used to split the available space into multiple horizontal and vertical panes. These panes are resizable and usually used in developing dashboards and administrative tools that must work across device types.

- ResponsiveLayout`sap.ui.layout.form.ResponsiveLayout`

  This isn't a standalone layout; instead, it's used with forms. Internally, this uses `ResponsiveFlowLayout` and helps in making the best use of available space while rendering a form. It arranges form containers as well as labels and input fields within them to suit the devices.

- ResponsiveGridLayout

  Like `ResponsiveLayout`, `sap.ui.layout.form.ResponsiveGridLayout` is also used with a form but uses a 12-column grid to position the form elements. There are several settings available to choose the number of form containers within a row and the way labels are aligned with the input fields.

Figure 3.26 shows the rendering of a form using responsive layouts.

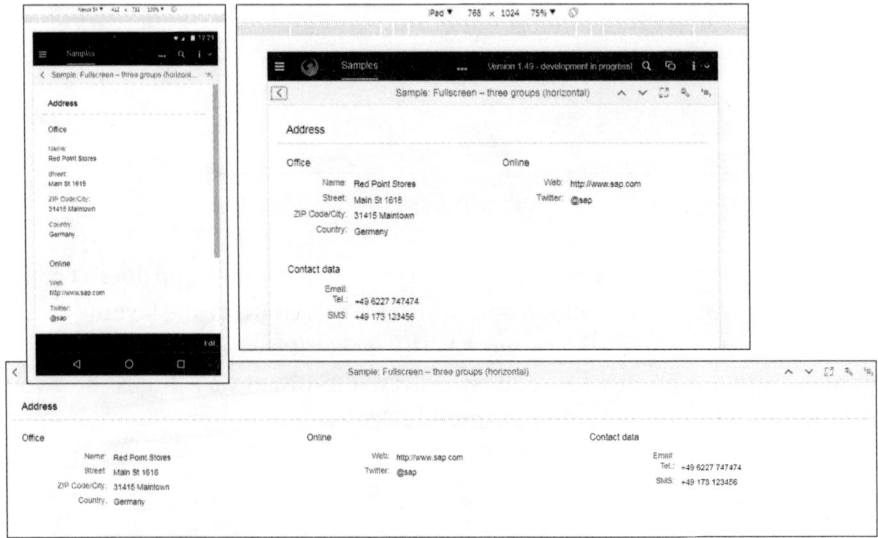

Figure 3.26 A Form Using ResponsiveGridLayout on Different Devices

Next, we'll discuss a few responsive SAPUI5 controls.

Responsive Table

Tables are an important UI component in displaying a set of data. But showing them on a mobile device would always be a challenge. CSS won't be of much help in fitting all the columns in a small screen.

SAPUI5 solves this problem with two strategies.

- **Ability to hide columns**
  Properties are available to hide specific columns based on device sizes, and table personalization can be used by the end user to choose the desired columns.

- **Pop in display**
  In this case, based on settings, multiple column values with labels will be shown in a single column, one below the other.

Figure 3.27 shows how a responsive table behaves under different screen sizes.

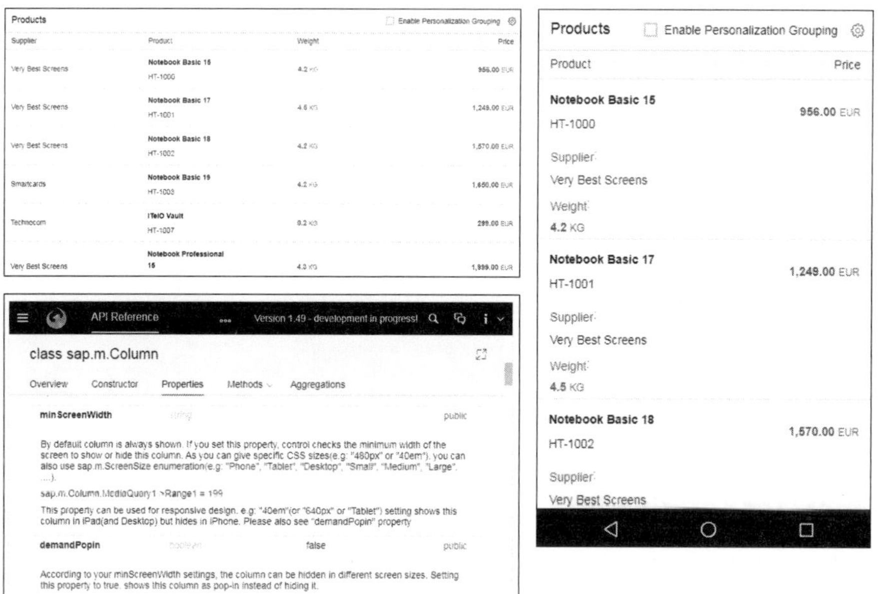

Figure 3.27 Responsive Table's Properties and Behavior across Devices

Properties minScreenWidth and demandPopin on sap.m.Column determine how a column behaves under various screen sizes. If the screen width is greater than or equal to the minScreenWidth, then the column is always shown. If the screen width of the device is less than `minScreenWidth`, then the property `demandPopin` is checked. If `demand-Popin` is true, then the column would appear as a pop in; otherwise, the column would be hidden.

Form Factors

SAPUI5 provides two form factors based on touch and nontouch interaction styles:

- **Cozy form factor**
  In touch devices, fingers are commonly used for interaction. If the controls aren't big enough, it can result in a bad experience. In earlier days, a stylus was used to handle such scenarios, but it may not be always handy for users to have a stylus with them. When an application uses the cozy form factor, controls will have a slightly bigger dimension to conveniently interact with fingers.

- **Compact form factor**
  When a user is using a bigger, nontouch screen, you can choose to have a smaller dimension so that information density can be increased on the screen.

Setting Form Factors

While defining an XML view, a class attribute can be used to set the form factor as follows:

```
<mvc:View class="sapUiSizeCompact" xmlns=....>
   ...
</mvc:View>
```

While using a JavaScript view, you can use the API `addStyleClass` to set the desired form factor:

```
this.addStyleClass("sapUiSizeCompact");
```

Important Terminology

In this chapter, the following terminology was used:

- **MVC**
  Model View Controller (MVC) is a popular architectural pattern for building web/mobile applications.

- **Binding**
  Binding is a technique in which data is bound to the UI so that any change to the

data in the model automatically gets displayed on the SAPUI5 control. In two-way binding, changes to the value of bound properties automatically flow to the model. With a simple API, these changes can hit the server.

- **Component**
  A component is a self-contained reusable part of an SAPUI5 application. Every SAP Fiori app is loaded as a component in the SAP Fiori architecture.

- **Application descriptor**
  An application descriptor is a JSON file that contains application-related configurations and metadata.

- **Routing**
  Routing is a technique of navigation across different views in an SAPUI5 application. Using routing, you can develop solutions to bookmark various states of the application (including popups) and return to these states directly using the URL.

- **.i18n localization**
  In this process, text literals used in the app are translated into other languages and stored in different language-dependent *i18n* files. The application fetches the language-dependent objects from here. *I18n* stands for "internationalization."

- **AMD**
  Asynchronous Module Definition (AMD) is a JavaScript specification for defining the code as small modules with dependencies specified so that these modules can be loaded asynchronously, improving app performance and user experience.

 Practice Questions

These practice questions will help you evaluate your understanding of the topics covered in this chapter. The questions shown are similar in nature to those found on the certification examination. Although none of these questions will be found on the exam itself, they will allow you to review your knowledge of the subject. Select the correct answers, and then check the completeness of your answers in the "Practice Question Answers and Explanations" section. Remember, on the exam, you must select all correct answers and only correct answers to receive credit for the question.

1. You need to set the binding context explicitly for a page and all its child controls. Which binding type would you use?

    ☐   A. Aggregation binding

    ☐   B. Element binding

    ☐   C. Property binding

    ☐   D. Resource binding

2. Which is a widely used SAPUI5 view type while building an SAP Fiori app?

    ☐   A. JSON view

    ☐   B. JavaScript view

    ☐   C. XML view

    ☐   D. HTML view

3. Which of the following is the file name for the descriptor for applications, components, and libraries?

    ☐   A. *app_descriptor.json*

    ☐   B. *manifest.json*

    ☐   C. *application.xml*

    ☐   D. *i18n.properties*

4. Which lifecycle event would you use if you need a hook every time a view is rendered?

    ☐   A. `onAfterRendering`

    ☐   B. `onAfterShow`

    ☐   C. `onInit`

    ☐   D. `onAfterViewRender`

5. Which model is used to fetch data from the server and update data into the server?

    ☐   A. OData model

    ☐   B. JSON model

    ☐   C. XML model

    ☐   D. Resource model

6. Which form factor is suggested for nontouch scenarios?

☐ A. Compact

☐ B. Compress

☐ C. Cozy

☐ D. Bigger

7. In a JavaScript view, this method returns a tree of SAPUI5 controls to be part of the view.

☐ A. `getContent`

☐ B. `buildControlTree`

☐ C. `getController`

☐ D. `createContent`

8. Which OData version is supported by SAPUI5 OData `sap.ui.model.odata.OData-Model`?

☐ A. V1

☐ B. V2

☐ C. V3

☐ D. V4

9. Which is the default file in the internationalization (*i18n*) folder?

☐ A. *i18n.properties*

☐ B. *i18n_default.properties*

☐ C. *i18n_en.properties*

☐ D. *i18n_de.properties*

10. Which of the following is *not* an advantage of an MVC pattern?

☐ A. Reusability

☐ B. Code readability

☐ C. Better performance

☐ D. Increased speed of development

11.   True or False: It's always better to use expression binding wherever possible.

☐   A. True

☐   B. False

12.   As of SAPUI5 version 1.44, which of the following is an advantage of using AMD syntax.

☐   A. Better performance

☐   B. Better code readability

☐   C. Future compatibility with asynchronous module loading

☐   D. Reduced bandwidth usage

13.   In this root tag of an XML view, which is the default namespace?

```
<mvc:View xmlns:mvc="sap.ui.core.mvc" xmlns="sap.m" xmlns:layout="sap.ui.com-
mons.layout" controllerName="ViewTypes.controller.View1" height="100%">
```

☐   A. `sap.ui.core.mvc`

☐   B. `sap.m`

☐   C. `sap.ui.commons.layout`

☐   D. `sap.ui.commons`

14.   Routing configuration can be specified in which two of the following places.

☐   A. `Controller`

☐   B. `Component`

☐   C. *manifest.json*

☐   D. *Index.htm*

15.   True or False: A fragment, when included as part of an existing view, inherits the model as well as the binding context.

☐   A. True

☐   B. False

Practice Answers and Explanations

1. Correct answer: **B**

    Element binding allows you to bind a page to a specific object of a model, which will create the binding context for the page and all its children.

2. Correct answer: **C**

    XML view types are widely used due to their simplicity when compared with other view types. Because XML views are declarative, this helps to avoid mixing the view logic and controller logic. Most SAP Fiori apps have their views built as XML views.

3. Correct answer: **B**

    manifest.json is the application descriptor file containing various application configurations and application metadata.

4. Correct answer: **A**

    `onAfterRendering` gets triggered every time a view is rendered. `onInit` gets called only the first time when the view is instantiated.

5. Correct answer: **A**

    The OData model represents an OData service, which is used for fetching data from the backend and updating data to the backend.

6. Correct answer: **A**

    The compact form factor is used for nontouch screens so that more data can fit into the screen to make good use of screen space. For touch scenarios, to accommodate the finger touch, a cozy form factor is used so that touch interactions become comfortable.

7. Correct answer: **D**

    The `createContent` method returns an SAPUI5 control class that can contain a single SAPUI5 control or a hierarchy of SAPUI5 controls.

8. Correct answer: **B**

    Both `sap.ui.model.odata.ODataModel` and `sap.ui.model.odata.v2.ODataModel` support OData Version 2.0.

9. Correct answer: **A**

    i18n.properties is the default file. If a literal key isn't found in the language-specific file, or the language-specific file isn't present at all, then the i18n.properties file will be considered.

10. Correct answer: **C**

    MVC doesn't guarantee better performance of the application. Reusability, code readability, and increased speed of development due to parallel development are advantages of an MVC pattern.

11. Correct answer: **B**

    False. For complex scenarios, it's better to use formatters from a readability and maintenance point of view.

12. Correct answer: **C**

    There is no immediate advantage of using AMD syntax because, as of version 1.44, SAPUI5 modules are still loaded synchronously. When asynchronous loading comes to SAPUI5, existing applications can make use of this advantage without any code change.

13. Correct answer: **B**

    In the XML view, the control tag without a prefix is considered as the default namespace. In the given example, `sap.m` doesn't have any prefix in the control tag.

14. Correct answer: **C**

    Routing configuration can be specified in either the component or manifest, but the recommendation is to use *manifest.json*.

15. Correct answer: **A**

    True. A fragment will inherit the model and binding of the parent control.

Take Away

You should now be able to explain the MVC architecture and know how to build an SAPUI5 application using it. You should be able to explain the general structure of an SAPUI5 application and its important parts. You can now describe the power of data binding and when to use various binding types with different models.

You're also aware of how to make the application available in other languages (localization). You should be able to explain how to use routing to navigate between various views and bookmark various states of the application.

You saw which controls to use for creating views with charts and graphs. We discussed the concepts of responsive design and explored which layouts and controls to use to build a responsive application.

Summary

In this chapter, you've learned the basics of SAPUI5 and its various concepts. You've also learned about the MVC architecture and how SAPUI5 follows it.

In the next chapter, we'll introduce SAP Cloud Platform and start using SAP Web IDE as recommended for SAPUI5/SAP Fiori development.

Chapter 4
SAP Cloud Platform and SAP Web IDE Basics

Techniques You'll Master:

- Understand SAP Cloud Platform
- Development with SAP Web IDE
- Extension with SAP Web IDE
- Packaging with SAP Web IDE
- Deployment tools with SAP Web IDE

In this chapter, we'll discuss SAP Cloud Platform and its capabilities. You'll see how the SAP Web IDE service can be used to develop, package, deploy, and extend SAP Fiori apps. We'll discuss packaging the application using Cordova and Kapsel plugins, and how to deploy the application to server environment for general use.

Real-World Scenarios

You're an SAP Fiori developer and need an Integrated Development Environment (IDE) for developing SAP Fiori apps. You also need capabilities to package and deploy the app to SAP Cloud Platform as well as the SAP Gateway server.

While developing, you want to use predefined templates to get a quick start on your application coding. You would also love to have a graphical editor ("what you see is what you get", or WYSIWYG) to speed up the view development.

As a Fiori developer, you need the capability to extend SAP Fiori applications as per customers' requirements using predefined extension points and other extension options. In this case, you would need an IDE that recognizes the SAP-provided extensibility options within the app and eases the process of implementing these extensions.

You also want to add mobile features to your apps, including scanners, camera, and sensors.

Objectives of This Portion of the Test

The objective of this portion of the SAP Fiori Certification Test is to test your understanding of SAP Cloud Platform and basics of SAP Web IDE. The certification test expects SAP Fiori developers to be knowledgeable in the following areas:

- SAP Cloud Platform
- Developing SAP Fiori apps with SAP Web IDE
- Extending an SAP Fiori app using SAP Web IDE
- Building and deploying an SAP Fiori app

Key Concepts Refresher

In this section, we'll discuss cloud computing and SAP's approach towards cloud computing by exploring the SAP Cloud Platform. After that, we'll explore SAP Web IDE, which is the SAP's cloud-based development tool for SAP Fiori applications. We'll review how to register and launch SAP Web IDE and all SAP Fiori-specific features including templates, layout editor, building, and deploying.

Cloud Computing

Cloud computing refers to the concept of delivering computing services such as storage, servers, software, databases, and networking over the Internet. Cloud computing is rapidly changing the way businesses buy and use technical resources. What started as a simple website hosting service has progressed into a wide variety of cloud services providing immense advantages to both small and large enterprises. Cloud computing offers the following benefits to businesses:

- **Cost benefit**

  Cloud computing reduces the up-front capital expenditures required for setting up servers, databases, and networks. This also reduces the barriers to innovation, allowing businesses to perform proof of concepts and experiments with minimum cost and embrace new technologies.

  Because of the reduced hardware and physical resources, there is less resource to power, no rent to be paid for data centers, and fewer physical devices to be maintained. Again, the number of IT staff required is smaller due to the reduced need for experts and resources for maintenance. Overall, cloud computing reduces the maintenance costs of the IT department.

- **Flexibility**

  As users for your applications grow, or as you need more server cores, RAM, and storage, you can subscribe just enough resources to run your application. In addition, you can downscale your resources whenever required to save costs. In some business applications, there will be times of the year when you have higher user activity and in other times lower user activity. Using cloud computing, you can always keep an optimum level of resources and be flexible.

- **Reliability**

  Most cloud providers provide 99.99% uptime using multiple redundancy, disaster recovery, and fail-safe mechanisms.

- **Security**

  Cloud service providers can provide high-end security features even for small enterprises that otherwise can't afford those products.

Cloud computing can be delivered at different abstraction levels. Services are usually offered at the following three levels:

- **Software-as-a-Service (SaaS)**

  This is the oldest form of cloud computing, where software applications are hosted by a third party, and customers are provided access to the application over the Internet. The applications range from simple applications, such as email services (e.g., Yahoo Mail and Gmail) and storage services (e.g., Box, Dropbox, and Google Drive), to complex enterprise applications such as SAP SuccessFactors, Concur, Workday, and Salesforce.

- **Platform-as-a-Service (PaaS)**

  In this form of cloud computing, a platform is provided as a service. Platform here can mean range of resources such as an operating system, a development environment, a set of development tools, a runtime environment, or an analytical platform. Resources provided here as a service are at a higher abstraction layer than a software application.

- **Infrastructure-as-a-Service (IaaS)**

  In this form of cloud computing, virtualized computing resources such as storage, servers, and other hardware resources are provided to users on demand. These resources are highly scalable, and this feature provides users with the ability to innovate, experiment, and handle unexpected loads on the infrastructure. IaaS users are usually charged on a per-user basis such as per hour, week, or month.

SAP Cloud Platform

SAP Cloud Platform is an open Platform-as-a-Service (PaaS) offering that provides a single PaaS to build, integrate, and extend apps for enterprises of all sizes. SAP Cloud Platform offers two environments to choose from: Cloud Foundry and Neo. You can choose the environments based on services offered, data center you want to use, and the technology with which you want to develop applications. Let's take a look at the two options:

- **Cloud Foundry**
  Cloud Foundry is an open source technology and is considered by many as a de facto industry standard for PaaS solutions. Cloud Foundry provides options to choose different IaaS providers such as Amazon Web Services (AWS) or Microsoft Azure. Currently, SAP Cloud Platform based on Cloud Foundry allows you to develop applications such as SAP HANA extended application services, advanced model (SAP HANA XSA), Internet of Things (IoT) scenarios, machine learning scenarios, and multiple other runtimes.

- **Neo**
  Neo is based on SAP's proprietary technology and requires you to use SAP as the IaaS provider. You can develop Java, SAP HANA extended application services (SAP HANA XS), and HTML5 applications.

SAP provides a free trial of the developer edition of SAP Cloud Platform, which you can use to explore its various features. To get the free trial, navigate to *https:// account.hanatrial.ondemand.com*. You'll see a home page as shown in Figure 4.1.

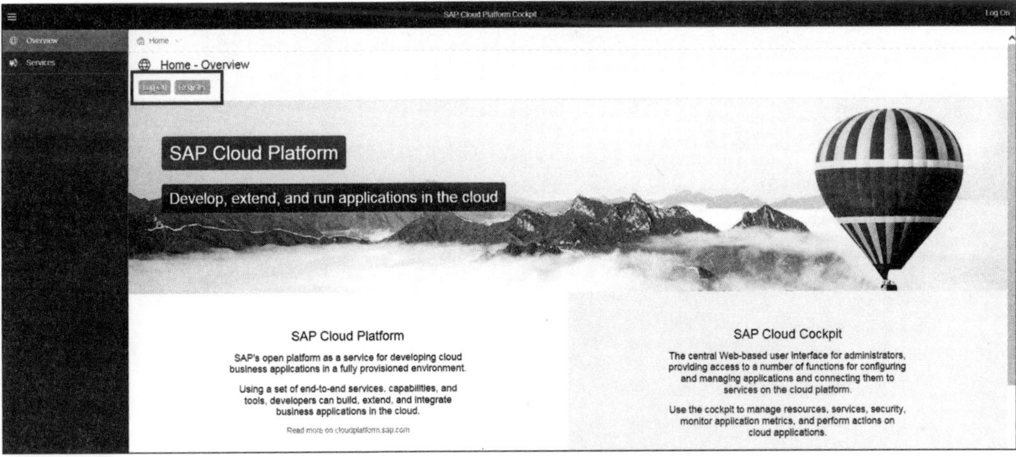

Figure 4.1 SAP Cloud Platform Home Page

If you already have an account with SAP, you can click on **Log On** and log in to SAP. To use SAP Cloud Platform, you need to agree to an additional set of terms and conditions as shown in Figure 4.2.

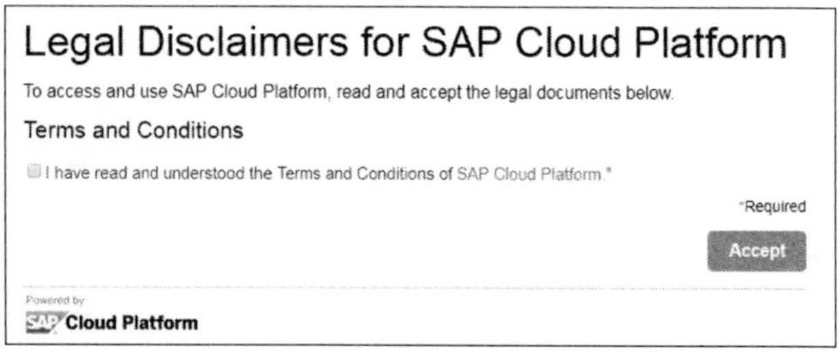

Figure 4.2 Additional Terms for Using Trial SAP Cloud Platform

If you're new to SAP, you can click on **Register** and fill in the details about yourself on the screen that appears, as shown in Figure 4.3.

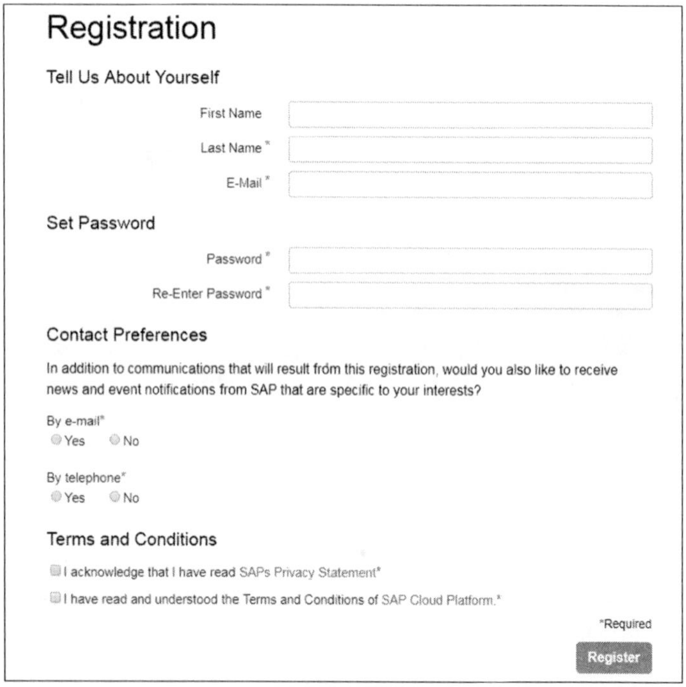

Figure 4.3 Registering for a New Account

Upon registering, you'll see the **SAP Cloud Platform Cockpit** screen shown in Figure 4.4. Note the IaaS provider name and the account number shown.

By default, the **Neo** environment gets chosen for you. You can choose to activate the Cloud Foundry environment by clicking on **Home ❶** and choosing **Start Cloud Foundry Trial ❷**, as shown in Figure 4.5.

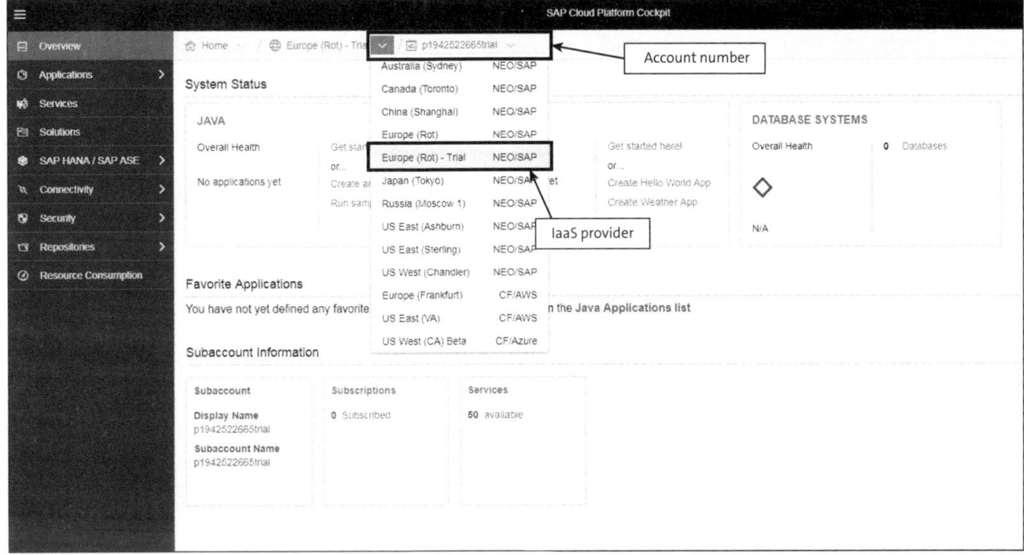

Figure 4.4 SAP Cloud Platform Trial: SAP Cloud Platform Cockpit

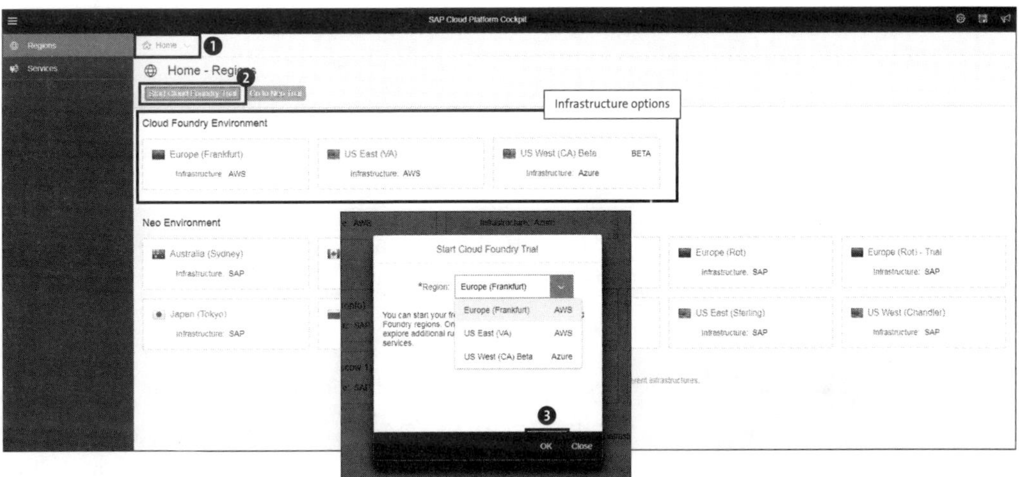

Figure 4.5 Enabling the Cloud Foundry Trial

Introduction to SAP Web IDE

SAP Web IDE is one of the important services offered by SAP Cloud Platform. It's a powerful, browser-based, end-to-end application development tool that enables you to develop, extend, build, and deploy SAP Fiori/SAPUI5 applications.

Since SAPUI5 was introduced, SAP has provided several tools for prototyping, developing, packaging, and deploying SAPUI5 applications. SAP Web IDE aims to be the default tool used by different roles (e.g., developers, designers, and business experts) and for different use cases (e.g., prototyping, developing, enhancing, packaging, and deploying). SAP Web IDE can be used in both on-premise and cloud systems, as well as for all the target devices such as mobile phones, tablets, and desktops.

To speed up the development of applications, SAP Web IDE provides the following features:

- A graphical editor with drag-and-drop features for building the user interface (UI)
- Multiple predefined templates for the most-used use cases
- Reference applications for developers regarding how to implement best practices
- Built-in app previewing ability with a feature to choose multiple devices, such as mobile phones, tablets, and desktops, as target environments
- Ability to run the application with mock data
- Git integration to enable developers to collaborate
- SAPUI5 code completion feature with configurable options
- SAP Web IDE able to be extended by developers by writing different plug-ins
- A Grunt task runner (only in multi-cloud version) for automating tasks and building add-ons

Next, let's walk through the activation and configuration of SAP Web IDE.

Activating the SAP Web IDE Service

The SAP Web IDE service needs to be activated before you start using it:

1. Go to **Home,** and then click on **Go to Neo Trial** to launch the **SAP Cloud Platform Cockpit** screen. You can also navigate directly to the **SAP Cloud Platform Cockpit** screen by going to *https://account.hanatrial.ondemand.com/cockpit.*
2. In the cockpit, click on the **Service** button ❶, as shown in Figure 4.6. This will load the catalog of all services available within the SAP Cloud Platform.
3. Search for "web ide" ❷, and you'll see that there are two versions of SAP Web IDE available (Figure 4.6).

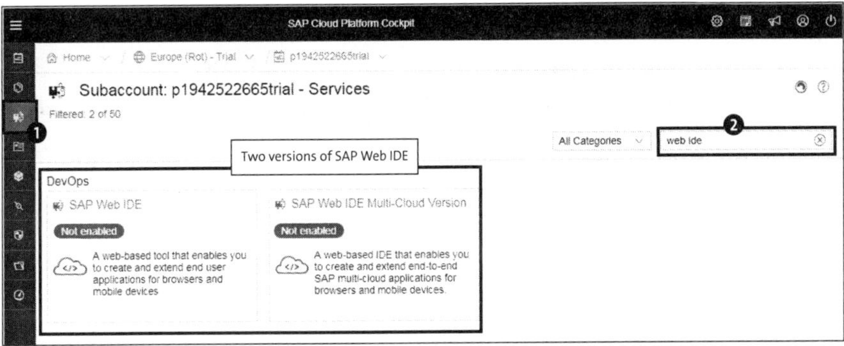

Figure 4.6 Searching for the SAP Web IDE Services

The SAP Web IDE multi-cloud version is the latest version and supports developing multitarget applications (MTA). A MTA includes multiple modules within a single project, each deployed to different runtimes using different programming languages. In addition to developing the UI, you can also develop the services required for your UI. Thus, the full-stack version supports both UI and sever logic development within the single IDE.

To activate these services, click on each of the SAP Web IDE services as shown in Figure 4.6, and then click on the **Enable** button ❶ (Figure 4.7). After enabled, you can click on **Go to Service** ❷ to launch the SAP Web IDE (Figure 4.7).

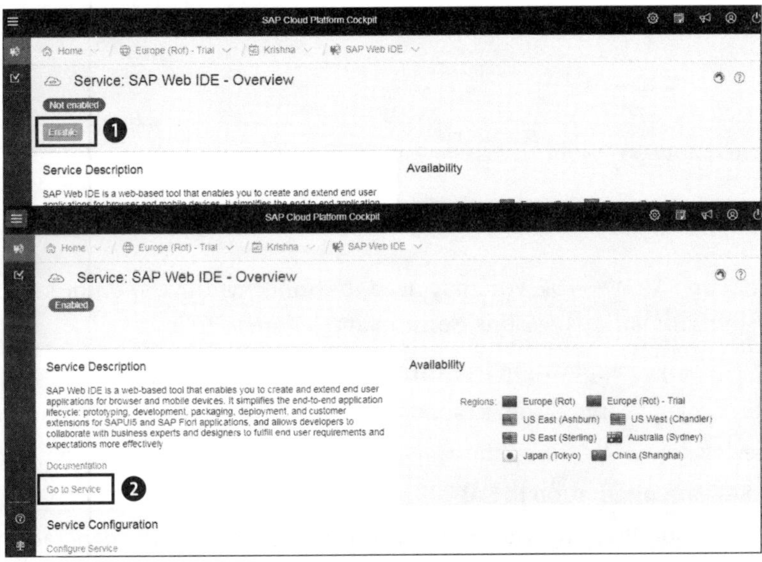

Figure 4.7 Enabling and Launching the SAP Web IDE Service

Tip

New features that get introduced will always go to the SAP Web IDE multi-cloud version, so it's better to start using it even if the classical version is still available.

Once the SAP Web IDE service is active, it needs to be configured. First, we'll configure permissions for limiting the Web IDE access to developers. Then, configure destinations for accessing the backend systems. Finally, we'll enable/disable plugins for activating/deactivating various features of SAP Web IDE.

Let us discuss how to perform these configurations.

Permissions

Access to SAP Cloud Platform services is controlled by roles and permissions. As shown in Figure 4.8, a permission **Web IDEPermission** must be assigned to all developer users through a role for the user to access the SAP Web IDE service. Upon activating the service, this permission is automatically assigned to the **AccountDeveloper** role. So, all users with the **AccountDeveloper** role in the SAP Cloud Platform will have access to the SAP Web IDE service. To access the configuration settings, click on the **Configure Service** link under **Service Configuration** as shown earlier in Figure 4.7.

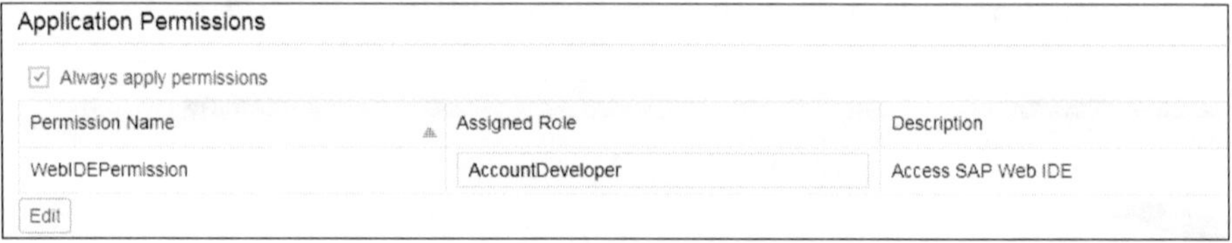

Figure 4.8 SAP Web IDE Access Control by Assigning Permission to a Role

Destinations

When you work on SAP Web IDE, you may need to connect with your on-premise or remote systems for various reasons. Some examples are as follows:

- Importing a deployed application from an SAP Gateway server
- Choosing an available service from a catalog of services in an SAP Gateway system
- Testing the developed SAPUI5 application, including data from the server
- Providing SAP Jam integration to SAPUI5 applications
- Using an SAP Cloud Platform translation service for automatically generating text string translations in the app

In this section, let's discuss how to create a destination for an SAP Gateway system so that SAP Web IDE can communicate with the on-premise system.

> **Note**
> To work with destinations, you should have either a developer or an administrator role on the SAP Cloud Platform.

The following list of Transaction SICF nodes need to be active for SAP Web IDE to communicate with the SAP Gateway system. These SICF nodes can be accessed with Transaction /nSICF. If any of these nodes are not active, you can activate it by selecting **Activate** in the context menu of the corresponding node.

- */sap/opu/odata*
  For connecting with SAP Gateway exposed services.

- */sap/bc/adt*
  For importing an SAP Fiori app into SAP Web IDE and for deploying a new or extended SAP Fiori app into the SAP Gateway system.

- */sap/bc/ui5_ui5*
  For running deployed applications from SAP Web IDE.

- */sapbc/bsp* and */sap/bc/ui2*
  For working with SAP Fiori fact sheet apps.

- */sap/hba*
  For connecting to the SAP HANA application server.

To see the existing destinations, go to the **SAP Cloud Platform Cockpit** screen, click on the **Connectivity** icon, and then select **Destinations** (Figure 4.9).

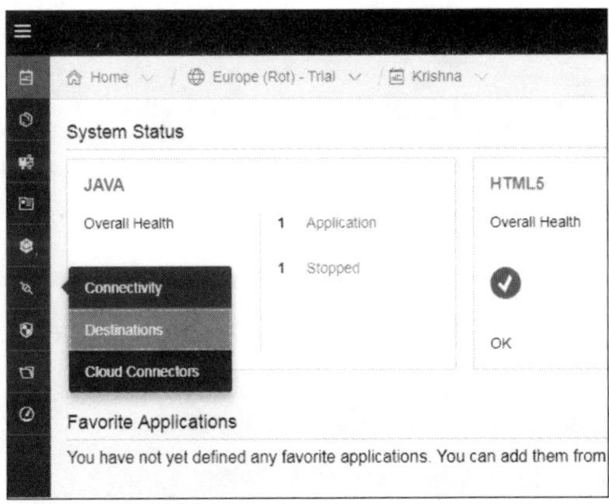

Figure 4.9 Navigating to Destinations within the SAP Cloud Platform Cockpit

Figure 4.10 shows the available destinations for the chosen subaccount. It's important to notice that you're in the context of **Subaccount: Krishna** while looking at destinations. This means that each subaccount can have its own set of destinations.

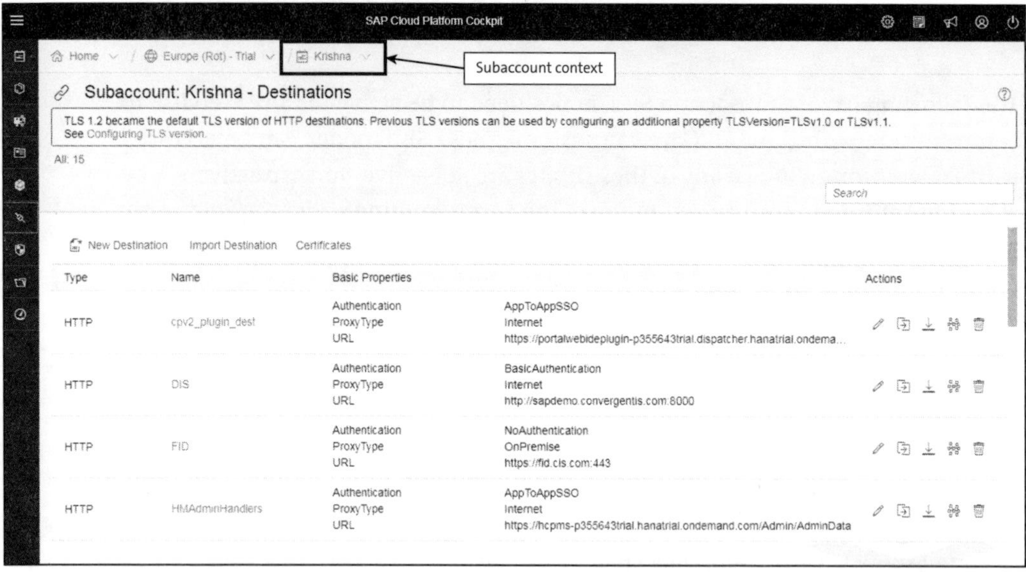

Figure 4.10 Available Destinations within a Subaccount

To create a new destination, select **New Destination** in Figure 4.10. This will open a form below the **Destination** list as shown in Figure 4.11.

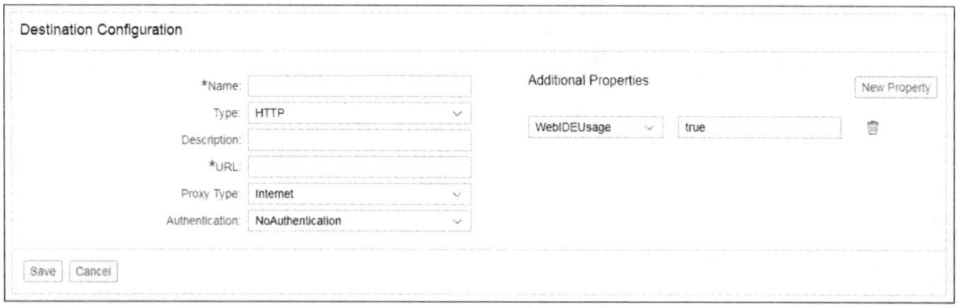

Figure 4.11 Form for Creating a New Destination

Fill in the form fields with the following details:

- **Name**

  Provide a unique technical name for the destination.

- **Type**
  SAP Cloud Platform allows several types of connections such as HTTP, Lightweight Directory Access Protocol (LDAP), Simple Mail Transfer Protocol (SMTP), and Remote Function Call (RFC). Select **HTTP** for connecting from SAP Web IDE to on-premise systems.

- **Description**
  This is the name that appears on SAP Web IDE while choosing a destination.

- **URL**
  Provide the host name and port number of the SAP Gateway system.

- **Proxy Type**
  This is a critical property. If the SAP Gateway system is exposed to the Internet, choose **Internet**; otherwise, choose **On-Premise**.

- **Authentication**
  Choose an authentication method that is configured for the SAP Gateway system.

- **Additional Properties**
  These provide additional information about the destination. The following properties are relevant:
  - **Web IDEEnabled**: Always choose **true** for using the destination from SAP Web IDE.
  - **Web IDESystem**: Provide the SAP system ID here.
  - **sap-client**: Provide the client of the SAP Gateway server for which you need to connect.
  - **Web IDEUsage**: This property enables different usages for the destination. The following values are relevant, and each can be entered separated by a comma:
    - **odata_abap**: For connecting to OData services from the SAP Gateway server.
    - **odata_gen**: For OData-related functionality.
    - **ui5_execute_abap**: For running SAP Fiori/SAPUI5 applications that are deployed on the SAP Gateway server.
    - **dev_abap**: For accessing standard applications for extensibility scenarios and to deploy the apps to the ABAP repository.

Figure 4.12 shows a sample destination connecting to an SAP Gateway system exposed to the Internet.

Figure 4.12 Destination Settings for an Internet-Exposed SAP Gateway System

Because SAP Web IDE is on the public Internet, it can connect easily to your on-premise system, provided your on-premise SAP Gateway system is exposed to the Internet as well. But this isn't a common scenario due to security concerns. Normally, SAP systems are inside a firewall or a Virtual Private Network (VPN). For such cases, SAP delivers the Cloud Connector tool, which acts as a link between the on-premise SAP Gateway system and SAP Cloud Platform.

Cloud Connector runs from within the VPN and has direct access to on-premise systems. From within the VPN, it opens a secure tunnel to SAP Cloud Platform so that applications can use this to communicate with on-premise systems, as shown in Figure 4.13.

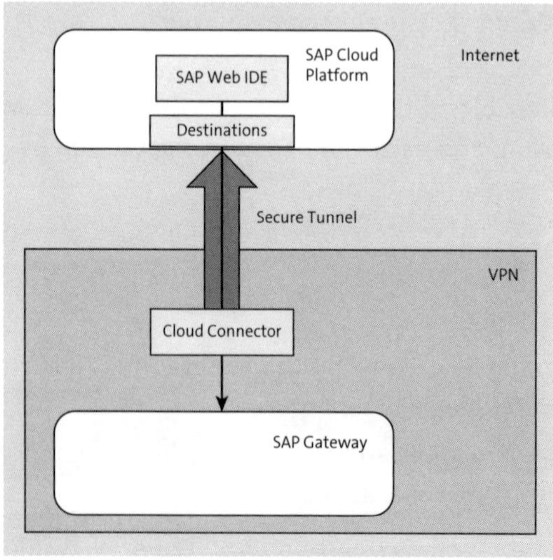

Figure 4.13 SAP Web IDE Communicating with SAP Gateway Using Cloud Connector

Note

Cloud Connector is a generic integration tool to be used with SAP Cloud Platform to connect to on-premise systems such as SAP Gateway, SAP ERP, or SAP HANA, and it isn't specific to SAP Web IDE. The installation and configuration of Cloud Connector is out of the scope of this book.

After the Cloud Connector is installed, the following steps need to be performed:

- Connect to SAP Cloud Platform by logging in using the subaccount. Only one Cloud Connector instance per subaccount can be connected at a time.

- Perform a virtual host mapping. Within the destination on SAP Cloud Platform, a virtual host name and port can be given, and this host and port can be mapped to an actual SAP Gateway host and port in the Cloud Connector.

- Expose required URL subpaths within the SAP Gateway system. By using this feature, you can restrict the access and selectively expose required URLs for the SAP Cloud Platform.

- For more detailed steps, go to *https://help.sap.com* and search for **SAP Cloud Platform Connectivity** and navigate to the **Cloud Connector** section.

Plug-Ins

SAP Web IDE is an extensible platform, which means that the tool can be extended by developers using plug-ins. Because these plug-ins are self-contained, this route allows developers to perform parallel development without stepping into other developers and inadvertently creating dependencies. SAP also uses this route to deliver new features to users in a speedy manner.

SAP publishes many beta-only plug-ins for developers to explore and report issues to SAP. These plug-ins can be disabled, so SAP doesn't need to worry about a non-productive plug-in interfering with the actual functioning of SAP Web IDE in a negative way.

Existing plug-ins can be viewed by navigating to **Tools • Preferences** and then choosing **Features** on the left pane, as shown in Figure 4.14.

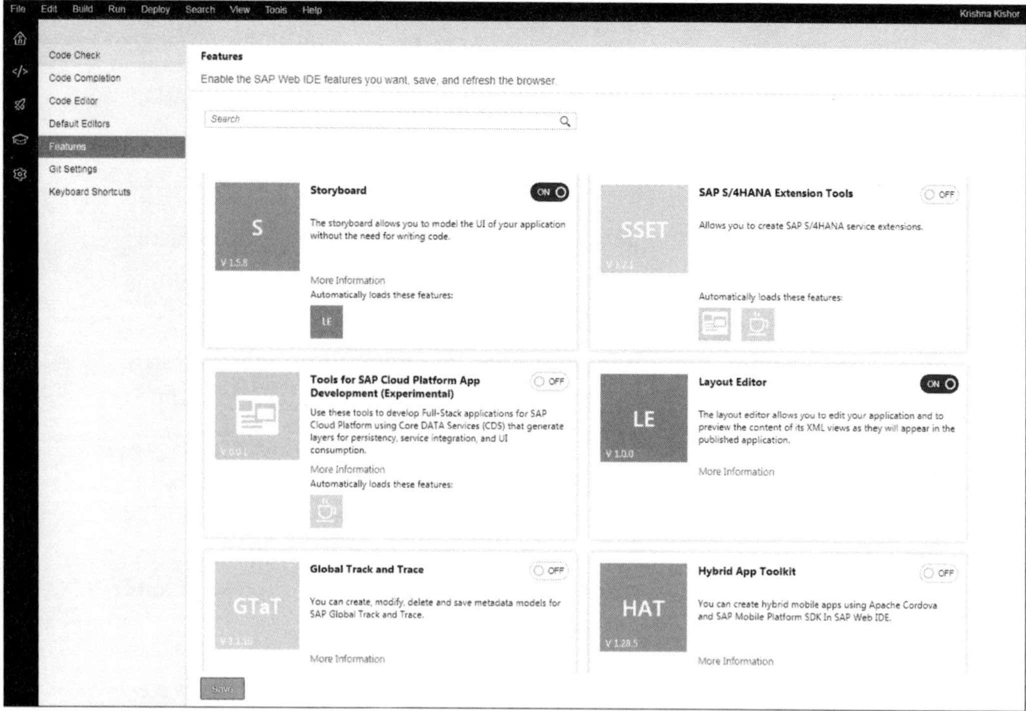

Figure 4.14 Plug-ins/Features Available within SAP Web IDE

You can filter and search the features using the search bar on the top. You can click on **More Information** on each of the plug-ins to see the SAP- or developer-provided documentation. The **On/Off** button on each of these tiles allows you to enable or disable these features.

Development with SAP Web IDE

Let's get started using the SAP Web IDE. In this section, we'll review how to launch the SAP Web IDE and how to use OData Model editor. We'll discuss creating a new SAP Fiori project from a template, sample application, or importing it from an SAP Build prototype. We will also review the layout editor, which speeds up building and extending SAPUI5 views.

Launching SAP Web IDE

To launch SAP Web IDE, navigate to the **SAP Cloud Platform Cockpit** screen, select **Services**, and search for "Web IDE" as shown earlier in Figure 4.6. Choose one of the SAP Web IDE versions, and click on **Go to Service**, as shown in Figure 4.15.

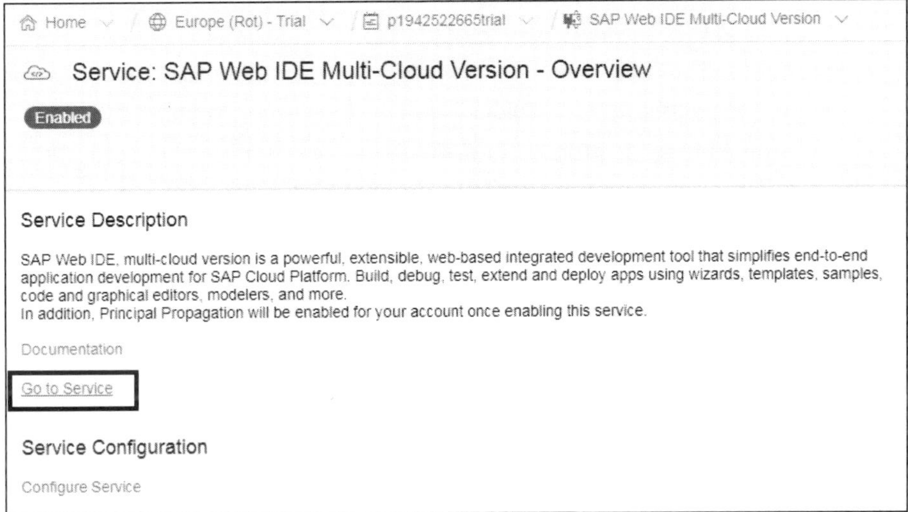

Figure 4.15 Launching SAP Web IDE

Real-World Scenario

Consider a scenario where it's required to create a simple SAP Fiori app to display a list of products and their details. You need to use SAP Web IDE templates to create this application quickly. Let's assume that the service isn't yet ready at the time of starting the SAPUI5 development.

OData Model Editor

Before using an SAP Fiori app template, you must have the metadata of the related OData service, so that the developer can select the available entity sets and properties for binding.

Because it's not always practical to have the OData service available beforehand, SAP Web IDE provides an OData model editor for developing the OData model and thus its metadata.

You need to enable the **OData Model Editor** feature from **Tool • Preferences • Features** (plug-ins) to make use of this tool. Refresh SAP Web IDE to make the changes take effect.

The metadata of an OData service is written in Common Schema Definition Language (CSDL) as an XML file. When stored in a file, the file extension is *.edmx*.

Let's create an OData model for our scenario by following these steps:

1. Create a new project by creating an empty folder from the **Workspace** context menu, and then choose **New • Folder**. Name it "FB_OData_Model".

2. Create a new file in this folder by using the folder's context menu and then choosing **New • File**. Name it "Product_Service.edmx".

3. Enter the XML namespaces, as shown in Figure 4.16.

```
Product_Service.edmx  ×

1 ▾  <edmx:Edmx Version="1.0" xmlns:edmx="http://schemas.microsoft.com/ado/2007/06/edmx">
2 ▾      <edmx:DataServices m:DataServiceVersion="2.0" xmlns:m="http://schemas.microsoft.com/ado/2007/08/dataservices/metadata">
3 ▾          <Schema xmlns="http://schemas.microsoft.com/ado/2008/09/edm" Namespace="ODATA_MODEL">
4
5              </Schema>
6          </edmx:DataServices>
7    </edmx:Edmx>
```

Figure 4.16 OData Metadata Namespaces

Now to create entities, you can make use of schema-based code assist, which helps in creating OData elements. Follow these steps:

1. Press ⟨Ctrl⟩+⟨Spacebar⟩ to open the schema-based code assist feature, providing context-specific help, as shown in Figure 4.17. As shown here, these are five different OData artifact types that can be added at this point.

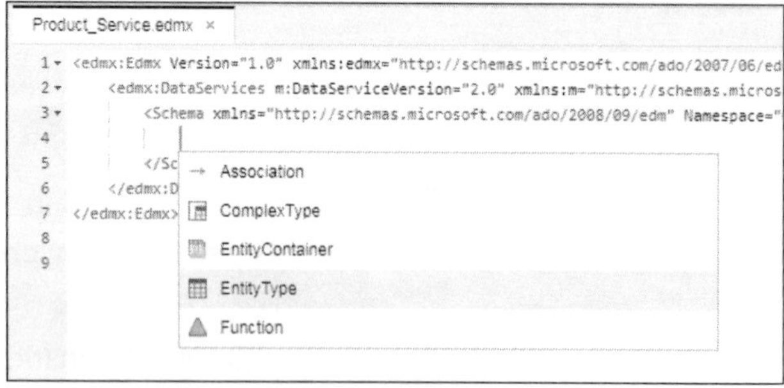

Figure 4.17 Schema-Based Code Assist

2. Next, add an entity and entity set for Products, as well as another entity and entity set for Order.

3. In addition, create an association between Products and Order so that a Navigation property can be created within the Product entity that allows related orders for a Product to be shown by navigation.

The data model with these artifacts is shown in Figure 4.18.

```
Product_Service.edmx  ×
 1  <edmx:Edmx Version="1.0" xmlns:edmx="http://schemas.microsoft.com/ado/2007/06/edmx">
 2    <edmx:DataServices m:DataServiceVersion="2.0" xmlns:m="http://schemas.microsoft.com/ado/2007/08/dataservices/metadata">
 3      <Schema xmlns="http://schemas.microsoft.com/ado/2008/09/edm" Namespace="ODATA_MODEL">
 4        <EntityType Name="Product">
 5          <Key>
 6            <PropertyRef Name="ProductID"/>
 7          </Key>
 8          <Property xmlns:p8="http://schemas.microsoft.com/ado/2009/02/edm/annotation" Name="ProductID" Type="Edm.Int32" Nullable="false"
 9              p8:StoreGeneratedPattern="Identity"/>
10          <Property Name="ProductName" Type="Edm.String" Nullable="false" MaxLength="40" Unicode="true" FixedLength="false"/>
11          <Property Name="SupplierID" Type="Edm.Int32" Nullable="true"/>
12          <Property Name="CategoryID" Type="Edm.Int32" Nullable="true"/>
13          <Property Name="QuantityPerUnit" Type="Edm.String" Nullable="true" MaxLength="20" Unicode="true" FixedLength="false"/>
14          <Property Name="UnitPrice" Type="Edm.Decimal" Nullable="true" Precision="19" Scale="4"/>
15          <Property Name="UnitsInStock" Type="Edm.Int16" Nullable="true"/>
16          <Property Name="UnitsOnOrder" Type="Edm.Int16" Nullable="true"/>
17          <Property Name="ReorderLevel" Type="Edm.Int16" Nullable="true"/>
18          <Property Name="Discontinued" Type="Edm.Boolean" Nullable="false"/>
19          <NavigationProperty Name="Order_Details" Relationship="ODATA_MODEL.FK_Order_Details_Products" FromRole="Products" ToRole="Order_Details"/>
20        </EntityType>
21        <EntityType Name="Order_Detail">
22          <Key>
23            <PropertyRef Name="OrderID"/>
24            <PropertyRef Name="ProductID"/>
25          </Key>
26          <Property Name="OrderID" Type="Edm.Int32" Nullable="false"/>
27          <Property Name="ProductID" Type="Edm.Int32" Nullable="false"/>
28          <Property Name="UnitPrice" Type="Edm.Decimal" Nullable="false" Precision="19" Scale="4"/>
29          <Property Name="Quantity" Type="Edm.Int16" Nullable="false"/>
30          <Property Name="Discount" Type="Edm.Single" Nullable="false"/>
31        </EntityType>
32        <Association Name="FK_Order_Details_Products">
33          <End Role="Products" Type="ODATA_MODEL.Product" Multiplicity="1"/>
34          <End Role="Order_Details" Type="ODATA_MODEL.Order_Detail" Multiplicity="*"/>
35        </Association>
36        <EntityContainer Name="ODATA_MODELEntities" m:IsDefaultEntityContainer="true">
37          <EntitySet Name="Order_Details" EntityType="ODATA_MODEL.Order_Detail"/>
38          <EntitySet Name="Products" EntityType="ODATA_MODEL.Product"/>
39        </EntityContainer>
40      </Schema>
41    </edmx:DataServices>
42  </edmx:Edmx>
```

Figure 4.18 Data Model

4. By clicking on the **Design** tab from *Products_Service.edmx*, you can see a visual representation of the OData model (Figure 4.19).

5. Export this model file into your local system by using the context menu on the *Product_Service.edmx* file and selecting **Export**.

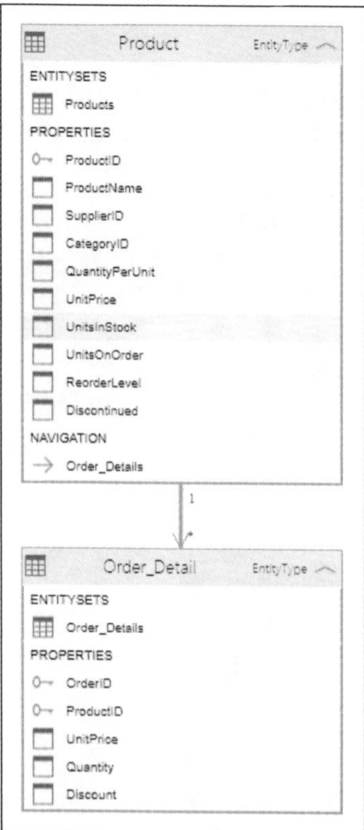

Figure 4.19 Data Model from the Design Tab

Creating New Projects

Projects inside SAP Web IDE reside in an area called the **Workspace**. This is the top-level folder under which all the projects reside. Currently SAP Web IDE supports only one **Workspace**, which is available by default.

Creating from Template

Let's use the model we created to make a simple app using SAP Fiori templates. SAP Web IDE provides multiple templates that can be used to fast-track SAP Fiori app development. Follow these steps:

1. Navigate to **File • New • Project from Template** to see the available templates.

2. Select the **SAP Fiori Worklist Application** template from the list shown in Figure 4.20.

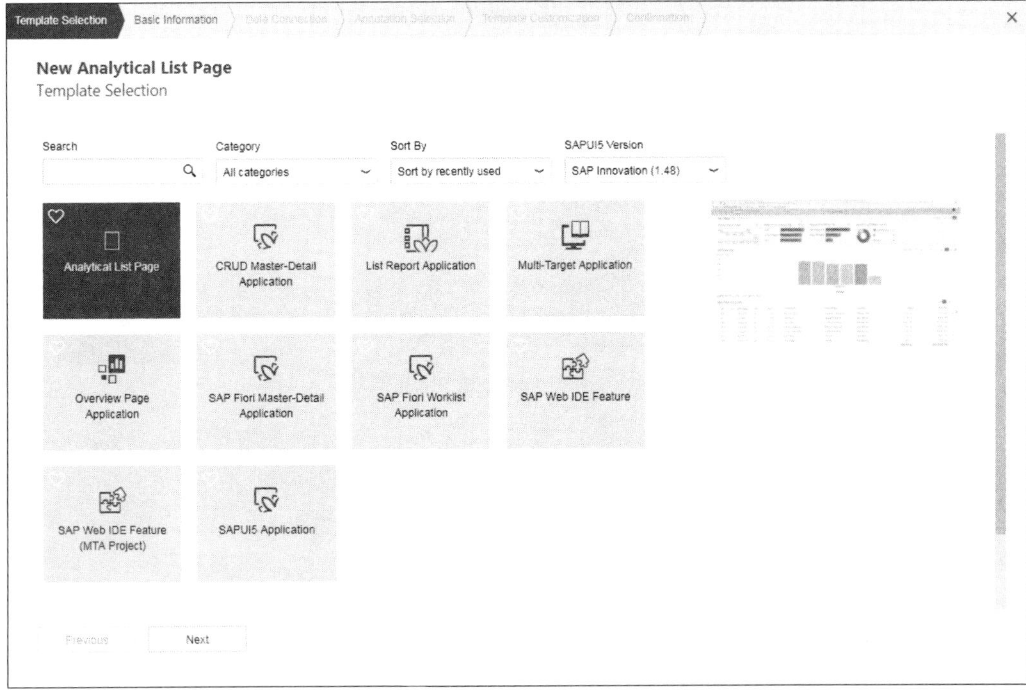

Figure 4.20 Templates in SAP Web IDE

3. Provide a name for the project, and click **Next** (Figure 4.21).

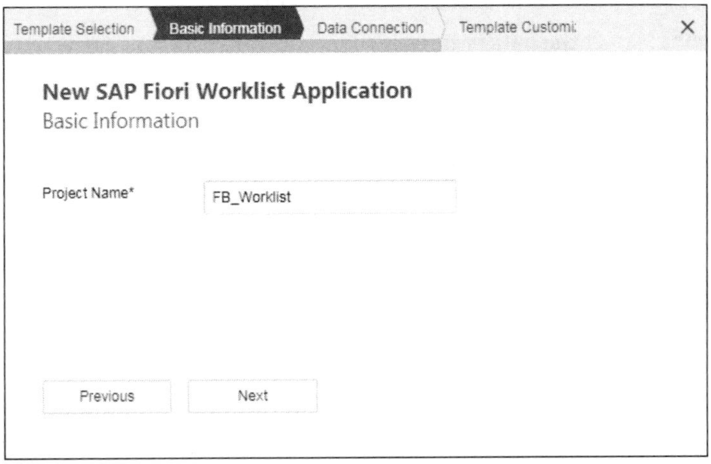

Figure 4.21 Providing a Name for the Project from Template

4. In the next screen, choose **File System** as the data source, and then choose the previously exported file **Products_Service (1).edmx**. SAP Web IDE will validate this file and show the artifacts within the file (Figure 4.22). Click **Next**.

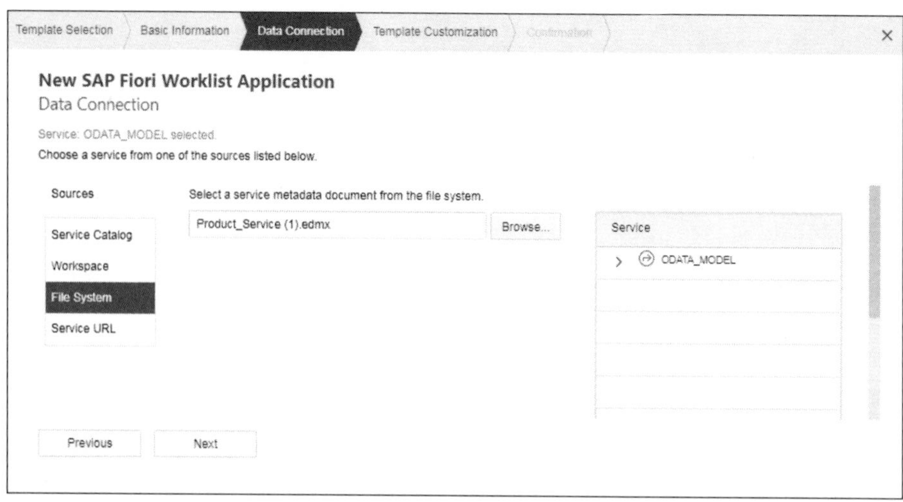

Figure 4.22 Selecting a Source from Local File System

5. Choose the entity set and the corresponding properties for various placeholders within the worklist template as part of **Template Customization** tab.

6. Under **Application Setting**, choose **App for SAP Fiori Launchpad** in the **Type** field, and provide a suitable **Title, Namespace,** and **Description**.

7. Under **Data Binding**, select the data to be shown on the home screen of this template. Provide an entity set name in the **Object Collection** field.

8. Select the **Products** entity set, and provide the suitable property names of the corresponding entity for various attributes of the object.

9. Click the **Finish** button. Figure 4.23 shows the data filled in the **Template Customization** screen.

A new project is available in the **Workspace** with the generated code. Although we don't have a working service linked at this point, we can run the application with mock data. To do so, right-click on the project, and then choose **Run • App in FLP Sandbox (Mock Server)** (Figure 4.24).

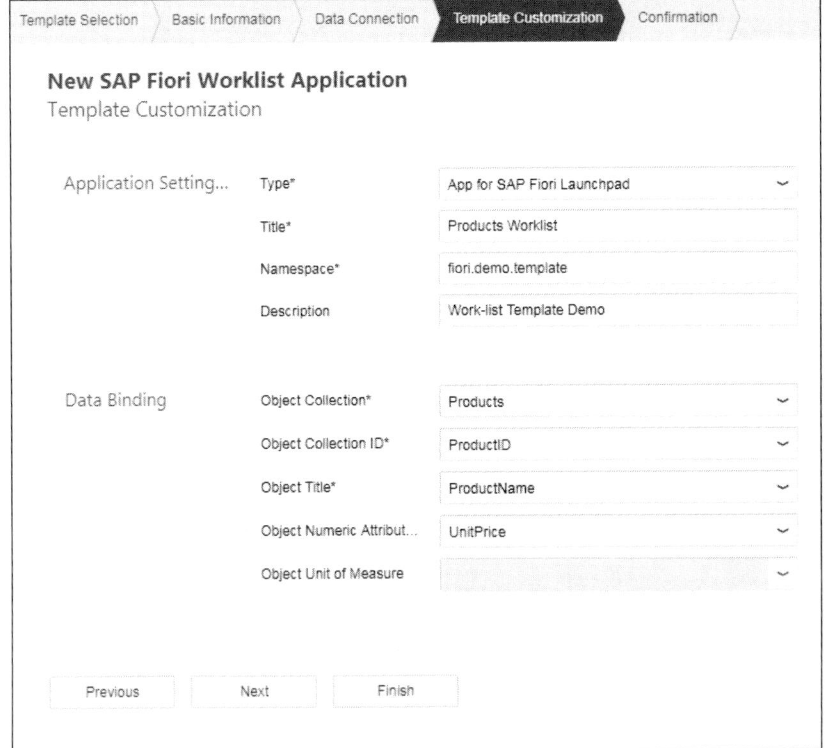

Figure 4.23 Template Customization

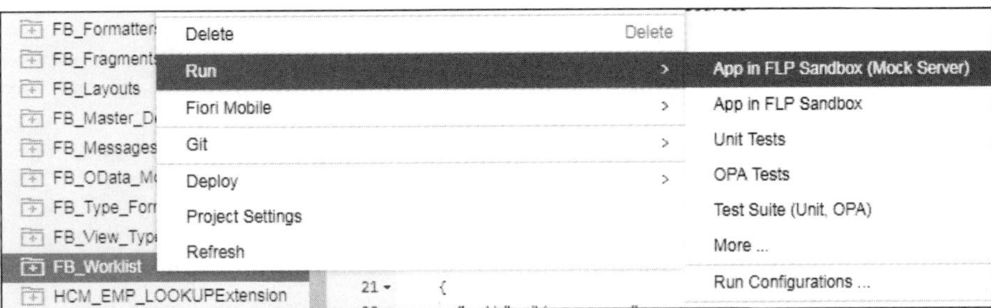

Figure 4.24 Running the App with Mock Data

The app with random generated mock data is shown in Figure 4.25.

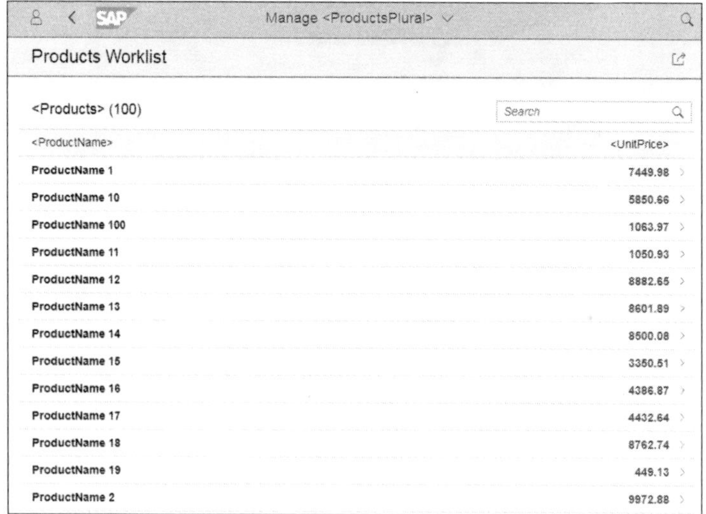

Figure 4.25 App with Mock Data

You might need to use more relevant data for demo purposes. For such scenarios, you can manually enter and prepare data by navigating inside the project to **webapp • LocalService • metadata.xml**. Right-click on **metadata.xml** and choose **Edit Mock Data**. Here you can maintain the mock data for each entity set as shown in Figure 4.26.

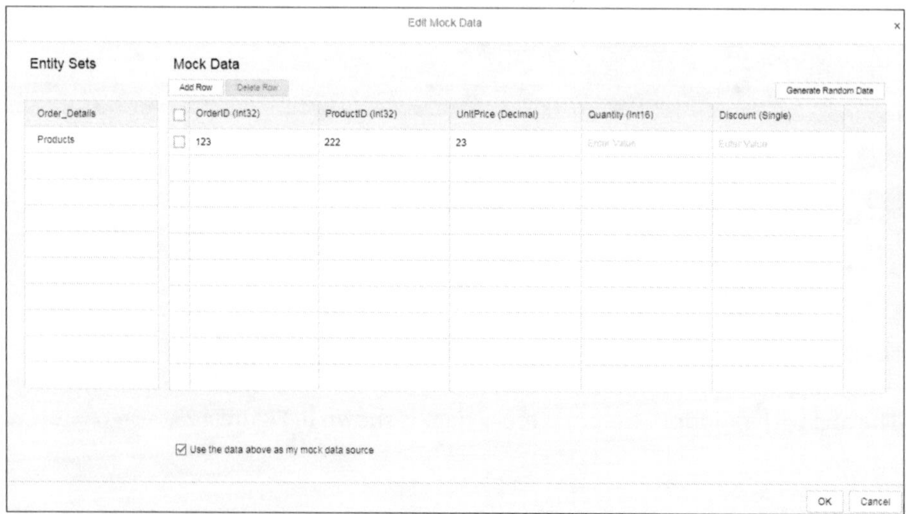

Figure 4.26 Editing/Entering Mock Data

Now let's connect the application with the service available at *http://services.odata.org/V2/Northwind/Northwind.svc* by following these steps:

1. Create a destination in SAP Cloud Platform for the *http://services.odata.org* as shown in Figure 4.27.

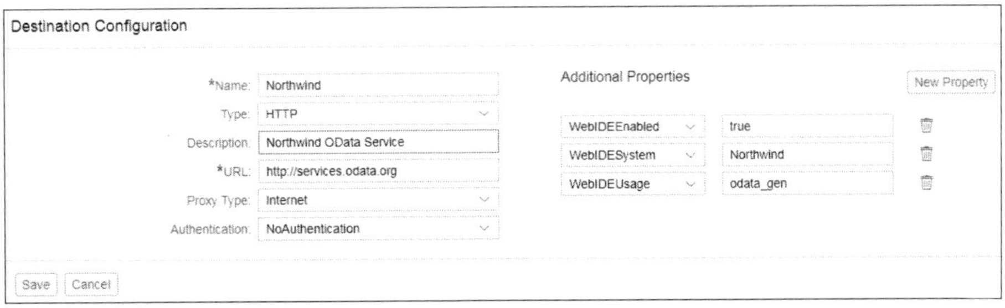

Destination Configuration
*Name: Northwind
Type: HTTP
Description: Northwind OData Service
*URL: http://services.odata.org
Proxy Type: Internet
Authentication: NoAuthentication
Additional Properties
New Property
WebIDEEnabled   true
WebIDESystem   Northwind
WebIDEUsage   odata_gen
Save   Cancel

Figure 4.27 Destination Pointing to Northwind OData Service

2. Specify the service in the application descriptor by navigating to *manifest.json* of the project and providing the service URL, as shown in Figure 4.28 under "dataSources".

```
"dataSources": {
    "mainService": {
        "uri": "/destination/Northwind/V2/Northwind/Northwind.svc",
        "type": "OData",
        "settings": {
            "odataVersion": "2.0",
            "localUri": "localService/metadata.xml"
        }
    }
},
```

Figure 4.28 Specifying the OData Service in manifest.json

3. Update *neo-app.json* and provide the right routing to the SAP Cloud Platform destination as shown in Figure 4.29. This code specifies that any URL starting with /destination/Northwind should be directed to the destination named Northwind.

```
{
    "path": "/destination/Northwind",
    "target": {
        "type": "destination",
        "name": "Northwind"
    },
    "description": "Northwind OData Service"
}
```

Figure 4.29 Routing the OData Service Call to the SAP Cloud Platform Destination in neo-app.json

Let's run the app now without using the mock data. Right-click on the project, and choose **Run • App in FLP Sandbox**. The app will make a call to the Northwind Service and show the output shown in Figure 4.30.

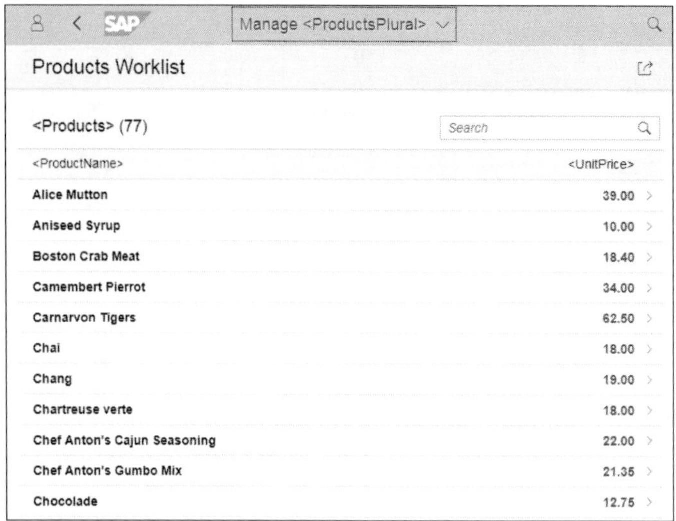

Figure 4.30 Running the App from Northwind OData Service

Creating from Sample Applications

SAP Web IDE provides four sample ready-to-run applications that act as reference implementations of SAP Fiori and SAPUI5 best practices. Two of these are freestyle applications, and the other two are SAP Fiori elements. You can also use these applications as startup code and modify them as required to your business requirements.

These applications rely on SAP's Enterprise Procurement Model (EPM) demo content. All these apps can be run using mock data so that you can navigate across screens and see the functionalities. If you want to connect to a real SAP Gateway server, you can either use your own backend system with EPM configured or use SAP's ES5 system to connect and run these applications. To get access to an ES5 system, navigate to *https://www.sap.com/developer/tutorials/ gateway-demo-signup.html*.

The following are the four available sample applications as shown in Figure 4.31:

- **Approve Purchase Orders**
  This app uses a split screen layout showing purchase orders on the left and purchase order details on the right.

- **Manage Products**
  This is an SAP Fiori elements-based application that uses the list report floor-plan as the home screen and then navigates to the object page floorplan for displaying the product.

- **Shop**
  This is a freestyle application that uses the worklist floorplan. This shows a list of products, allowing you to select and add them to a shopping cart and then check out.

- **Procurement Overview**
  This is an SAP Fiori elements-based application that uses the overview page floorplan. This provides data analysis about suppliers, comparing them, and providing details about trends on total revenue.

To create a project from a sample application, navigate to **File Menu • New • Project from Sample Application**.

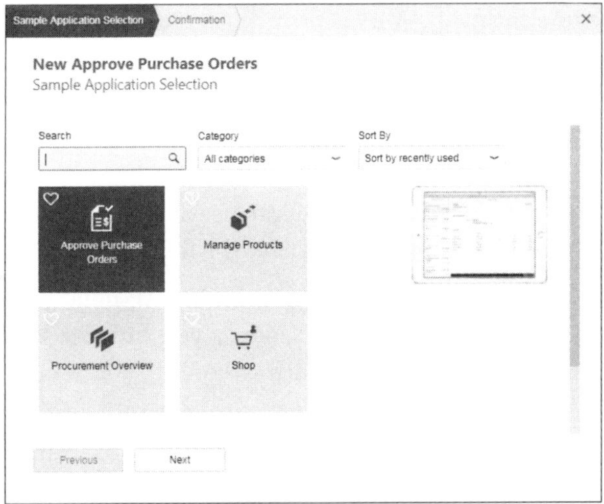

Figure 4.31 SAP Web IDE Sample Applications

Select **Approve Purchase Orders**, and click **Next**. In the next screen, read the SAP Evaluation License Agreement, and then click the **Finish** button.

A new project will get created in your **Workspace** called **sample.ApprovePurchseOrders**. This reference application also comes with mock data under the **localService** folder. You may need to run the app to better understand the reference code in this application. To run the app with mock data, right-click on **flpSandboxMockServer.html**, and choose **Run • Run as • Web Application** (Figure 4.32).

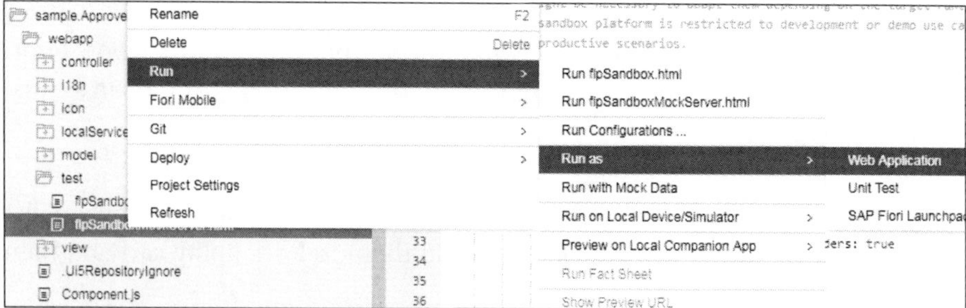

Figure 4.32 Running Application with Mock Data

This will open an SAP Fiori launchpad with other sample applications. When you click the new reference application tile in the **My Home** group, the app will open with mock data.

Tip

You can also run these sample applications with a real backend. You can use SAP's demo SAP Gateway server ES5 or your on-premise SAP Gateway system with the minimum of SAP_BASIS 7.51 SP02.

Importing from SAP Build

When you create prototypes from the SAP Build tool, you can use it to directly generate startup code within SAP Web IDE. The process involves the following steps:

1. Create destinations within SAP Cloud Platform to connect to SAP Build. The required destinations are automatically created whenever you buy the SAP Build license and connect with your SAP Cloud Platform account.

2. Enable the SAP Build service in SAP Cloud Platform.

3. Enable the SAP Build plug-in in SAP Web IDE.

4. Import the SAP Build prototype as a project to SAP Web IDE.

More details about each of these steps can be found here: *https://www.sap.com/developer/tutorials/build-import-webide.html.*

Collaborative Development

Git is a distributed versioning system allowing you to perform collaborative development. SAP Web IDE allows you to collaborate with other developers by providing an integration with Git servers.

You can host a Git repository inside your local server, host on public servers such as GitHub, or create a repository in SAP Cloud Platform.

Let's create a Git repository in SAP Cloud Platform and push an SAPUI5 app to it by following these steps:

1. Navigate to the **SAP Cloud Platform Cockpit** screen, and choose **Repositories • Git Repositories**. This will show a list of existing repositories in the subaccount (Figure 4.33).

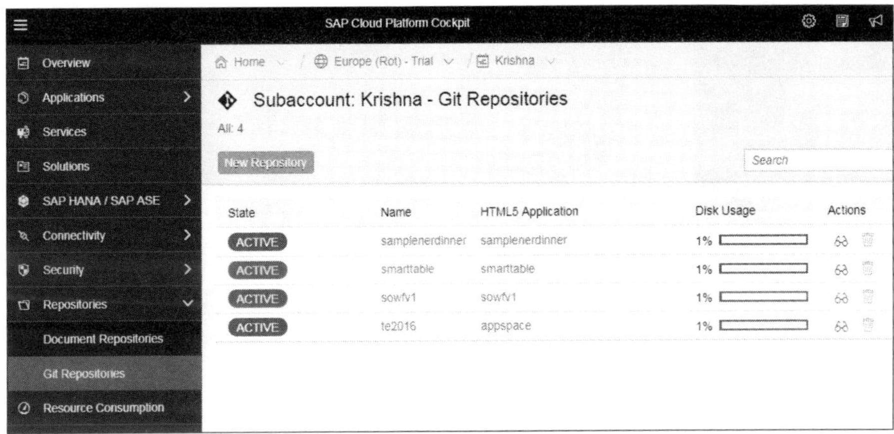

Figure 4.33 Git Repositories in SAP Cloud Platform

2. Click on **New Repository** to create a new repository.

3. Enter "gitdemo" as the repository **Name,** and click **OK** (Figure 4.34). This will create a Git repository. Click on the repository name to see more details. Note that you'll need the **Repository URL** value shown here later in step 4.

4. Go to SAP Web IDE, and initialize the local repository by right-clicking on the project and choosing **Git • Initialize Local Repository**.

5. Set the remote repository by right-clicking on the project and choosing **Git • Set Remote**. Provide the **Repository URL** that you saw in Step 1, and click **OK**.

6. Open the **Git Pane** by clicking on the **Git** icon on the right toolbar.

7. Click on the **Merge** button.

8. Click on the **Stage All** checkbox, provide a **Commit Description**, and click **Commit and Push** (Figure 4.35).

9. Click on **master** branch in the next popup, and then click **OK**.

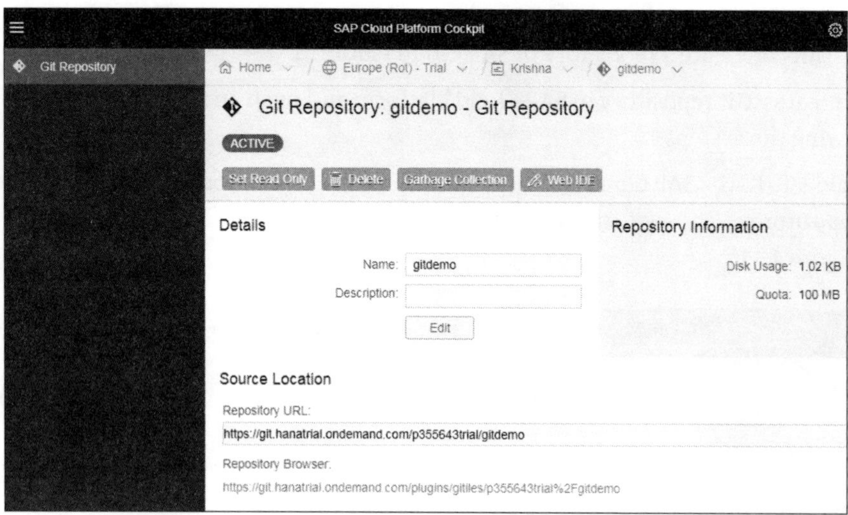

Figure 4.34 Details of Git Repository in SAP Cloud Platform

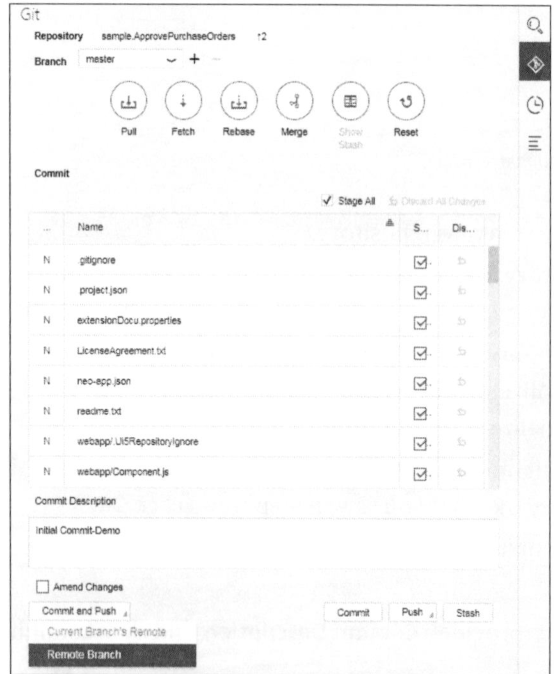

Figure 4.35 Committing and Pushing the Project to a Git Repository on SAP Cloud Platform

This will send the current project to the Git repository.

Importing Projects

You can import projects in the following four ways:

- **From a local system**
  You can import an existing project from the Git repository by cloning it within SAP Web IDE. Let's import an existing repository on GitHub:

  Click on **Clone from Git Repository** in the SAP Web IDE home screen. Provide the **Repository URL** (*https://github.com/SAP/openui5-sample-app*), and click **Clone**. When the cloning finishes, the content of the repository appears in the **Workspace** as a project (Figure 4.36).

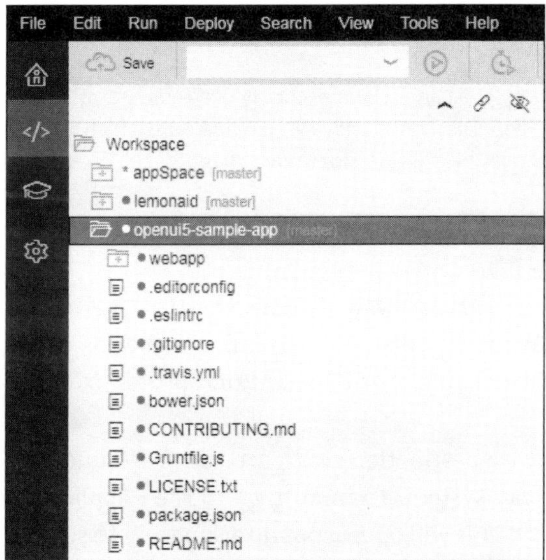

Figure 4.36 Cloned Repository as a Project

- **Importing from a local system**
  You can import an existing archive of an SAPUI5 project into SAP Web IDE.

  In the **Home** screen of SAP Web IDE, under **Import an Application**, select **Archive**. This opens a prompt to choose an archive from your local computer. Choose an archive, and provide a project where the contents should be extracted to (Figure 4.37). If you provide the name of a nonexisting folder/project, this folder will be created within the SAP Web IDE **Workspace**.

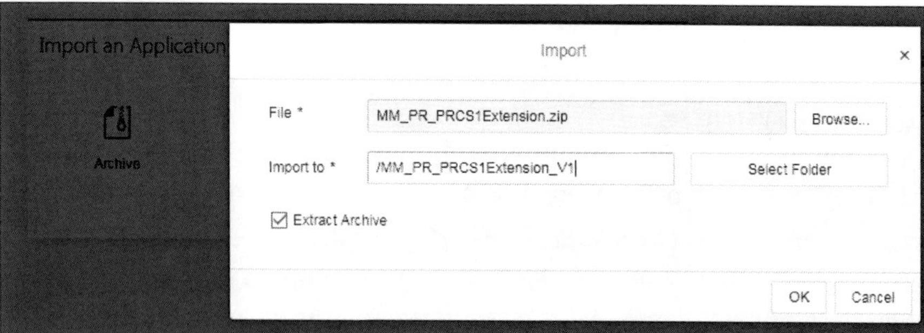

Figure 4.37 Importing an SAPUI5 Project from an Archive

Tip

When you import an SAPUI5 project as an archive, you may not always be able to run the application from SAP Web IDE. This is because *neo-app.json*, which is the **Project Settings** file, may not have the right destinations and routes that are suitable to the current SAP Web IDE.

- **Importing from an ABAP server (SAP Gateway system)**
  An existing deployed project in an SAP Gateway system's SAPUI5 ABAP repository can be imported into SAP Web IDE. This can be useful in scenarios where you want to read and analyze the existing code of an SAPUI5 app, for example, for extension scenarios.

  As a prerequisite you need to have a destination configured on SAP Cloud Platform pointing to the SAP Gateway system. To import, go to **File • Application** from the SAPUI5 ABAP repository. This will open a popup asking you to select a destination. After you select a destination from the dropdown, all SAPUI5 projects in the SAP Gateway system will be listed as shown in Figure 4.38. Choose one of the SAPUI5 projects and click **OK** so that the SAPUI5 app gets added to your **Workspace** as a project.

- **Importing from SAP Cloud Platform**
  Consider that you want to work on an SAPUI5 application that is already deployed to SAP Cloud Platform. You can import that to your **Workspace** and start working on it. To import, go to **File • Import • Application from SAP Cloud Platform**. It will open a popup that lists all the applications deployed on the SAP Cloud Platform as shown in Figure 4.39. Choose an application and click **OK** so that the application gets added to the **Workspace** as a project.

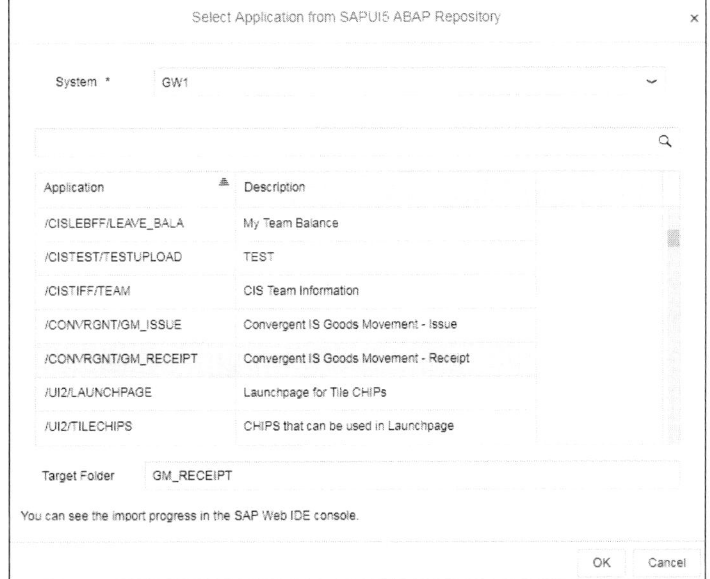

Figure 4.38 Importing an SAPUI5 Project from an SAP Gateway System

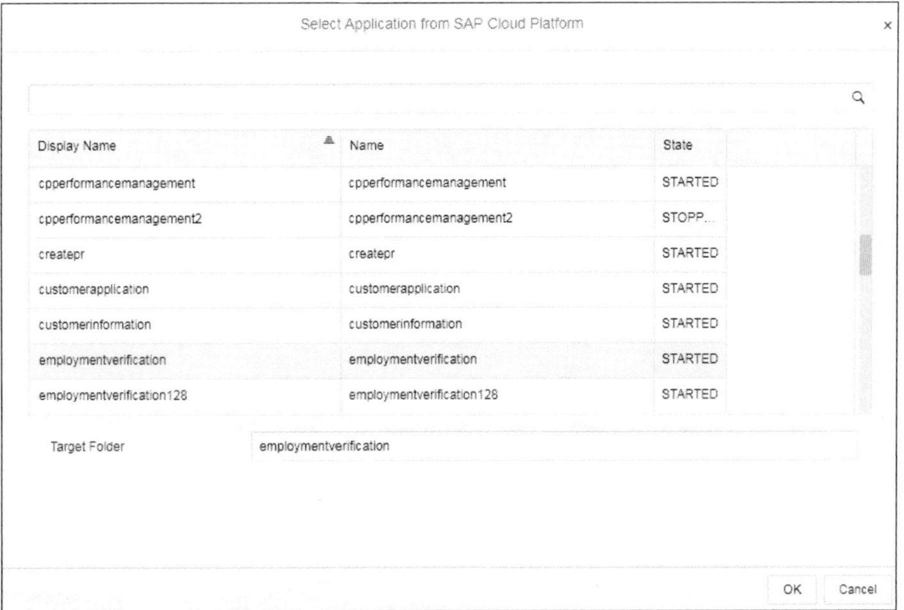

Figure 4.39 Importing an Application from SAP Cloud Platform

Layout Editor

The layout editor can open an XML view, providing a graphical view of how the XML view would look in an application (Figure 4.40). In addition, you can drag and drop to move SAPUI5 controls within the layout editor, so that corresponding XML view gets updated suitably. This can speed up XML view development considerably.

Any existing XML view can be opened using the layout editor by right-clicking on the XML view and choosing **Open with • Layout Editor**.

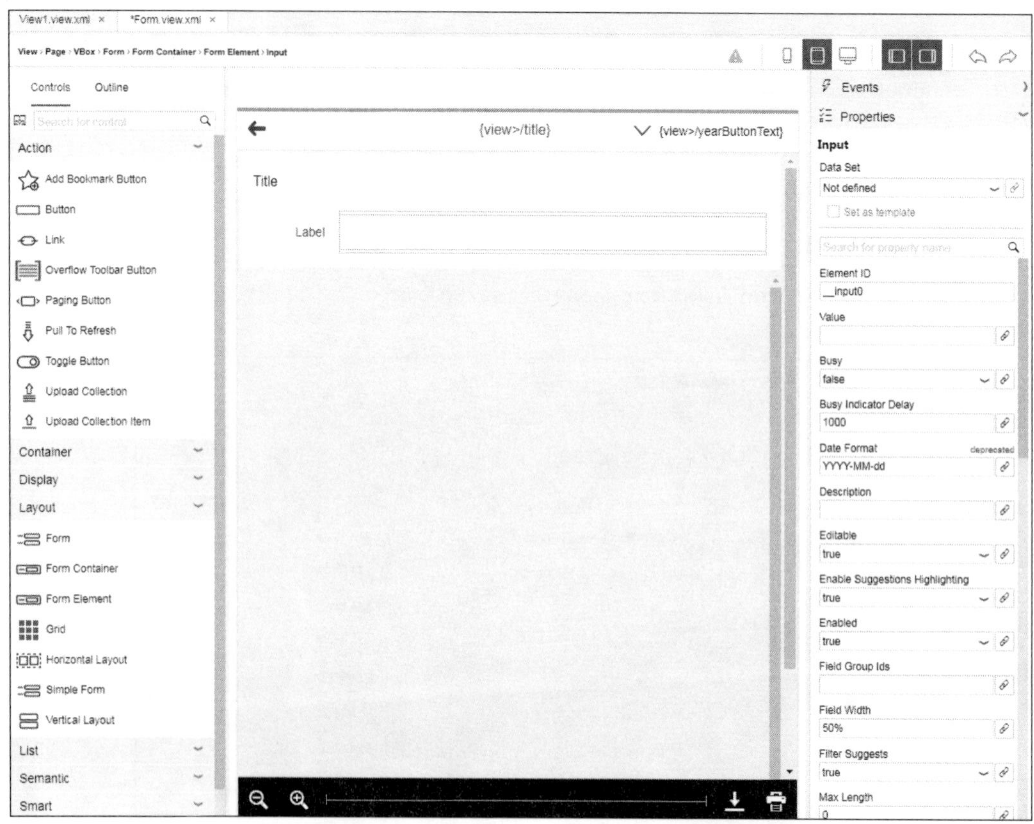

Figure 4.40 Layout Editor Panes

This editor has a canvas in the center, which represents the content of the XML view. The pane on the left contains two tabs. The **Controls** tab lists all the SAPUI5 controls that can be dragged and dropped in the center canvas. The **Outline** tab helps you visualize the XML view hierarchy. By clicking on each hierarchy element, the element gets highlighted on the canvas.

The right side of the canvas contains a pane with properties and events of the SAPUI5 control that is selected on the canvas/outline. You can enter values for these properties and specify the binding entity set and properties, including *i18n* translation texts. Under **Events**, you can specify the event-handling functions available in the controller.

Layout Editor also has a toolbar that enables you to preview the view in desktops, tablets, and mobile screens.

As you build the view on the canvas, the XML view gets built in the background.

Warning

The layout editor works only in Google Chrome. In addition, not all SAPUI5 controls are supported. These controls appear with the label **unsupported** in the **Outline** pane.

Extension with SAP Web IDE

SAP Web IDE provides tools to extend the SAP-delivered SAP Fiori apps that are deployed either on SAP Gateway or SAP Cloud Platform.

To create an extension project, go to **File • New • Extension Project** or click on **New Extension Project** on the home screen. This step opens a popup where you need to select the original SAPUI5/SAP Fiori app that you want to extend. You can either select an **SAPUI5 ABAP Repository** system or **SAP Cloud Platform** at this point, as shown in Figure 4.41.

If you choose **SAPUI5 ABAP Repository**, you need to choose a destination in the next step and subsequently choose an original SAPUI5 application from the list of available applications. If you choose **SAP Cloud Platform**, it will show a list of available SAPUI5 applications, and you need to choose the original application from there.

After choosing the original application, you need to provide name for the extension project and click **Next**. Click **Finish** on the next screen, and this will create an extension project within **Workspace**.

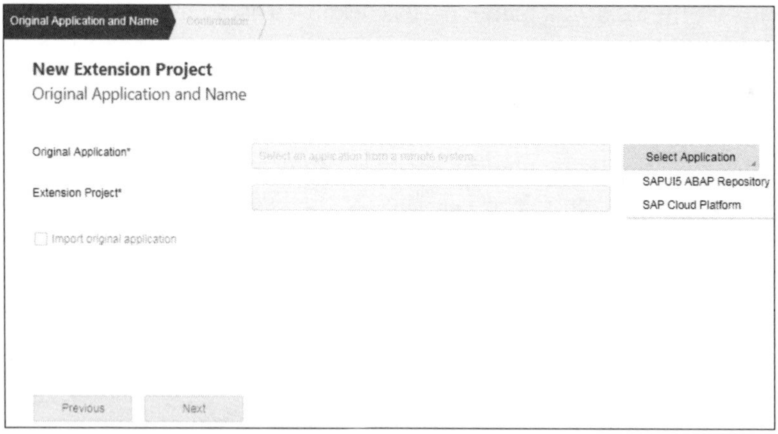

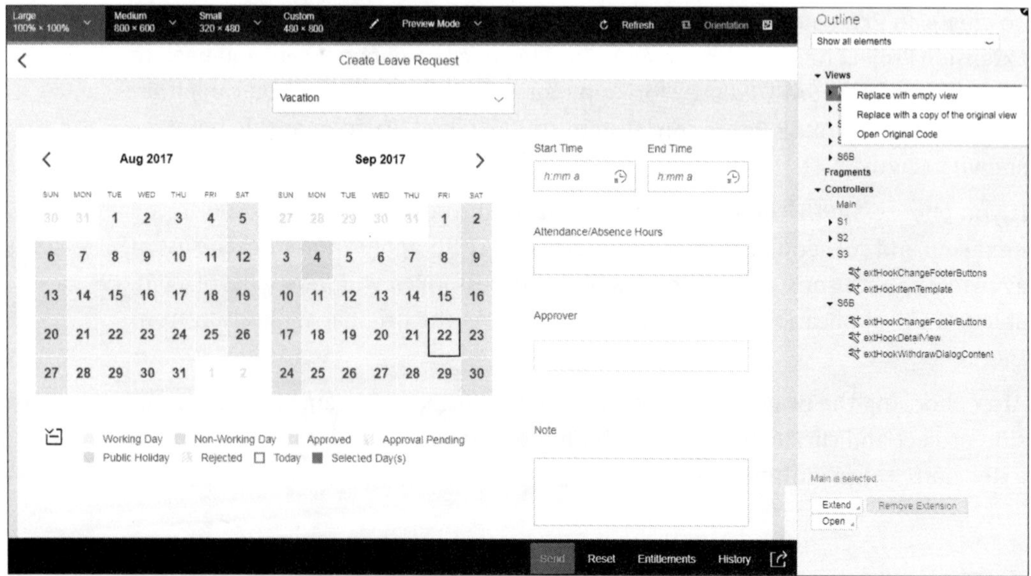

Figure 4.41 Extension: Choosing the Source of Original Application

The extensibility pane is a graphical tool to perform various extensions on the original application. Upon performing extensions using the extensibility pane, it creates the required code in the backend.

To open the extensibility pane, select the extension project, and choose **Tools • Extensibility Pane**. This will open the original application within the extensibility pane as shown in Figure 4.42.

Figure 4.42 Extensibility Pane Showing Original Application

Extensibility has a canvas area that displays the original application. On the right pane, there is an outline area that lists all the views with its contents and controllers within the app.

The toolbar on the extensibility pane has different buttons for viewing the application with different screen sizes. You can choose these buttons, and the application reloads with those screen dimensions. The toolbar also has a button to choose between **Preview Mode** and **Extensibility Mode**. **Preview Mode** runs the original application and allows you to work with the app and navigate to different screens. After you navigate to the screen that you want to enhance, you can switch to **Extensibility Mode**. Now you can select different UI controls in the screen by either clicking on the control or choosing it from the **Outline** pane. You can click on the **Extend** button, which lists the possible extension operations on the UI control. Figure 4.43 lists the various extensions possible within a view.

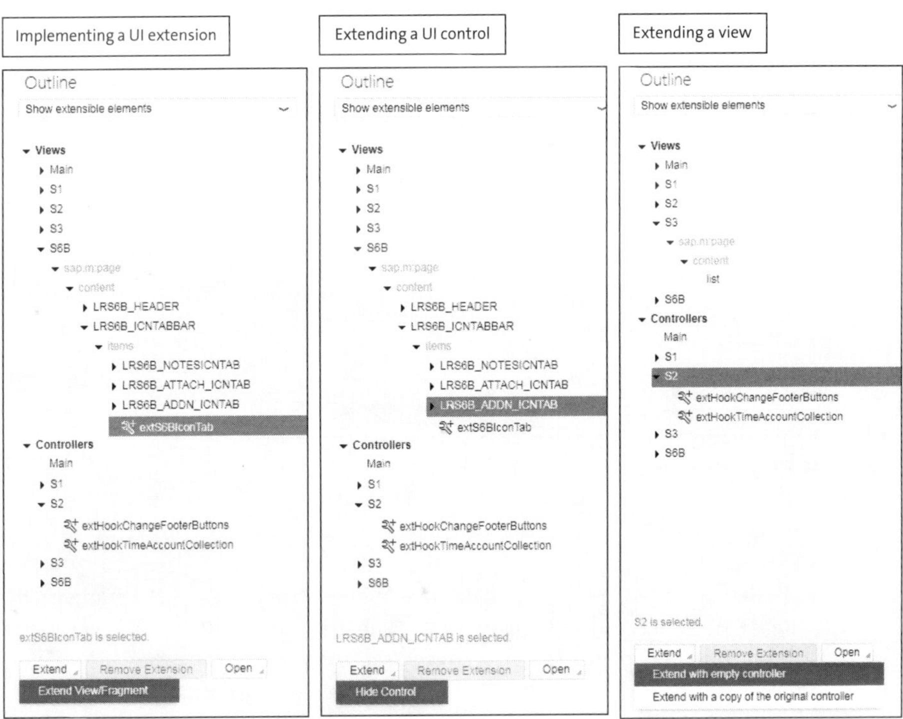

Figure 4.43 View Extensions with the Extensibility Pane

You can use the **Outline** pane to choose different controllers in the app as well. You can replace the controllers or implement SAPUI5 controller hooks as shown in Figure 4.44.

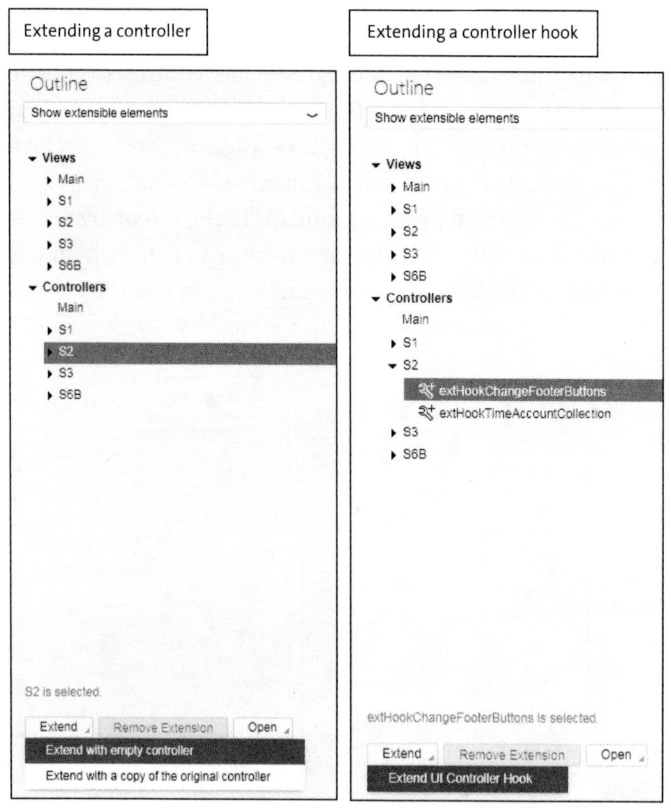

Figure 4.44 Controller Extensions in the Extensibility Pane

Note

For extending SAP Fiori apps, SAP-delivered SAP Fiori apps need not be imported into SAP Web IDE. While running the extension app within SAP Web IDE, SAP Web IDE loads the SAP-delivered app from the source system and applies the extensions.

You can refer to Chapter 6 for more details on extension concepts within SAP Fiori/SAPUI5.

Build and Deployment with SAP Web IDE

Code in the SAPUI5 application is arranged in folders, and the code in these files are readable (with tabs, spaces, and line breaks) for the use of the developer and others while developing the application. However, browsers don't need these to be in a human-readable format. Applications can be optimized greatly by making changes to the way code is organized and delivered to the browser. This process is called application build.

If configured, application build happens automatically before the project is deployed either to SAP Gateway or SAP Cloud Platform.

SAP Web IDE has a built-in tool for building SAPUI5 applications. To enable this for any project, you need to navigate to project settings by right-clicking on the project, choosing **Project Settings • Project Types**, and selecting **SAPUI5 Client Build** (see Figure 4.45).

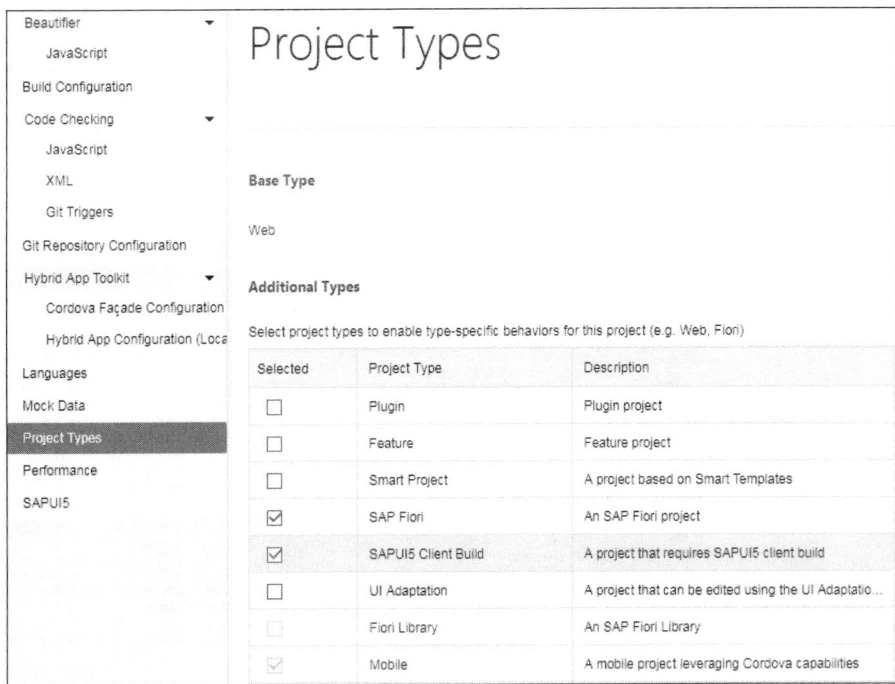

Figure 4.45 Enabling Client Build for a Project

SAPUI5 client build does the following to an SAP Fiori project:

- A *dist* (distributable) folder is created. that is optimized and can be shared with others without the need for further optimizations. This folder will have an optimized copy of all resource files.

- Application minification is performed by creating a *Component-preload.js* inside the *dist* folder. This is the most important function of application build. *Component-preload.js* contains all the resources of the application in a single file, optimized, thus reducing the number of round trips to the server and the amount of data moved over the network.

- A *project.json* file of the application is updated with application build details.

- A *resource.json* file is created within the *dist* folder providing details of all the project resources.

Warning

Contents of the *dist* folder should never be altered because it will be overwritten every time an application build is performed.

Figure 4.46 shows a project with application build artifacts along with original artifacts. It also shows a *Component-preload.js* file where you can see an optimized version of project files.

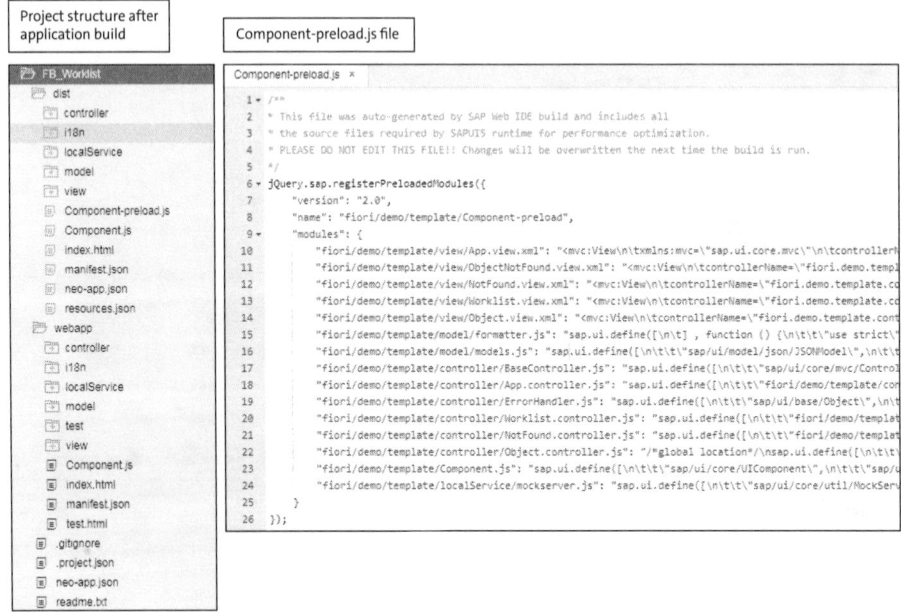

Figure 4.46 Application Build Artifacts and Component-preload.js file

> **Tip**
> Grunt task runner is available with the multi-cloud (full stack) version of SAP Web IDE, so you need to enable the corresponding Grunt plug-in to perform application build. The previously mentioned SAPUI5 client build is no longer available with the multi-cloud version of SAP Web IDE.

An SAP Fiori app that is developed on SAP Web IDE needs to be available on a server so that it can be accessible using a URL. Moving the application from the development environment to a server is called deployment.

Deployment will be discussed further in Chapter 7.

Important Terminology

This chapter covered the following terminology:

- **Cloud computing**
  An IT paradigm of delivery of computing services—be it a platform, an application, or an infrastructure—over the Internet on a pay-per-use basis.

- **Cloud Connector**
  A lightweight Java server that runs within the on-premise network and allows SAP Cloud Platform to connect to on-premise systems.

- **Cloud Foundry**
  Cloud Foundry is an open source community as well as an open source Platform-as-a-Service technology. SAP is a founding member of this foundation, and SAP Cloud Platform has a Cloud-Foundry based version which will be the primary technology behind SAP Cloud Platform, going forward.

- **Common Schema Definition Language (CSDL)**
  Format used for defining OData model or metadata.

- **Destination**
  A configuration object on SAP Cloud Platform that can be used across applications to connect to systems outside SAP Cloud Platform.

- **Git**
  Most popular open source, distributed version-controlling system.

- **Infrastructure as a Service (IaaS)**
  IaaS is a type of cloud computing that provides computing infrastructure like servers and databases over the internet.

- **Neo**
  This is the original technology on which SAP Cloud Platform was built on. Neo allows users develop HTML5, Java, and SAP HANA extended application services applications.

- **Platform as a Service (PaaS)**
  PaaS is a type of cloud computing which provides access to a platform over the internet for developing, running, and managing applications.

- **Software as a Service (SaaS)**
  SaaS is a type of cloud computing which provides access to an application like email over the internet.

- **Version-controlling system**
  A system to maintain different versions of a file or a piece of code to be able to load previous versions of the file or code whenever required.

Practice Questions

These practice questions will help you evaluate your understanding of the topics covered in this chapter. The questions shown are similar in nature to those found on the certification examination. Although none of these questions will be found on the exam itself, they will allow you to review your knowledge of the subject. Select the correct answers, and then check the completeness of your answers in the "Practice Question Answers and Explanations" section. Remember, on the exam, you must select all correct answers and only correct answers to receive credit for the question.

1.   Which is the recommended tool for developing and extending SAP Fiori apps?

☐   A. Eclipse Mars

☐   B. SAP Web IDE

☐   C. SAP Cloud Connector

☐   D. Git

2.   Which of the following is *not* a benefit of cloud computing?

☐   A. Scalability

☐   B. Cost benefit

☐   C. Reliability

☐   D. Application performance

3. Which of the following is *not* offered as a of cloud service?

☐   A. Platform

☐   B. Software

☐   C. Training

☐   D. Infrastructure

4. Neo is an SAP Cloud Platform environment based on open source technology and standard. True or False?

☐   A. True

☐   B. False

5. Which of the following is *not* a feature provided by SAP Web IDE?

☐   A. Multiple workspaces to manage and organize your code

☐   B. Ability to perform Application Build

☐   C. Provides a graphical editor to create an XML view

☐   D. Provides a mock server to work with test data

6. When you want to update the committed code in your local repository into the remote repository, which command would you run?

☐   A. `Commit`

☐   B. `Pull`

☐   C. `Push`

☐   D. `Update`

7. Which of the following is a valid way to import applications into SAP Web IDE?

☐   A. Import from Eclipse SAPUI5 plug-in

☐   B. Import from a different SAP Web IDE's workspace

☐   C. Import from a different SAP Cloud Platform's Git repository

☐   D. Import from subversion (SVN)

8.   What is the extension of an OData model metadata file?

☐   A. *.edmx*

☐   B. *.xml*

☐   C. *.json*

☐   D. *.exe*

9.   Which file contains the minified version of application files?

☐   A. *application-preload.js*

☐   B. *library-preload.js*

☐   C. *project-preload.js*

☐   D. *component-preload.js*

10.   Which folder contains the file component *preload.json*?

☐   A. *dist*

☐   B. *webapp*

☐   C. *project*

☐   D. *app*

11.   Which view type can be visualized from layout editor?

☐   A. JSON

☐   B. JavaScript

☐   C. XML

12.   Which of the following is not a feature of SAP Web IDE multi-cloud version on SAP Cloud Platform?

☐   A. Grunt task runner available

☐   B. A Multitarget application can be created

☐   C. Register the app to On-premise SAP Fiori launchpad

☐   D. Import from SAP Build

Practice Answers and Explanations

1. Correct answer: **B**

    SAP Web IDE is an SAP recommended tool for developing and extending SAP Fiori apps. Even though you can install the SAPUI5 development toolkit on Eclipse, it doesn't provide all the features and tools available with SAP Web IDE.

2. Correct answer: **D**

    Application performance need not improve with a cloud computing service. The remaining options are clear advantages of cloud computing.

3. Correct answer: **C**

    Though trainings are offered as a traditional service in a traditional business model, it's not a technical service provided or referred on cloud computing.

4. Correct answer: **B**

    False. Cloud Foundry is one of the environments available with SAP Cloud Platform and is an open source platform and technology. Neo is an SAP proprietary environment and technology.

5. Correct answer: **A**

    SAP Web IDE currently provides only one workspace to organize your projects.

6. Correct answer: **C**

    Committed changes are updated to the remote repository using the Push command.

7. Correct answer: **C**

    Among the options provided, you can only import from an SAP Cloud Platform Git repository. Other options aren't supported.

8. Correct answer: **A**

    OData metadata is stored in a file with extension *.edmx*.

9. Correct answer: **D**

    component-preload.js contains the minified version of the file. This gets created when the application build happens.

10. Correct answer: **A**

    Upon application build, the *dist* folder gets created, and *component-preload.js* gets generated with other files.

11. Correct answer: **C**

    The layout editor can visualize only an XML view. All changes done within the layout editor will also be updated in the XML view.

12. Correct answer: **C**

    SAP Web IDE cannot be used for registering the app to SAP Fiori launchpad.

Take Away

In this chapter, you learned about SAP Cloud Platform and its capabilities. We discussed various features of SAP Web IDE focusing on developing new SAP Fiori apps using templates, sample applications, and layout editor. We also covered enhancement techniques using the extension pane. We ended the chapter by going through tooling for the application build when optimizing the loading and running of SAP Fiori apps.

Summary

SAP Web IDE is an indispensable SAP Cloud Platform service for an SAPUI5/SAP Fiori developer. SAP Web IDE helps developers immensely in being efficient both while creating new SAP Fiori apps and enhancing SAP-provided SAP Fiori apps. Now you should be familiar with SAP Web IDE and how to use it for your development.

In the next chapter, you'll learn about OData and how to implement complex operations such as deep insert, expand, and changeset processing. You'll find out how to trigger these calls from SAPUI5 code.

Chapter 5
OData and Advanced Data Handling

Techniques You'll Master:

- Understand OData and its purpose

- Understand concepts of data binding

- Implement `Create`, `Read`, `Update`, and `Delete` operations

- Perform complex operations such as `Deep Insert` and batch programming

- Implement a facet filter control in your app

- Use in-app navigation and deep linking

In this chapter, we'll introduce OData and discover its capabilities. We'll also discuss data binding in SAPUI5 and specific to XML views. We'll explore how to write data to databases using SAPUI5 application programming interfaces (APIs). During a deep dive into OData, you'll learn how to implement various operations using SAP Gateway. You'll also learn complex operations, including `Deep Insert` and `$batch`. We'll cover facet filters and how to implement them in your application. You'll also see how to navigate from one app to another, how to open a specific app and a view directly by navigating to an app, and how to open a view within that app by using deep linking.

Real-World Scenarios

As a developer, you want to understand OData because it's the preferred way of exchanging data between a server and an SAPUI5 app. You want to understand how to trigger various operations from the user interface (UI) and implement these operations in the ABAP system.

When you deal with a huge amount of data, it's common to need to apply multiple filters for various attributes or facets of the dataset. You want to understand how to use and implement the facet filter for such a requirement.

In business applications, it's common to navigate from one business transaction to another transaction or to a business object, as well as to a specific view in the target application.

Objectives of This Portion of the Test

The objective of this portion of the SAP Fiori Certification Test is to test the understanding of the following:

- Basics of OData and performing various simple and complex operations
- Concept of two-way data binding
- Facet filter and its implementation
- Concepts of intent-based navigation and deep linking

Key Concepts Refresher

OData services are one of the most important parts of an SAP Fiori application. They supply the business data to the UI controls and carry out business transactions. OData model is a key integration point between UI layer and the backend layer. Skills in modeling of OData artifacts, mapping the right OData operations for the UI actions and implementing those identified operations is very important for developing an efficient and maintainable SAP Fiori application. In this chapter, we will get introduced to the OData concepts and then deep dive into advanced concepts which are useful in practical scenarios.

OData Services

For business applications, it's common to get the data from a server over HTTP. However, a standard must be defined for all the communications between the application and the server for efficient communication.

SAP has chosen OData, which is an ISO/IEC-approved standard and OASIS standard defining best practices for building REST APIs. OData lets you focus on the business logic, while it defines standards for request/response payloads, request URLs, formats for exchanging media types, response status codes, standard error responses, and a way to send multiple requests in a single HTTP request.

OData Data Model

OData defines several data model artifacts for defining the data model.

Entity and Entity Sets

An entity is a group of related properties that usually represents a business object and is one of the central objects in data modeling. One or more of these properties is marked as key properties, identifying an instance of an entity. Examples of OData entities are `SalesOrderHeader`, `SalesOrderItem`, `Material`, `Plant`, and so on. The OData code includes feeds, or collections of entity sets, that represent a collection of entities, while adding a business context if required. For example, `User` can be an entity, whereas `Managers` and `Developers` can be entity sets linked to the `User` entity.

Service Operations

Operations aren't always on entities. When a service requires a behavior to be modeled by taking few inputs and returning none or many entity instances, you can make use of `Service` operations.

Associations and Navigations

Associations and navigations relate entities to each other. They help to navigate using a URL from an entity set to a linked entity set. Associations define the relationship between two entities and define the cardinality of the relationship. Navigation properties, on the other hand, refers to a defined association and defines a one-way navigation (navigation property in the source entity) from a source entity to a target entity. For navigating in the reverse direction, another navigation property will be required in the source entity.

Metadata

Metadata is information about the OData service describing the containing artifacts. OData allows you to define two types of metadata documents:

- **Service document**
  This document lists all the high-level artifacts such as entity sets and `Service` operations. A service document is usually available at the service root of the OData service.

- **Service metadata document**
  This document describes the complete data model listing of each of the OData artifacts involved from properties to `Service` operations.

Figure 5.1 shows the metadata of the publicly available Northwind OData service (*http://services.odata.org/V2/Northwind/Northwind.svc/$metadata*).

```
←  →  C   ⓘ services.odata.org/V2/Northwind/Northwind.svc/$metadata

This XML file does not appear to have any style information associated with it. The document tree is sh

▼<edmx:Edmx xmlns:edmx="http://schemas.microsoft.com/ado/2007/06/edmx" Version="1.0">
  ▼<edmx:DataServices xmlns:m="http://schemas.microsoft.com/ado/2007/08/dataservices/metadata
    ▼<Schema xmlns:d="http://schemas.microsoft.com/ado/2007/08/dataservices" xmlns:m="http://
      ▼<EntityType Name="Category">
        ▼<Key>
            <PropertyRef Name="CategoryID"/>
          </Key>
          <Property xmlns:p8="http://schemas.microsoft.com/ado/2009/02/edm/annotation" Name="Ca
          <Property Name="CategoryName" Type="Edm.String" Nullable="false" MaxLength="15" Unico
          <Property Name="Description" Type="Edm.String" Nullable="true" MaxLength="Max" Unicod
          <Property Name="Picture" Type="Edm.Binary" Nullable="true" MaxLength="Max" FixedLengt
          <NavigationProperty Name="Products" Relationship="NorthwindModel.FK_Products_Categori
        </EntityType>
      ▶<EntityType Name="CustomerDemographic">...</EntityType>
      ▶<EntityType Name="Customer">...</EntityType>
      ▶<EntityType Name="Employee">...</EntityType>
      ▶<EntityType Name="Order_Detail">...</EntityType>
      ▶<EntityType Name="Order">...</EntityType>
      ▶<EntityType Name="Product">...</EntityType>
      ▶<EntityType Name="Region">...</EntityType>
      ▶<EntityType Name="Shipper">...</EntityType>
      ▶<EntityType Name="Supplier">...</EntityType>
      ▶<EntityType Name="Territory">...</EntityType>
      ▶<EntityType Name="Alphabetical_list_of_product">...</EntityType>
      ▶<EntityType Name="Category_Sales_for_1997">...</EntityType>
      ▶<EntityType Name="Current_Product_List">...</EntityType>
      ▶<EntityType Name="Customer_and_Suppliers_by_City">...</EntityType>
      ▶<EntityType Name="Invoice">...</EntityType>
      ▶<EntityType Name="Order_Details_Extended">...</EntityType>
      ▶<EntityType Name="Order_Subtotal">...</EntityType>
      ▶<EntityType Name="Orders_Qry">...</EntityType>
      ▶<EntityType Name="Product_Sales_for_1997">...</EntityType>
      ▶<EntityType Name="Products_Above_Average_Price">...</EntityType>
      ▶<EntityType Name="Products_by_Category">...</EntityType>
      ▶<EntityType Name="Sales_by_Category">...</EntityType>
      ▶<EntityType Name="Sales_Totals_by_Amount">...</EntityType>
      ▶<EntityType Name="Summary_of_Sales_by_Quarter">...</EntityType>
      ▶<EntityType Name="Summary_of_Sales_by_Year">...</EntityType>
      ▶<Association Name="FK_Products_Categories">...</Association>
      ▶<Association Name="FK_Orders_Customers">...</Association>
      ▶<Association Name="FK_Employees_Employees">...</Association>
      ▶<Association Name="FK_Orders_Employees">...</Association>
      ▶<Association Name="FK_Order_Details_Orders">...</Association>
      ▶<Association Name="FK_Order_Details_Products">...</Association>
      ▶<Association Name="FK_Orders_Shippers">...</Association>
      ▶<Association Name="FK_Products_Suppliers">...</Association>
      ▶<Association Name="FK_Territories_Region">...</Association>
      ▶<Association Name="CustomerCustomerDemo">...</Association>
      ▶<Association Name="EmployeeTerritories">...</Association>
      </Schema>
    ▶<Schema xmlns:d="http://schemas.microsoft.com/ado/2007/08/dataservices" xmlns:m="http://
    </edmx:DataServices>
  </edmx:Edmx>
```

Figure 5.1 Metadata of Northwind Service

SAP Gateway Service Builder and OData Implementation

Before we learn more about OData services, let's discuss the implementation architecture of OData services in the on-premise systems. Next, we'll cover how SAP Gateway Service Builder helps you create these components.

Implementation Architecture of an OData Service

As you can see in Figure 5.2, the data provider class (DPC) and model provider class (MPC) are the only programming artifacts involved in the architecture. The MPC determines the metadata of the service, whereas the DPC contains the implementation of various OData operations (Read, Query, Update, Create, Delete, etc.).

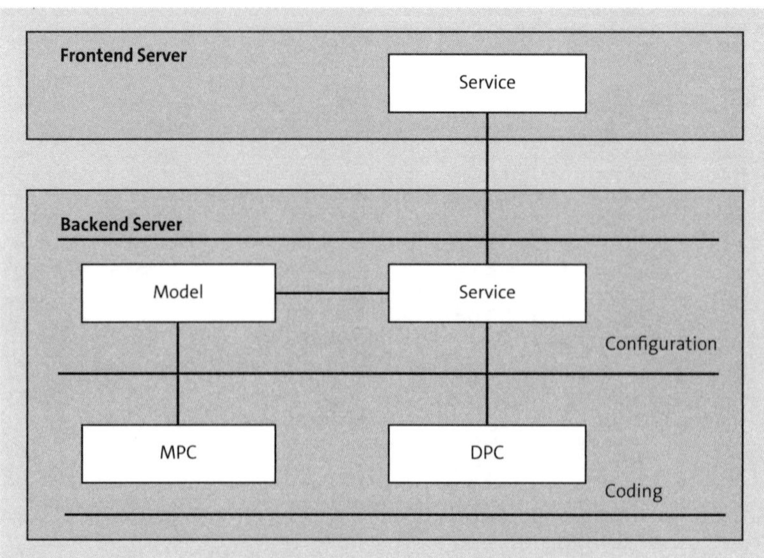

Figure 5.2 OData Service Implementation Architecture

SAP Gateway Service Builder

SAP Gateway Service Builder, as the name suggests, helps you in the process of building an OData service. It has no role in the runtime of an OData service as shown previously in the architecture in Figure 5.2. It gives you a UI to create metadata for your project and automates several steps of OData service creation, thus improving the developer productivity.

Before the introduction of the SAP Gateway Service Builder, developers used to hand code the MPC and DPC classes from scratch in a tedious process. SAP Gateway Service Builder gives you a jump start in the service building process by automatically creating classes, codes, and configuration entries.

In SAP Gateway Service Builder, you start by creating a project and building the data model of your service. As shown in Figure 5.3, SAP Gateway Service Builder provides a visual UI for building the metadata of your service.

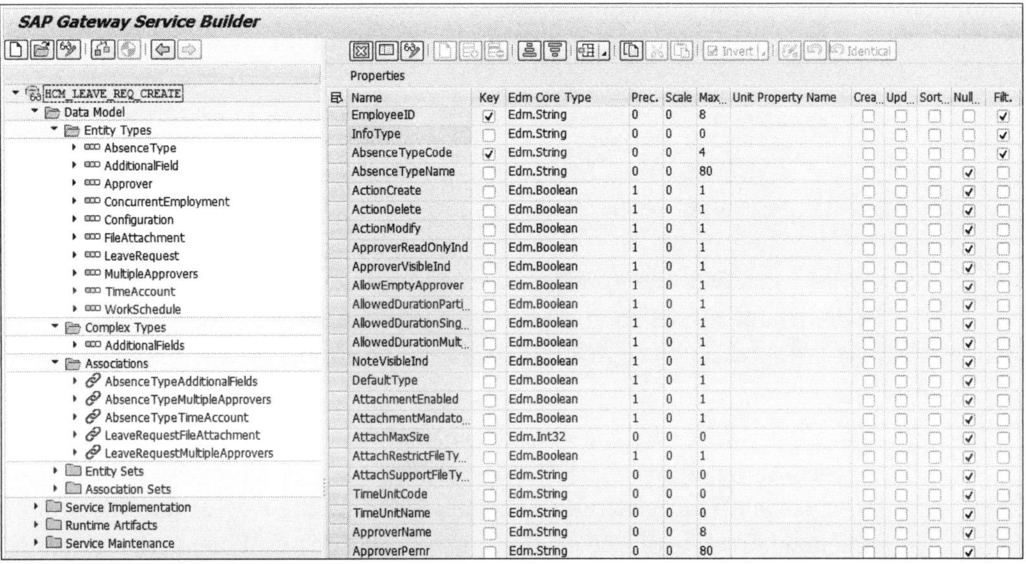

Name	Key	Edm Core Type	Prec.	Scale	Max...	Unit Property Name	Crea...	Upd...	Sort...	Null...	Filt.
EmployeeID	✓	Edm.String	0	0	8						✓
InfoType		Edm.String	0	0	0						✓
AbsenceTypeCode	✓	Edm.String	0	0	4						✓
AbsenceTypeName		Edm.String	0	0	80					✓	
ActionCreate		Edm.Boolean	1	0	1					✓	
ActionDelete		Edm.Boolean	1	0	1					✓	
ActionModify		Edm.Boolean	1	0	1					✓	
ApproverReadOnlyInd		Edm.Boolean	1	0	1					✓	
ApproverVisibleInd		Edm.Boolean	1	0	1					✓	
AllowEmptyApprover		Edm.Boolean	1	0	1					✓	
AllowedDurationParti...		Edm.Boolean	1	0	1					✓	
AllowedDurationSing...		Edm.Boolean	1	0	1					✓	
AllowedDurationMult...		Edm.Boolean	1	0	1					✓	
NoteVisibleInd		Edm.Boolean	1	0	1					✓	
DefaultType		Edm.Boolean	1	0	1					✓	
AttachmentEnabled		Edm.Boolean	1	0	1					✓	
AttachmentMandato...		Edm.Boolean	1	0	1					✓	
AttachMaxSize		Edm.Int32	0	0	0					✓	
AttachRestrictFileTy...		Edm.Boolean	1	0	1					✓	
AttachSupportFileTy...		Edm.String	0	0	0					✓	
TimeUnitCode		Edm.String	0	0	0					✓	
TimeUnitName		Edm.String	0	0	0					✓	
ApproverName		Edm.String	0	0	8					✓	
ApproverPernr		Edm.String	0	0	80					✓	

Figure 5.3 SAP Gateway Service Builder Tool

Under the **Service Implementation** node, you can define the data source for various operations on the entity. You can choose a Business Object Repository (BOR) object, remote function call (RFC) function module, or a search help as your data source.

Tip

You'll rarely find a standard SAP Fiori OData service using BORs or RFCs as data sources in Transaction SEGW because practical scenarios will usually be complex and can't be handled by simple mapping of data sources. "Search Helps" are widely used as data sources because of simplicity in their requirements.

After you're defining the data model and mapping the data sources, you need to click on the **Generate runtime objects**' button, which will generate classes and configurations for the OData service. Figure 5.4 shows the classes generated for the standard My Leave Request SAP Fiori app's service.

*MDL and *SRV are the proxies to MPC and DPC, respectively, and are used in configurations to relate MPC and DPCs. In addition, *SRV is the name of the service that will get used by the developers.

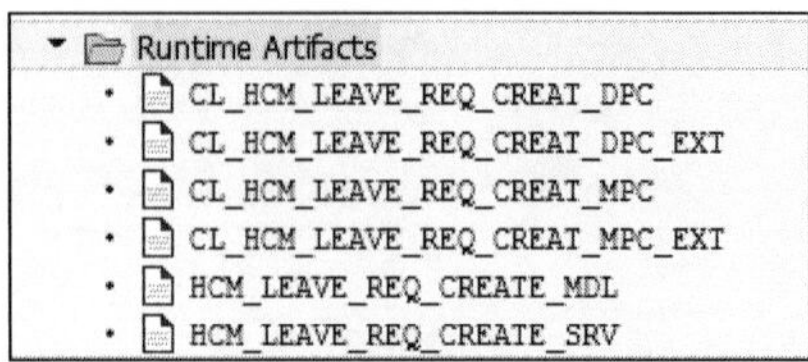

Figure 5.4 Generated Runtime Artifacts

As you can see here, there are two pairs of classes generated here instead of one. As the name suggests, CL_HCM_LEAVE_REQ_CREAT_DPC is the parent of CL_HCM_LEAVE_REQ_CREAT_DPC_EXT, and CL_HCM_LEAVE_REQ_CREAT_MPC is the parent of CL_HCM_LEAVE_REQ_CREAT_MPC_EXT.

So, let's see why we need the additional pair of classes. The child classes are empty, and the SAP Gateway Service Builder writes code into the parent classes. If the developer wants any code-based changes (either to the metadata or the runtime implementation), it can be written in the child classes. Whenever a developer makes changes in the SAP Gateway Service Builder tool and regenerates runtime objects the next time, SAP Gateway Service Builder will only update the parent classes, thus safeguarding any of the developer's coding changes done in the child classes. If you code your changes in the *MPC classes (or in DPC), those will be lost whenever the developer generates runtime objects the next time. This is the reason all custom changes need to always be made in *PC_EXT classes.

Tip
SAP Gateway Service Builder is just a design-time tool and has no role during runtime of the OData service. Runtime is taken over by the generated classes such as MPC and DPC.

Model Provider Class

The structure of an MPC is shown in Figure 5.5.

Method	Level	Visibility	M...	Description
DEFINE	Instance Method	Public		Define method for model - needs to be implemented
GET_LAST_MODIFIED	Instance Method	Public		Returns the last modification of model class
DEFINE_COMPLEXTYPES	Instance Method	Private		DEFINE_COMPLEXTYPES
DEFINE_ABSENCETYPE	Instance Method	Private		DEFINE_ABSENCETYPE
DEFINE_ADDITIONALFIELD	Instance Method	Private		DEFINE_ADDITIONALFIELD
DEFINE_MULTIPLEAPPROVERS	Instance Method	Private		DEFINE_MULTIPLEAPPROVERS
DEFINE_CONFIGURATION	Instance Method	Private		DEFINE_CONFIGURATION
DEFINE_CONCURRENTEMPLOYMENT	Instance Method	Private		DEFINE_CONCURRENTEMPLOYMENT
DEFINE_FILEATTACHMENT	Instance Method	Private		DEFINE_FILEATTACHMENT
DEFINE_APPROVER	Instance Method	Private		DEFINE_APPROVER
DEFINE_LEAVEREQUEST	Instance Method	Private		DEFINE_LEAVEREQUEST
DEFINE_TIMEACCOUNT	Instance Method	Private		DEFINE_TIMEACCOUNT
DEFINE_WORKSCHEDULE	Instance Method	Private		DEFINE_WORKSCHEDULE
DEFINE_ASSOCIATIONS	Instance Method	Private		DEFINE_ASSOCIATIONS
LOAD_TEXT_ELEMENTS	Instance Method	Public		LOAD_TEXT_ELEMENTS

Figure 5.5 Structure of a Model Provider Class

DEFINE is the entry method, which gets called whenever the service's metadata is queried. This method contains the code to define various artifacts within the service. The DEFINE method subsequently calls various other methods listed in the class as shown in Figure 5.6. You can see that there is a method each for each of the entities in the service. Each such method contains code for defining each property inside the entity and annotations for those properties.

Method DEFINE_ASSOCIATIONS has the code to define all the associations between various entities and navigation properties for all the entities. DEFINE_COMPLEXTYPES has the code to define all the required complex types for the model.

MPC also has type declarations for each entity of the service, one each for a flat type and for a table type. These types can be used while coding the runtime implementation (DPC) of the service. Figure 5.7 shows these types.

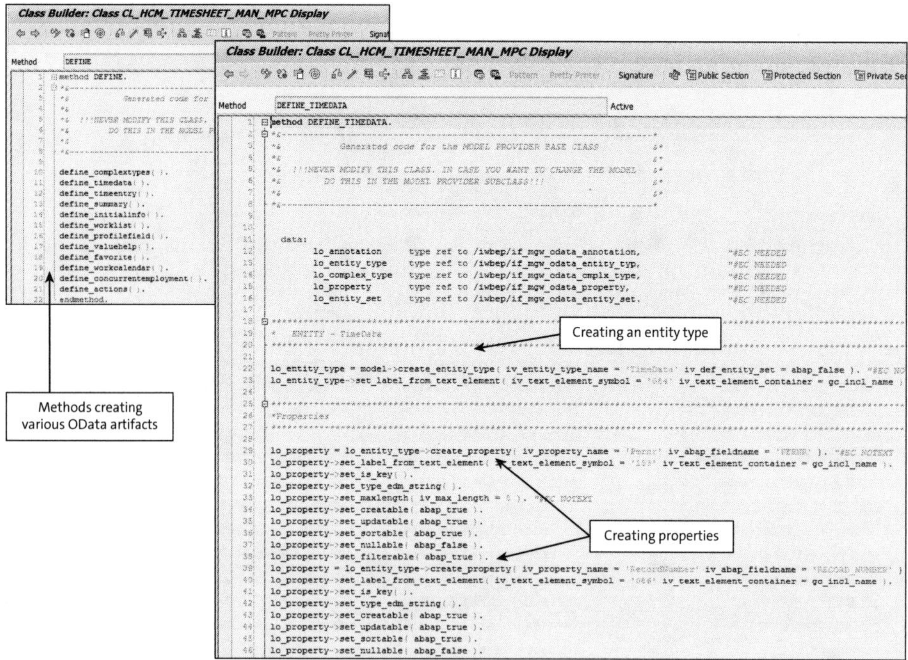

Figure 5.6 "Define" Method Dispatching Calls to Other Methods

Figure 5.7 Type Declarations in MPC for All the Entities in the Service

Data Provide Class

Now let's discuss the structure of a DPC. Unlike MPC, there are multiple entry methods in this class. Based on the operation called on the service, different methods of DPC are called. For example, if you're reading a single record, then method `/IWBEP/IF_MGW_APPL_SRV_RUNTIME~GET_ENTITY` is called. If you're creating an entity, then `/IWBEP/IF_MGW_APPL_SRV_RUNTIME~CREATE_ENTITY` is called. If you're getting a file downloaded, then method `/IWBEP/IF_MGW_APPL_SRV_RUNTIME~GET_STREAM` is called. Figure 5.8 shows the various dispatching methods of the DPC.

Figure 5.8 Dispatching Methods of a DPC

When the SAP Gateway Service Builder generates runtime objects, it creates additional methods for different operations of each entity. Dispatcher methods call these additional methods whose aim is code refactoring to keep the number of lines of code in dispatcher methods to a minimum and manageable. Figure 5.9 shows these utility methods.

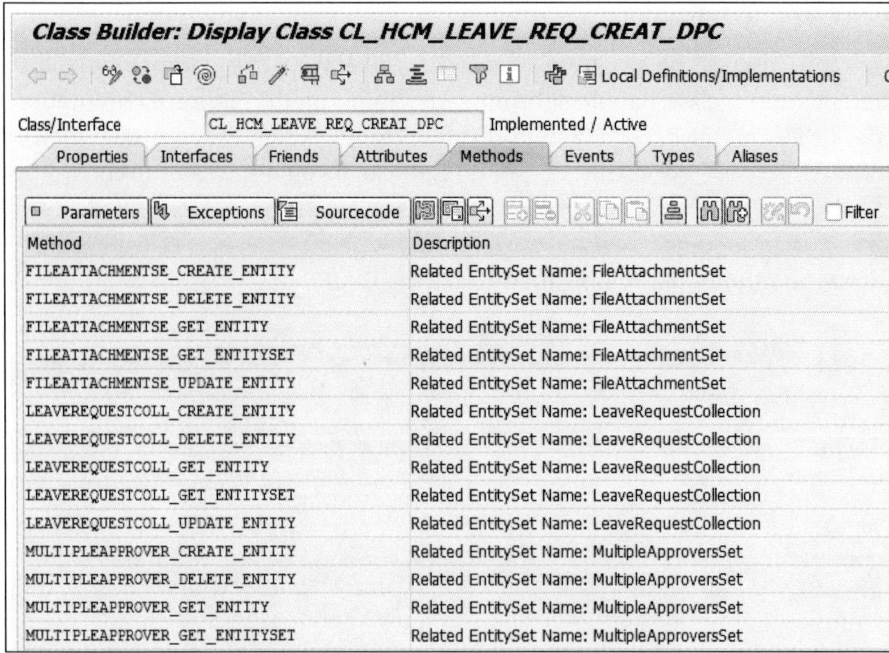

Figure 5.9 SAP Gateway Service Builder Generated Utility Methods in the DPC

OData URLs and Payload

OData provides standards on how OData URLs should be constructed. We'll use the examples from the Northwind service to explore various supported URLs. *OData.org* lists all the supported URLs for both V2 and V4 of OData as listed here:

- **OData V2**
  http://www.odata.org/documentation/odata-version-2-0/uri-conventions/
- **OData V4**
  http://docs.oasis-open.org/odata/odata/v4.0/csprd02/part2-url-conventions/ odata-v4.0-csprd02-part2-url-conventions.html

We'll go through few important URLs in this section.

Query

Querying the feed is the most basic OData operation. It's used to get a list of instances of business objects, such as employees, products, orders, and so on. The following are a few examples from the Northwind service:

- **List of orders**
  http://services.odata.org/V2/Northwind/Northwind.svc/Orders

- **List of customers**
  http://services.odata.org/V2/Northwind/Northwind.svc/Customers

- **List of products**
  http://services.odata.org/V2/Northwind/Northwind.svc/Products

The query result is always going to be a `<feed> </feed>` with multiple `<entry></entry>` records that represent individual records (see Figure 5.10).

```xml
<?xml version="1.0" encoding="utf-8" standalone="yes"?>
<feed xml:base="http://services.odata.org/V2/Northwind/Northwind.svc/" xmlns:d="http://schemas.microsoft.com/ado
  <title type="text">Customers</title>
  <id>http://services.odata.org/V2/Northwind/Northwind.svc/Customers</id>
  <updated>2017-11-23T11:48:55Z</updated>
  <link rel="self" title="Customers" href="Customers" />
  <entry>
    <id>http://services.odata.org/V2/Northwind/Northwind.svc/Customers('ALFKI')</id>
    <title type="text"></title>
    <updated>2017-11-23T11:48:55Z</updated>
    <author>
    <link rel="edit" title="Customer" href="Customers('ALFKI')" />
    <link rel="http://schemas.microsoft.com/ado/2007/08/dataservices/related/Orders" type="application/atom+xml
    <link rel="http://schemas.microsoft.com/ado/2007/08/dataservices/related/CustomerDemographics" type="applic
    <category term="NorthwindModel.Customer" scheme="http://schemas.microsoft.com/ado/2007/08/dataservices/sche
    <content type="application/xml">
      <m:properties>
        <d:CustomerID m:type="Edm.String">ALFKI</d:CustomerID>
        <d:CompanyName m:type="Edm.String">Alfreds Futterkiste</d:CompanyName>
        <d:ContactName m:type="Edm.String">Maria Anders</d:ContactName>
        <d:ContactTitle m:type="Edm.String">Sales Representative</d:ContactTitle>
        <d:Address m:type="Edm.String">Obere Str. 57</d:Address>
        <d:City m:type="Edm.String">Berlin</d:City>
        <d:Region m:type="Edm.String" m:null="true" />
        <d:PostalCode m:type="Edm.String">12209</d:PostalCode>
        <d:Country m:type="Edm.String">Germany</d:Country>
        <d:Phone m:type="Edm.String">030-0074321</d:Phone>
        <d:Fax m:type="Edm.String">030-0076545</d:Fax>
      </m:properties>
    </content>
  </entry>
  <entry>
  <entry>
  <entry>
  <entry>
  <entry>
  <entry>
  <entry>
  <entry>
  <entry>
    <link rel="next" href="http://services.odata.org/V2/Northwind/Northwind.svc/Customers?$skiptoken='ERNSH'" />
</feed>
```

Figure 5.10 OData Query/Feed Output Showing `<feed></feed>`

Filtering

Note that in the preceding URLs, the last part of the URL is an entity set name. You can also filter the resulting feed by adding filters. The following URL filters customers from the country of Mexico only:

http://services.odata.org/V2/Northwind/Northwind.svc/Customers?
$filter=Country eq 'Mexico'

Paging

When requesting a feed, it's common for the user to request only a fixed number of records first and then request the next set of values when scrolling through them. This is called lazy loading. The OData service handles these kinds of requests with `$top` and `$skip`. `$top` indicates the number of records to be fetched in one go, while `$skip` mentions the number of records to be skipped from the top before fetching `$top` number of records. The following URL fetches the top 20 records starting from the 81st record (up to 10th record):

http://services.odata.org/V2/Northwind/Northwind.svc/Customers?$top=20&
$skip=80

Implementation: SAP Gateway

`Query` operations end up at the main dispatching method:

```
/IWBEP/IF_MGW_APPL_SRV_RUNTIME~GET_ENTITYSET
```

This method in the data provider class will have a generated code that will direct calls to entity-specific query methods, which are usually implemented in `DPC_EXT` classes.

Implementation: SAPUI5

Let's consider `oModel` as an instance of `sap.ui.model.odata.v2.ODataModel` throughout this chapter. A query can be triggered using the `read` method of the `oModel`:

```
oModel.read("/SalesOrders", {success: mySuccessHandler, error: myErrorHandler});
```

`SalesOrders` is the name of the entity set in the OData model. `/SalesOrders` will be concatenated with model URL to arrive at the URL to be called. `mySuccessHandler` and `myErrorHandler` are names of the success and error handler functions, respectively.

In addition to event handlers, sorters and filters can also be sent to the backend with the read API. You can also trigger a query using aggregation binding in the views.

Read

A read request is used to retrieve a single record by sending all the keys for that entity record. The following URL fetches a customer with `CustomerID` = 'TRAIH':

http://services.odata.org/V2/Northwind/Northwind.svc/Customers('TRAIH')

The response to a read request will be an `<entry></entry>` implying that a single record is fetched, as shown in Figure 5.11.

```xml
<?xml version="1.0" encoding="utf-8" standalone="yes"?>
<entry xml:base="http://services.odata.org/V2/Northwind/Northwind.svc/" xmlns:d="http://schem
  <id>http://services.odata.org/V2/Northwind/Northwind.svc/Customers('TRAIH')</id>
  <title type="text"></title>
  <updated>2017-11-23T11:59:37Z</updated>
  <author>
    <name />
  </author>
  <link rel="edit" title="Customer" href="Customers('TRAIH')" />
  <link rel="http://schemas.microsoft.com/ado/2007/08/dataservices/related/Orders" type="appl
  <link rel="http://schemas.microsoft.com/ado/2007/08/dataservices/related/CustomerDemographi
  <category term="NorthwindModel.Customer" scheme="http://schemas.microsoft.com/ado/2007/08/d
  <content type="application/xml">
    <m:properties>
      <d:CustomerID m:type="Edm.String">TRAIH</d:CustomerID>
      <d:CompanyName m:type="Edm.String">Trail's Head Gourmet Provisioners</d:CompanyName>
      <d:ContactName m:type="Edm.String">Helvetius Nagy</d:ContactName>
      <d:ContactTitle m:type="Edm.String">Sales Associate</d:ContactTitle>
      <d:Address m:type="Edm.String">722 DaVinci Blvd.</d:Address>
      <d:City m:type="Edm.String">Kirkland</d:City>
      <d:Region m:type="Edm.String">WA</d:Region>
      <d:PostalCode m:type="Edm.String">98034</d:PostalCode>
      <d:Country m:type="Edm.String">USA</d:Country>
      <d:Phone m:type="Edm.String">(206) 555-8257</d:Phone>
      <d:Fax m:type="Edm.String">(206) 555-2174</d:Fax>
    </m:properties>
  </content>
</entry>
```

Figure 5.11 Read Request Response Showing <entry></entry>

Implementation: SAP Gateway

`Query` operations end up at the main dispatching method:

```
/IWBEP/IF_MGW_APPL_SRV_RUNTIME~GET_ENTITY
```

This method in the data provider class will have a generated code in that will direct calls to an entity-specific query methods, which are usually implemented in `DPC_EXT` classes.

Implementation: SAPUI5

Just like the query, a read call can also be initiated using the `read` API of the `oModel`.

Navigations

Navigations are one of the most important features of OData. Navigations let you know all the possible relationships from the current record and help you fetch further related records to show on-screen.

When you consider details of a customer as shown in Figure 5.11, you might be interested in looking at all the orders of this customer. You just need to add the navigation property name to the preceding URL to derive the following URL to provide the required list of customer's orders. `Orders` is the name of the navigation property here.

http://services.odata.org/V2/Northwind/Northwind.svc/Customers('TRAIH')/ Orders

The result of the preceding URL can either be a `<feed>` or an `<entry>`. This is decided by the association between the `Customer` and `Order` entity. If the target cardinality of the relationship is * (or `N`), the response will be a feed; if the target cardinality is `1` (or `0` to `1`), the response will be of type `<entry>`. Because a customer can have more than one order, target cardinality in this case is *; thus, the response of the preceding navigation will be a `<feed></feed>`.

Tip

Both `Read` and `Query` operations, when successful, will return **200** as the HTTP response code.

Implementation: SAP Gateway

Based on the cardinality just described, one of dispatching methods `/IWBEP/IF_MGW_APPL_SRV_RUNTIME~GET_ENTITYSET` or `/IWBEP/IF_MGW_APPL_SRV_RUNTIME~GET_ENTITY` will be called, and, from there, the next corresponding entity-specific method will be called.

Implementation: SAPUI5

Navigations can also be initiated using the `read` API of the `oModel`. However, they are usually triggered by relative bindings. Let's see an example:

Consider a table, whose items are bound as follows:

```
<Table items="{LineItems}" >
........................
---------
</Table>
```

If the page containing this table is bound to "/SalesOrders(12344321)", then the preceding table binding will trigger a navigation call with the following URL:

"/SalesOrders(12344321)/LineItems"

Create

The Create operation lets you create new instances of an entity. Such an operation will be an HTTP POST operation, and the data to be created will be supplied as a request body.

The URL for the Create operation will be the same as that of a Query operation; that is, the URL will end with the entity set name of which instance is getting created. The request body will be provided in an <entry></entry> tag, which represents the new instance to be created.

Because *Northwind.svc* doesn't support any Edit operations, we'll use SAP's demo service /IWFND/RMTSAMPLEFLIGHT for performing all the Edit operations.

Figure 5.12 shows the creation of a new travel agency. The URL ends with the entity set name TravelAgencyCollection. You can also see that the HTTP response status code for a successful create is 201-Created. The response body contains the newly created record.

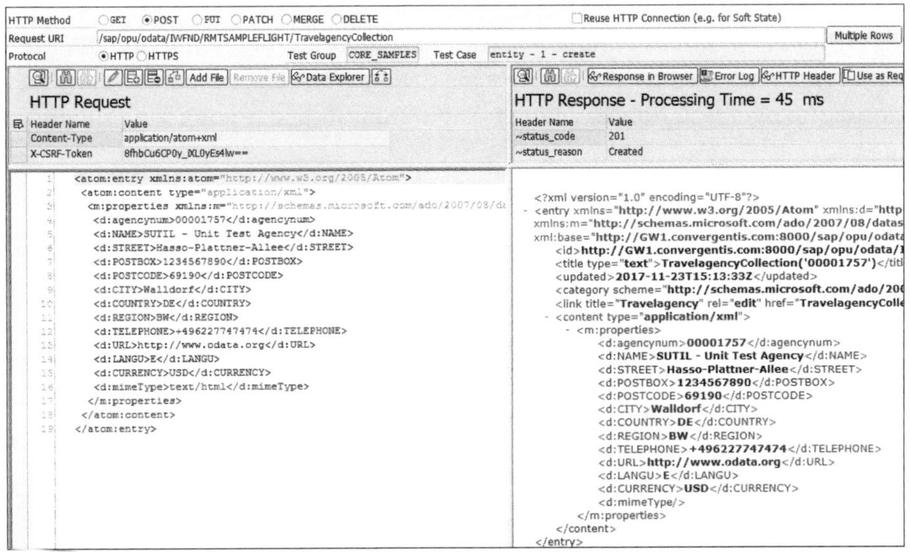


```xml
 1  <atom:entry xmlns:atom="http://www.w3.org/2005/Atom">
 2    <atom:content type="application/xml">
 3     <m:properties xmlns:m="http://schemas.microsoft.com/ado/2007/08/da
 4      <d:agencynum>00001757</d:agencynum>
 5      <d:NAME>SUTIL - Unit Test Agency</d:NAME>
 6      <d:STREET>Hasso-Plattner-Allee</d:STREET>
 7      <d:POSTBOX>1234567890</d:POSTBOX>
 8      <d:POSTCODE>69190</d:POSTCODE>
 9      <d:CITY>Walldorf</d:CITY>
10      <d:COUNTRY>DE</d:COUNTRY>
11      <d:REGION>BW</d:REGION>
12      <d:TELEPHONE>+496227747474</d:TELEPHONE>
13      <d:URL>http://www.odata.org</d:URL>
14      <d:LANGU>E</d:LANGU>
15      <d:CURRENCY>USD</d:CURRENCY>
16      <d:mimeType>text/html</d:mimeType>
17     </m:properties>
18    </atom:content>
19  </atom:entry>
```

```xml
<?xml version="1.0" encoding="UTF-8"?>
<entry xmlns="http://www.w3.org/2005/Atom" xmlns:d="http
  xmlns:m="http://schemas.microsoft.com/ado/2007/08/datas
  xml:base="http://GW1.convergentis.com:8000/sap/opu/odata
  <id>http://GW1.convergentis.com:8000/sap/opu/odata/1
  <title type="text">TravelagencyCollection('00001757')</titl
  <updated>2017-11-23T15:13:33Z</updated>
  <category scheme="http://schemas.microsoft.com/ado/200
  <link title="Travelagency" rel="edit" href="TravelagencyColle
  <content type="application/xml">
    <m:properties>
      <d:agencynum>00001757</d:agencynum>
      <d:NAME>SUTIL - Unit Test Agency</d:NAME>
      <d:STREET>Hasso-Plattner-Allee</d:STREET>
      <d:POSTBOX>1234567890</d:POSTBOX>
      <d:POSTCODE>69190</d:POSTCODE>
      <d:CITY>Walldorf</d:CITY>
      <d:COUNTRY>DE</d:COUNTRY>
      <d:REGION>BW</d:REGION>
      <d:TELEPHONE>+496227747474</d:TELEPHONE>
      <d:URL>http://www.odata.org</d:URL>
      <d:LANGU>E</d:LANGU>
      <d:CURRENCY>USD</d:CURRENCY>
      <d:mimeType/>
    </m:properties>
  </content>
</entry>
```

Figure 5.12 Request and Responses of a OData Create Operation

Implementation: SAP Gateway

The main dispatching method for `Create` operations is `/IWBEP/IF_MGW_APPL_SRV_RUN-TIME~CREATE_ENTITY`. This method will further navigate to entity-specific methods.

Implementation: SAPUI5

A create OData request (HTTP method POST) can be triggered using an API such as the following:

```
oModel.create("/SalesOrders", oSalesOrder, {success: mySuccessHandler, error:
myErrorHandler});
```

`SalesOrders` is the name of the entity set, and `oSalesOrder` is an object containing data to be sent as the request body.

Update

The `Update` operation, as the name suggests, updates a single record's properties. The URL used in an `Update` operation should point to the unique record that is getting updated. (This URL is the same as that of a read request.) `Update` operations should also use HTTP method `PUT` while performing an update. The request body of the `PUT` operations should contain all the properties of the entity, including those being changed.

As Figure 5.13 shows, the URL contains the complete key to the `TravelAgencyCollection` to uniquely identify the record being updated. The response status code for a successful update is **204-No Content**. There is no response body for a successful update.

Implementation: SAP Gateway

The main dispatching method for `Update` operations is `/IWBEP/IF_MGW_APPL_SRV_RUN-TIME~UPDATE_ENTITY`. This method will further navigate to entity-specific methods.

Implementation: SAPUI5

The following code triggers an update (`PUT` or `MERGE` based on model settings):

```
oModel.update("/SalesOrders(1234532)", oSalesOrder, {success: mySuccessHandler,
error: myErrorHandler});
```

The URL (path attribute) in this case refers to a specific instance of the business object that needs to be edited by specifying the entity's key. oSalesOrder contains the data to be updated.

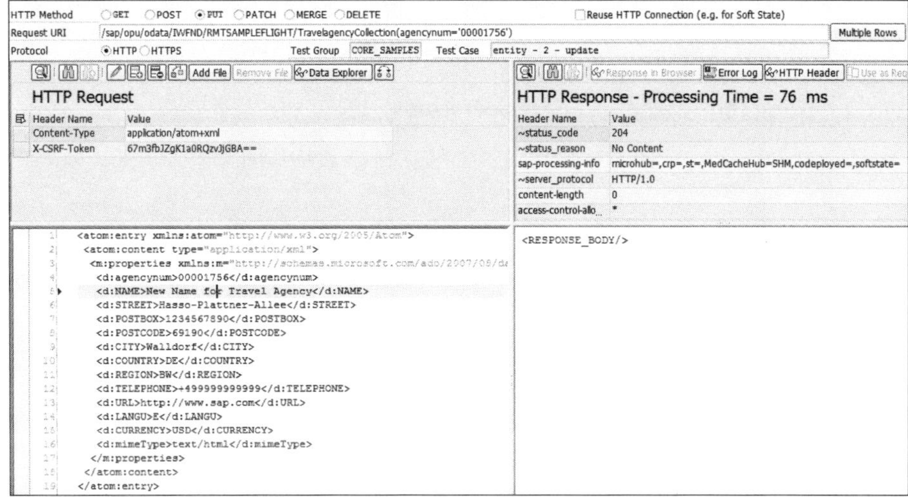

Figure 5.13 Request and Response of an OData Update Operation

Delete

The Delete operation deletes the instance of an entity set. Just like Read and Update, the URL of a Delete operation should contain the keys and thus uniquely identify the record to be deleted. This URL is called with HTTP method DELETE for the Delete operation. The Delete operation doesn't require any request body because all required information is available in the request URL.

As shown in Figure 5.14, a successful Delete operation results in HTTP status code **204-No Content** and an empty response body.

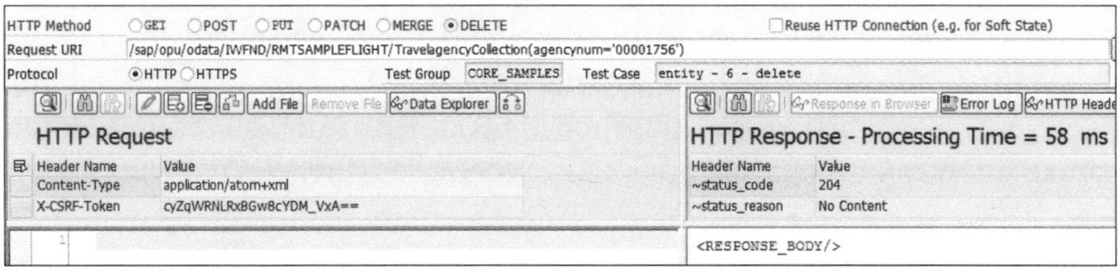

Figure 5.14 Delete Operation in OData

Implementation: SAP Gateway

The main dispatching method for `Delete` operations is `/IWBEP/IF_MGW_APPL_SRV_RUN-TIME~DELETE_ENTITY`. This method will further navigate to entity-specific methods.

Implementation: SAPUI5

The following code triggers a `Delete` operation (HTTP `DELETE`):

```
oModel.remove("/SalesOrders(1234532)", {success: mySuccessHandler, error:
myErrorHandler});
```

The path attribute in this case refers to a specific instance of the business object that needs to be deleted.

$Expand

Many times, it's not enough just to fetch a record, but its children must be fetched as well in a single call. For example, while fetching details of a single customer, you can fetch all the corresponding orders as well. This can be helpful in reducing the number of HTTP calls and thus improving overall performance. OData provides a technique called as $expand for performing this operation.

The URL of such an operation is like a `Read` operation, but it has an additional attribute called $expand that contains all the navigation properties to be fetched. The following URL fetches details of a customer and all the orders by this customer:

http://services.odata.org/V2/Northwind/Northwind.svc/Customers('TRAIH')?$expand=Orders

Expanded data will appear inside `<inline></inline>` tags.

$Expand can also be used with multiple navigation properties (separated by commas), so that multiple dimensions can be fetched at a time.

In the preceding example, we've performed an $expand while reading a `Customer` instance; however, $expand can also be used while performing a query. That is, while fetching a feed on a customer, each of the required subnodes can be fetched. This is rarely used in practical scenarios though because it's not required. In addition, such a query can be performance intensive because it involves querying a lot of data.

Implementation: SAP Gateway

The `Expand` operation on a read request triggers method `/IWBEP/IF_MGW_APPL_SRV_RUN-TIME~GET_EXPANDED_ENTITY`.

The `Expand` operation on a query request triggers method `/IWBEP/IF_MGW_APPL_SRV_RUNTIME~GET_EXPANDED_ENTITYSET`.

The preceding methods need to be implemented based on the requirements for getting the results. However, SAP Gateway's framework provides a default implementation for these operations. This has few prerequisites, however. Consider the following URL:

/sap/opu/odata/IWFND/RMTSAMPLEFLIGHT/FlightCollection?$expand=FlightCarrier

For the framework implementation expand to work, the query on `Flight` and read on `Carrier` entity are required because the URL requires a feed of `Flight` while reading a single carrier for each flight.

Consider another URL:

/sap/opu/odata/IWFND/RMTSAMPLEFLIGHT/CarrierCollection('AA')?$expand=carrierFlights

For the framework implementation of this URL, the `Read` implementation on `CarrierCollection` and `Query` implementation on the `Flight` entity are required. This is because the preceding URL needs to read a single record for carrier `AA`, and then needs to fetch flights for this carrier.

The framework implementation of `$expand` can give poor performance at times. In such cases, developers need to implement the methods mentioned earlier.

Implementation: SAPUI5

There are several ways to call an expand URL. You can use the `urlParameters` attribute to pass the `$expand` as follows:

```
oModel.read("/
CarrierCollection('AA')", {urlParameters:{$expand:"carrierFlights"}, success: mySucc
essHandler, error: myErrorHandler});
```

However, expand is also called usually in bindings. In element binding, the following code shows binding to a page instance `oPage`:

```
oPage.bindElement("/CarrierCollection('AA')", {expand:"carrierFlights"});
```

In aggregation binding, this makes sense when one of the table's columns needs data from a navigation property, and the cardinality to the child entity is 1. Consider a table showing a list of products from the Northwind service. One of the columns of this table is the name of the supplier. You can use an aggregation binding as follows:

```
oTable.bindRows({
    path: "/Products",
    parameters: {expand: "Supplier"}
});
```

In an XML view, expand can be bound as shown in Listing 5.1. The `parameters` property is used to add the expand call, while binding a slash (`Supplier/Name`) is used to navigate to the child entity.

```
<Table:Table rows="{path:'/Products', parameters:{expand:'Supplier'} }">
    <Table:columns>
        <Table:Column>
            <Table:label>
                <Label text="Product ID" />
            </Table:label>
            <Table:template>
                <Label text="{ID}" />
            </Table:template>
        </Table:Column>
        <Table:Column>
            <Table:label>
                <Label text="Supplier Name from Expanded entity" />
            </Table:label>
            <Table:template>
                <Label text="{Supplier/Name}" />
            </Table:template>
        </Table:Column>
    </Table:columns>
</Table:Table>
```

Listing 5.1 Triggering an $expand by Binding and Referencing the Deep/Child Properties

Deep Insert

In the `Create` operation, we created a single record. Many times, you may need to create a parent node instance as well as child node instances. For example, you may want to create a purchase order along with its items. This operation of creating a parent node along with child nodes is called `Deep Insert`.

The URL for a `Deep Insert` operation remains the same as that of a regular create request. That is, the URL ends with the entity set name of the parent entity set. The main difference is in the request body. The request body of a `Deep Insert` call has one single `<entry></entry>` node, but it also specifies child nodes using the navigation property names pointing to child entity sets/nodes.

Figure 5.15 shows how a `Deep Insert` is performed. This request creates a purchase requisition along with two requisition items. `Items` is name of the navigation property in entity `PR`, pointing to `PRItem`. The request body is represented in JavaScript Object Notation (JSON) format here. Just like the regular `Create` operation, upon a successful create, a status code of **201-Created** will be returned, and the requested complete entry will be returned as the response body.

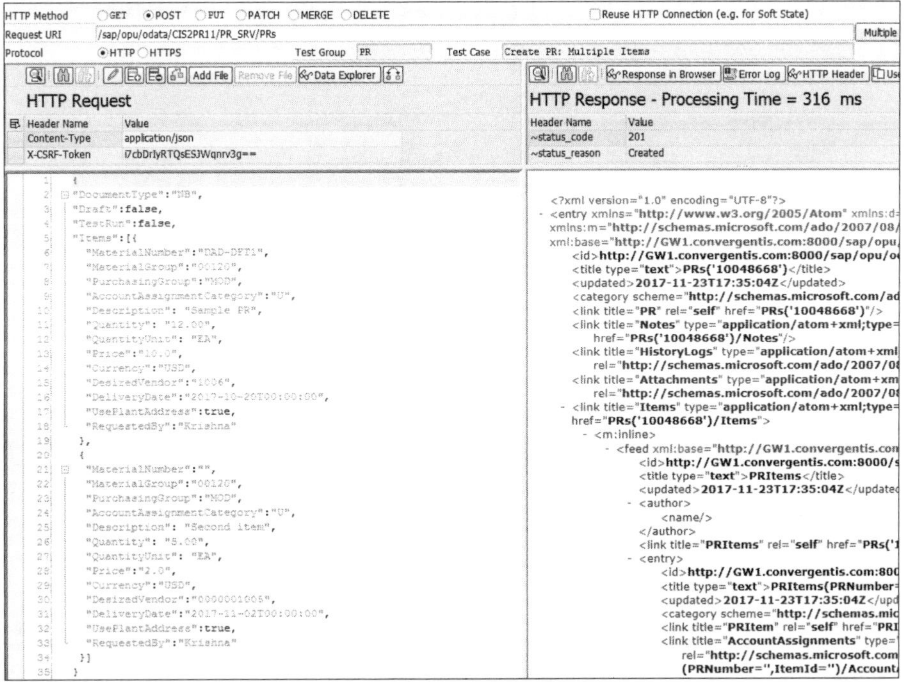

Figure 5.15 Deep Insert Operation in OData

Implementation: SAP Gateway

When the request body contains a deep data (hierarchical data), method `/IWBEP/IF_MGW_APPL_SRV_RUNTIME~CREATE_DEEP_ENTITY` will be triggered. Inside this method, to get the input data, a structure needs to be created so that it can receive the data. Figure 5.16 shows how to declare this structure and how to use it to fetch the data.

```
"Data Structure to receive the data
DATA:BEGIN OF ls_payload.
INCLUDE TYPE /cis2pr11/cl_pr_mpc=>ts_pr.
DATA: items TYPE STANDARD TABLE OF /cis2pr11/cl_pr_mpc=>ts_item.

DATA: END OF ls_payload.


"Fetch the data
io_data_provider->read_entry_data( IMPORTING es_data = ls_payload ).
```

Figure 5.16 Code Declaring the Data Structure and Fetching Data

In the declaration of structure `ls_payload` shown in Figure 5.16, `items` is the technical name of the navigation property from entity `PR` to entity `PRItem`.

Warning

In the `Deep Insert` implementation, special care must be taken in declaring the structure for receiving the deep data. All the property names within the structure, including the navigation property names, should be the technical names. Otherwise, data won't be available in those properties.

Implementation: SAPUI5

The SAPUI5 code for triggering a `Deep Insert` is the same as the code that was used for the `Create` operation. The only difference is that the request body will contain a hierarchical structure, containing the parent as well as child entities.

$Batch

In many scenarios, the UI is ready to make multiple calls to the backend for fetching data or updating multiple pieces of information in one go. In such cases, you can use a batch request. Batch requests combine multiple requests into one HTTP POST request. By eliminating multiple HTTP requests, $batch can speed up the user experience. A batch request body can contain multiple Query and Change operations.

In addition, there are scenarios in which to maintain data consistency, a set of change requests needs to either all be successful or if any one of them fails, then all other requests should roll back as well. Such a single group of requests is called a changeset. A single changeset can't contain retrieve requests and can't contain other changesets.

The response body of the batch request will contain responses to each Retrieve and Change operation. The response status code will always **202–Accepted**, as long as the backend is able to process the batch request (individual request statuses don't matter).

The response body of a changeset request is either a single response indicating success or failure, or, in the case of successful processing, it can have one response to each changeset operation inside. If any of the changeset requests within fail, then there will be only one response with errors.

Implementation: SAP Gateway

No implementation is required for batch calls. The SAP Gateway framework will call the corresponding APIs for each Retrieve or Update operation. Because multiple Retrieve operations within a batch request are independent of each other, they are executed in parallel to optimize performance. Parallelization can be disabled either for a service or in the entire system using configurations.

If an entire set of operations within a changeset can be handled using a single API in the backend, it can be beneficial from a performance point of view (e.g., creating multiple PR items in one go). For each such entity whose multiple operations can be handled in one go, the SAP Gateway framework needs to be informed so that it doesn't automatically call the regular operation performing methods for such calls. This is done in method CHANGESET_BEGIN by setting a variable called CV_DEFER_MODE. After the variable CV_DEFERRED_MODE is set as true, then method CHANGESET_PROCESS is called by the framework to execute the corresponding implementation code, as shown in Figure 5.17.

Finally, in the method CHANGESET_END, COMMIT WORK is called to commit all the changes.

Implementation: SAPUI5

In sap.ui.model.odata.v2.ODataModel, all calls to the backend are sent as batch requests by default. This can be disabled using parameter useBatch while instantiating the OData model. This can also be entered in the *manifest.json* file in SAP Fiori apps.

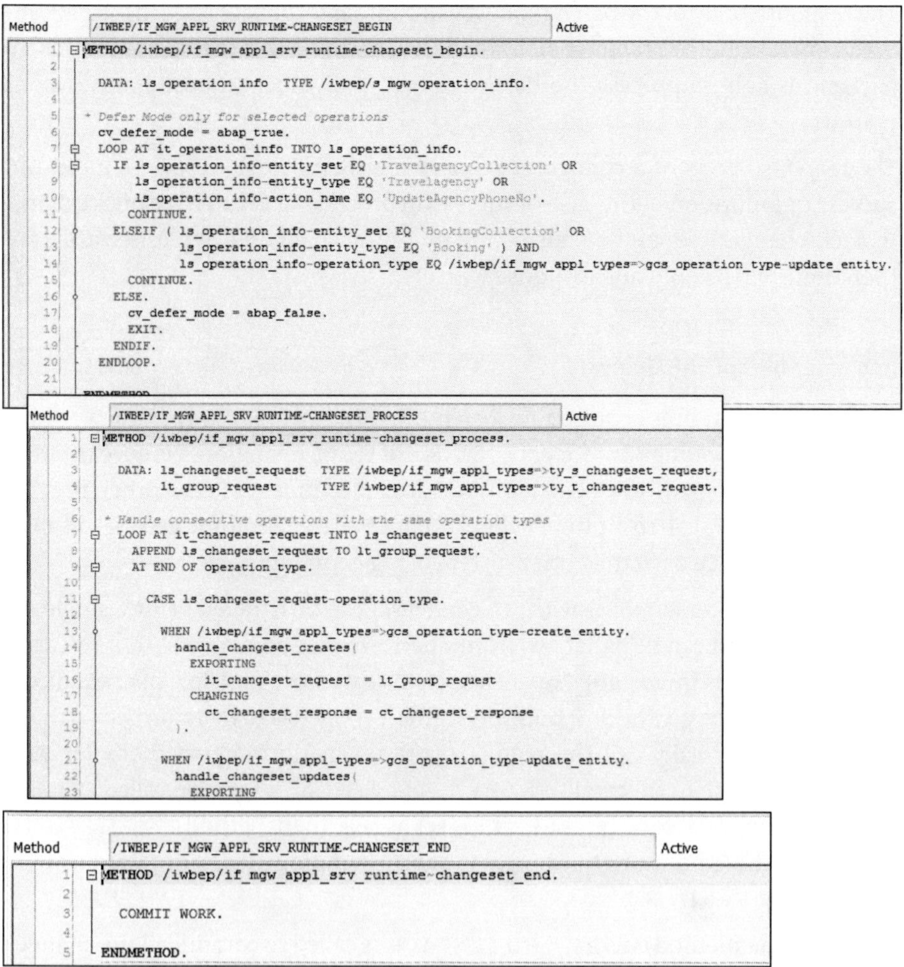

Figure 5.17 Changeset BEGIN/PROCESS/END Implementations

Grouping Batch Calls

Whenever an operation is triggered using any of the OData V2 model's APIs such as create, update, remove, and read, each of these APIs have a parameter called `groupId`. This can be used to group OData calls as batches. Operations with the same `groupId` will be bundled as a single batch request to the backend.

`groupIds` can be assigned to bindings as well, as shown here, so that all requests triggering from the bindings with the same `groupIds` are sent together:

```
{path:"/SalesOrders", parameters: {groupId: "myFirstGroup"}}
```

In these cases, all batch requests are formed and sent at the end of the current call stack. All operations that don't have a `groupId` assigned are grouped together with a default `groupId`. However, you might require a better control on batch requests and might want to trigger a batch request only at a specific instance. SAP provides an API for this. All the `batchIds` that need to be triggered in a controlled manner must be specified in an API `setDeferredGroups` as follows:

```
oModel.setDeferredGroups(["myFirstGroup", "myThirdGroup"]);
```

Now, to trigger a batch request for a specific `groupId`, you need to call an API `submitChanges` and specify the `groupId` under which all the requests are grouped. Here is a sample `submitChanges` call:

```
oModel.submitChanges({groupId:"myFirstGroup",success: mySuccessHandler, error: myErr
orHandler});
```

In the preceding case, only requests with `batchId` as `myFirstGroup` will be sent as a single batch request.

Change Sets

Consider a scenario where you need to send multiple `Change` operations (`Create/Delete/Update`) as a single logical unit of an operation, which means that either all of them should succeed or none of them should succeed to keep the data consistent.

For such scenarios, SAPUI5 offers the concept of changesets, which are similar to `groupIds`. With all the `Change` operations, you can specify a `changeSetId` in addition to `groupId`.

All the `Change` operations with the same `changeSetId` will be sent as a single changeset within a batch request. If `changeSetId` isn't specified, then each change will have its own `changeSetId`.

Download/Get File

It's a common requirement to show or download an attachment from the server. An entity needs to model for media operations with properties describing the content of the download. This entity needs to be marked as **Media** as shown in Figure 5.18.

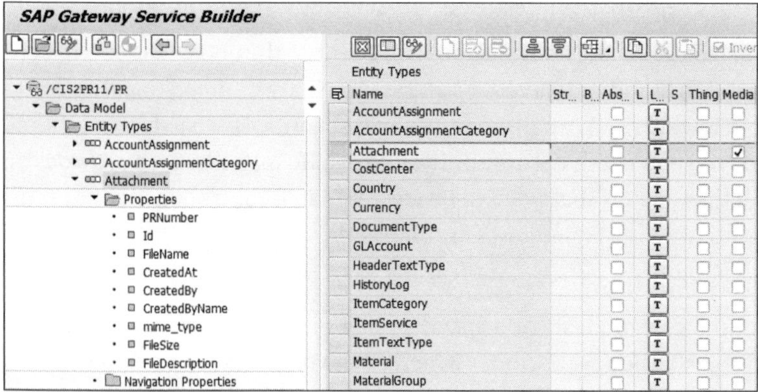

Figure 5.18 "Media" Entity with Properties

The URL for fetching an attachment ends with the $value:

/sap/opu/odata/CIS2PR11/PR_SRV/Attachments(PRNumber='0010047959',Id= 'FOL18%20%20%20%20%20%20%20%20%20%204%20EXT42000000000044')/ $value

Implementation: SAP Gateway

When the preceding URL gets called, method /IWBEP/IF_MGW_APPL_SRV_RUNTIME~GET_ STREAM gets triggered in the DPC. In the implementation, and the xstring content of the attachment needs to be returned along with the mime type.

Implementation: SAPUI5

The xstring content of a file isn't usually read using any of the OData model's APIs. Rather the URL for fetching the file content is used as value of the src property in an HTML iframe tag, so that the file either displays in the iframe or gets downloaded based on the type of the file.

Create/Upload Media

Another common requirement is to upload an attachment to a server. The URL for uploading an attachment will end with the Media entity set. This will be an HTTP POST request with the request body as the attachment content. The HTTP request header should contain a **Content-Type** header indicating the mime type of the attachment. The slug header should contain the complete name of the file being uploaded. Figure 5.19 shows an example file upload in the SAP Gateway client. Upon successful attachment, the HTTP response code **201–Created** will be returned with details about the uploaded attachment.

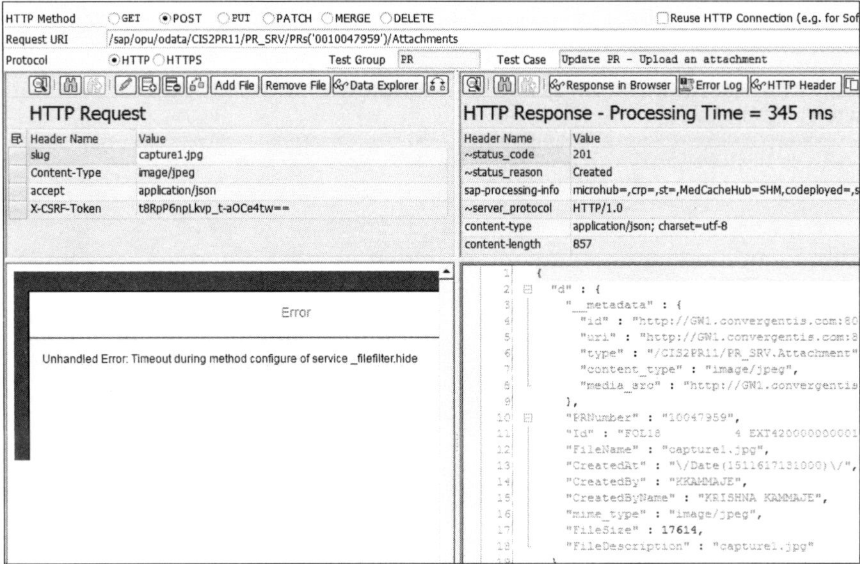

Figure 5.19 OData Operation for Uploading Media Content

Implementation: SAP Gateway

The preceding request will trigger method /IWBEP/IF_MGW_APPL_SRV_RUNTIME~CREATE_ STREAM in the DPC. Input structure IS_MEDIA_SOURCE contains the media content along with the mime type.

Implementation: SAPUI5

Creating a request to upload a file usually happens from an SAPUI5 file upload control such as sap.ui.unified.FileUploader with the event uploadOnChange.

Service Operations

When any of the preceding operations on an entity don't suit the requirements, you can use Service operations or function imports. These requests don't have a request body but can be of type GET (retrieve and nonmodifying) or POST (modifying). Service operations can have input parameters, which will be specified while calling them. The following is a sample Service operation that performs a currency conversion operation:

```
/sap/opu/odata/CIS2PR11/PR_SRV/ConvertCurrency?SourceAmount=25.00m&SourceCurrency=
'USD'&TargetCurrency='CAD'ration calling URL.
```

The output of a Service operation can be a complex type, entity type, or a feed. Successful execution of a Service operation will return HTTP status code **200–OK**, as shown in Figure 5.20.

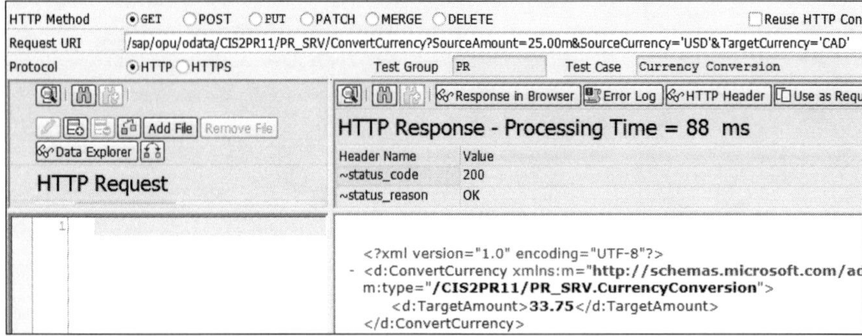

Figure 5.20 An OData Service Operation

Implementation: SAP Gateway

Triggering a Service operation will invoke the method /IWBEP/IF_MGW_APPL_SRV_RUN-TIME~EXECUTE_ACTION in DPC. Based on the Service operation name, different implementations can be written here.

Implementation: SAPUI5

Listing 5.2 shows how to call a Service operation with the name CheckFlightFare, which has three parameters. Data returned by the Service operation can be accessed in the Success handler function.

```
oModel.callFunction(
  "/CheckFlightFare", {
      method: "GET",
      urlParameters: {
         carrierid: carrid,
         connectionid: connid,
         flightdate: fldate
       },
      success: function(oData, response) {
        ..........
```

```
    },
  error: function(oError) {
    . . . . . . . . . .
    }
});
```

Listing 5.2 Calling a Function Import and Service Operation

OData Two-Way Binding

In Chapter 3, we discussed data binding and how to implement various bindings. Earlier we discussed `changeSetId`, so now let's dig deeper into implementing and working with two-way binding.

Two-way binding is supported in the V2 version of the OData model, although one-way binding is the default. As discussed in Chapter 3, two-way binding results in changes being recorded whenever values in a bound control are changed. By default, all these model changes resulting from two-way binding are deferred. They use a common group called `changes`. Whenever `submitChanges()` is called, the `changes` group gets submitted to the backend with all changes.

SAPUI5 provides ways to group all the operations resulting from the two-way binding as groups and changesets as shown here:

```
oModel.setChangeGroups({
    "SalesOrder": {
        groupId: "myChangeGroup",
        changeSetId: "AllItemUpdates",
        single: false
    }
);
```

In this code, we're specifying that all change requests resulting from two-way binding of entity type `SalesOrder` should have a `groupId` as `myChangeGroup` and `change-SetId` as `AllItemUpdates`. If `single` is set to `true`, then `changeSetId` is ignored, and each change request will have its own `changeSetId`.

Just like other batch requests, if the corresponding `groupIds` aren't deferred, then each change will hit the backend immediately, defeating the purpose of having a changeset. Thus, in this scenario, it makes sense to have `groupId` `myChangeGroup` deferred.

There might be scenarios where you have to discard all the changes made by the user and don't issue any batch requests to the backend. In such cases, you can call the API `resetChanges` to reset all the changes in the model. You can also selectively reset the changes of an entity set by specifying the path for which changes need to be reset:

```
resetChanges(["/Products", "/SalesOrder"]);
```

Implement a Facet Filter

The facet filter control (`sap.m.FacetFilter`) is usually used on huge sets of data, when users want to dynamically filter this data along multiple facets or data values to find the data they need.

The filters used in the facet filter control can be dependency managed; that is, upon selecting a filter, filters in another facet list can be enabled or disabled.

Types of Facet Filter

The `FacetFilter` supports two variants, which can be switched by using the property `type` on the `FacetFilter`'s instance:

- **Simple type**
  This is the default type of facet filter and is available only for desktops and tablets. The active facets are available as clickable buttons on the toolbar. Any of these facets can be clicked on to adjust the filter values as shown in Figure 5.21.

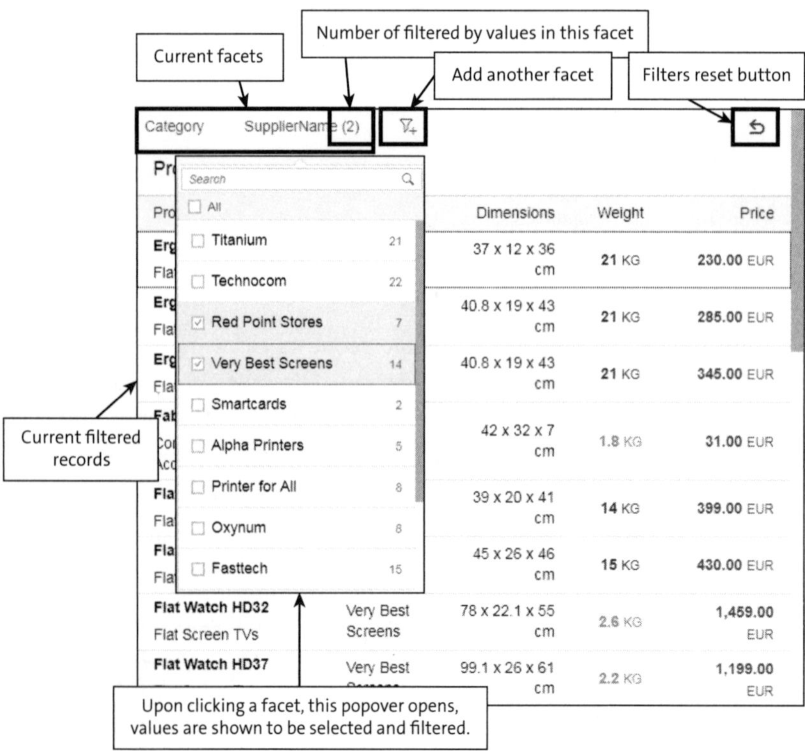

Figure 5.21 Features of a Simple Type Facet Filter

- **Light type**

  This is enabled automatically on mobile-sized devices; however, it's available on desktops and tablets as well. There is a summary bar on top of the facet filter that shows the list of current facets and values of these facets. Upon clicking the summary bar, you'll see a list of facets available for filtering. When you select any of the facets, all the possible values are shown and can be filtered (Figure 5.22):

  - `showReset="true"` will show the filter **Reset** button.

  - `showPopoverOKButton="true"` shows an **OK** button to close the facet popover.

  - `showPersonaliation="True"` will show the **Remove Facet List** and **Add Facet List** buttons so that the number of facets can be personalized.

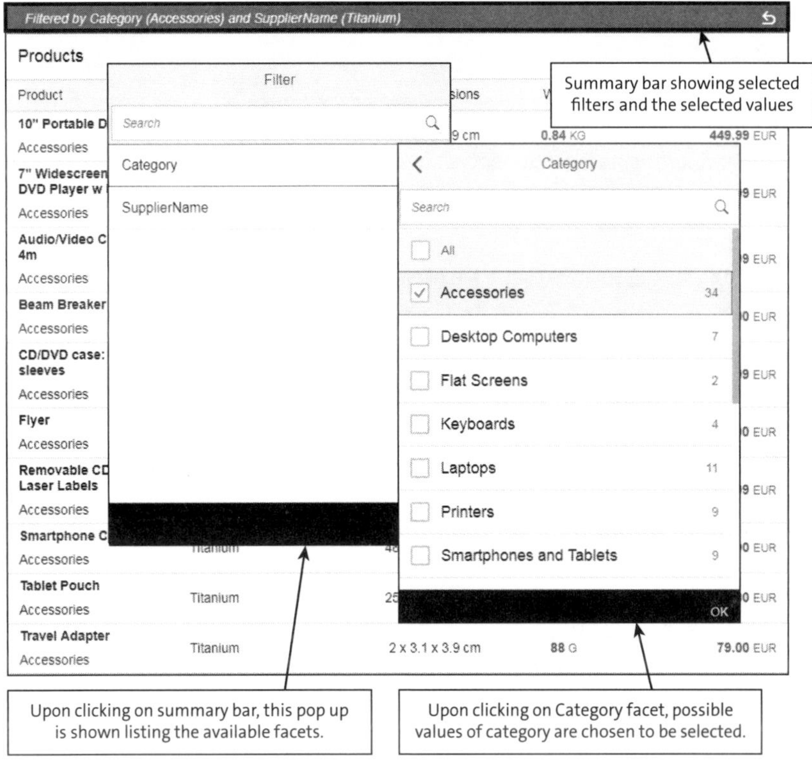

Figure 5.22 Light Type Facet Filter

As you can see in Figure 5.22, the main difference between simple and light types is in how they show the facets. The simple type lets you select a facet directly;

however, clicking on the summary bar in the light type always opens the same popup listing all the facets.

Content of Facet Filter

The number of facets in a facet filter is defined by the aggregation lists. Each item in this aggregation is of type `sap.m.FacetFilterList`. The number of allowed facets are usually static in a facet filter, so instances of `FacetFilterList` are manually created and added to the lists aggregation. Another common way is to have a JSON model that contains one entry for each allowed facet and bound to aggregation lists. However, the number of facets can be completely dynamic by binding it to an OData collection, just like any other aggregations of an SAPUI5 control.

`sap.m.FacetFilterList` extends `sap.m.List`. Table 5.1 provides a list of important properties of this class.

Property	Description
title	Provides the name that appears for each facet.
mode	Determines if only one (`SingleSelectMaster`) or multiple facets (`MultiSelect`) can be active at a time.
sequence	Controls the relative sequence of the active facets in the toolbar.
active	Determines that only active facets appear on the simple type's toolbar.
allCount	Displays the number of records in the dataset that match if all the filter items are selected.

Table 5.1 Facet Filter Properties

The number of valid values for a facet is defined by the aggregation `items` within `FacetFilterList`. Because the valid values can be huge, items aggregation is usually bound either to a JSON model or to an OData model collection. Each item in the aggregation `items` is going to be of type `sap.m.FacetFilterItem`.

`sap.m.FacetFilterItem` extends `sap.m.ListItemBase`. This class has two important properties:

- key

  A unique identifier for each item in the facet filter.

- text

  The title/name of each item.

Implementing a Facet Filter

In this section, we'll explore modelling an OData model as well as a JSON model for a facet filter. We'll also discuss how to code view and controller for a facet filter.

Using the OData Model

If the number of facets is going to be dynamic and needs to be derived from the OData service, then there should be an entity/entity set for fetching the facets. This entity can have navigation property Values, which will provide valid values for each of these facets. In this case, both FacetFilterList and FacetFilterItem are populated by OData aggregation binding as shown in Figure 5.23.

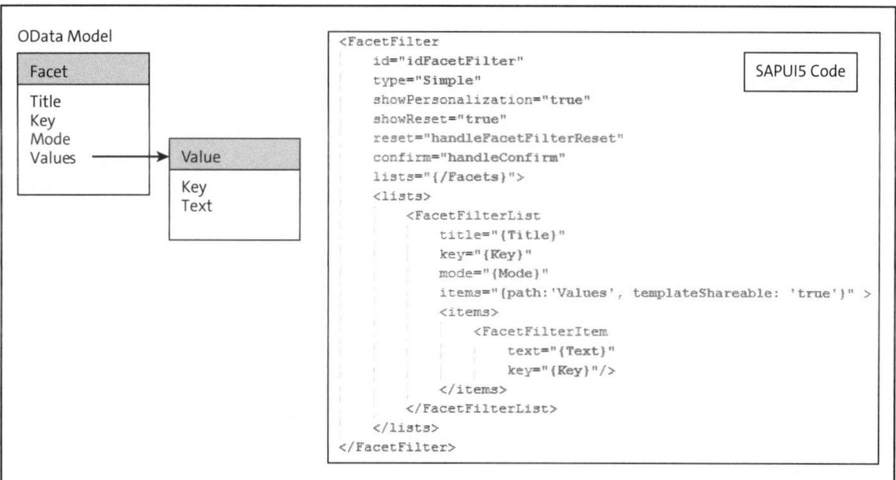


```
<FacetFilter
    id="idFacetFilter"
    type="Simple"
    showPersonalization="true"
    showReset="true"
    reset="handleFacetFilterReset"
    confirm="handleConfirm"
    lists="{/Facets}">
    <lists>
        <FacetFilterList
            title="{Title}"
            key="{Key}"
            mode="{Mode}"
            items="{path:'Values', templateShareable: 'true'}" >
            <items>
                <FacetFilterItem
                    text="{Text}"
                    key="{Key}"/>
            </items>
        </FacetFilterList>
    </lists>
</FacetFilter>
```

Figure 5.23 OData Binding and UI Code for Facet Filter

Using the JSON Model

The JSON model can also be used whenever the valid values of facet filters are static and limited. Figure 5.24 shows a JSON model for populating a facet filter.

```
{
  "Facets": [
    {
      "Title": "Categories",
      "Values": [
        {
          "Key": "Accessories",
          "Text": "Accessories"
        },
        {
          "Key": "DC",
          "Text": "Desktop Computers"
        },
        {
          "Key": "FS",
          "Text": "Flat Screens"
        },
        {
          "Key": "KB",
          "Text": "Keyboards"
        }
      ]
    },
    {
      "Title": "Products",
      "Values": [
        {
          "Key": "TT",
          "Text": "Titanium"
        },
        {
          "Key": "TC",
          "Text": "Technocom"
        },
        {
          "Key": "SC",
          "Text": "Smartcards"
        },
        {
          "Key": "PR",
          "Text": "Printers"
        }
      ]
    }
  ]
}
```

Figure 5.24 JSON Model for Populating a Facet Filter

User Interface Code for Facet Filter

In practical scenarios, however, the number of facets is usually static and known, while the number of valid values for each facet is usually fetched from the backend server.

Let's use the SAP-delivered OData service /IWBEP/GWSAMPLE_BASIC to create a facet filter. The number of facets is static and created as shown in Figure 5.25. Valid values for each facet are fetched by aggregation binding as shown. Before we continue further with the coding, let's understand the events involved with the facet filter.

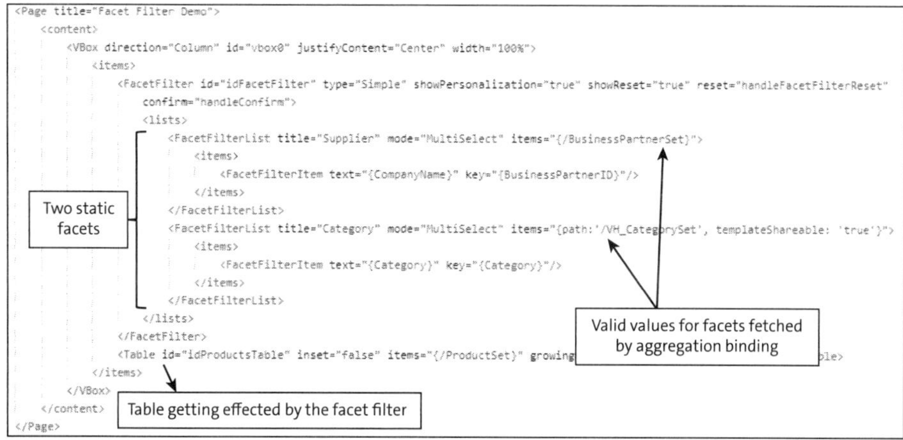

Figure 5.25 SAPUI5 Code for Creating a Facet Filter

Events in a Facet Filter

These events are available on the on `sap.m.FacetFilter`:

- `Confirm`

  This event gets fired when the user makes his selections and closes the facet filter list popup either by clicking **OK** (if configured) or by clicking outside the popup. You can use this event to look for all the selected facets and filter the main list.

- `Reset`

  This event gets fired when the user clicks on the **Reset** icon if enabled. This button is intended to clear all the facet filter selections. You can use this event to clear all the filters that filter the binding of the main list.

In addition, these events are available on `sap.m.FacetFilterList`:

- `Reset`

  Like the event on the facet filter, the `reset` event is triggered by the **Reset** icon on the facet filter's toolbar. This event handler is expected to remove all the current applied filters. You can use the method `removeSelections(true)` to remove all the filters.

- `List Close`

  This event is triggered when the user completes the selection and closes the popup list of facet filter items. This event is like the `Confirm` event on the facet filter, however, by triggering different methods by different facet filter lists, you can write facet-specific coding using this event.

- `List Open`

  This event gets triggered just before the facet filter popup gets opened. This event can be used to influence the valid filter items within a facet. For example, consider two facets, **Category** and **Supplier**. Whenever one or more items in the **Category** facet is chosen, and the user opens the **Supplier** facet, only suppliers supplying products in those categories will be shown. The `listOpen` event can be used to handle these kind of dependencies and filter items in a facet filter list popup.

Controller Coding for the Facet Filter

Figure 5.26 explains the `confirm` event handler. `handleConfirm` is the event handler for the `confirm` event. When this event occurs, all the facets are checked for the selected filter values, and an SAPUI5 filter object is created. An `OR` statement is used to combine selections within a facet, and an `AND` is used for selections between different facets.

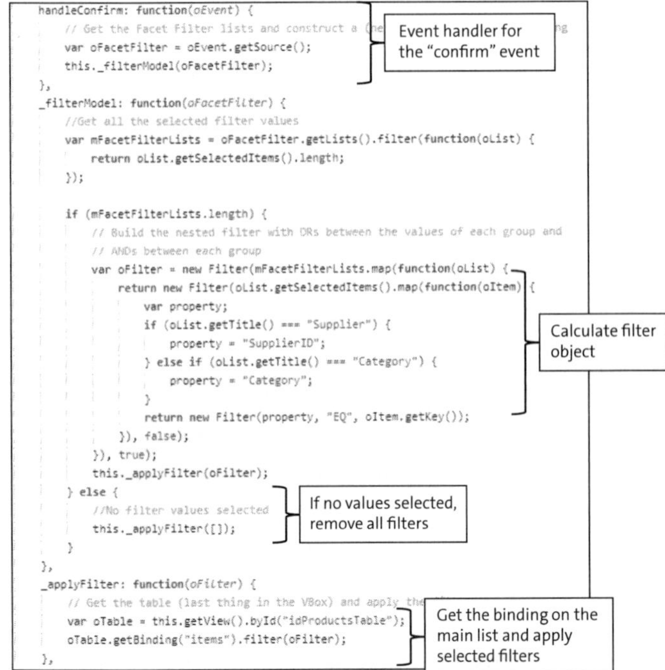


```javascript
handleConfirm: function(oEvent) {
    // Get the Facet Filter lists and construct a (he...
    var oFacetFilter = oEvent.getSource();
    this._filterModel(oFacetFilter);
},
_filterModel: function(oFacetFilter) {
    //Get all the selected filter values
    var mFacetFilterLists = oFacetFilter.getLists().filter(function(oList) {
        return oList.getSelectedItems().length;
    });

    if (mFacetFilterLists.length) {
        // Build the nested filter with ORs between the values of each group and
        // ANDs between each group
        var oFilter = new Filter(mFacetFilterLists.map(function(oList) {
            return new Filter(oList.getSelectedItems().map(function(oItem) {
                var property;
                if (oList.getTitle() === "Supplier") {
                    property = "SupplierID";
                } else if (oList.getTitle() === "Category") {
                    property = "Category";
                }
                return new Filter(property, "EQ", oItem.getKey());
            }), false);
        }), true);
        this._applyFilter(oFilter);
    } else {
        //No filter values selected
        this._applyFilter([]);
    }
},
_applyFilter: function(oFilter) {
    // Get the table (last thing in the VBox) and apply the...
    var oTable = this.getView().byId("idProductsTable");
    oTable.getBinding("items").filter(oFilter);
},
```

Figure 5.26 Confirm Event Handler

Figure 5.27 explains the reset event's handler. The application needs to handle the functionality of this event. First, all the facet filter lists are fetched, and selected keys are cleared off. In the next step, an empty error is passed to _applyFilter (implemented as shown in Figure 5.27) to remove the filters on the main list's item binding.

```
handleFacetFilterReset: function(oEvent) {
    //Remove all the selections from facets
    var oFacetFilter = sap.ui.getCore().byId(oEvent.getParameter("idFacetFilter"));
    var aFacetFilterLists = oFacetFilter.getLists();
    for (var i = 0; i < aFacetFilterLists.length; i++) {
        aFacetFilterLists[i].setSelectedKeys();
    }
    //Remove all filters
    this._applyFilter([]);
},
```

Figure 5.27 Reset Event Handler

Figure 5.28 shows the resulting facet filter along with the main table.

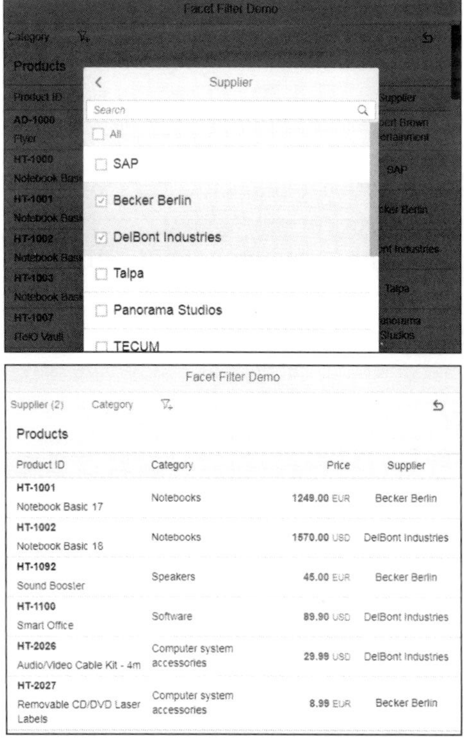

Figure 5.28 Facet Filter Selection and Results

In-App Navigation

SAP Fiori uses a Single Page Application (SPA) framework, which means that there is only one HTML page involved—*Fiorilaunchpad.html*. So how does one see different content within the same page? This is possible due to hash-based navigation. The page and the URL remain as *Fiorilaunchpad.html*, but the hash keeps changing. The hash indicates which view or content to show on the page. The SAPUI5 routing concept analyzes the hash and renders the corresponding SAPUI5 view based on routing configurations. This concept of hash-based navigation is also called intent-based navigation. Let's discuss what the hash/intent contains.

An intent starts after a # and consists of three parts with the following syntax.

```
<semantic object - <action> ? <parameter> = <parameter value>
```

Semantic Object

This is a string that represents a business object. Having a meaningful name here helps users make sense of the URL. If you're working on a purchase order app, you may have the semantic object as `PurchaseOrder`. Other examples are `SalesOrder`, `Employee`, and `Material`.

Action

This string, which follows the semantic object with a hyphen, indicates the action that will happen on the semantic object in the current application. Example actions can be `Create`, `Delete`, `Update`, and `Display`. A combination of semantic object and action must be unique for an SAP Fiori app. For example, a purchase order creating application will have it as `PurchaseOrder-Create`. Other examples of semantic object-action combination are `Material-View`, `Employee-Hire`, and `SalesOrder-Delete`. The semantic object and action are linked to an SAP Fiori app using target mapping in an SAP Fiori catalog. You can see more about this in Chapter 2.

Parameters

Parameters are used to specify an instance of the business object and to open a specific instance of this business object on the screen. However, parameters are optional. Without parameters, the default screen of the application opens.

An example of an SAP Fiori URL with intent is as follows:

```
/sap/bc/ui5_ui5/ui2/ushell/shells/abap/Fiorilaunchpad.html?#PurchaseOrder-Display?
OrderNumber=23443211
```

By looking at the URL, the user can imply that this opens an SAP Fiori app, which displays details of a purchase order with ID 23443211.

Routing

Routing is a concept in SAPUI5 that allows you to navigate within the SAP Fiori app (in-app navigation). Routing configurations are entered in the *manifest.json* file, which is called the application descriptor of the application.

The entire routing configuration is within the `routing` property under the `sap.ui` part of *manifest.json* as shown in . Routing contains three important subsections as discussed in the following.

config

This part of the routing configuration contains the main routing configuration and default values for routes and targets. `routerClass` specifies a class that contains the definition of standard APIs within routing. SAP provides a standard `routerClass` `sap.m.routing.Router`, which can be used here for getting the standard functionality. `sap.ui.core.routing.Router` is another SAP-delivered router class. However, `sap.m.routing.Router` contains features specific to mobile apps, such as transition direction while navigating from a master to detail and vice versa. However, you can always have a custom class extending a standard class to enhance the functionalities.

Other properties under `config`, such as `viewType`, `viewPath`, `controlId`, and `ControlAggregation`, specify default values for these properties under `routes` and `targets`. You'll learn more about these properties in the following sections.

routes

`routes` specify a list of all the possible navigations within the app. Each route specifies a name, a routing `pattern`, and one or more `targets` to be rendered whenever the `pattern` is matched. The name of the route can be used to programmatically navigate to the route without changing the hash of the URL.

The sequence of the routes definition in a routing configuration is important while pattern matching. After the first match, router configurations aren't evaluated, and the matched route is navigated to.

Route patterns can also include mandatory parameters. For example, a pattern `PurchaseOrder/{OrderID}` would match the hash `PurchaseOrder/23123123` or `PurchaseOrder/23123123`. However, hash `PurchaseOrder` would not match because the parameter is mandatory for this pattern.

Parameters can be optional as well. The pattern for the optional parameter is `PurchaseOrder/:OrderID:`. This pattern would match the hash `PurchaseOrder` because the parameter is optional.

Using query parameters is another powerful way to pass context-specific data. Consider a pattern `PurchaseOrder{?query}`. This will match the URL hash `PurchaseOrder?OrderID=12345`. It also matches `PurchaseOrder?OrderID=12345&Plant=1000`. You can have multiple query parameters, but a query parameter is mandatory to match the preceding pattern. If you want to match an optional query parameter, you can use the pattern `PurchaseOrder:?query:`.

Property `bypassed` in `config` can be used to specify a target that will be called when none of the configured routes can be matched.

You can programmatically navigate to any of the routes using the following code:

```
this.getOwnerComponent().getRouter().navTo("employeeDetails");
```

`this.getOwnerComponent().getRouter()` gets the instance of the router class, while `navTo("employeeDetails");` navigates to a route with name "`employeeDetails`".

You can also navigate to routes with the following parameters. This code navigates to hash `PurchaseOrder/23123123`.

```
this.getOwnerComponent().getRouter().navTo("PurchaseOrder", {
    OrderID: "23123123"
});
```

After a route is matched, event `routeMatched` gets triggered, which can be handled. The following code shows how a `routeMatched` event is handled and how the routing parameter (if available) is fetched.

```
Var oRouter = this.getOwnerComponent().getRouter();
oRouter.attachRouteMatched(function (oEvt){
    var orderId = oEvt.getParameter("OrderID");
});
```

However, the preceding code will be run for *all* the routes in the system, and you may want to react to only specific routes. In such a case, you can check the route name in the handler function and react only if interested.

Another way to react only to a specific route is as follows using the `attachMatched` API on the route instance:

```
oRouter.getRoute("employeeDetails").attachMatched(function(oEvt){
    //Write your code here.
});
```

> **Tip**
> SAPUI5 includes open source JavaScript library *Corssroad.js* for handling and parsing URL hashes.

targets

`targets` specify all the possible views where a route can end up. Targets are linked to one or more routes to specify the destination of the route. When a `target` is chosen, the corresponding view specified by `viewName` is initialized and added to the aggregation specified by `ControlAggregation` of the control with ID `controlId`. While looking for the view, the router looks for the view of type `viewType` in the `viewPath`. The property `transition` allows you to specify how the transition to the new view should happen. You can choose one of `slide` (default), `flip`, `fade`, and `show` for the transition value. The `transition` property uses the `viewLevel` property to determine the transition to use.

Properties such as `transition`, `ControlAggregation`, `controlId`, `viewPath`, and `viewType` are usually defaulted in the `config` of the router.

A `target` can be directly navigated to without hitting a route or changing the URL hash by calling an API in the controller:

```
this.getOwnerComponent().getRouter().getTargets().display("home");
```

`this.getOwnerComponent().getRouter()` gets the instance of the router class. `getTargets()` gets all the targets, and `display("home")` displays the target with name "home".

Deep Linking

Though SAP Fiori follows an SPA framework, hash-based navigation along with the SAPUI5 routing concept allows users to bookmark various stages in the application. For example, if you're using a Sales Order SAP Fiori app to view a sales order of interest, you can bookmark the URL to come back to it later. This ability to bookmark various statuses of the app is called deep-linking.

In this section, we'll cover how to use the routing concept to bookmark various statuses of the application.

Bookmarkable Views and Business Objects

Consider a scenario in which you want to have a bookmarkable URL that displays the details of a specific sales order. The following steps are involved:

1. Design a hash/route that has a specific pattern as well as a mandatory parameter for specifying the sales order number. We'll use the following hash for this navigation: `SalesOrderDetail/2344321`.

2. In the router configuration, specify the pattern and route to a target that shows a sales order display view. Part of the routing configuration from *manifest.json* is shown in Listing 5.3.

```
"sap.ui5": {
   …..
      "routing":{
         "config"  :{
            …….
         },
         "routes":[
            {
                "pattern":"",
                "name":"home",
                "target":"home"
            },
            {
                "pattern":"SalesOrderDetail/{OrderID}",
                "name":"detail",
                "target":"detail"
            }
         ],
         "targets":{
            "home": {
                "viewName":  "Home",
                "viewLevel": 1
            },
            "details": {
                "viewName":  "OrderDetail",
                "viewLevel": 2
            }
```

```
        }
    }
}
```

Listing 5.3 Routing Configuration for Deep Linking

As you can see in this configuration, pattern "`SalesOrderDetail/{OrderID}`" when matched, will hit the target "`details`", which will show the view "`OrderDetail`".

3. In the controller of the view, listen to the `attachPatternMatched` event of the designed route. In the event handler, fetch the sales order number. Use the `bindElement` method to bind the view using the sales order number.

Listing 5.4 shows the relevant code in the controller of the view "OrderDetail":

```
onInit: function () {
    var oRouter = this.getRouter();
    oRouter.getRoute("detail").attachMatched(this._onRouteMatched, this);
},
_onRouteMatched : function (oEvent) {
            var oArgs, oView;
            oArgs = oEvent.getParameter("arguments");
            oView = this.getView();

            //Using the OrderID set the binding for the
//OrderDetail view
            oView.bindElement({
                path :"/SalesOrders(" + oArgs.OrderID + ")",
                events : {
                    dataRequested: function (oEvent) {
                        oView.setBusy(true);
                    },
                    dataReceived: function (oEvent) {
                        oView.setBusy(false);
                    }
                }
            });
}
```

Listing 5.4 Handling Deep Linking and Binding the Context to the View

In the `onInit` event handler, an event handler `_onRouteMatched` is attached when the route `detail` is matched. In the method `_onRouteMatched`, `oEvent.getParameter("arguments")` fetches all the routing parameters (only one in this example). These routing parameters are used to form a binding path, which is used to bind to the `orderDetail` view using the `bindElement` API.

Bookmarkable Tabs

Consider a scenario in which the preceding orderDetail view contains multiple tabs to organize the sales order information. Consider a use case where there is important information in the fourth tab, and you want to get a URL link to share with a colleague that should directly navigate to the fourth tab of the sales order detail.

We'll realize this requirement in this section by using optional query parameters to navigate to the specific tab of the control IconTabBar. The query parameter is optional as we should be able to navigate to the detail without having to specify any tab.

Follow these steps to do so:

1. Design a hash. Consider the hash "SalesOrderDetail/{OrderID}/:?query:". Here, query parameters are optional because it's defined as :?query:. To configure a mandatory query parameter, you can specify it as "SalesOrderDetail/{OrderID}/{? query}".

   All the following hashes should navigate to the right tabs. In addition, any invalid tabs selected through the URL should show the first tab.

   SalesOrderDetail/12345/?Tab=History

   SalesOrderDetail/12345/?Tab=Info

   SalesOrderDetail/12345/?Tab=Items

   SalesOrderDetail/12345/?Tab=Customers

   SalesOrderDetail/12345/?Tab=Invalid (invalid tab in the hash)

   Note

   :?query: allows you to pass as many query parameters as required. For example, it matches SalesOrderDetail/12345/?Tab=History as well as SalesOrderDetail/12345/ ?Tab=History&Action=edit.

2. In the routing configuration, specify the preceding pattern as shown in Listing 5.5. Only the routes property is shown here for simplicity.

```
"routes":[
    {
        "pattern":"",
        "name":"home",
        "target":"home"
    },
    {
        "pattern":"SalesOrderDetail/{OrderID}",
        "name":"detail",
```

```
                  "target":"detail"
            },
            {
            "pattern":"SalesOrderDetail/{OrderID}/

}/:?query:

",
                  "name":"detailTab",
                  "target":"detailTab"

            }
      ],
```

Listing 5.5 Deep Linking Tabs

3. In the view, it's important that the URL reflects the tab selection whenever the user selects one of these tabs. Therefore, the event select needs to be listened to on the IconTabBar. In addition, property selectedTabKey is used (bound) to influence the selected key of the tab IconTabBar. This will allow you to influence the selected tab based on the URL hash. The relevant part of the view looks like Figure 5.29. The contents of IconTabFilter are kept simple in the XML view, and ideally it would contain the relevant tab content.

```
<IconTabBar
    id="iconTabBar"
    select="onTabSelect"
    selectedKey="{uiModel>/selectedTabKey}">
    <items>
        <IconTabFilter id="infoTab" text="{i18n>Info}" key="Info">
            <Text text="{Info}" />
        </IconTabFilter>
        <IconTabFilter id="itemsTab" text="{i18n>Items}" key="Items">
            <Text text="{Items}" />
        </IconTabFilter>
        <IconTabFilter id="customerTab" text="{i18n>Customer}"  key="Customer">
            <Text text="{Customer}" />
        </IconTabFilter>
        <IconTabFilter id="historyTab" text="{i18n>History}" key="History">
            <Text text="{History}" />
        </IconTabFilter>
    </items>
</IconTabBar>
```

Figure 5.29 Part of the View Showing select and selectedKey for IconTabFilter

4. In the view's controller, you need to perform the following tasks:
   - Listen to the matched event on the route. On the event handler, fetch the sales order number and bind the view to the sales order as we did in the previous exercise. In addition, fetch the query parameters from the route, fetch the parameter for the Tab key, and update the uiModel's property selectedKey

so that `selectedKey` of `IconTabBar` gets updated triggering a navigation to the relevant tab.

- Use an array `_aValidTabKeys` to store all the relevant tab keys and ensure that URL contains only the allowed tab keys. If any invalid tab keys are used, then navigate to the first valid tab key. Ideally this variable is defined in the `onInit` method of the view.

- Implement `onTabSelect`, which is a listener for select events of the `IconTabFilter`. When the user clicks anywhere on the tab, use `navTo` API on the router to navigate to the right URL. It's important to mention the right route and pass the sales order number and the ⌈Tab⌋ key as a query parameter during the `navTo` API call. This will update the URL to reflect the right tab the user is in.

The code in Figure 5.30 displays part of the controller code that is relevant and performs these actions.

```javascript
onRouteMatched : function (oEvent) {
        var oArgs, oView, oQuery, _aValidTabKeys;
        //All the possible tab keys
        _aValidTabKeys = ["Info", "Items", "Customer", "History"];
        oArgs = oEvent.getParameter("arguments");
        oView = this.getView();
        oView.bindElement({
            path :"/SalesOrders(" + oArgs.OrderID + ")",
            events : {
                dataRequested: function (oEvent) {
                    oView.setBusy(true);
                },
                dataReceived: function (oEvent) {
                    oView.setBusy(false);
                }
            }
        });
        oQuery = oArgs["?query"];
        if (oQuery && _aValidTabKeys.indexOf(oQuery.Tab) > -1){
            oView.getModel("uiModel").setProperty("/selectedTabKey", oQuery.Tab);
        } else {
            // the default tab to be navigated to,
            //if no valid tab key was fetched; Goto first tab
            this.getRouter().navTo("detailTab", {
                OrderID : oArgs.OrderID,
                query: {
                    Tab : _aValidTabKeys[0]
                }
            });
        }
},

        onTabSelect : function (oEvent){
            var oBindingContext = this.getView().getBindingContext();
            //Update the OrderID as well as Tab
            this.getRouter().navTo("detailTab", {
                OrderID : oBindingContext.getProperty("OrderID"),
                query: {
                    Tab : oEvent.getParameter("selectedKey")
                }
            });
        });
    }
```

Figure 5.30 Relevant Controller Code for Navigating to a Specific Tab of IconTabFilter

Bookmarkable "Search" Results

Consider a scenario in which you search for a sales order in the master list and want to have a URL to share the search results. An optional query parameter can be used in this scenario as well for capturing the search term. Broad steps involved remain the same as for bookmarkable tabs that we discussed earlier. For this reason, we won't look at the code but just list the steps involved:

1. Create a new route or modify the existing route of the master list that shows a list of sales orders to handle an optional query parameter to hold the search string.

2. In the `_onRouteMatched` function, get the query parameter for search, and filter the binding of the master list using this search term.

3. When the users directly enter a search term for searching the sales orders, you need to update the URL so that this search can be bookmarked. In this case, identify the search event, and, in its handler, call the `navTo` API of the router, and navigate to the route specified in step 1. Remember to pass the search term as the query parameter so that the URL reflects the search being carried out.

Bookmarkable Dialogs

Dialogs are important components of the UI. There might be use cases in which you want to bookmark or share a link to the application when it is showing a specific dialog. This use case is also achieved using an optional query parameter, and the basic technique remains the same as we did earlier. Consider a use case where there is a value help dialog for choosing a material. You need the URL that opens this dialog upon running the URL. Here are the steps involved:

1. Edit an existing route or add a new route, with an optional query parameter, for example, `showMaterialDialog`.

2. In the `_onRouteMatched` function, get the query parameter and get the value of `showMaterialDialog`. If it's `true`, write the code to open the material dialog.

3. When the user manually clicks on the value help button to open the dialog, use the `navTo` API to navigate to the route while passing the query parameter `showMaterialDialog` as `true`.

4. When the user manually closes the dialog, navigate to the same route, but don't pass the query parameter to indicate that the dialog isn't open.

As you've seen, optional query parameters can be used to achieve various use cases of deep linking. In addition to these use cases, scenarios such as table sorting, filtering, and various other statuses can be bookmarked.

Important Terminology

This chapter covered the following terminology:

- **OData metadata**
  Metadata lists all the OData artifacts within a service. Metadata helps to understand the OData service and its capabilities.

- **SAP Gateway Service Builder**
  This is a tool within the SAP ABAP server and is opened by Transaction SEGW. This tool helps to build OData services and provides various features to build the OData artifacts as well as implement the runtime of the service.

- **Model provider class (MPC)**
  This class contains the code that defines every OData artifact, including entities, properties, associations, `Service` operations, and others. This class and the code inside it are usually generated by the SAP Gateway Service Builder tool based on the data modeling done on SAP Gateway Service Builder.

- **Data provider class (DPC)**
  This class contains the OData implementation code for each operation of the OData service. Like MPC, this class also can be generated by the SAP Gateway Service Builder tool. Implementation code is usually written manually for each operation.

- **Deep Insert**
  `Deep Insert` is a special `Create` operation in an OData Service. This operation creates an entity instance as well as one or more child instances. The code for implementing this operation needs to be written explicitly.

- **Facet filter**
  This is an SAPUI5 control that can be used for filtering a list or a table. The facet filter can be configured to have multiple, as well as dynamic facets or filters. Valid values for each of these facets can be dynamic, sourced from an OData service, or static.

- **In-app navigation**

  Navigation inside an SAP Fiori app occurs using SAPUI5 routing concepts. The routing concept allows an SAPUI5 application to access the URL hash and render various SAPUI5 views without changing the HTML page.

- **Deep linking**

  Deep linking refers to URLs that allow bookmarking various application statuses. For example, bookmarking a tab in an `IconTabFilter`, bookmarking a dialog, bookmarking a table with filters/sorters, and so on. This is achieved by SAPUI5 routing concepts.

 Practice Questions

These practice questions will help you evaluate your understanding of the topics covered in this chapter. The questions shown are similar in nature to those found on the certification examination. Although none of these questions will be found on the exam itself, they will allow you to review your knowledge of the subject. Select the correct answers, and then check the completeness of your answers in the "Practice Question Answers and Explanations" section. Remember, on the exam, you must select all correct answers and only correct answers to receive credit for the question.

1. In an OData service, this is usually cached in the browser as well as in the SAP Gateway layer.

    ☐ A. Query

    ☐ B. Service operation

    ☐ C. Metadata

    ☐ D. Read

2. Which of the following *cannot* be bookmarked in an SAP Fiori app?

    ☐ A. Filters

    ☐ B. Dialogs

    ☐ C. Tabs

    ☐ D. None

3.   Which of the following concepts is used to group multiple OData change requests as a single logical operation?

☐   A. Batch

☐   B. Group

☐   C. Change set

☐   D. Expand

4.   If an OData operation does *not* fit into any of `Create/Read-Query/Update/Delete`, then which of the following options can be used?

☐   A. Function modules

☐   B. `Service` operations

☐   C. Metadata update

☐   D. `Deep Insert`

5.   Within the MPC, which of the following methods is triggered upon metadata request.

☐   A. `DEFINE`

☐   B. `GET_METADATA`

☐   C. `DEFINE_META`

☐   D. `GET_ENTITIES`

6.   An `$expand` URL will contain which of the following to represent the child entities?

☐   A. Child entity set name

☐   B. Navigation property name

☐   C. Association name

☐   D. Child entity name

7.   How does the SAP Gateway framework determine if the create request is a single entity create or a `Deep Insert`?

☐   A. URL contains navigation properties

☐   B. HTTP headers

☐   C. URL ends with key word "Deep"

☐   D. Request body contains the parent as well as child Entity data

8.   Which is the right place to declare router configurations?

☐   A. *manifest.json*

☐   B. *index.html*

☐   C. *Component.js*

☐   D. *router.js*

9.   Which events get triggered in a facet filter upon the user completing the selection of facet filter values (or closing the facet filter dialog)? (2 possible answers)

☐   A. `Confirm`

☐   B. `ListOpen`

☐   C. `ListClose`

☐   D. `Reset`

Practice Answers and Explanations

1.   Correct answer: **C**
     OData metadata is usually cached because it doesn't change often during the runtime of a service. However, all other operations aren't cached, as they need to deliver real-time data to the user.

2.   Correct answer: **D**
     All filters, dialogs, and tabs can be bookmarked.

3.   Correct answer: **C**
     Change sets are used to group multiple changes into a single logical group. However, change sets have to be inside a batch request.

4.   Correct answer: **B**
     Any operation not suiting the CRUD framework can be modeled using a `Service` operation (or function import). It can be both a read only (`GET`) and a change operation (`POST`).

5. Correct answer: **A**

    The `DEFINE` method will be triggered on a metadata call. It will contain the code for defining all the artifacts within the OData service and is usually the code inside it's generated from the SAP Gateway Service Builder tool.

6. Correct answer: **A**

    An `$expand` call URL will have navigation properties to the child entities specified in the URL.

7. Correct answer: **D**

    The SAP Gateway framework detects that the request is a `Deep Insert` by looking at the request body. Based on this detection, it triggers the right method in the DPC.

8. Correct answer: **A**

    Manifest.json is the right place to declare router configuration. Although it can be defined within *Component.js*, this technique is currently deprecated.

9. Correct answers: **A, C**

    When the facet filter's dialog is closed, facet filter's `confirm` event as well as `Facet-FilterList`'s `ListClose` event will get triggered.

Take Away

In this chapter, we discussed OData and various operations that are supported in an OData service. We covered how each of these operations can be triggered as well as implemented. We also explored batch calls and how logical groupings of change operations can be done.

We also considered SAP Gateway Service Builder and how its data model is defined. You saw the utility of the SAP Gateway Service Builder tool in generating classes and code to make it easier to develop OData services.

The very useful SAPUI5 facet filter control was discussed, including how it can be implemented using OData services as well as when there are static facets.

Finally, we saw how navigations happen within an SPA. We discussed several techniques to generate bookmarkable URLs for various statuses of the application.

Summary

Now that you've understood SAPUI5 in previous chapters and advanced techniques in data handling in the current chapter, you should be able to create new SAP Fiori apps. In the next chapter, we'll discuss various techniques for extending the SAP-delivered SAP Fiori apps using extensibility concepts.

Chapter 6
Extensibility in SAPUI5

Techniques You'll Master:

- Concept of extension in SAPUI5
- Implementing a view extension
- Implementing a view modification
- Implementing a view replacement
- Implementing a controller extension
- Implementing a translation extension
- Implementing a service replacement

In this chapter, we'll start with discussing SAP's extensibility concept for SAPUI5 and find out why it's better than modifying an SAP-delivered SAP Fiori app. We'll cover the various types of extension use cases for an SAPUI5 application and strategies to achieve them using extension concepts. You'll also see how translation texts can be extended by replacing existing translations or adding additional translations. Finally, you'll learn how to find information about extension options for a specific SAP Fiori app.

Real-World Scenarios

You've implemented multiple SAP-delivered SAP Fiori apps in your organization's landscape. While testing, business users have requested additional information be shown within the app. Some of the additional information would require a new screen to be shown by navigating from the existing screens.

You want to explore options to ensure that after adding additional features to the SAP Fiori app, you can still retain SAP support; that is, any bug fixes released by SAP can still be applied and made available to users.

To do so, you need to check the documentation and see what extension scenarios are supported for a specific SAP Fiori app. You also need to know the extension options if SAP didn't foresee an extension use case within an SAP Fiori app.

Objectives of This Portion of the Test

The objective of this portion of the SAP Fiori Certification Test is to test your understanding of how to extend the functionality of an SAP Fiori app in a modification-free way. The certification test expects SAP Fiori developers to be knowledgeable in the following areas.

- Difference between extension and modification
- Architecture of extension concepts
- View extension
- Controller extension
- Controller replacement
- Translation extension

Key Concepts Refresher

Let's discuss the concept of extensions in SAP Fiori apps and find out how they're different from modification. We'll also explore various extensions that are possible in an SAP Fiori application while using the SAP Web IDE.

Introduction to Extensibility in SAPUI5

SAP currently provides several hundred SAP Fiori apps. Each of these apps is built with certain business roles in mind and SAP's generic understanding of a business process. However, it's very common for businesses to perform a single business process in different ways due to preference, history, local conditions, and economic reasons. Different legal requirements across countries will add additional restrictions on how businesses operate. SAP Fiori key principles such as "role based" and "simple" make the SAP Fiori apps usually provide only one method and style of performing a business process.

Due to these conditions, it's very common for customers to make alterations to SAP-provided SAP Fiori apps to suit their needs. While making these alterations, it's important to ensure that these changes don't completely block new bug fixes and enhancements that SAP releases for these apps. Any modification, that is, direct change to SAP-delivered code will make the app incompatible to receive bug fixes and enhancements from SAP.

To achieve the objectives of modification-free enhancements to the SAP Fiori apps, SAP provides several recommended enhancement methods. All of these recommendations involve creating a new SAPUI5 application in the customer namespace, which will refer to the SAP-delivered app. Because the component is the entry point to an SAP Fiori app, the extension is done through inheritance of components (Figure 6.1).

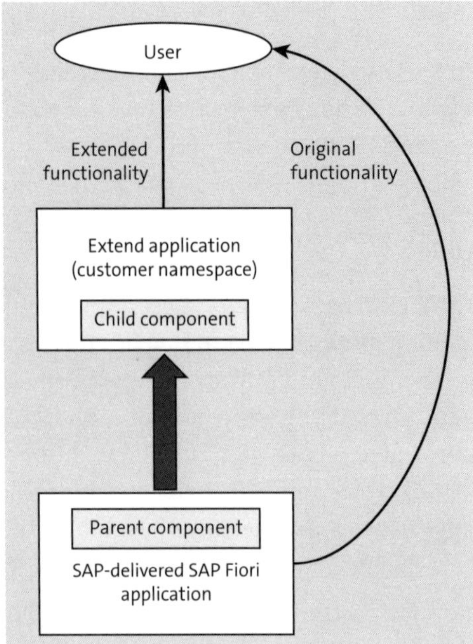

Figure 6.1 Extending an SAP Fiori App

Because the SAP-delivered code isn't modified, it can still receive any new features and bug fixes delivered by SAP (through support packs or SAP Notes), and the extension application will get these features and bug fixes due to the inheritance concept.

The newly created extension application becomes the startup application. Whenever it's called, it loads the parent component (application), and then loads the customizations coded within it. Even after extension, if you refer to the parent application directly, you still get the SAP-delivered functionality without any extensions.

Let's go over the various types of extensions, which will be discussed in further detail in later sections:

- **View modification**
  This allows you to hide the available user interface (UI) controls within an SAP-delivered view.

- **View extension**
  This allows you to implement standard UI hooks provided by SAP to add or replace UI controls within the view.

- **View replacements**
  If you require huge changes that aren't supported by view extensions, then you can replace the SAP-delivered view with your own.

- **Controller extensions**
  This concept allows you to enhance the SAP-delivered SAPUI5 controllers with your own controllers.

- **Controller replacement**
  This concept allows you to replace a controller in cases where a controller can't be extended.

- **Translation extension**
  Text elements or static texts of the standard app can be added or changed with this concept.

- **Service replacement**
  With this concept, the standard OData service used by the application can be replaced with a custom service (usually an extension service).

For any of these extensions, the first steps are to create an extension project and the component configuration, as we'll discuss in the following subsections.

Creating an Extension Project

To create an extension project, follow these steps:

1. Select **Extension Project** from the **File** menu as shown in Figure 6.2.

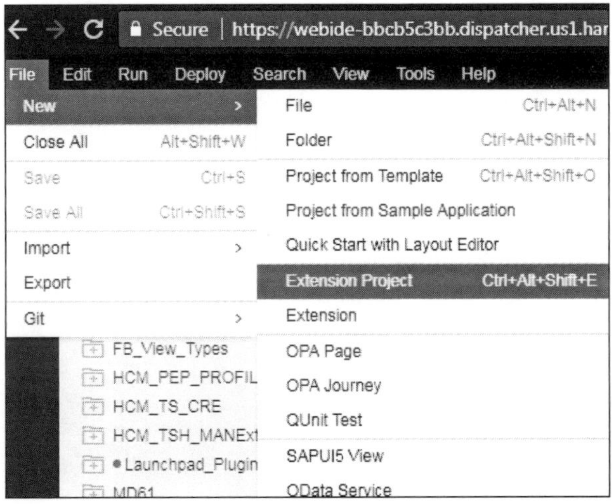

Figure 6.2 Creating an Extension Project

2. SAP Web IDE allows you to extend SAPUI5 applications that are deployed either in an SAP Gateway system (**SAPUI5 ABAP Repository**) or in **SAP Cloud Platform**. In this screen, you need to select the location of the SAP-delivered application that you're going to extend as shown in Figure 6.3.

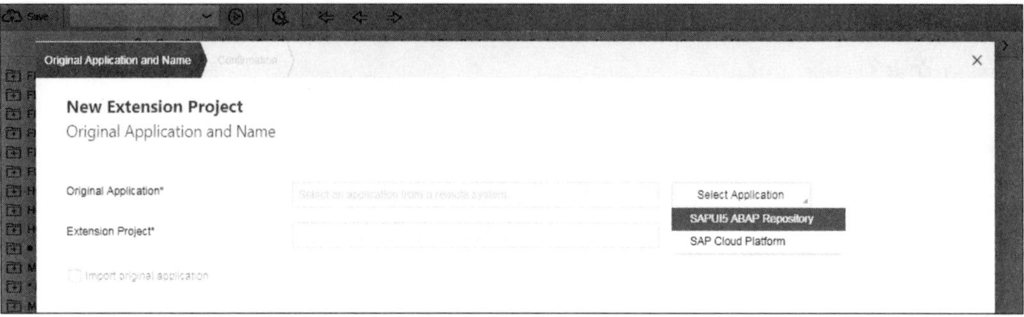

Figure 6.3 Choosing the Location of the Original Application

3. Upon selecting **SAPUI5 ABAP Repository**, you need to select an ABAP system where the SAP-delivered app is deployed. These systems need to be configured as destinations in the **SAP Cloud Platform Cockpit** screen. Upon selecting the system, you can filter the available projects and select the standard app, as shown in Figure 6.4.

   You can also choose **SAP Cloud Platform** if the app that you want to extend is deployed on the current instance of the cloud. All the current deployed apps will be shown, and you can select the app and continue (Figure 6.4).

4. After selecting the application to be enhanced (here, we've chosen the Manage Supplier Invoices app), you can provide a name for the extension application and click **Finish** on the wizard. The new extension project will be available in the SAP Web IDE as shown in Figure 6.5.

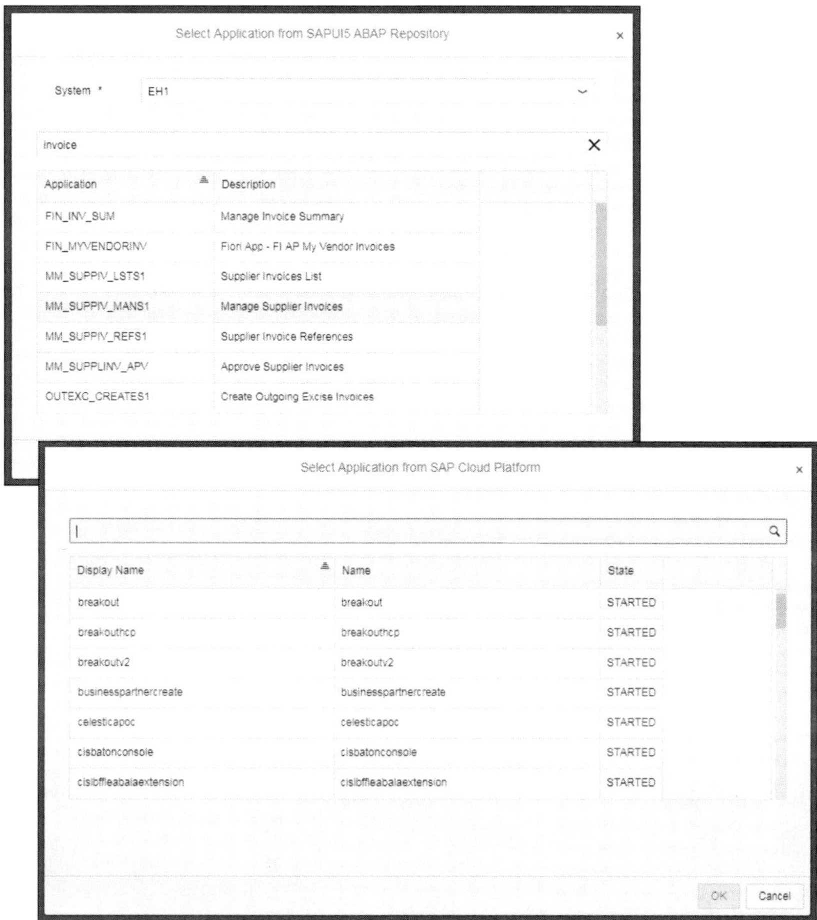

Figure 6.4 Selecting the Application to be Enhanced: from ABAP System and from SAP Cloud Platform

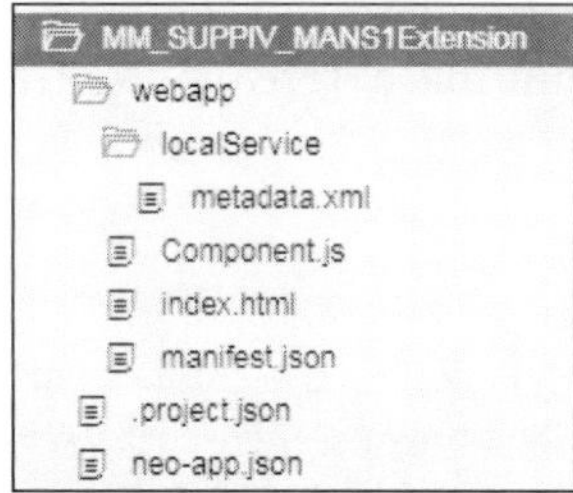

Figure 6.5 Extension Project in SAP Web IDE

Metadata of the original service is available as an XML file under folder *localService*, so that mock data can be created for running the application. An *index.html* file is available for running the application standalone.

The file *Component.js* defines a new component while inheriting the parent component. As shown in Figure 6.6, the code from line number 4 to 10 loads the component of the SAP-delivered app. At line number 12, it defines the new component as a child of the standard component by using the extend API.

```
1    jQuery.sap.declare("ui.s2p.mm.supplinvoice.manage.s1.MM_SUPPIV_MANS1Extension.Component");

2
3    // use the load function for getting the optimized preload file if present
4 ▾  sap.ui.component.load({
5        name: "ui.s2p.mm.supplinvoice.manage.s1",
6        // Use the below URL to run the extended application when SAP-delivered application is deployed on SAPUI5 ABAP Repository
7        url: "/sap/bc/ui5_ui5/sap/MM_SUPPIV_MANS1"
8            // we use a URL relative to our own component
9            // extension application is deployed with customer namespace
10   });
11
12 ▾  this.ui.s2p.mm.supplinvoice.manage.s1.Component.extend("ui.s2p.mm.supplinvoice.manage.s1.MM_SUPPIV_MANS1Extension.Component", {
13 ▾      metadata: {
14            manifest: "json"
15        }
16   });
```

Figure 6.6 Generated Component.js of the Extension Project

You can run this application using the **Run** button on the SAP Web IDE, and the extension application will work just like the standard application because no extension has been added to the extension project.

Component Configuration

Component configuration is part of the metadata of the extension app's component (*manifest.json*) that lists information about various extensions performed on the parent component. It describes various objects that are replaced and extended. In Figure 6.7, the component configuration is showing multiple extensions for the People Profile SAP Fiori app.

Tip

Starting from SAPUI5 1.30, metadata of the component, including the component configuration, has moved to *manifest.json*. For the earlier versions, metadata was defined within the *Component.js* file.

```
1   jQuery.sap.declare("hcm.people.profile.HCM_PEP_PROFILEExtension1.Component");
2   jQuery.sap.registerModulePath("sap.hcm.lib.common", "/sap/bc/ui5_ui5/sap/hcm_common/sap/hcm/lib/common/");
3   // use the load function for getting the optimized preload file if present
4   sap.ui.component.load({
5       name: "hcm.people.profile",
6       // Use the below URL to run the extended application when SAP-delivered application is deployed on SAPUI5 ABAP Repository
7       url: "/sap/bc/ui5_ui5/sap/HCM_PEP_PROFILE" // we use a URL relative to our own component
8           // extension application is deployed with customer namespace
9   });
10  this.hcm.people.profile.Component.extend("hcm.people.profile.HCM_PEP_PROFILEExtension1.Component", {
11      metadata: {
12          version: "1.0",
13          config: {
14              "sap.ca.i18Nconfigs": {
15                  "bundleName": "hcm.people.profile.HCM_PEP_PROFILEExtension1.i18n.i18n"
16              }
17          },
18          customizing: {
19              "sap.ui.viewReplacements": {
20                  "hcm.people.profile.blocks.Salary": {
21                      "viewName": "hcm.people.profile.HCM_PEP_PROFILEExtension1.blocks.SalaryCustom",
22                      "type": "XML"
23                  },
24                  "hcm.people.profile.blocks.TimeBalance": {
25                      "viewName": "hcm.people.profile.HCM_PEP_PROFILEExtension1.blocks.TimeBalanceCustom",
26                      "type": "XML"
27                  }
28              },
29              "sap.ui.controllerExtensions": {
30                  "hcm.people.profile.blocks.SalaryController": {
31                      "controllerName": "hcm.people.profile.HCM_PEP_PROFILEExtension1.blocks.SalaryControllerCustom"
32                  },
33                  "hcm.people.profile.view.Profile": {
34                      "controllerName": "hcm.people.profile.HCM_PEP_PROFILEExtension1.view.ProfileCustom"
35                  },
36                  "hcm.people.profile.blocks.TimeRecordingController": {
37                      "controllerName": "hcm.people.profile.HCM_PEP_PROFILEExtension1.blocks.TimeRecordingControllerCustom"
38                  },
39                  "hcm.people.profile.blocks.VacationsController": {
40                      "controllerName": "hcm.people.profile.HCM_PEP_PROFILEExtension1.blocks.VacationsControllerCustom"
41                  }
42              }
43          }
44      }
45  });
```


Figure 6.7 Component Configuration within Component.js

View Modification

View modification involves changing properties of controls that are part of the view. However, currently only the "visible" property of the controls can be changed using this technique. This extension is available for XML views, JavaScript views, and HTML views. Let's see an example of how to achieve this in an XML view.

Listing 6.1 represents a simple SAPUI5 view from an SAP-delivered SAPUI5 application containing three input controls.

```
<mvc:View xmlns="sap.m" xmlns:mvc="sap.ui.core.mvc">
<Input type="Text"/>
<Input type="Number"/>
<Input id="inputCanBeHidden" type="Text"/>
</mvc:View>
```

Listing 6.1 A Simple SAPUI5 View

Consider a case where you need to hide the last input control within the view, as shown in Listing 6.2. This can be achieved with the following entry at `sap.ui5/extends/extensions` on *manifest.json* of the extension application.

```
"sap.ui5":{
  "_version": "1.1.0",
  "dependencies": {
    "minUI5Version": "1.40.3"
  },
  "extends" :{
    "component": "samples.modify",
    "extensions": {
      "sap.ui.ViewModifications": {
        "samples.modify.View.S1": {
          "inputCanBeHidden": {
            "visible": false
          }
        }
      }
    }
  }
}
```

Listing 6.2 manifest.json Specifying the Hiding of the UI Control

Here is the explanation of the preceding listing:

- `extends` indicates that the current component extends the component named `samples.modify`.
- The `extensions` property lists all the extensions within the component/application.
- `sap.ui.ViewModifications` is the type of SAPUI5 extension.
- `samples.modify.View.S1` is the name of the view that has been extended.
- `inputCanBeHidden` is the ID of the control that is undergoing modification (getting hidden).
- The `visible` property of the control is set to `false`.

Note

If the SAPUI5 control in the standard view doesn't have an explicit ID, then the control can't be uniquely identified by the extension framework and hence can't be hidden. The other two input controls in the preceding sample view can't be hidden for the same reason.

SAP Web IDE makes it easier to create extensions using the *extensibility pane*.

To open the extensibility pane, click on the extension project, and choose **Tools •
Extensibility Pane** from the menu bar, as shown in Figure 6.8. (Chapter 4 explains
the capabilities of the extensibility pane in detail.)

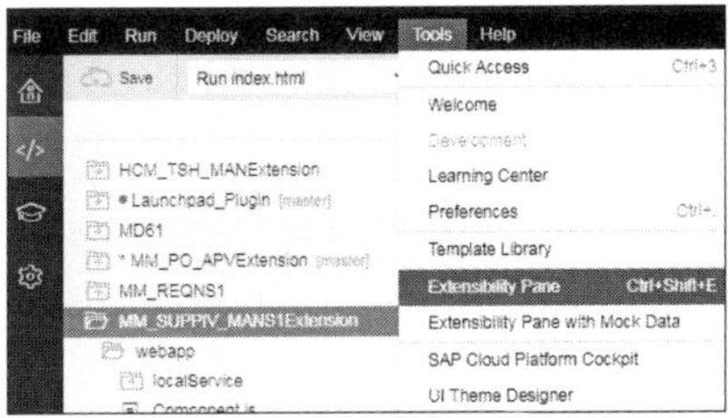

Figure 6.8 Opening the Extensibility Pane

Now that you have the extensibility pane open, follow these steps to create an
extension:

1. Select **Extensibility Mode** under the **Preview Mode** dropdown.

2. On the **Outline** pane on the right, choose **Show extensible elements** from the
   dropdown so only relevant controls that can be extensible are shown.

3. Select the control you want to hide on the **Outline** pane (in this example, we're
   hiding the **Hold** button) or click on the control in the main pane itself.

4. Click on the **Extend** button, and then click **Hide Control** as shown in Figure 6.9.

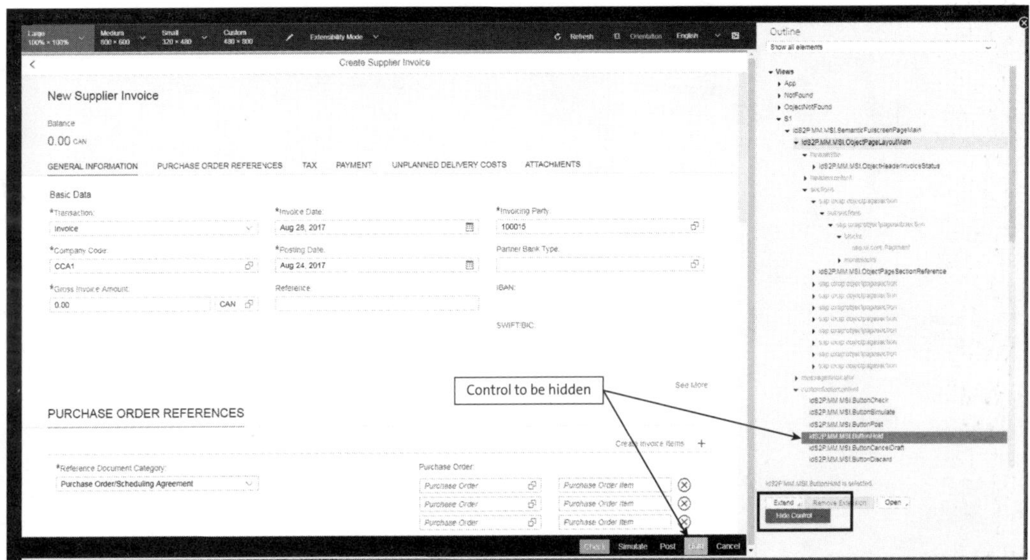

Figure 6.9 Selecting and Hiding a Control in the Extensibility Pane

5. In the confirmation box that appears (Figure 6.10), click on **Open Extension Code** to view the generated code.

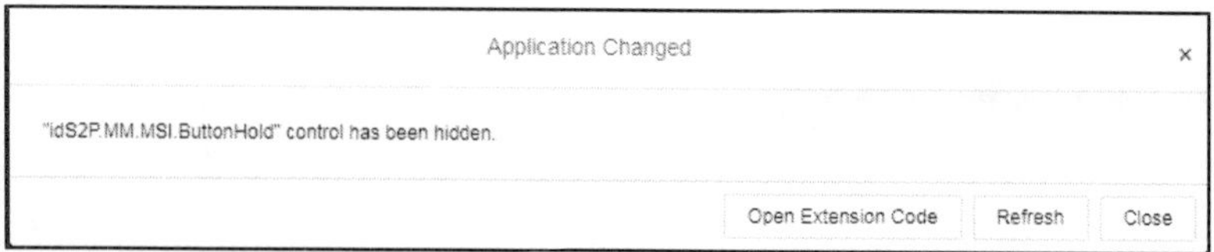

Figure 6.10 Confirmation of Hiding the Control

6. Click on the **Open Extension Code** button to go to *manifest.json* to see the generated code (Figure 6.11).

```
manifest.json  ×

 2        "_version": "1.1.0",
 3 ▾      "sap.app": {
 4            "_version": "1.1.0",
 5            "id": "ui.s2p.mm.supplinvoice.manage.s1.MM_SUPPIV_MANS1Extension",
 6            "type": "application",
 7 ▾          "applicationVersion": {
 8                "version": "1.0"
 9            },
10            "title": "{{appTitle}}"
11        },
12 ▾      "sap.ui": {
13            "_version": "1.1.0",
14            "technology": "UI5",
15 ▾          "icons": {
16                "icon": "",
17                "favIcon": ""
18            },
19 ▾          "deviceTypes": {
20                "desktop": true,
21                "tablet": true,
22                "phone": false
23            },
24 ▾          "supportedThemes": [
25                "sap_hcb,sap_bluecrystal"
26            ]
27        },
28 ▾      "sap.ui5": {
29            "_version": "1.1.0",
30 ▾          "dependencies": {
31                "minUI5Version": "1.40.3"
32            },
33 ▾          "extends": {
34                "component": "ui.s2p.mm.supplinvoice.manage.s1",        →  Component name
35 ▾              "extensions": {
36 ▾                  "sap.ui.viewModifications": {
37 ▾                      "ui.s2p.mm.supplinvoice.manage.s1.view.S1": {   →  View name
38 ▾                          "idS2P.MM.MSI.ButtonHold": {               →  ID of the 'Hold' button
39                                "visible": false                       →  'visible' to false => Hide
40                            }
41                        }
42                    }
43                }
44            },
```

Figure 6.11 Generated Extension Settings in manifest.json (Component Descriptor)

Tip

If the minimum SAPUI5 version supported by the standard application (`sap.ui5/dependencies/minUI5Version`) is less than 1.30, then SAP Web IDE creates extension metadata inside the *Component.js* instead of *manifest.json*.

View Extension

View extensions or extension points are predefined places within SAP-delivered SAPUI5 views where custom controls can be inserted by customers. Developers of SAP-delivered SAP Fiori apps need to carefully consider probable scenarios for providing extension points within the delivered views.

Let's see how to find these extension points, and what they look like in an SAPUI5 view. We'll also look at a few examples of how they're implemented.

Finding Extension Points

The SAP Fiori apps reference library (*https://fioriappslibrary.hana.ondemand.com*) is the best place to find available extensions within an SAP Fiori app. Let's search for extensions points in the SAP-delivered Employee Lookup SAP Fiori app.

Figure 6.12 shows that the Employee Lookup app has 11 **View** extensions and 1 **Controller** extension.

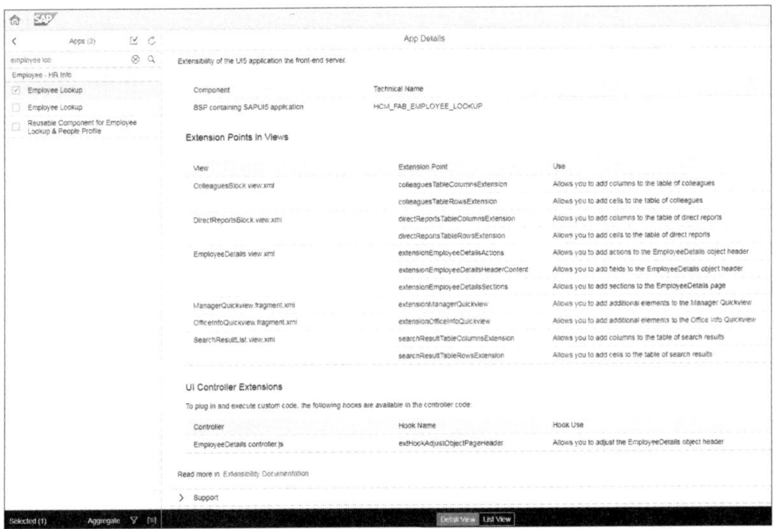

Figure 6.12 SAP Fiori App Reference Library Showing UI Extension Points

Extension Point Examples

The sample code in Listing 6.3 shows how SAP delivers extension points in XML views.

```
<mvc:View xmlns="sap.m" xmlns:mvc="sap.ui.core.mvc" xmlns:core="sap.ui.core">
<core:ExtensionPoint name="ExtensionBefore"/>
<Input type="Number"/>
<core:ExtensionPoint name="ExtensionAfter"/>
</mvc:View>
```

Listing 6.3 Extension Points in a View

Note that extension points have the property `name`, which is used by the framework to uniquely identify an extension point while implementing it. This also means that `name` must be unique within a view.

Extension points can contain default content, so this concept can be used to replace existing controls within a standard SAPUI5 view. Standard application developers can wrap any control in the `<core:ExtensionPoint>` tag and that control or set of controls will be easily replaceable by customers. This also means that content in the `<core:ExtensionPoint>` tag is the default content visible if the customer decides not to implement the extension point.

Listing 6.4 is an example of an extension point with default content.

```
<mvc:View xmlns="sap.m" xmlns:mvc="sap.ui.core.mvc" xmlns:core="sap.ui.core">
<core:ExtensionPoint name="ExtensionReplaceable"/>
<Label text="Name"/>
<Input type="Number"/>
</core:ExtensionPoint/>
</mvc:View>
```

Listing 6.4 An Extension Point with Default Content

In this case, there is a label control and an input control within the extension point, and customers can replace them with their own set of controls.

Implementing an Extension Point

Like view modifications, view enhancements are also implemented by making entries in manifest.json, as shown in Listing 6.5.

```
"sap.ui5":{
  "_version": "1.1.0",
  "dependencies": {
    "minUI5Version": "1.40.3"
  },
  "extends" :{
    "component": "samples.modify",
```

```
    "extensions": {
      "sap.ui.ViewExtesnions": {
          "samples.modify.View.S1": {
            "ExtensionBefore": {
 Classname: "sap.ui.core.Fragment",
 fragmentName: "ext.samples.View.extensionFrag"
    type: "XML"
      },
      "ExtensionReplaceable": {
 Classname: "sap.ui.core.mvc.View",
 ViewName: "ext.samples.View.extensionView1"
 type: "XML"
      }
          }
        }
      }
    }
}
```

Listing 6.5 View Extensions Specified in manifest.json

Let's break down this example:

- Within the extensions property, `sap.ui.ViewExtesnions` indicates the type of view extension we're dealing with.
- The `samples.modify.View.S1` property indicates the name of the view that we're extending.
- `ExtensionBefore` is the name of the extension point.
- Value of property `Classname` indicates if extension is performed using a view or a fragment.
- Next, you can use property `fragmentName` or `ViewName` to specify the name of the fragment or view that will contain the controls of the extension.
- Property `type` indicates the type of view or fragment used for the extension.

Extension points can be implemented using either the extensibility pane or the extensibility wizard. Let's take a look at both methods.

Using the Extensibility Pane

The extensibility pane helps you speed up the implementation of extension points by generating extension metadata in *manifest.json* (or *Component.js*) and by creating an empty XML fragment to contain the extension point content. Let's consider the SAP-provided People Profile SAP Fiori app for implementing an extension point using the extensibility pane.

From the SAP Fiori apps reference library, you can see that there is an **Extension Point** available for the header area of the app in the **Profile.view.xml** as shown in Figure 6.13.

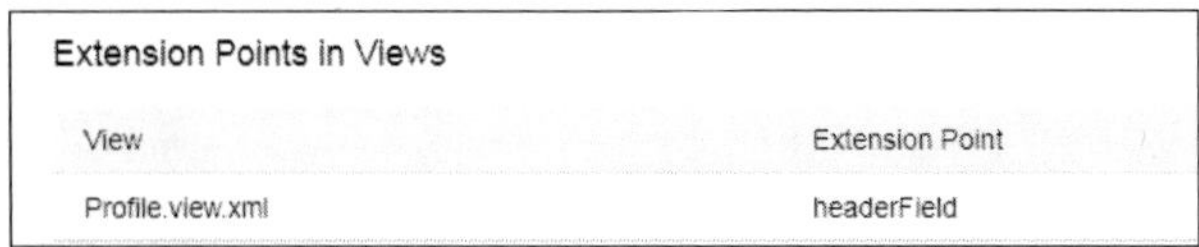

Figure 6.13 Extension Point in the People Profile App

Implementing this extension involves creating an extension project and working with the extensibility pane. Here are the steps involved:

1. Create an extension project from the People Profile app.
2. Open the extensibility pane, and switch to **Extensibility Mode**.
3. In the **Outline** panel, open **Profile View**, and select the available extension.
4. Click on the **Extend** button, and choose **Extend View/Fragment** (see Figure 6.14).

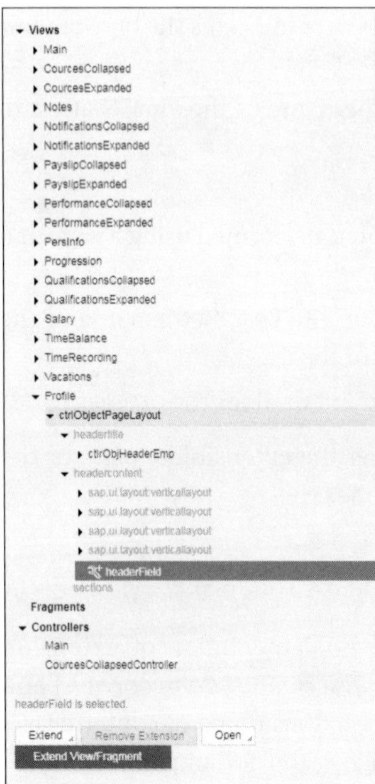

Figure 6.14 Implementing an Extension Point Using the Extensibility Pane

5. Click on **Open Extension Code** in the subsequent popup shown in Figure 6.15.

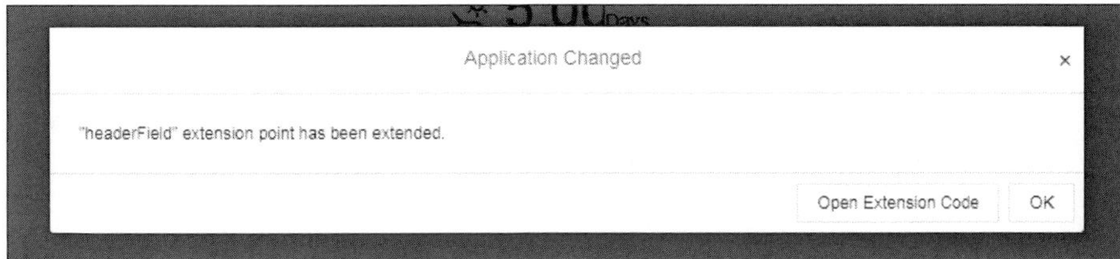

Figure 6.15 Clicking on the Open Extension Code Button to See the Generated Default Code

You can see the generated fragment, and it also provides sample content as commented code (Figure 6.16).

```
Component.js  ×      Profile_headerFieldCustom.frag...  ×

1 ▾ <core:FragmentDefinition xmlns:core="sap.ui.core" xmlns:suite="sap.suite.ui.commons" xmlns:bl="sap.uxap.blocks" xmlns:f="sap.ui.layout.form"
2       xmlns:html="http://www.w3.org/1999/xhtml" xmlns:layout="sap.ui.layout" xmlns:m="sap.m" xmlns:mvc="sap.ui.core.mvc"
3       xmlns:pp="hcm.people.profile.blocks" xmlns:uxap="sap.uxap" xmlns:viz="sap.viz.ui5.controls">
4       <!-- This extension point can be used to add fields to uxap:headerContent -->
5       <!--<layout:VerticalLayout xmlns:layout="sap.ui.layout">
6             <m:Label xmlns:m="sap.m" id="lblCountryLocation_clone"/>
7             <m:Label xmlns:m="sap.m" id="lblTime_clone"/>
8          </layout:VerticalLayout> -->
9    </core:FragmentDefinition>
```

Figure 6.16 Generated Fragment with Commented Default Code

Because the minimum required SAPUI5 version of the People Profile app must be earlier than version 1.30, the extension metadata gets created within the *Component.js* instead of *manifest.json*. See Figure 6.17 for the generated metadata.

Tip

If your current SAPUI5 landscape version is higher or equal to 1.30, you can manually move the generated extension metadata from *Component.js* to *manifest.json*.

6. Uncomment the available sample in Figure 6.16, and provide texts to labels.

7. Reopen the **Extensibility Mode**, or run the project to see the results. See Figure 6.18 for details.

```
Component.js  ×    Profile_headerFieldCustom.frag...  ×

 1   jQuery.sap.declare("hcm.people.profile.HCM_PEP_PROFILEExtension1.Component");
 2   (function() {
 3       jQuery.sap.registerModulePath("sap.hcm.lib.common", "/sap/bc/ui5_ui5/sap/hcm_common/sap/hcm/lib/common/");
 4   }());
 5   // use the load function for getting the optimized preload file if present
 6   sap.ui.component.load({
 7       name: "hcm.people.profile",
 8       // Use the below URL to run the extended application when SAP-delivered application is deployed on SAPUI5 ABAP Repository
 9       url: "/sap/bc/ui5_ui5/sap/HCM_PEP_PROFILE" // we use a URL relative to our own component
10           // extension application is deployed with customer namespace
11   });
12   this.hcm.people.profile.Component.extend("hcm.people.profile.HCM_PEP_PROFILEExtension1.Component", {
13       metadata: {
14           version: "1.0",
15           config: {},
16           customizing: {
17               "sap.ui.viewExtensions": {
18                   "hcm.people.profile.view.Profile": {
19                       "headerField": {
20                           "className": "sap.ui.core.Fragment",
21                           "fragmentName": "hcm.people.profile.HCM_PEP_PROFILEExtension1.view.Profile_headerFieldCustom",
22                           "type": "XML"
23                       }
24                   }
25               }
26           }
27       }
28   });
```

```
"sap.ui5": {
    "_version": "1.1.0",
    "dependencies": {
        "minUI5Version": "1.28.5"
    },
```

Figure 6.17 Extension Metadata Auto-Generated within Component.js

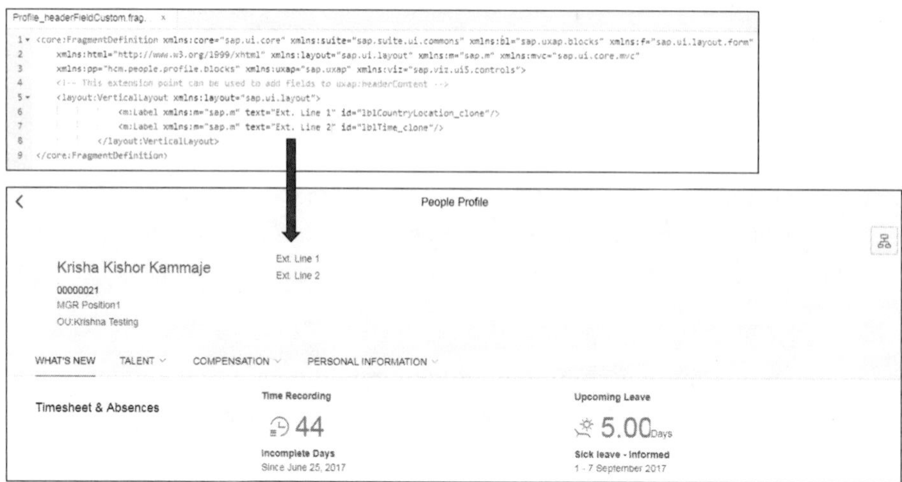

Figure 6.18 Result of Implementing the Extension Point

Tip

If you have a complex implementation involving more controls and lots of controller logic, you can choose to implement the extension point using a view (instead of a fragment). In this case, you need to manually code the extension metadata and view/controller because the SAP Web IDE always generates a fragment.

Using the Extensibility Wizard

The SAP Web IDE extensibility wizard can also be used to implement an extension point by following these steps:

1. Create an extension project if it doesn't already exist.

2. Create a new extension using the context menu on the extension project as shown in Figure 6.19.

Figure 6.19 Creating a New Extension

3. Confirm the **Extension Project** in which the new extension is to be created on the screen shown in Figure 6.20. Click **Next**.

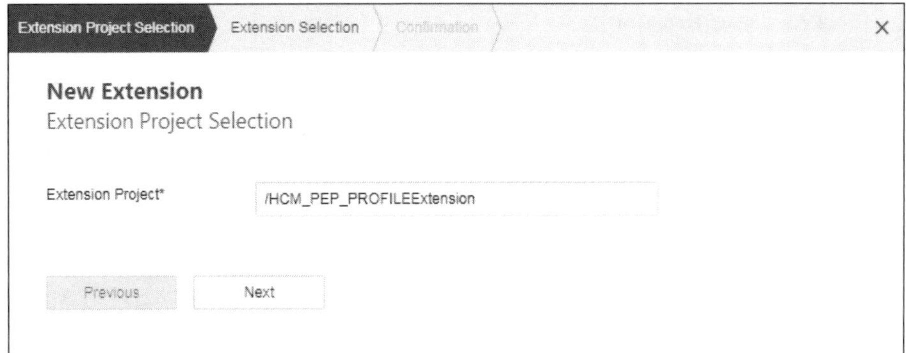

Figure 6.20 Extension Project for the Extension

4. Select **Extend View/Fragment** in the next screen (shown in Figure 6.21) and click **Next**.

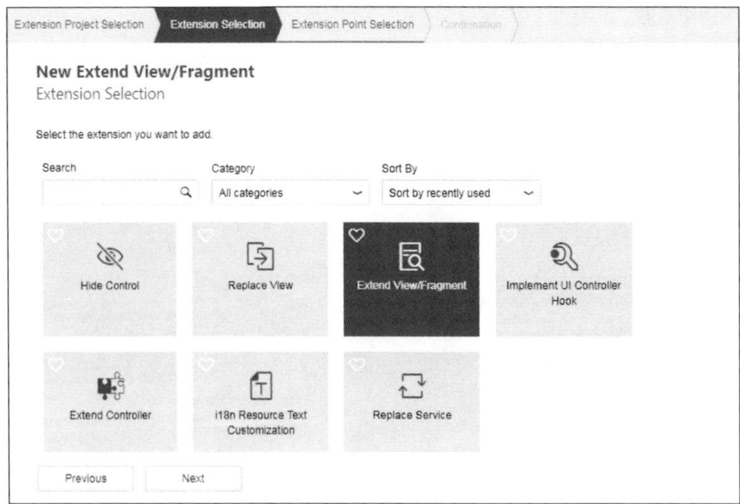

Figure 6.21 Selection for Implementing an Extension Point

5. In the next screen shown in Figure 6.22, select the **View** that needs to be extended. If there are no extensions available within the selected view, a message indicates it.

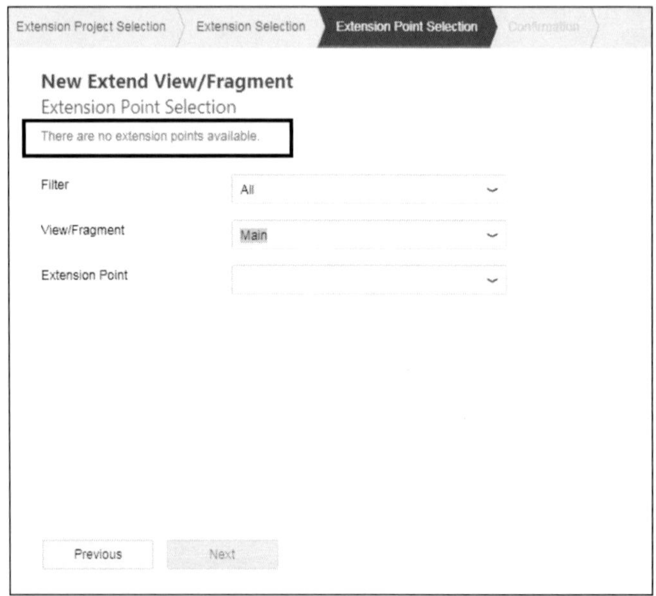

Figure 6.22 Message Indicating There Are No Extension Points Available

Figure 6.23 indicates the available extension points in a view. Select one from the **Extension Point** field, and click **Next**.

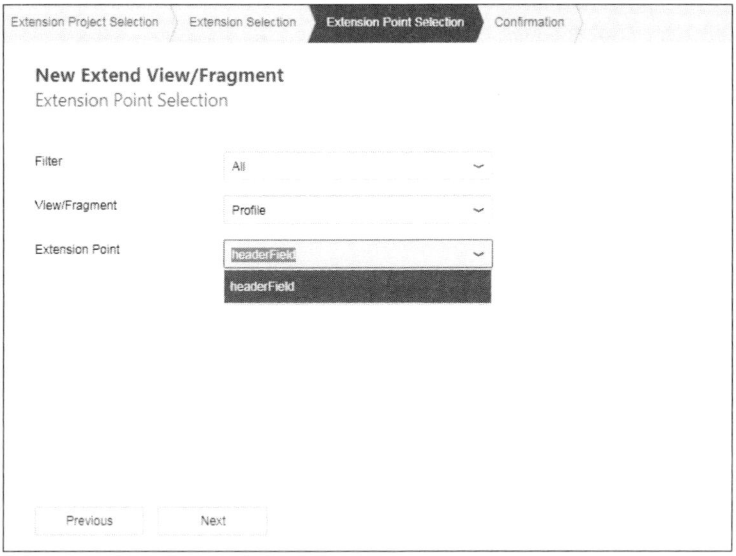

Figure 6.23 One Extension Point Available within the Profile View

6. Click **Finish** in the next screen.

Just like the extensibility pane, the wizard also creates extension metadata and a fragment with default content for the developer to code.

View Replacement

It's very common to not have extension points to all the extension scenarios you need. This can be because you have a unique scenario or the product developer at SAP didn't foresee your requirements.

When you have scenarios that can't be achieved by view modification or view extension, you can replace the SAPUI5 view with your own custom view. Because this is a custom view, you'll have all the freedom to edit the view per your requirements.

> **Warning**
>
> When you do a view replacement, you'll no longer see the effect of bug fixes that SAP releases on the replaced view because the SAP-delivered view is ignored, and only the custom view is considered by the framework. Therefore, it's wise to implement all the SAP Notes relevant to the SAP Fiori app, copy the SAP-delivered view into your custom view, and make the required changes. This way all the known defects until the time of extension are addressed. Because of this, a view replacement should be considered only if no other extension can fulfill the custom requirement.

Unlike extension points, any view can be replaced by a custom view in the extension application. Like other extensions, component metadata (in *Component.js* or *manifest.json*) will indicate if any views have been replaced in the extension app.

Listing 6.6 from the component metadata shows how a replaced view is represented.

```
"sap.ui.ViewReplacements": {
    "samples.modify.View.S1": {
        "ViewName": "ext.samples.View.S1",
        "type": "XML"
    }
}
```

Listing 6.6 View Replacement Configuration in manifest.json

Let's break down this example:

- `sap.ui.ViewReplacements` indicates the type of the enhancement as the view replacement.
- `samples.modify.View.S1` is the original view in the standard application, while `ext.samples.View.S1` is the name of the replacing view.
- `type` is the type of the replacing view.

To perform a view replacement using the extensibility pane, follow these steps:

1. Create a new extension project.
2. Open the extensibility pane, and select **Extensibility Mode**.
3. From the **Outline** pane, select the view, and then select **Extend • Replace with a copy of the original view** (Figure 6.24).

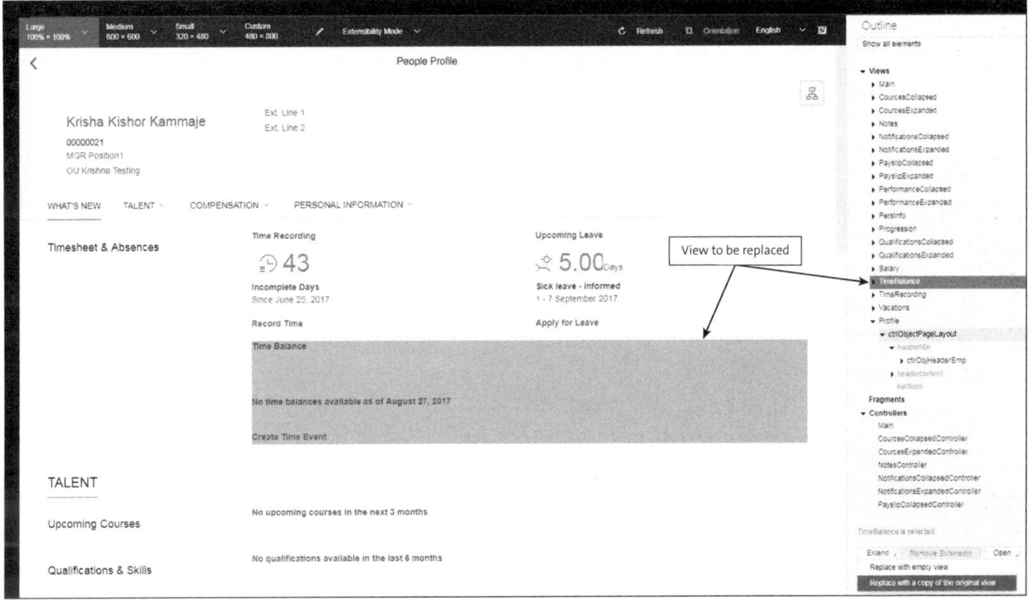

Figure 6.24 Selecting and Replacing a View in the Extensibility Pane

4. A popup appears, as shown in Figure 6.25, indicating the new view that was created. It also warns that any new changes made to the original view (by SAP Notes or upgrades) won't be reflected in the new custom view.

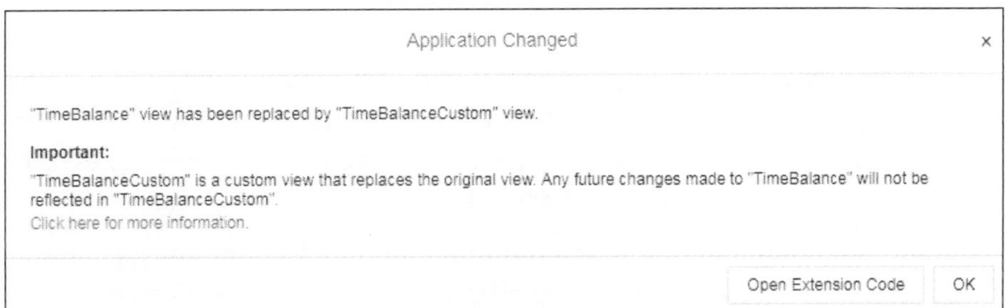

Figure 6.25 Popup Providing Extension Information

The new view has been created along with a new folder called **blocks** (see Figure 6.26).

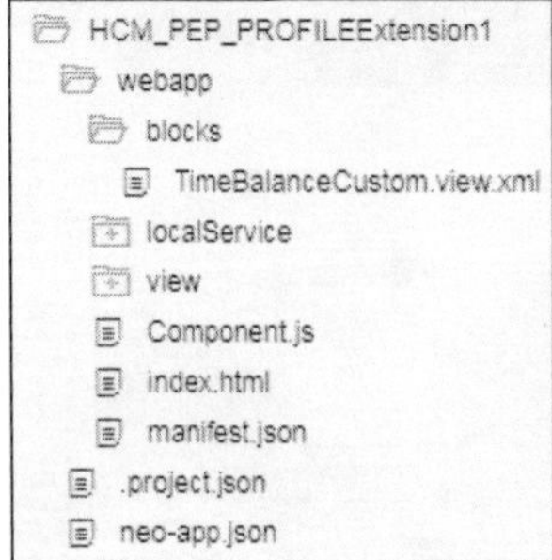

Figure 6.26 New Blocks Folder and the New Replacement View

Figure 6.27 shows the generated metadata for the recent view replacement. Although the type of the extended view here is **XML**, you can manually create other types of views to replace existing views.

```
"sap.ui.viewReplacements": {
    "hcm.people.profile.blocks.TimeBalance": {
        "viewName": "hcm.people.profile.HCM_PEP_PROFILEExtension1.blocks.TimeBalanceCustom",
        "type": "XML"
    }
}
```

Figure 6.27 Metadata Generated for the View Replacement

Controller Extension

SAPUI5's controller extension object allows you to extend the functionality of a controller by creating a custom controller with additional functionality. At runtime, both controllers are merged, and the functionalities of both controllers are available. However, if both controllers have methods with the same names, then methods from the custom controller will override those of the standard controller.

Let us see how controller extensions work and how is it different than the inheritance concept of object-oriented programing. Let us also explore how to identify and implement controller hooks, the predefined enhancement options provided by SAP.

Merging Controllers

Merging controllers (or controller extensions) is a powerful extension method that allows you to add new methods (new functionality) to the controller and override current methods (change functionality).

Listing 6.7 shows how a controller extension is implemented.

```
customizing: {
    "sap.ui.ControllerExtensions": {
"samples.modify.View.S1": {
            ControllerName: "ext.samples.Controller.S1"
        }
    }
```

Listing 6.7 Specifying a Controller Extension in Component.js

The preceding metadata in the component results in merging controllers `samples.modify.View.S1` and `ext.samples.Controller.S1` (extension).

Figure 6.28 shows how the non-lifecycle methods are treated when same name methods are available in both standard and extended (custom) controllers.

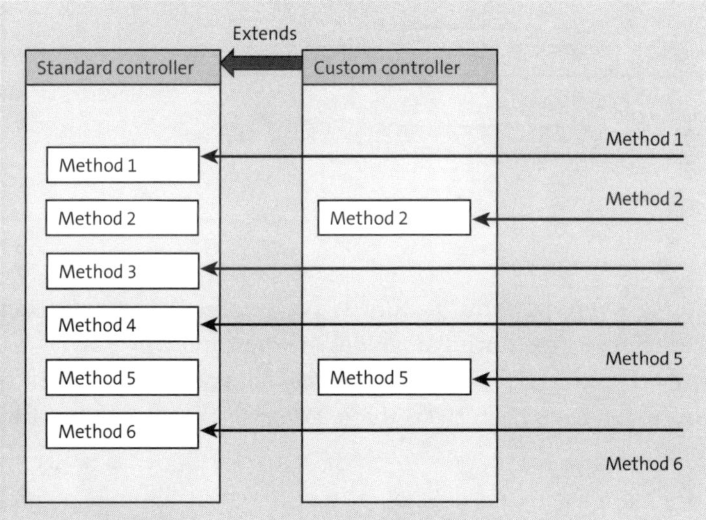

Figure 6.28 Controller Extension Impact on Non-lifecycle Methods

Methods from both the controllers are available to be called during the runtime. If the extended controller has a method which has the same name as one of the methods in the standard controller, then method in the extended controller will be called (like if the standard controller's method is overwritten). This is very similar to inheritance concept in classes, however, there are significant differences when it comes to the lifecycle methods of the controller.

Figure 6.29 shows how the controller's lifecycle methods are called in an extension scenario. For the `onInit` and `onAfterRendering` methods, the custom controller's methods are called after the standard controller. For `onBeforeRendering` and `onExit`, the custom controller's methods are called before that of the standard controller.

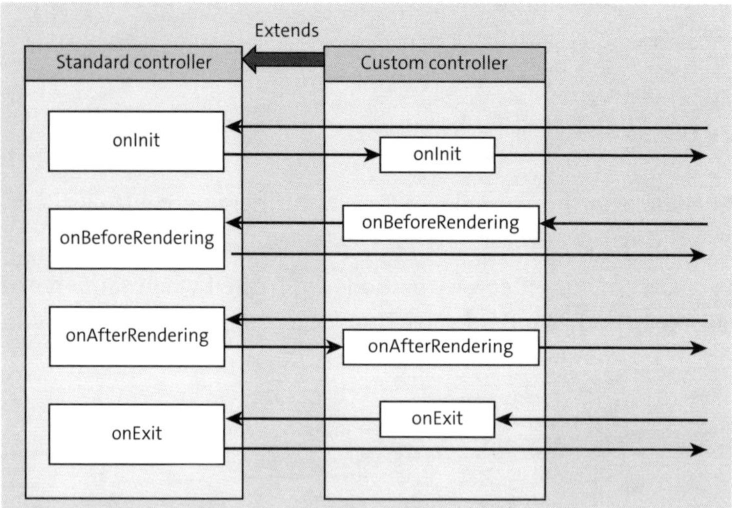

Figure 6.29 Order of Call of Controller's Lifecycle Methods in an Extension Scenario

Controller Hooks

Controller extension is a very powerful feature as you've seen. However, it can break in several scenarios such as during upgrades or when applying SAP Notes. This is because SAP Fiori product developers at SAP may not know how and which methods of the controller have been overridden. *Controller hooks* are used to address this situation.

Controller hooks are like view extension points that are available only at predefined places in the controller. SAP ensures that the applications using these hooks will be stable through upgrades and updates.

Listing 6.8 shows how a controller hook is defined within a standard controller. In this example, this piece of code decides what to show as a person's profile picture.

```
if (this.customProfilePicture){
    this.customProfilePicture(oPerson);
}
else{
    this.defaultProfilePicture();
}
```

Listing 6.8 customProfilePicture, a Controller Hook

customProfilePicture is the name of the method (hook), which is defined but not implemented in the standard controller. The standard controller checks if the method is implemented by the extension controller. If yes, then that method will be called, and the customer can have the code to fetch the person's profile picture within this hook implementation. If the method isn't implemented, that is, no hook extension is defined, then the standard controller calls a method to get the default profile picture.

Listing 6.9 shows how a hook is implemented in an extension controller. This is the same as how any method is defined in a controller. First you'll create a custom controller as an extension of the standard controller and define the method called customProfilePicture to fetch the profile picture.

```
customProfilePicture: function(oData){
    //Code to get profile picture
}
```

Listing 6.9 Implementing a Controller Hook

Next, we'll cover how to find controller hooks and implement them using the extensibility pane.

Finding Controller Hooks

Just like view extensions, controller hooks/extensions are also documented in the SAP Fiori app reference library. In Figure 6.30, you see the list of controller extensions for the My Leave Request (Version 2) app.

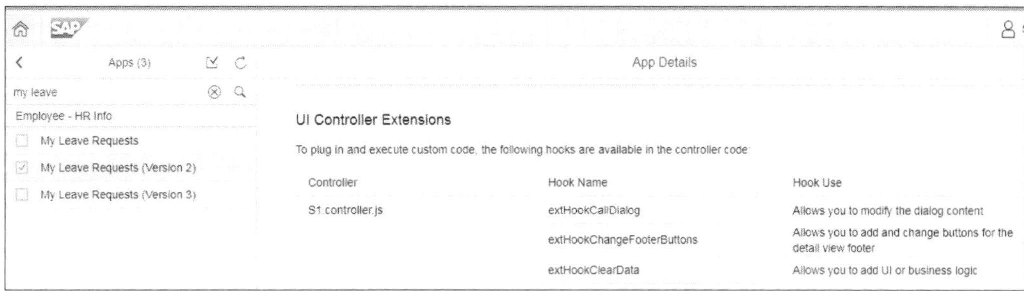

Figure 6.30 Documented Controller Hooks in the SAP Fiori App Reference Library

Using the My Leave Request app, consider a scenario where we need to add a new button in the initial screen (**S1 View**) as an extension.

As you can see in Figure 6.31, a hook named extHookChangeFooterButtons is available to add or remove buttons in the footer. This is from the standard controller.

```
S1-dbg.controller.js  ×

 1 ▾ /*
 2      * Copyright (C) 2009-2014 SAP SE or an SAP affiliate company. All rights reserved
 3      */
 4     jQuery.sap.require("sap.ca.scfld.md.controller.BaseFullscreenController");
 5     jQuery.sap.require("hcm.myleaverequest.utils.Formatters");
 6     jQuery.sap.require("hcm.myleaverequest.utils.UIHelper");
 7     jQuery.sap.require("sap.m.MessageBox");
 8     jQuery.sap.require("hcm.myleaverequest.utils.DataManager");
 9     jQuery.sap.require("hcm.myleaverequest.utils.ConcurrentEmployment");
10     jQuery.sap.require("hcm.myleaverequest.utils.CalendarTools");
11     jQuery.sap.require("sap.ca.ui.dialog.factory");
12     jQuery.sap.require("sap.ca.ui.dialog.Dialog");
13     jQuery.sap.require("sap.m.MessageToast");
14     jQuery.support.useFlexBoxPolyfill = false;
15     jQuery.sap.require("sap.ca.ui.model.format.FileSizeFormat");
16     jQuery.sap.require("sap.ca.ui.message.message");
17     jQuery.sap.require("sap.ui.thirdparty.sinon");
18     //jQuery.sap.require("sap.m.UploadCollectionParameter");
19     //jQuery.sap.require("sap.m.UploadCollection");
20
21     /*global hcm window setTimeout sinon:true*/
22 ▾ sap.ca.scfld.md.controller.BaseFullscreenController.extend("hcm.myleaverequest.view.S1", {
23
24         extHookChangeFooterButtons: null,
25         extHookRouteMatchedHome: null,
26         extHookRouteMatchedChange: null,          ┐
27         extHookClearData: null,                   │
28         extHookInitCalendar: null,                │
29         extHookTapOnDate: null,                   ├─ Declaring the hooks
30         extHookSetHighlightedDays: null,          │
31         extHookDeviceDependantLayout: null,       │
32         extHookSubmit: null,                      │
33         extHookOnSubmitLRCfail: null,             │
34         extHookOnSubmitLRCsuccess: null,          │
35         extHookCallDialog: null,                  ┘
36
37 ▾     onInit: function() {
38             sap.ca.scfld.md.controller.BaseFullscreenController.prototype.onInit.call(this);
39             this.oApplication = this.oApplicationFacade.oApplicationImplementation;
```

```
S1-dbg.controller.js  ×

185     |
186 ▾       /**
187          * @ControllerHook Modify the footer buttons
188          * This hook method can be used to add and change buttons for the detail view footer
189          * It is called when the decision options for the detail item are fetched successfully
190          * @callback hcm.myleaverequest.view.S1~extHookChangeFooterButtons
191          * @param {object} Header Footer Object
192          * @return {object} Header Footer Object
193          */
194 ▾       if (this.extHookChangeFooterButtons) {
195             this.objHeaderFooterOptions = this.extHookChangeFooterButtons(this.objHeaderFooterOptions);
196         }
197     },                                            ◄── Using the hooks
198
```

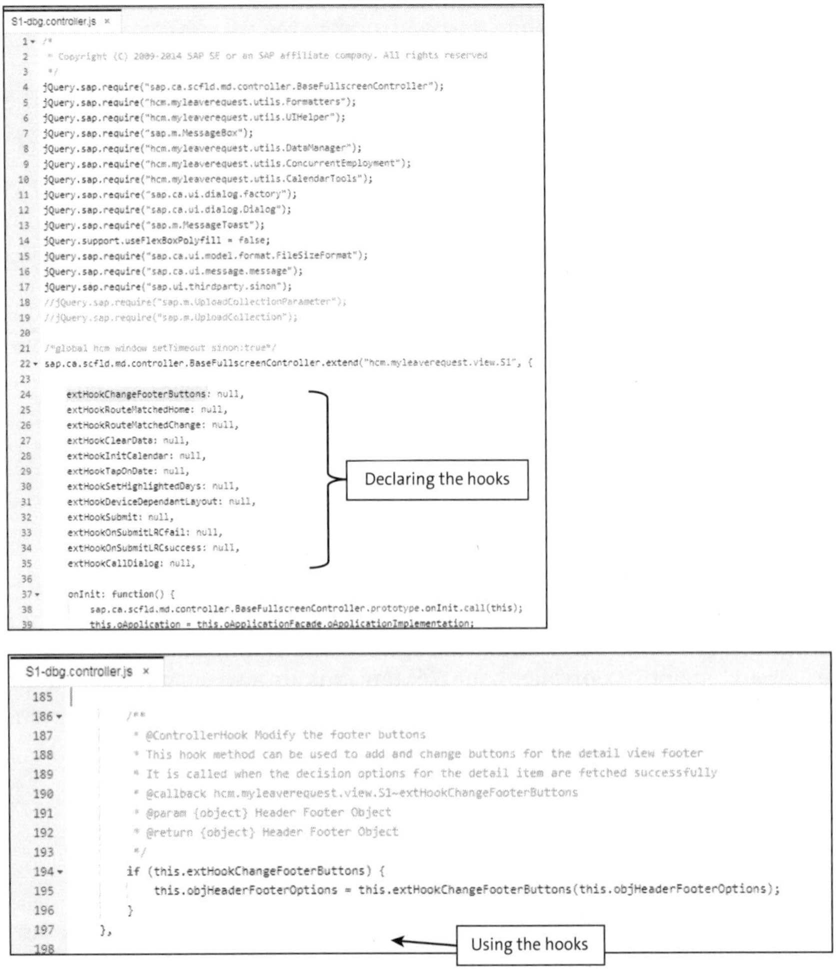

Figure 6.31 Hook Declaration and Usage in the Standard Controller

Using the Extensibility Pane

Let's use the extensibility pane to implement the hook by following these steps:

1. Create a new extension project.

2. Open the extensibility pane, and select **Extensibility Mode**.

3. From the **Outline** pane, select the hook **extHookChangeFooterButtons** under **Views • S1**.

4. Click the **Extend** dropdown button, and choose **Extend UI Controller Hook** as shown in Figure 6.32.

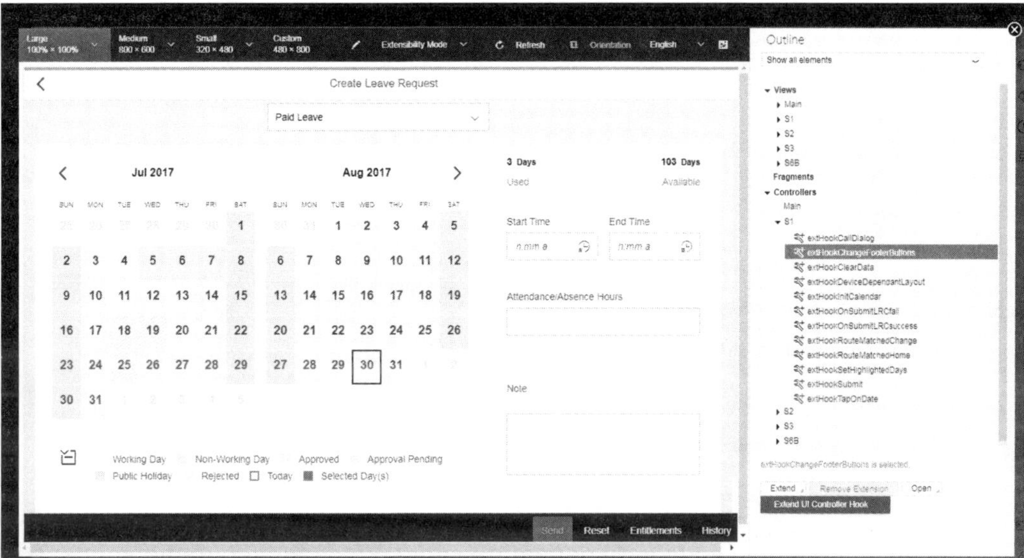

Figure 6.32 Implementing a Controller Hook

5. In the popup that appears, select **Open Extension Code** to view the generated code.

It has created a controller extension by creating custom controller `hcm.myleaverequest.HCM_LRQ_CREExtension.View.S1Custom` and specified it in the component metadata. The generated controller has defined an empty method with called `extHookChangeFooterButtons`. This method gets an array as the input that contains all the buttons to be shown on the screen's footer.

Figure 6.33 shows the generated artifacts while implementing a controller extension. A new extension controller, `S1Custom.controller.js`, was created along with an empty hook implementation for extension hook `extHookChangeFooterButtons`. In the component metadata, a new entry was added under customizing, to inform the SAPUI5 runtime about the controller extension.

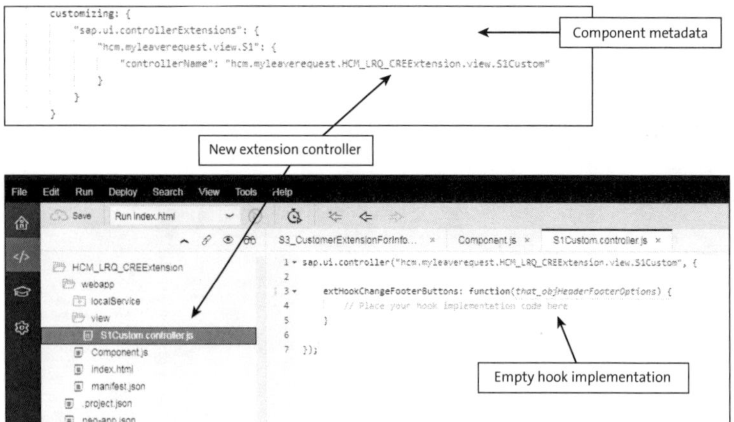

Figure 6.33 Generated Code/Controller for the Hook Implementation

6. Write the code to add the button, and run the extension project. Figure 6.34 shows the extension code and the result.

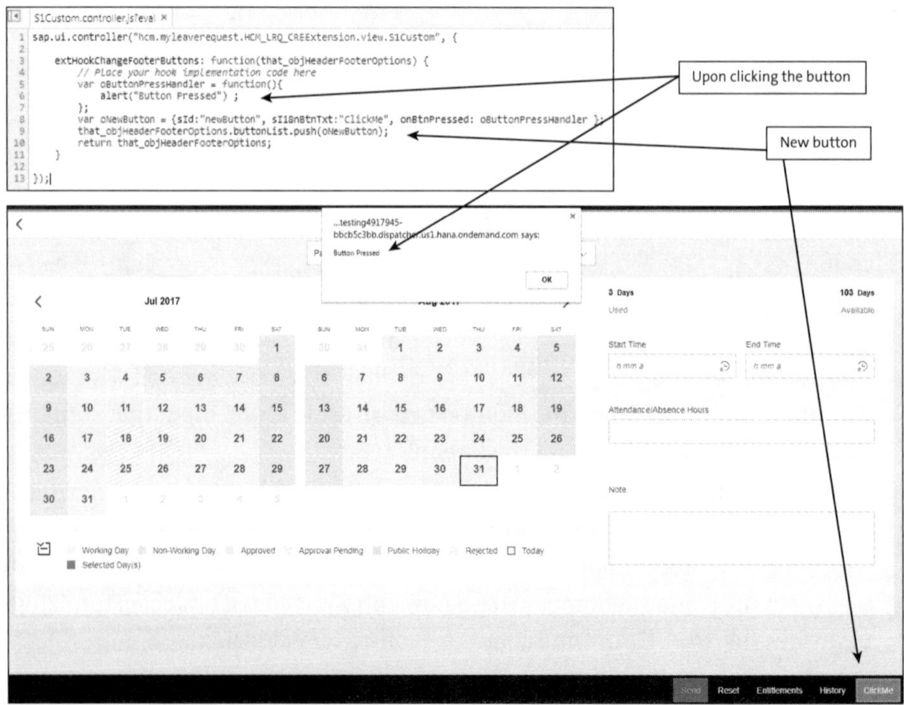

Figure 6.34 Hook Extension Code and the Result

Controller Replacement

Consider a scenario where you want to enhance a controller, but you don't want to use any of the controller's lifecycle methods. In this case, you can use the controller replacement strategy, in which the existing controller is completely replaced by a new custom controller. Controller replacement can be achieved using configuration options; however, this option isn't currently supported using SAP Web IDE's extensibility wizard.

The component metadata in Listing 6.10 can replace a standard controller with a custom controller.

```
customizing: {
    "sap.ui.ControllerReplacements": {
        "ui.ssuite.s2p.mm.pur..View.S2": "ui.ssuite.s2p.mm.pur.MM_PR_PRCS1Extension_
v1.View.S2Custom"
    }
```

Listing 6.10 Controller Replacement Configuration in manifest.json

In Listing 6.10, `ui.ssuite.s2p.mm.pur.View.S2` is the name of the standard controller, while `ui.ssuite.s2p.mm.pur.MM_PR_PRCS1Extension_v1.View.S2Custom` is the controller in the extension application that will replace the standard controller.

Typed Controllers and Extension

One of the limitations of controller extension configuration (merging controllers) concept is not supported for typed controllers. Typed controllers are the ones which are defined using `extend` keyword as shown in Listing 6.11. Listing 6.11 shows examples of both typed and non-typed controllers.

```
// This is not a 'Typed' controller
sap.ui.controller("samples.components.standard.sap.Main", {
        onInit: function() { /* do something */ },
        function1: function() { /* do something */ },
        function2: function() { /* do something */ },
        onExit: function() { /* do something */ }
});

//This is a 'Typed' controller
sap.ui.define([
    "sap/ui/core/mvc/Controller"
], function(Controller) {
    "use strict";
```

```
    return Controller.extend("samples.components.standard.sap.Main", {
        onInit: function() { /* other code */ },
        function1: function() { /* other code */ },
        function2: function() { /* other code */ },
        onExit: function() { /* other code */ }
    });
});
```

Listing 6.11 Typed and Non-typed Controllers

In the case of typed controllers, controller replacement has to be used for extending it. Here are the steps involved.

1. Create a new controller, which extends the SAP-delivered typed controller.

2. Note that even though the new controller extends the standard controller, lifecycle functions of the standard controller will not be called by the SAPUI5 runtime. If you need to call those methods, you can call them using the apply API as shown in Listing 6.12.

```
sap.ui.define([
    "samples/components/standard/sap/Main"
], function(StandardController) {
    "use strict";

    return StandardController.extend("samples.components.ext.cust.CustomMain", {
        onInit: function() {
    //Calling standard controller's init
            StandardController.prototype.onInit.apply(this, arguments);
            /* other code */
        },
    //This function overwrites the function
    //with the same name in the standard controller
    function1: function() {
        /* other code */
    },
        onExit: function() {
            /* other code */
    //Calling standard controller's onExit
            CustomController.prototype.onExit.apply(this, arguments);
        }
    });
});
```

Listing 6.12 Replacement Controller Calling the Standard Controller's Lifecycle Method

In the Component Configuration, specify the controller replacement as shown in Listing 6.13.

```
customizing: {
    "sap.ui.controllerReplacements": {
        "samples.components.standard.sap.Main": "samples.components.ext.cust.CustomM
ain"
    }
```

Listing 6.13 Component Configuration for Controller Replacement

Translation Extension

At times, you might need to change the labels and strings within an SAP-delivered SAPUI5 application. You may also want to add new strings and labels for your new view extension.

By performing an i18n resource text customization extension, SAP Web IDE allows you to copy the *i18n* folder of the standard application into the extension app. You can add more strings or edit the existing strings. These strings in the extension app will take precedence over those in the standard app.

You can create an i18n resource text customization extension by following these steps:

1. Create an extension project that refers to an SAP-delivered SAP Fiori app.
2. Create an extension by using the context menu of the project and then clicking **New • Extension**.
3. Confirm the **Extension Project** name.
4. In the available extensions, select **i18n Resource Text Customization** (Figure 6.35).
5. Click on **Finish** in the subsequent screen.

This will copy the *i18n* folder from the standard app into the extension app. Now you can make your changes in these files and push the changes to the SAP Gateway server.

A new entry will be created in the component metadata to refer to the new location (within the extension application) for fetching the strings (see Listing 6.14).

```
config: {
    "sap.ca.i18Nconfigs": {
      "bundleName": "hcm.myteamcalendar.ZHCM_TEAM_CAL.i18n.i18n"
    }
}
```

Listing 6.14 Generated Configuration to Instruct the SAPUI5 Runtime to Fetch the i18n Files from the Extension Application

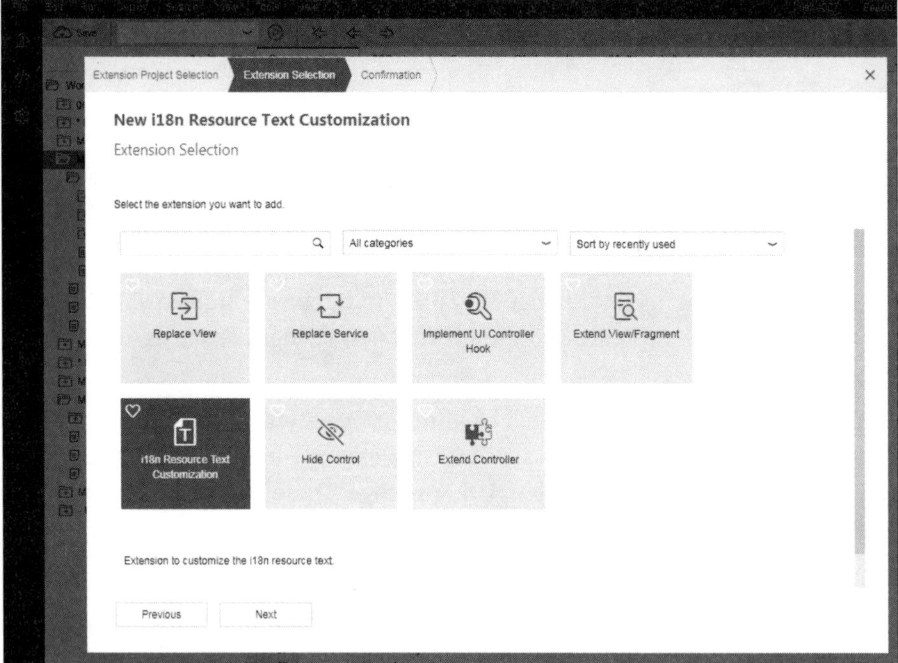

Figure 6.35 Selecting the Option for Translation Extension

Note

In this extension, though SAP Web IDE copies all the i18n files into extension project, it is not needed. You can choose to have only one i18n file with the changed i18n keys and texts in the extension project. The SAPUI5 runtime will look for texts in the i18n file of the extension project first. If it does not find the key, then the SAPUI5 runtime will fetch the text from the standard application.

Service Replacement

When you extend the SAP Fiori app's OData service, you'll end up having a new OData service in the customer's namespace. To make the SAP Fiori app use the new service, you must create an extension. The metadata of the newly created extension app will represent the new service to be used.

Perform a replace service extension by following these steps:

1. Create a new extension project that refers to the standard application.
2. Right-click on the extension project, and choose **New • Extension**.
3. Confirm the **Extension Project** name, and click **Next**.
4. In the **Extension Selection** screen, choose **Replace Service** as shown in Figure 6.36.

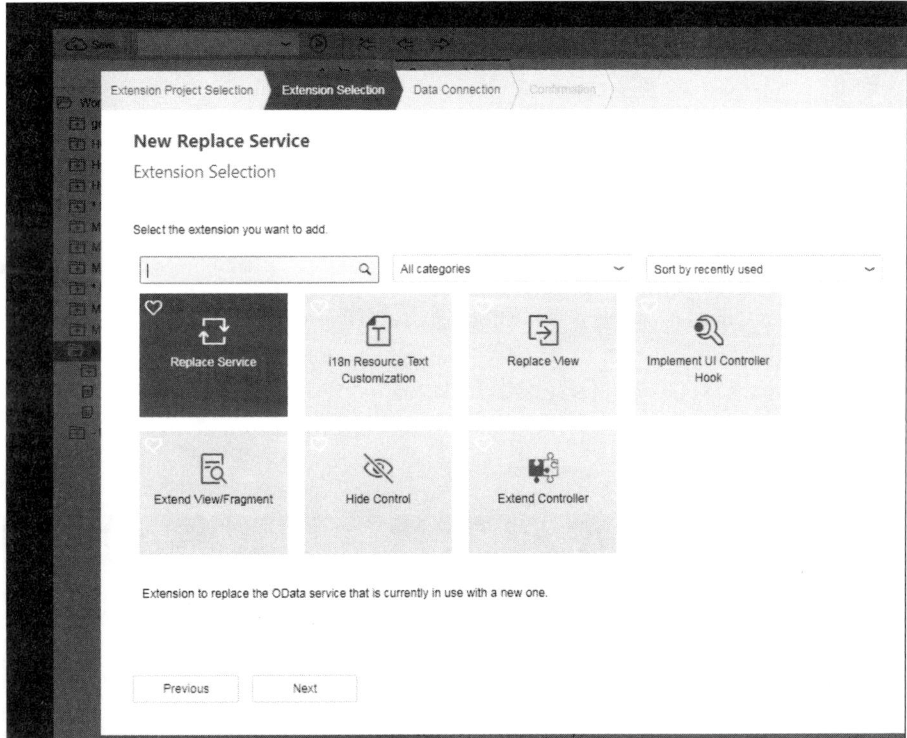

Figure 6.36 Choosing the Replace Service Extension

5. Here you have multiple ways to choose your replacement service:
   - **Service Catalog**: You can select one of the SAP Gateway destinations, and a catalog of all the OData services exposed by that server will be shown as in Figure 6.37.

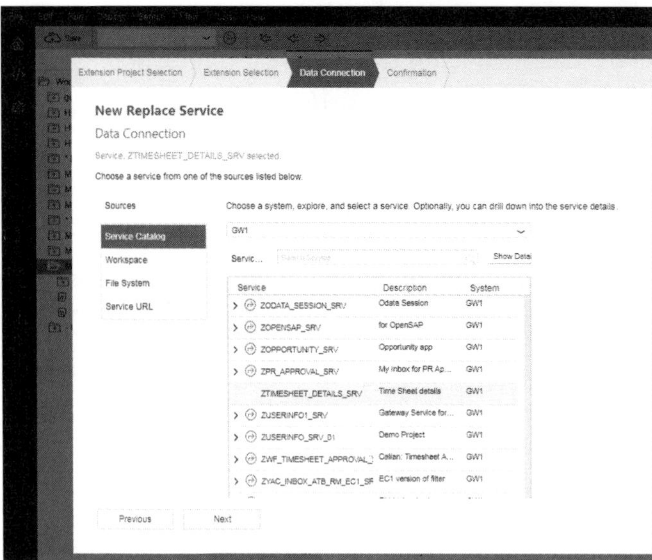

Figure 6.37 Selecting a Replacement Service from Service Catalog

> – **Workspace**: You can select an XML file from one of the folders in the SAP Web IDE workspace. This XML file must contain the metadata of an OData service (see Figure 6.38).

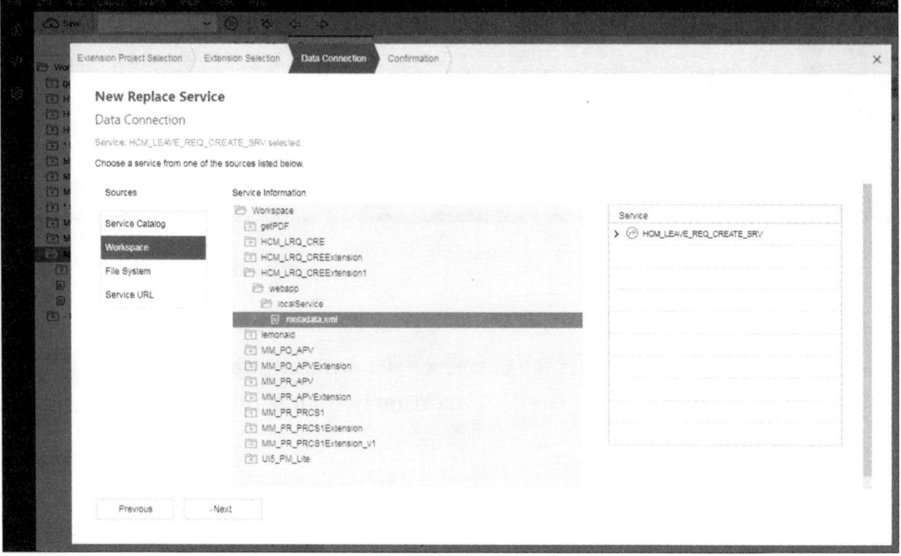

Figure 6.38 Selecting an OData Metadata File from a Folder in the SAP Web IDE Workspace

– **File System**: In this option, you can choose an OData metadata file from your local PC's file system (see Figure 6.39).

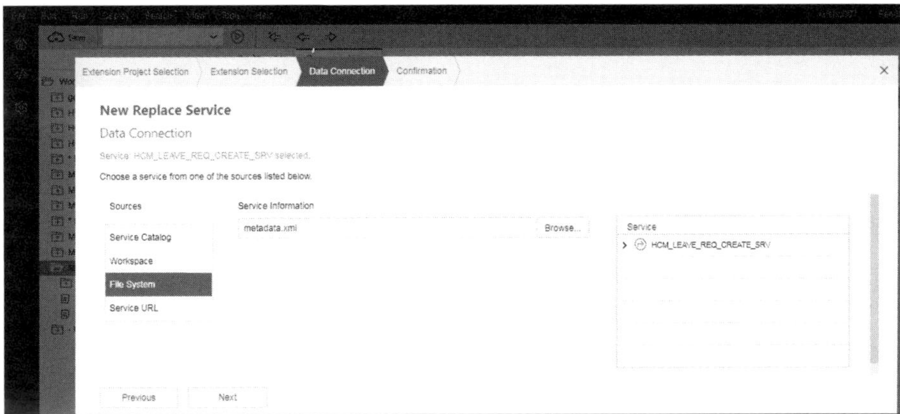

Figure 6.39 Selecting a Metadata File from the Local PC's File System

– **Service URL**: Similar to the **Service Catalog** option, you choose an SAP Gateway server destination and provide a relative URL of the location of the OData service. In Figure 6.40, the same service as chosen in the **Service Catalog** option is chosen.

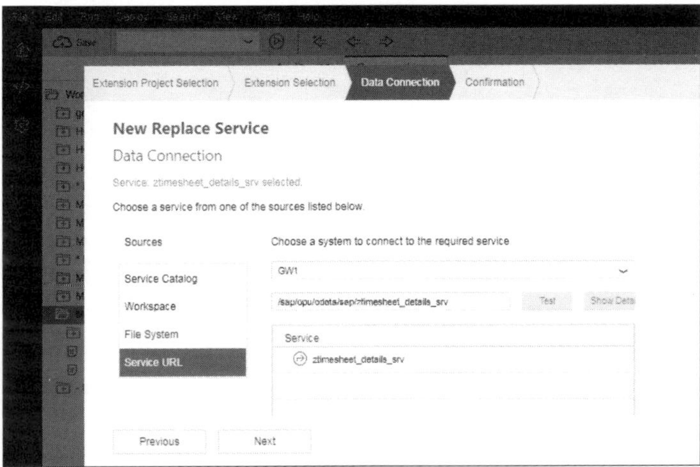

Figure 6.40 Selecting a Service by Providing the Service URL

6. After you make your choice of source, click **Next**. Then click **Finish** in the next screen to complete the process.

The standard app had the configurations shown in Listing 6.15 in the `manifest.json` at `sap.app.dataSources`.

```json
"dataSources": {
    "MM_PUR_PR_PROCESS": {
        "uri": "/sap/opu/odata/sap/MM_PUR_PR_PROCESS/",
        "settings": {
            "localUri": "model/mockData/metadata.xml"
        }
    }
}
```

Listing 6.15 Configuration for OData Service Specification in the Standard Application

The extension service has the settings shown in Listing 6.16 generated after Step 5.

```json
"dataSources": {
    "MM_PUR_PR_PROCESS": {
        "uri": "/sap/opu/odata/sap/ZMM_PUR_PR_PROCESSV1_SRV/",
        "settings": {
            "localUri": "./localService/metadata.xml"
        }
    }
}
```

Listing 6.16 Configuration for OData Service Specification in the Extended Application

As you can see, the "uri" property has the replacement service's URL as its value.

Apps that have the minimum-supported SAPUI5 library version as lower than 1.30 will have the extension configured in *Component.js*, as shown in Listing 6.17.

```js
metadata: {
    version: "1.0",
    config: {
        "sap.ca.serviceConfigs": [{
            "name": "GBAPP_POAPPROVAL",
            "serviceUrl": "/sap/opu/odata/sap/ZPO_EX_SRV/",
            "isDefault": true,
            "mockedDataSource": "./localService/metadata.xml"
        }]
    }
```

Listing 6.17 Generated Component Metadata within the Component.js for SAPUI5 Versions Lower than 1.30

When a service is replaced, a new folder named *localService* is created in the extension service that contains the metadata of the replaced service. This can be used to run the application with mock data and generate and edit mock data.

Tip

The new/replacement OData service need not always be an extension of the standard OData service. But because the views are usually dependent on the standard service's model structure (metadata), any incompatible difference in the new service's model will break the app. So, it's convenient to extend the existing standard service.

Adding a Custom View

In addition to the previously discussed extension options, you can also add a new view to the application. This can be for providing an additional functionality to the standard app.

Follow these steps to add a custom view:

1. Create an extension project.
2. In the context menu of **webapp**, select **New • SAPUI5 View**.
3. Provide the **View Type**, **Namespace**, and **View Name** as shown in Figure 6.41.

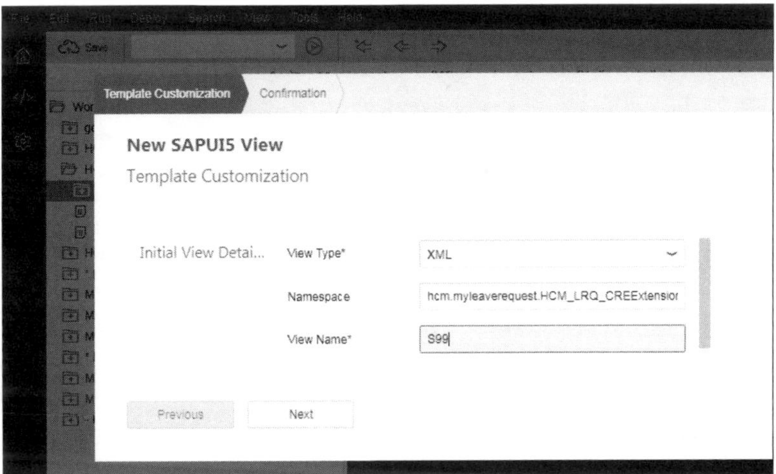

Figure 6.41 Details of the New View to Be Created

4. Click **Finish** in the subsequent screen. One file each for the view and controller is created within the extension application as shown in Figure 6.42.

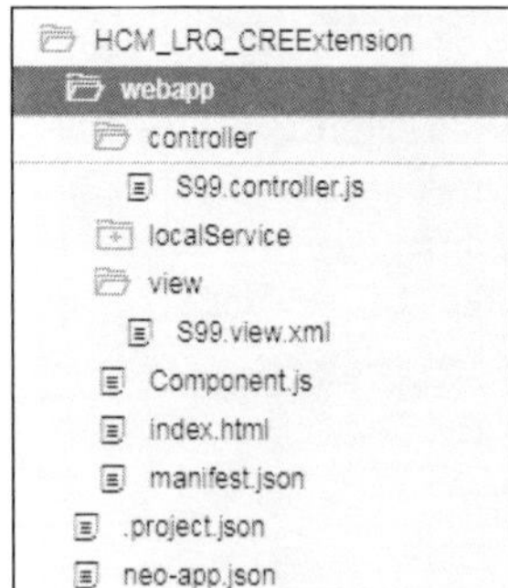

Figure 6.42 Newly Created View and Controller

5. A startup code for both view and controller will be provided, and you can code your actual logic in these files.

Although we've created a view and a controller, there is no way to navigate to the app. Routing configuration needs to be defined suitably in the `sapui5.routing` parameter in the component metadata.

You need to define the triggering button or action that will result in the navigation to the new app. To achieve this you may have to extend the existing view or controller.

Deploying the Extension Application

After the extension project is ready and tested in the preview mode of the controller, you can deploy the application into the application server (SAP Cloud Platform or SAP Gateway Server), so that a new tile can be created for it and can be made available in the SAP Fiori launchpad.

Important Terminology

This chapter covered the following terminology:

- **Controller hooks**
  Controller hooks are predefined and documented enhancement options which are documented and promised to be stable across application lifecycle. A new documented function name is used as a hook, and the developer needs to implement (code) this function in the custom controller.

- **Controller replacement**

  In the controller replacement technique, standard controller is replaced by a custom controller in the extension project. A typed controller can be extended only using this technique.

- **Extension project**

  This is a new SAPUI5 project in a customer's namespace, where all extension-related artifacts are stored. The component of the extension project extends the standard component.

- **Extension point**

  These are predefined places within the SAPUI5 code acting as anchor points for extensions. These are documented and kept safe so that extensions created by customers are safe across upgrades.

- **UI controller hooks**

  This is a type of extension point for the controller. These are methods within the standard controller that allow customers to define its content.

- **View extension**

  View extension is a technique of using extension points to enhance views. An extension point is assigned to a custom view or a fragment, whose content will be plugged into the enhanced view.

- **View modification**

  This is one of the view enhancement techniques which involves changing properties of the view by customizing entries in `manifest.json` file of the app. However, `visible` is the only property that can be influenced with the latest version of SAPUI5.

- **View replacement**

  As the name suggests, this technique is used to replace the standard view with a custom view. Developer has a complete freedom to define content of the custom view. This technique is suitable whenever any of the standard enhancement options do not suit the requirements.

 **Practice Questions**

These practice questions will help you evaluate your understanding of the topics covered in this chapter. The questions shown are similar in nature to those found on the certification examination. Although none of these questions will be found on the exam itself, they will allow you to review your knowledge of the subject. Select the correct answers, and then check the completeness of your answers in the "Practice Question Answers and Explanations" section. Remember, on the exam, you must select all correct answers and only correct answers to receive credit for the question.

1.   An SAP Fiori app's component is made up of which of the following files? (2 correct answers)

□   A. *index.html*

□   B. *Component.js*

□   C. *manifest.json*

□   D. *resources.json*

2.   An SAP Fiori app needs to be available in at least one of these two places for it to be supported by the SAP Web IDE's extensibility wizard while creating an extension project. (2 correct answers)

□   A. SAPUI5 ABAP repository

□   B. Tomcat server

□   C. SAP Cloud Platform

□   D. SAP Web IDE's workspace

3.   The component configuration contains which of the following?

□   A. Default properties of the component

□   B. Information about extensions performed

□   C. Application-related information

□   D. Inheritance information of the component

4.   View modifications can be done only if the SAPUI5 control has an explicit ID.

□   A. True

□   B. False

5.   All extension points within an SAP Fiori app are documented in which of the following?

□   A. *support.launchpad.com*

□   B. *sap.com*

  ☐ C. *answers.sap.com*

  ☐ D. *fioriappslibrary.hana.ondemand.com*

6. When you need to hide a UI element, would you choose view modification or view replacement?

  ☐ A. View modification

  ☐ B. View replacement

7. Which of these isn't a valid option while choosing a replacement service?

  ☐ A. Service URL in a destination

  ☐ B. PC's file system

  ☐ C. Direct URL to an OData service

  ☐ D. Service catalog of an SAP Gateway system

8. When an i18n resource text customization extension is performed, what is the result?

  ☐ A. A new empty *i18n* folder is created on the extension app

  ☐ B. A new *i18n* folder is created on the extension app with content copied from the standard app

9. When you use a controller replacement strategy, which of the following is true about lifecycle methods?

  ☐ A. `onInit` and `onAfterRendering` methods are called after the standard controller while `onBeforeRendering` and `onExit` are called before

  ☐ B. Lifecycle methods aren't called

10. When you want to replace the existing label of a screen element, what is the right extension to use?

  ☐ A. View extension

  ☐ B. Controller extension

  ☐ C. i18n extension

  ☐ D. Extension point

11.   SAPUI5 controller extensions use the inheritance concept. True or False?

☐   A. True

☐   B. False

Practice Answers and Explanations

1.   Correct answers: **B, C**

An SAP Fiori app's component is made up of *Component.js*, which is the component controller, and *manifest.json*, which is the component descriptor containing metadata and other objects.

2.   Correct answers: **A, C**

While creating a new extension project using menu option **File • New • Extension Project**, the extension project can be created only for the applications deployed in SAPUI5 ABAP repository or SAP Cloud Platform.

3.   Correct answer: **B**

The component configuration contains the extension metadata that indicates which extensions are performed on the standard application. Because of this reason, it is recommended to provide IDs to different UI controls wherever possible.

4.   Correct answer: **A**

True. SAPUI5 controls without an explicit ID in the view can't be hidden because the framework can't uniquely identify the control. Because of this reason, it is recommended to provide IDs to different UI controls wherever possible.

5.   Correct answer: **D**

SAP Fiori app reference library (*fioriappslibrary.hana.ondemand.com*) contains a list of extension points for each SAP Fiori app delivered by SAP.

6.   Correct answer: **A**

View modification is the correct choice because view replacement should always be a last option due to various associated caveats. For example, any enhancements/fixes done to the view in the standard view will no longer be available to the extended application.

7.   Correct answer: **C**

The direct URL of an OData service can't be provided as a replacement service. The browser would stop the application from making call to an external service due to same-origin-policy.

8. Correct answer: **B**

   A new *i18n* folder with all the standard content is created. You can change all the existing entries in addition to creating existing entries.

9. Correct answer: **B**

   When you use a controller replacement, the lifecycle methods are never called.

10. Correct answer: **C**

    The i18n extension is used to extend the translation objects. It copies the *i18n* folder to the extension app, and any changes made to the files within the folder are reflected in the app.

11. Correct answer: **B**

    False. SAPUI5 controller extensions do not use the inheritance concept. Rather, they merge both the standard and extension controllers. Methods for both of the controllers are available at the runtime. However, if both controllers have a method with the same name, then the extension controller will overwrite the method of the standard controller.

Take Away

In this chapter, you learned about the concept of extensibility within SAP Fiori and why it's better than modifying an SAP-provided application.

We discussed the role of component metadata in an extension project. You learned that a view can be enhanced in three ways/types, as well as why view replacement should be the last option when extending a view.

Every method in a controller can be extended using a controller extension, but there are risks with controller extensions, so we also discussed why controller hooks should be preferred if available.

We discussed how to perform a translation extension and noted that upon extension, the *i18n* folder and its contents are copied to the extension project.

Replacing an existing OData service with a custom service was explored, including the various options available to specify the custom service.

Throughout performing various extensions, you saw the role of component metadata and how it gets generated by the SAP Web IDE.

Summary

SAPUI5 provides multiple ways to extend an SAP-provided SAP Fiori app. It's important to understand which method is superior when an extension objective can be achieved in more than one way.

In the next chapter, we'll see how to deploy an SAP Fiori application to the ABAP server or to SAP Cloud Platform.

Chapter 7
Deployment

Techniques You'll Master:

- Deploy applications to an ABAP server
- Configure the app to the SAP Fiori launchpad
- Deploy applications to SAP Cloud Platform
- Configure the app to SAP Fiori launchpad on SAP Cloud Platform

In this chapter, we'll explore the techniques to deploy an SAP Fiori web app to an ABAP server and to SAP Cloud Platform. You'll also see how to register the deployed application to SAP Fiori launchpad on SAP Cloud Platform and to the on-premise SAP Fiori launchpad.

Real-World Scenario

You've built an SAP Fiori app using the SAP Web IDE, and now you want other users to access this application. For other users to access this app, the app needs to be deployed into a server environment. You want to explore options for deploying to an ABAP server and to SAP Cloud Platform. You also want to configure the deployed app in the SAP Fiori launchpad on-premise as well on SAP Cloud Platform.

Objectives of This Portion of the Test

The objective of this portion of the SAP Fiori Certification Test is to test your knowledge on various options to deploy an SAP Fiori app. The important objectives are as follows:

- Deployment options for an SAP Fiori app
- Registering and accessing the SAPUI5 app from SAP Fiori launchpad

Key Concepts Refresher

After an SAP Fiori app or an extension application is developed and unit tested, it can be deployed either to SAP Cloud Platform or the SAPUI5 ABAP repository. Once the application is deployed to a server environment, you can give the users a URL for directly accessing the application. You can also configure this application in the SAP Fiori launchpad and let the users access the application via the SAP Fiori launchpad.

Deploying to SAPUI5 ABAP Repository

To deploy your application to the SAP Gateway system, right-click on the project, and then choose **Deploy • Deploy to SAPUI5 ABAP Repository**. This opens a popup prompting you to select a previously configured SAP Cloud Platform destination (pointing to on SAP Gateway system) as shown in Figure 7.1. You also need to choose if you want to create a new Business Server Page (BSP) application to store the SAPUI5 application or if you want to overwrite an existing application. If you're deploying the application for the first time, you need to choose **Deploy a new application**; otherwise, choose **Update an existing application**. Click **Next**.

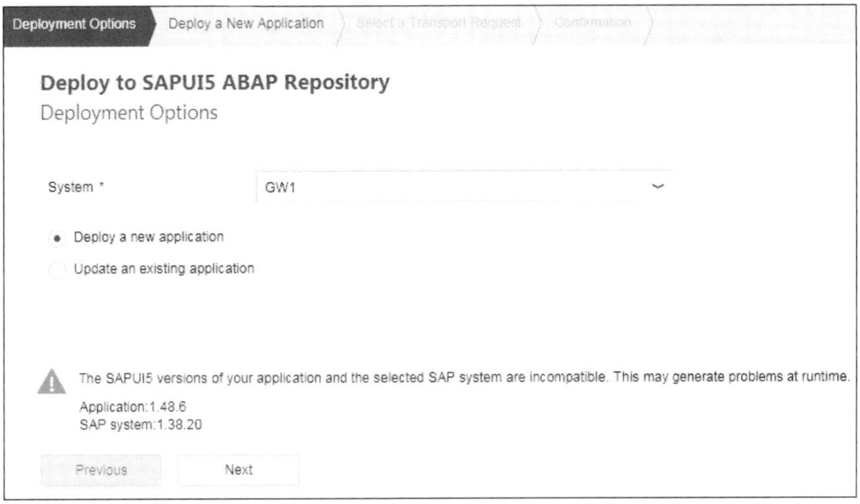

Figure 7.1 Deploying a Project to an SAPUI5 ABAP Repository

If you choose **Deploy a new application**, you need to select a **Name**, **Description**, and **Package**. To select a package, you can click the **Browse** button and choose an existing **Package** in the SAP Gateway system. Click **Next**.

> **Tip**
> The name of the new application should be in a customer namespace. That is, it should either start with a "Z" or "Y" in most cases, unless you're using a preregistered customer namespace. The name can't exceed 15 characters because it's a limit on the underlying ABAP system.

Now the SAP Web IDE presents you a list of transports with your participation from the backend. You are either an owner of the transport or an owner of one of the tasks under the transport. You can choose one of the existing transports or choose to create a new transport. Click **Next**, and then click **Finish** in the next screen. The app is deployed, and a success message will be displayed in the status bar on the SAP Web IDE.

Alternatively, if you had chosen **Update an existing application**' in the previous step, as shown earlier in Figure 7.1, you'll be presented with a list of currently deployed applications from the SAPUI5 repository. Choose the right application. Click **Next**, and then click **Finish** in the next screen to confirm deployment to the SAP Gateway system. At this point, SAP Web IDE will contact the SAPUI5 ABAP repository and make a list of files to be deleted, overwritten, and created and provide that information to the user to confirm as shown in Figure 7.2.

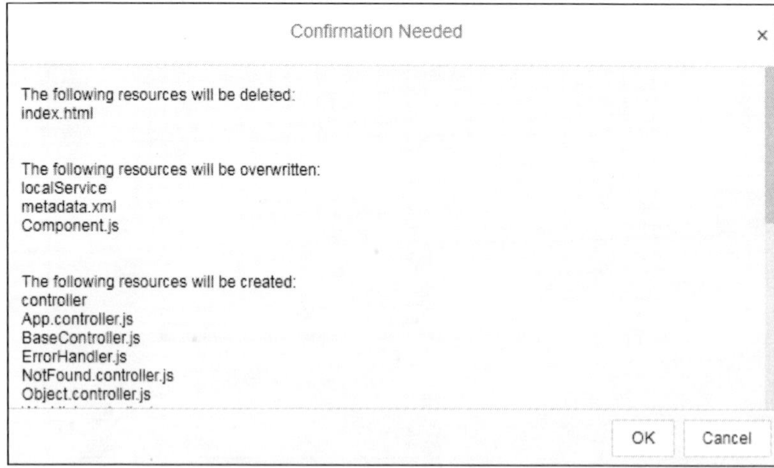

Figure 7.2 Confirmation for Various Operations Done while Deploying with the Update an Existing Application Option

It is important to note that even though this was an update, and majority of the files remain unchanged. We see that we get a confirmation query asking if we want to overwrite all the files. This is because the ABAP repository does not have the full features of a version management system for determining every change and maintaining versions. The ABAP repository will just overwrite the files every time you deploy or update the application. Because of this, it's recommended to make use of SAP Web IDE's Git integration and use Git for complete version management features. You can refer Chapter 1 for more information regarding Git integration.

Click **OK** to start the process of deployment, and you'll receive a confirmation message on the status bar.

Viewing on the Server

After an SAPUI5 app is uploaded into the SAP Gateway server, it's stored in the SAPUI5 ABAP repository. All the SAP-delivered and customer-created apps are stored in this repository. Technically, this repository is based on the BSP repository. When you see a deployed SAPUI5 application, it's represented by a BSP application in the ABAP **Object Navigator** shown in Figure 7.3.

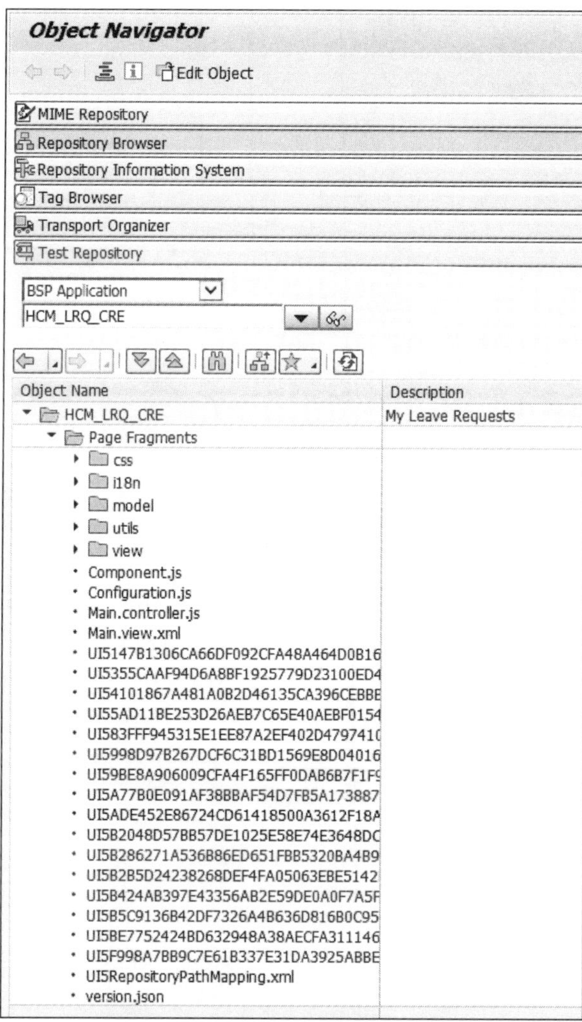

Figure 7.3 BSP Repository Storing an SAPUI5 Application

Go to Transaction SE80, and open the My Leave Requests app HCM_LRQ_CRE in the BSP repository.

In addition to the BSP application, Transaction SICF nodes are also created so that the SAPUI5 application can be accessed over the Internet (see Figure 7.4). The SICF node under */sap/bc/ui5_ui5/sap/zworklist* is the one which is required for running the SAPUI5 application. The other node under */sap.bc/bsp/sap/zworklist* gets created as this is technically a BSP application as well, however it is not of any significance and it is not used by the SAP Fiori runtime.

Virtual Hosts / Services	Documentation	Re
▼ default_host	VIRTUAL DEFAULT HOST	
▼ sap	SAP NAMESPACE; SAP IS OBLIGED NOT T…	
▼ bc	BASIS TREE (BASIS FUNCTIONS)	
▼ bsp	BUSINESS SERVER PAGES (BSP) RUNTIME	
▼ sap	NAMESPACE SAP	
• zworklist	Demo	
▼ ui5_ui5	SAPUI5 Application Handler SAPUI5 Applic…	
▼ sap	sap Namespace for SAPUI5 Applications	
• zworklist	Demo	

Figure 7.4 Transaction SICF Nodes Created upon Deploying the SAPUI5 Application

Registering to SAP Fiori Launchpad on SAP Gateway

The deployed application needs to be registered on the SAP Fiori launchpad, so that user can access it from there. If the application has an index.html file, then the application can be accessed directly using a URL.

Registration is done in the SAP Fiori admin page, which is available at *https://<host>:<port>/sap/bc/ui5_ui5/sap/arsrvc_upb_admn/main.html?scope=CUST*. Registering to SAP Fiori launchpad has many steps involved, which we'll explore in the following sections.

Add an SAP Fiori Catalog as a Tile

An SAP Fiori catalog is a group of SAP Fiori apps to be assigned to a specific role. After you're in the SAP Fiori admin page, you can use an existing catalog or create a new catalog, as shown in Figure 7.5.

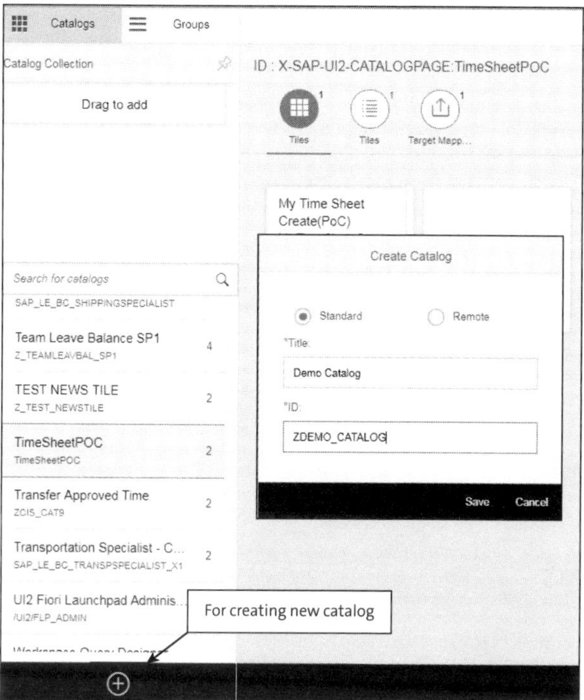

Figure 7.5 Creating a New Catalog

Create a Target Mapping

After the new catalog is created, select it on the master list, navigate to **Target Mapping**, and click on **Create Target Mapping** on the page footer, which opens a new page.

Semantic Object and **Action** are fields used to uniquely identify an SAP Fiori app. You can use an existing semantic object or create a new semantic object in Transaction /UI2/SEMOBJ and provide it here. **Action** can be a string of your choice, but you must ensure that the combination of **Semantic Object** and **Action** is unique within an SAP Fiori launchpad environment. The rest of the fields should be filled in as follows (Figure 7.6):

- **Application Type**
  Enter "SAPUI5 Fiori App".
- **Title**
  Enter a title for the target mapping.

- **URL**
  This should be a link to the SAPUI5 app without host and port name.
- **ID**
  Enter the component name within the SAP Fiori app.

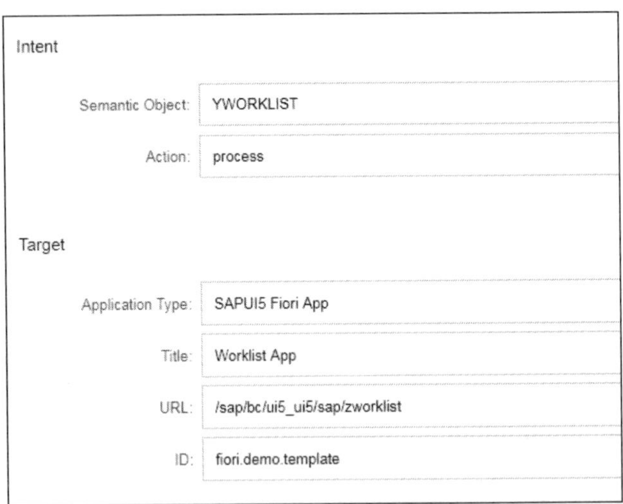

Figure 7.6 Creating a Target Mapping

Create a Tile

Next you need to create a tile by following these steps:

1. Navigate to the tile within the SAP Fiori catalog. Click on the tile with the **+** button to create a new tile.

   In the next screen, you'll see the following three types of tiles to choose from as shown in Figure 7.7:
   - **App Launcher – Dynamic**: This type can create a tile with some dynamic content from the backend server, especially a number in the tile, such as number of pending requests for approval and number of PRs created today.
   - **News Tile**: This can be used to display dynamic headlines from a news feed.
   - **App Launcher – Static**: This can be used to create a tile with static content.

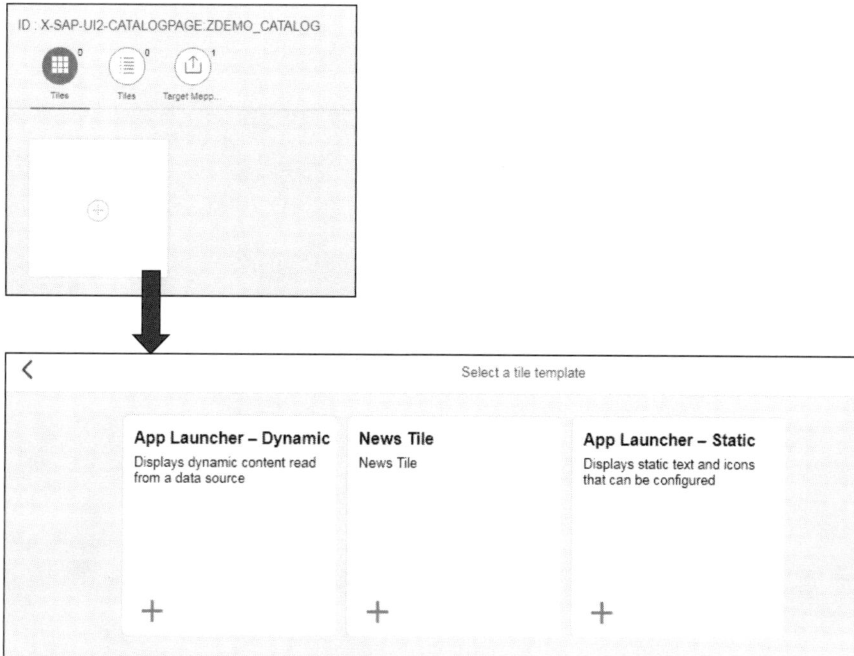

Figure 7.7 Creating a New Tile

2. Choose **App Launcher – Static** for our new tile. This will open a form to fill in the details of the tile as shown in Figure 7.8.

3. Under **General**, enter a suitable title to be shown on the tile. You may also enter an icon and information to be shown on the tile.

4. Under the **Navigation** section, select the **Use semantic object navigation** checkbox, and enter the **Semantic Object** and **Action** you provided in target mapping. Click on **Save**

Now you have an SAP Fiori catalog with a **Worklist** tile as shown in Figure 7.9.

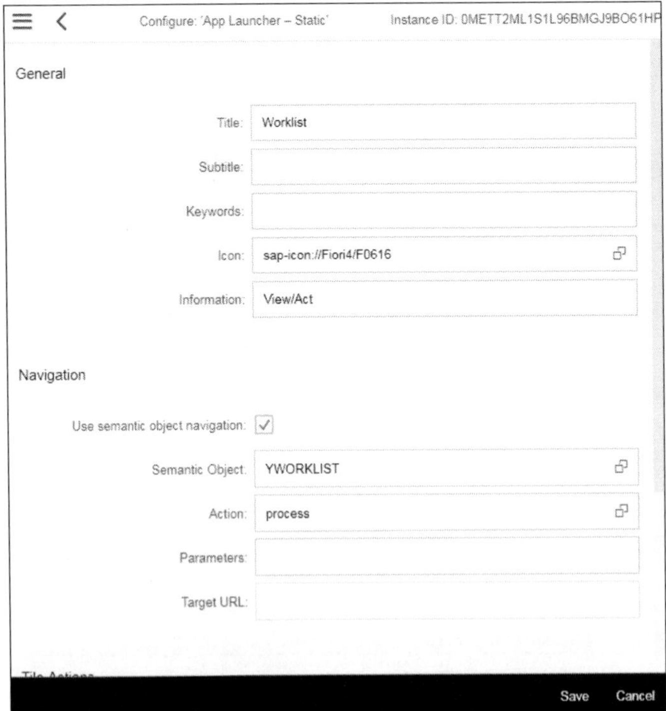

Figure 7.8 Creating a Tile Referring to the Target Mapping

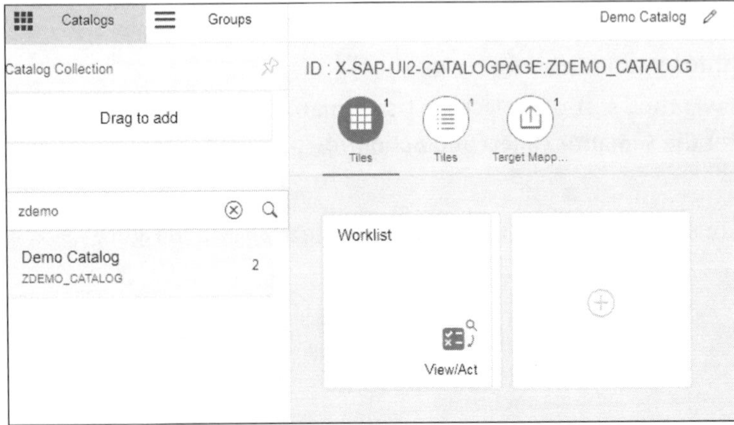

Figure 7.9 Tile within the Catalog

Now we need to create an SAP Fiori group and add the recently created tile into it.

Add an SAP Fiori Group

Navigate to see a list of groups by clicking on the **Groups** tab on top of the master list. You can create a new group by clicking on the **+** button on the master page's footer. Add a **Title** and **ID** to the group as shown in Figure 7.10.

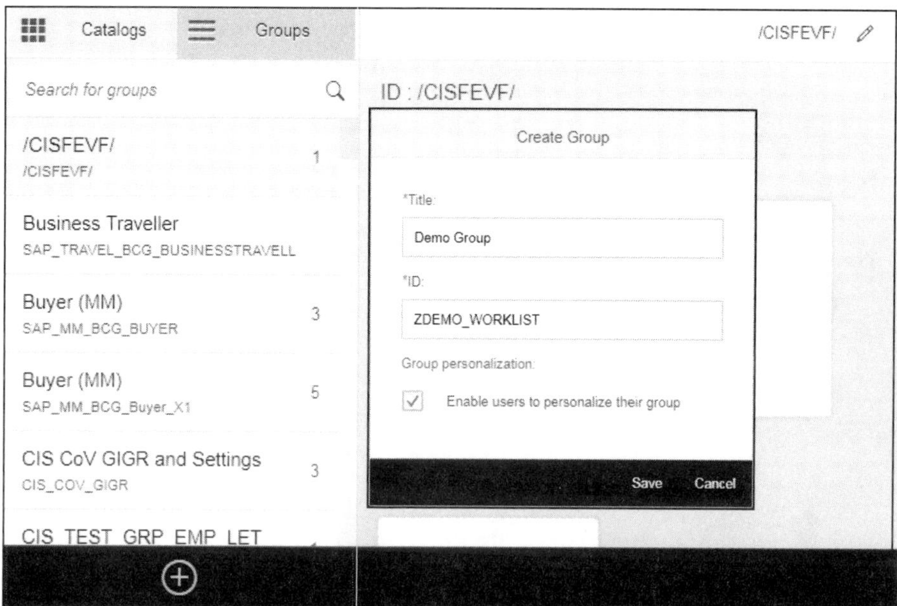

Figure 7.10 Creating a Group

After the group is created, you need to add tiles into it:

1. Click on the **Add Tile** button (Figure 7.11, ❶), which will show a screen to add the tile into the group.

2. In this screen, select the catalog that contains the tile to be added to the group. Select the **Demo Catalog**, which you created earlier ❷, and this will show the tile that you created earlier for the **Worklist** as shown in Figure 7.11.

3. Select the tile, and this will add the tile to the group ❸.

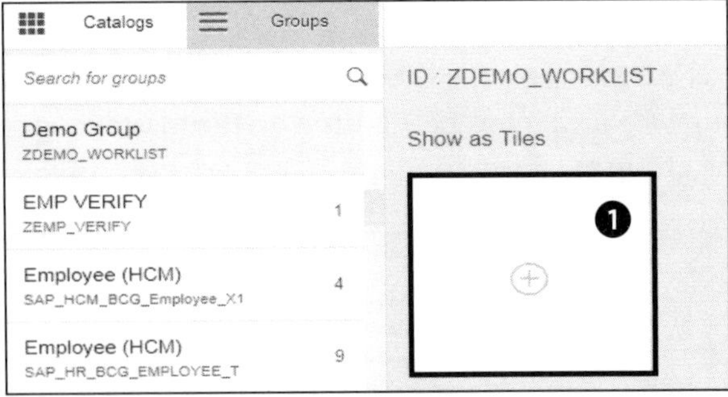

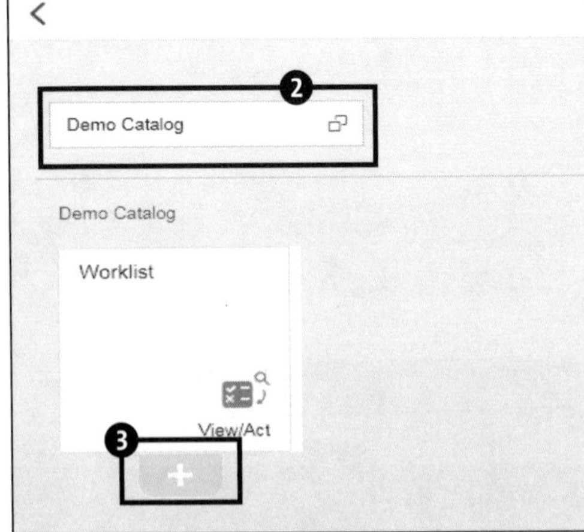

Figure 7.11 Adding a Tile to the Group

Add Catalog and the Group to a Role

Now that we have both the catalog and group, we need to add these to a role so that role can be used to assign the contained tile to the user. You can add both the catalog and the group to an existing role or to a new role. To do so, follow these steps:

1. Open the role in edit mode, and navigate to the **Menu** tab.

2. Clicking on the **Insert Node** icon, and choose **SAP Fiori Tile Catalog** as shown in Figure 7.12 ❶.

3. Provide the catalog name in the subsequent popup ❷, and click the **OK** icon ❸ to add the catalog to the role.

4. Repeat these steps for **SAP Fiori Tile Group** to add the group to the role.

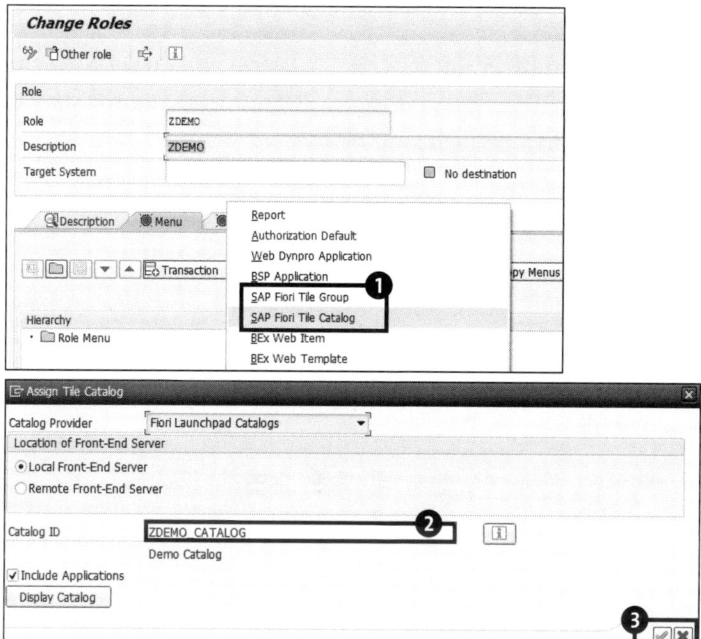

Figure 7.12 Adding an SAP Fiori Catalog to a Role

After adding both the SAP Fiori catalog and SAP Fiori group, the role looks as shown in Figure 7.13.

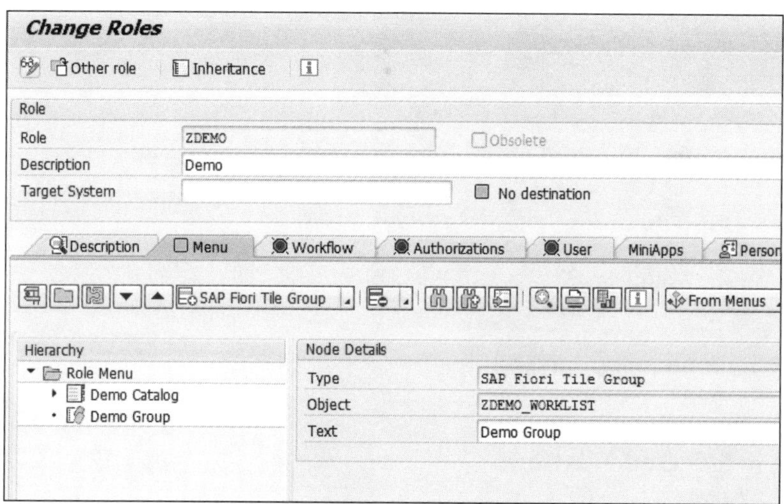

Figure 7.13 Role with the Added Catalog and Group

Add the Role to a User

By adding this role to a user, authorization to access SAP Fiori app ZWORKLIST can be provided to a user. Open the **User** tab under role **ZDEMO**, and add the user to whom the access is to be given as shown in Figure 7.14.

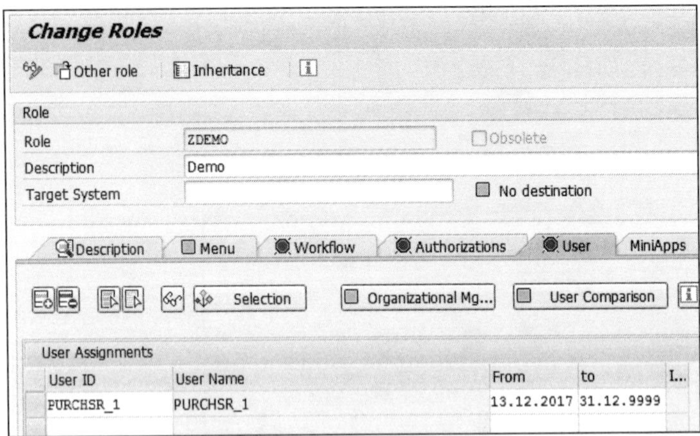

Figure 7.14 Adding a Role to the User

Figure 7.15 shows the user's launchpad with the tile for the ZWORKLIST app.

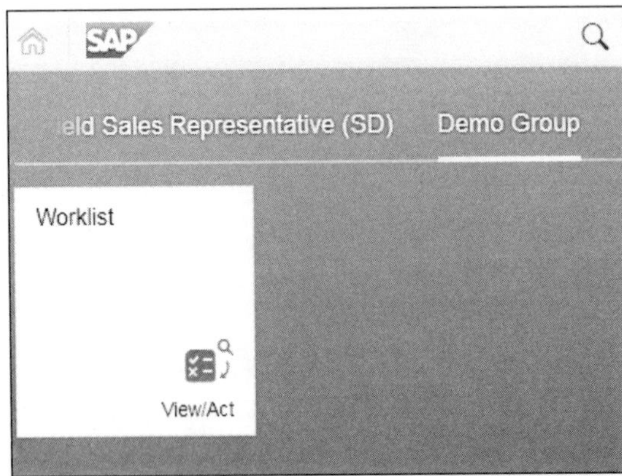

Figure 7.15 Tile Appearing in the User's SAP Fiori Launchpad

Deploying to SAP Cloud Platform

To deploy a project into SAP Cloud Platform, right-click on the project and then choose **Deploy • Deploy to SAP Cloud Platform**. This will display a popup with options to **Deploy a new application** and **Update an existing application** on SAP Cloud Platform as shown in Figure 7.16.

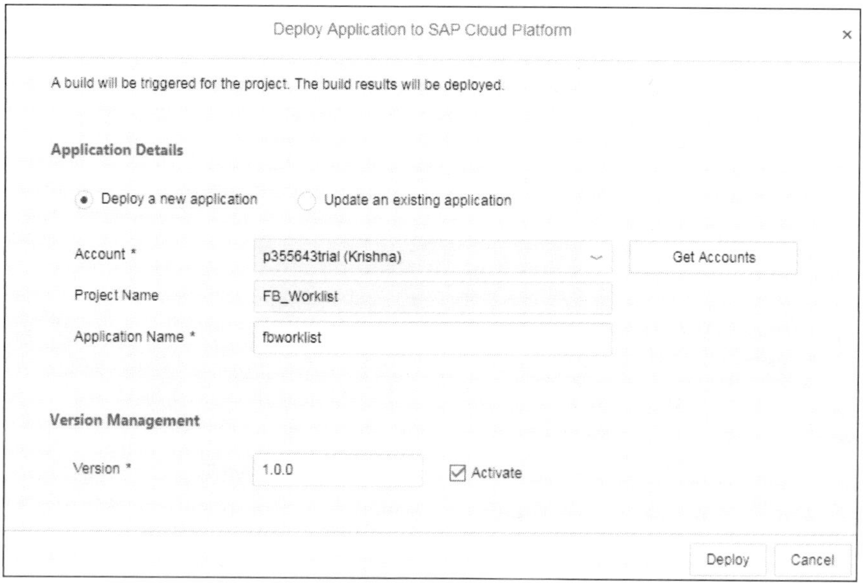

Figure 7.16 Option while Deploying to SAP Cloud Platform

Figure 7.16 Option while Deploying to SAP Cloud Platform

Note that under **Account**, you have options to deploy this project to other SAP Cloud Platform subaccounts under your organization. (Trial SAP Cloud Platform has only one subaccount, however). You can provide an **Application Name** with which the new app will be stored in SAP Cloud Platform and provide a suitable **Version**.

If you're updating an existing application, **Application Name** will be a dropdown from which you need to choose an existing application available on SAP Cloud Platform. Upon selecting an application, previous versions of the app will be displayed for information, and **Version** will be defaulted with an increment to the previously deployed version number.

Click **Deploy** to start your deployment. Upon completion, you'll get a popup confirmation as shown in Figure 7.17 with an option to register the application to the SAP Fiori launchpad on SAP Cloud Platform. You can register your application to SAP Fiori launchpad on SAP Cloud Platform provided your SAP Cloud Platform account has a subscription to the SAP Fiori launchpad service on SAP Cloud Platform.

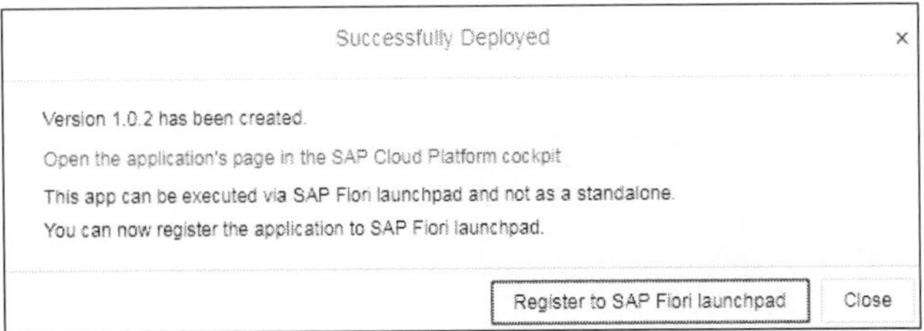

Figure 7.17 Confirmation Popup upon Deployment to SAP Cloud Platform

Tip

The popup in Figure 7.17 informs the user that the app can't be run standalone because SAP Web IDE didn't find an *index.html* file in the *webapp* folder of the project.

The deployed app can be seen in SAP Cloud Platform's list of HTML5 applications. Go to the **SAP Cloud Platform Cockpit** screen, and click on **HTML5** as shown in Figure 7.18. This will show a list of all available deployed HTML5 applications within SAP Cloud Platform.

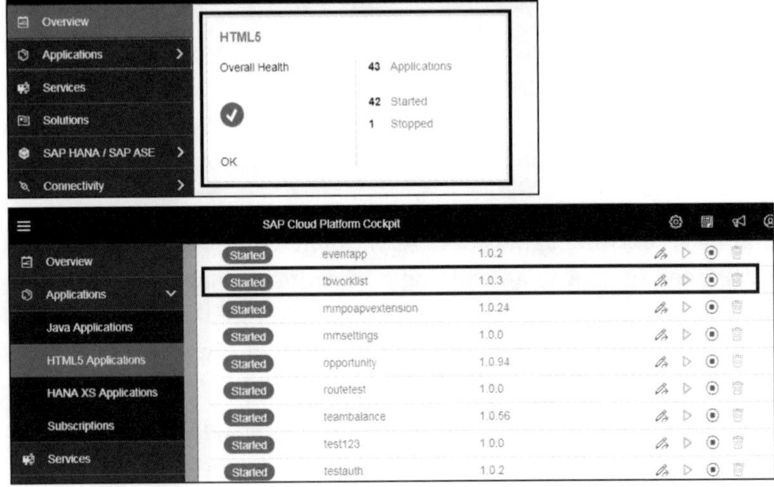

Figure 7.18 Deployed Apps within SAP Cloud Platform

Upon a deploying a new application, it will also get a Git repository of its own on SAP Cloud Platform. From the cockpit you can click on **Repositories • Git Repositories** and see that a new Git repository was created for the application.

Here you'll find a disk usage of each repository and an option to delete the repository as well. By clicking on the spectacles icon near the Git repository name (just before the trashcan icon), you can view the Git branches, the repository, versions and the code in each version of the application.

SAP Fiori Launchpad on SAP Cloud Platform

In this section, We'll explore SAP Cloud Platform's portal service and create an SAP Fiori launchpad on SAP Cloud Platform. We will also use the SAP Fiori configuration cockpit to configure the SAP Fiori launchpad and add an SAP Cloud Platform deployed application as a tile.

Portal Service

If the SAPUI5 application is deployed into SAP Cloud Platform, it can be registered to an SAP Fiori launchpad on SAP Cloud Platform. However, to achieve this, you need to create and configure the SAP Fiori launchpad as a prerequisite.

SAP Fiori launchpad on SAP Cloud Platform is created as part of an SAP Cloud Platform portal service. Using this service, you can create multiple business sites, which are either freestyle HTML sites or sites based on SAP Fiori launchpad. Within a freestyle site, you can even embed an SAP Fiori launchpad, in addition to other HTML contents.

To access the portal service, navigate to **Services** on the **SAP Cloud Platform Cockpit** screen, and choose **Portal'** service as shown in Figure 7.19.

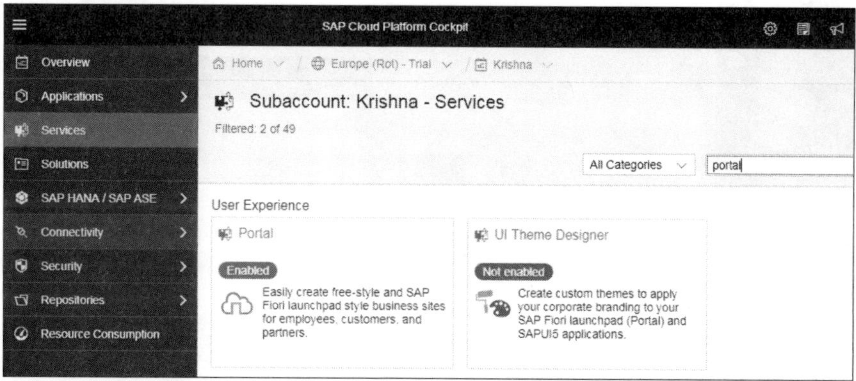

Figure 7.19 Portal Service in SAP Cloud Platform

Click on the **Portal** service, and then click on **Go to Service**' in the resulting screen. This will launch the portal service's admin page as shown in Figure 7.20.

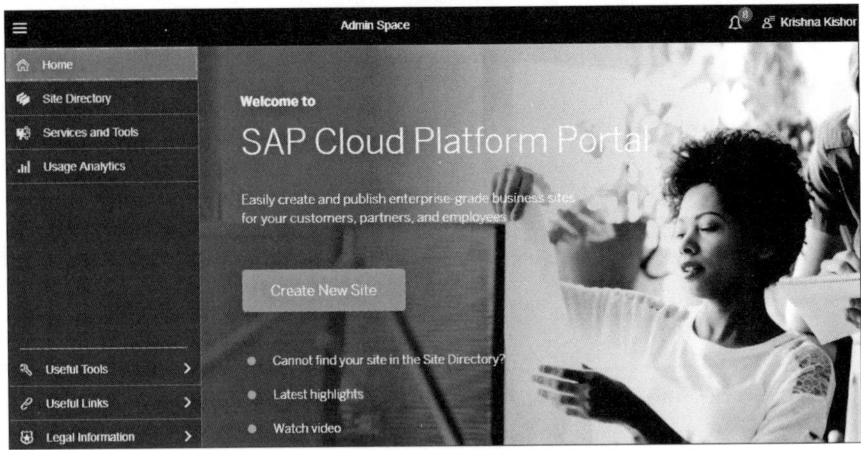

Figure 7.20 Home Page of the Portal Service

Clicking on the **Site Directory** on the master menu shows all the existing sites on the portal service as shown in Figure 7.21. By clicking on the **+** sign, you can create a new site.

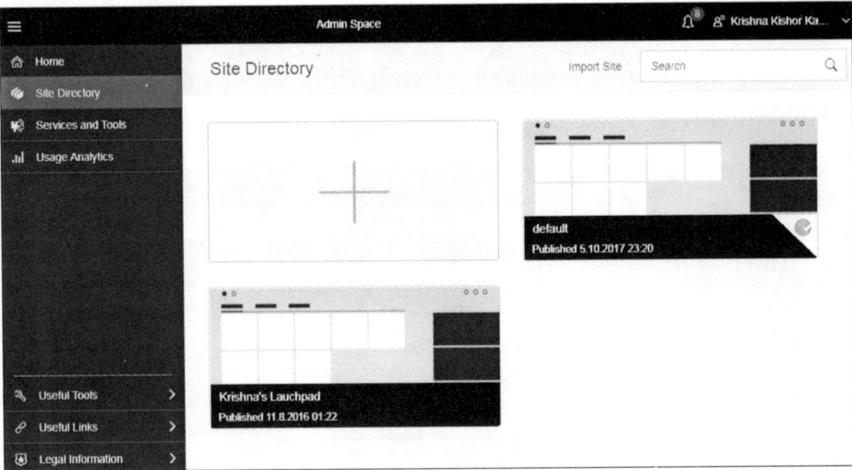

Figure 7.21 Site Directory of the Portal Service

Upon selecting **Create Site**, you'll be shown a popup screen where you can provide a **Site Name** for the new site. You can also use predefined templates for your site as shown in Figure 7.22. For this example, choose the **SAP Fiori Launchpad** template for the site. Click **Create**.

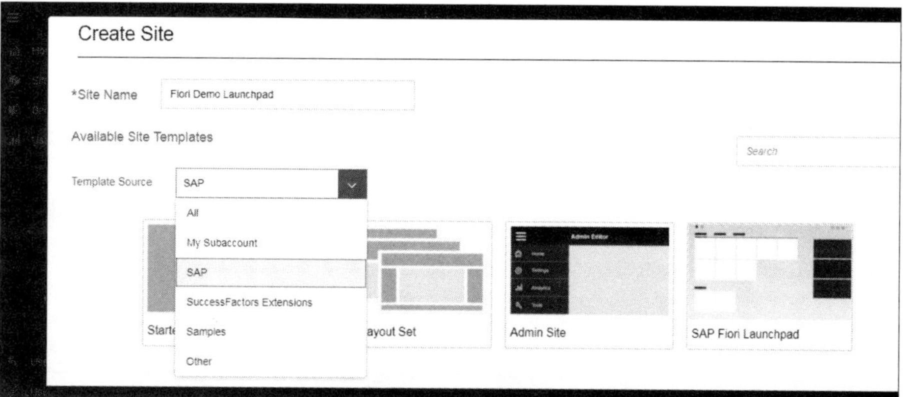

Figure 7.22 Available Templates for the New Site

Now you'll see the new site in the **Site Directory**. Upon moving the mouse cursor over the new site, you'll see an **Edit** button. Click on it to configure the site. This will open the **Fiori Configuration Cockpit** screen in a new browser tab for the new site that you created, as shown in Figure 7.23.

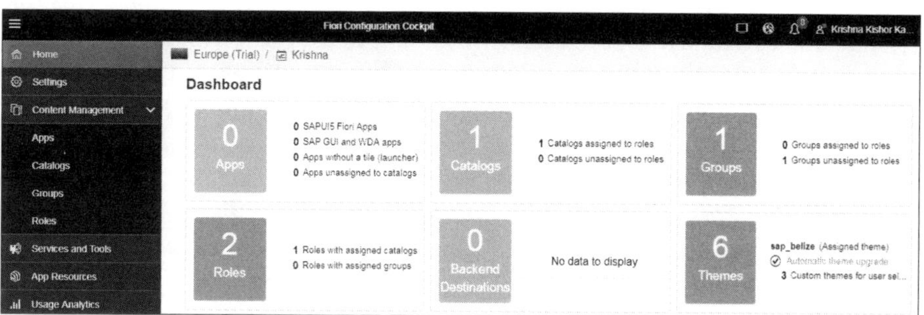

Figure 7.23 Fiori Configuration Cockpit

As you can see, the **Fiori Configuration Cockpit** screen, it already has a catalog and a group created by default.

You can click on the **Catalogs** under **Content Management** to see the default catalog as shown in Figure 7.24. You'll see that there are no apps associated with this catalog, and this catalog is assigned to a role named **Everyone**. You can edit this catalog by clicking on the **Edit** button on the footer, or you can create more catalogs using the **+** button on the footer.

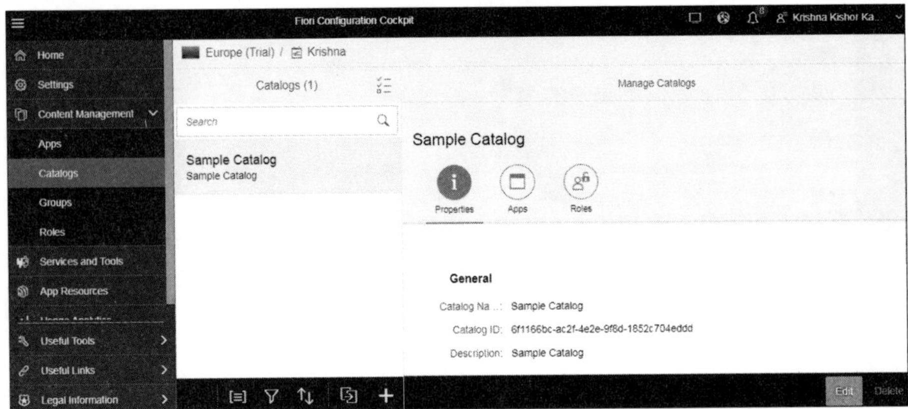

Figure 7.24 Catalogs within the Site

You can click on **Groups** under **Content Management** to see the default **Sample Group** as shown in Figure 7.25. You'll see that this group isn't associated to any role. Click on the **Edit** button to edit the group. Navigate to the **Roles** tab, click on the **+** button above the roles list, and choose the **Everyone** role. **Everyone** is a default role available in the SAP Cloud Platform and also in the SAP Fiori launchpad. This role is by default assigned to all the users. If you want to use custom roles, you need to create the role first in the SAP Cloud Platform cockpit, and then add that role in the Fiori launchpad. Click on the **Save** button to save the assignment of the group to the role.

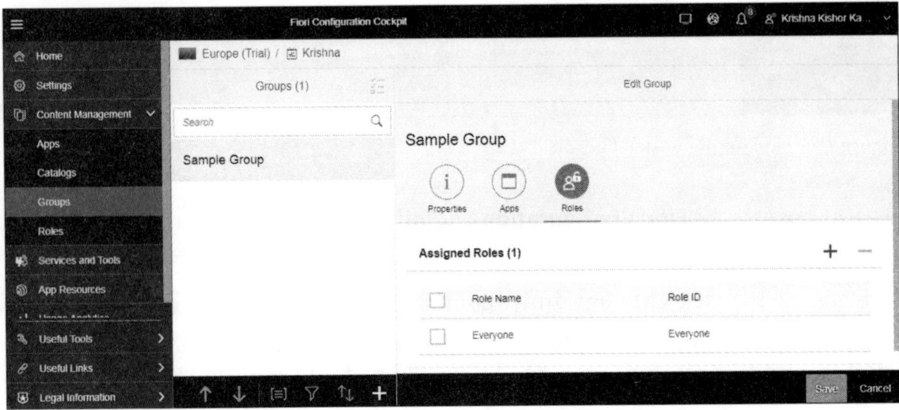

Figure 7.25 Groups within the Site

Register to SAP Fiori Launchpad

Now we need to register our application to the SAP Fiori launchpad. To do this, you can select the option available upon deploying to SAP Cloud Platform as shown earlier in Figure 7.4. You can also right-click on the application and choose **Deploy • Register to SAP Fiori Launchpad** as shown in Figure 7.26.

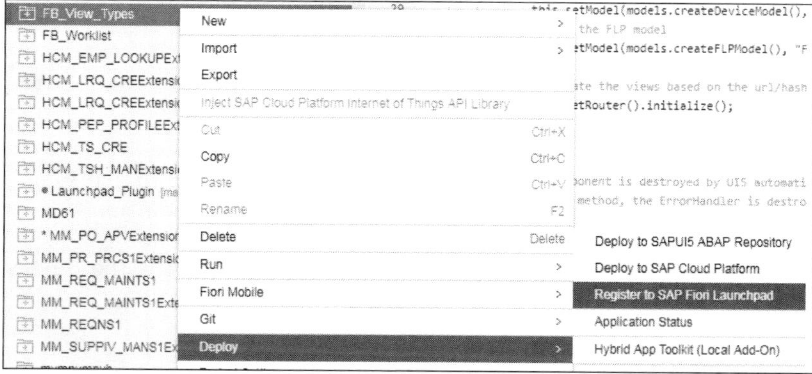

Figure 7.26 Registering to SAP Fiori Launchpad

You'll see a form as shown in Figure 7.27 for providing various details.

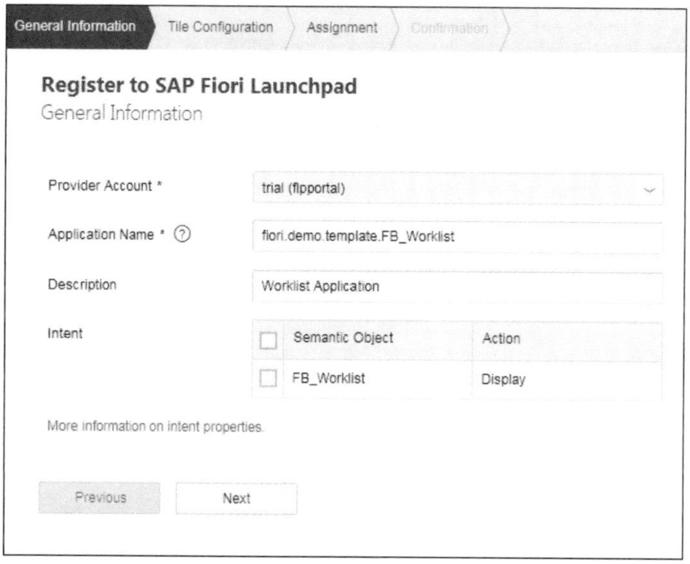

Figure 7.27 Specifying Provider Account and Application Name for Registering the App to SAP Fiori Launchpad

The details are as follows:

- **Provider Account**
  We're using an SAP Cloud Platform trial account for this exercise so the **Provider Account** defaults to that of the trial account.

- **Application Name**
  SAP Web IDE defaults a name, and you can retain it or provide a new application name.

- **Description**
  Text describing the application.

- **Intent**
  SAP Web IDE automatically creates a semantic object and action, so that intent-based navigation can be done.

Click **Next** to go the **Tile Configuration** tab where you provide the tile details. Choose **Static** as the tile **Type** and enter a **Title**. You can also provide the optional **Subtitle** and **Icon** for the tile as shown in Figure 7.28.

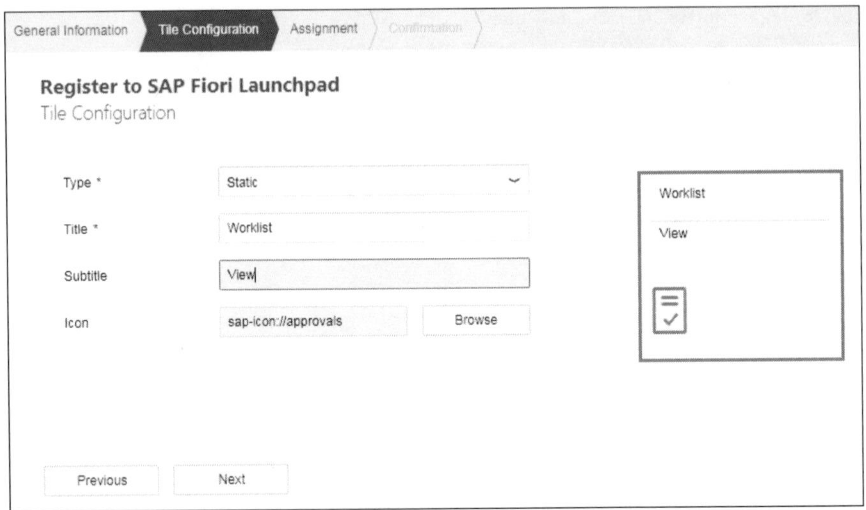

Figure 7.28 Tile Definition within SAP Fiori Launchpad

Click **Next** to go to the **Assignment'** screen where you assign the tile to **Site, Catalog**, and **Group** as shown in Figure 7.29:

- **Site**
  Choose the previously created site **Fiori Demo Launchpad** here.

- **Catalog/Group**
  These are similar concepts that are available in the on-premise SAP Fiori launchpad. Default catalogs and groups available in the site are chosen.

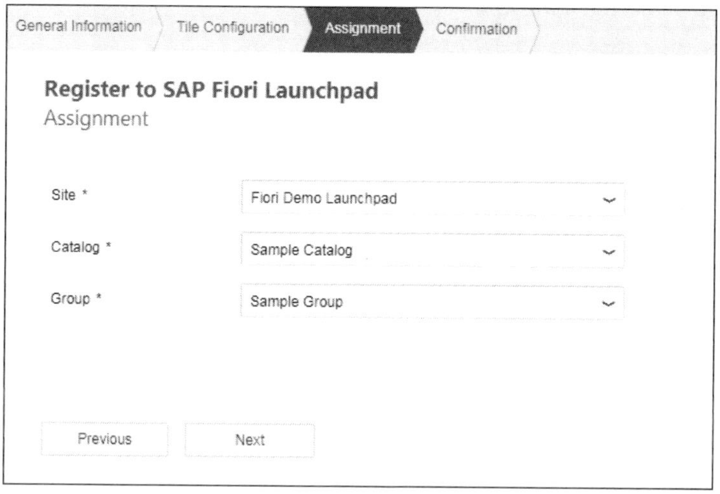

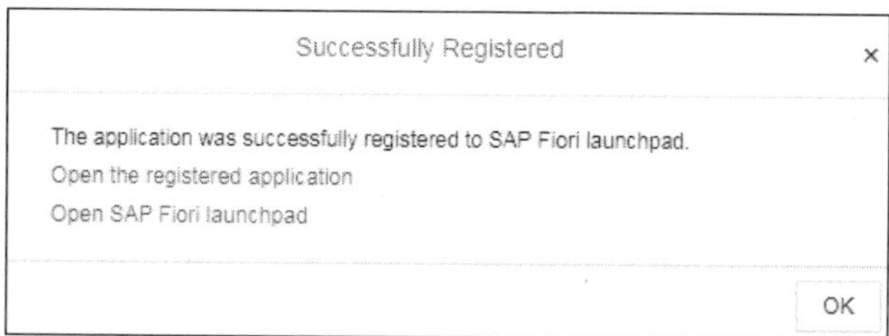

Figure 7.29 Assignment of the Tile within SAP Fiori Launchpad

Click **Next** to see the confirmation page, and click **Finish** to complete the process. You'll get a confirmation page as shown in Figure 7.30, which has a link to the SAP Fiori launchpad. Click on it to see the SAP Fiori launchpad.

Figure 7.30 Confirmation Popup with Link to the SAP Fiori Launchpad

Figure 7.31 shows the SAP Fiori launchpad with the Worklist app successfully added to it.

After the app is registered with SAP Fiori launchpad, a new configuration file gets inside the project in SAP Web IDE. This will give information about the SAP Fiori launchpad registration of the app as shown in Figure 7.32.

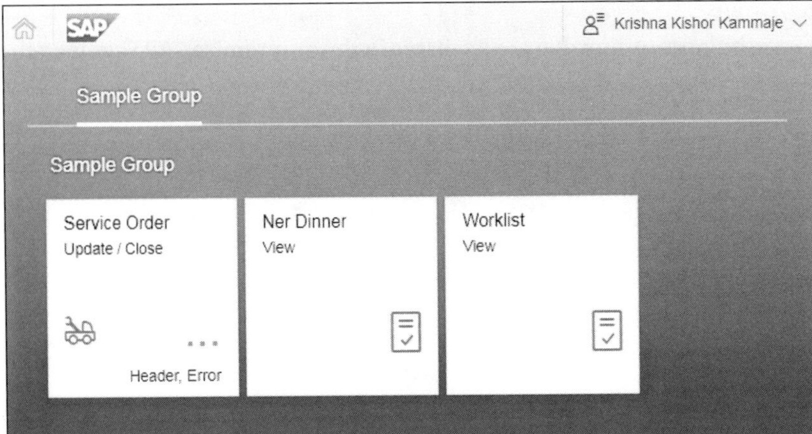

Figure 7.31 Successfully Added the Worklist App to SAP Fiori Launchpad

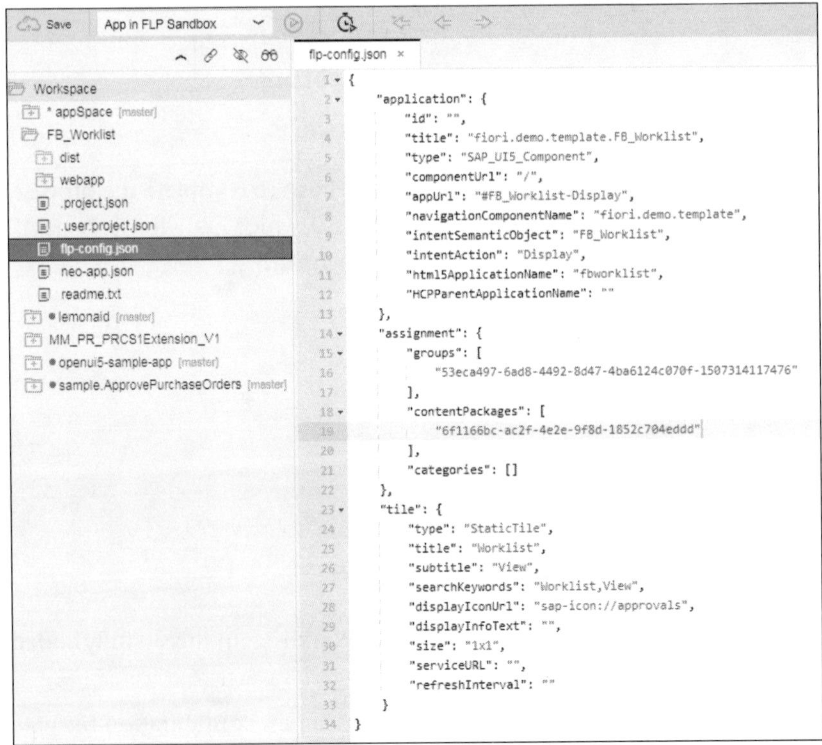


```json
{
    "application": {
        "id": "",
        "title": "fiori.demo.template.FB_Worklist",
        "type": "SAP_UI5_Component",
        "componentUrl": "/",
        "appUrl": "#FB_Worklist-Display",
        "navigationComponentName": "fiori.demo.template",
        "intentSemanticObject": "FB_Worklist",
        "intentAction": "Display",
        "html5ApplicationName": "fbworklist",
        "HCPParentApplicationName": ""
    },
    "assignment": {
        "groups": [
            "53eca497-6ad8-4492-8d47-4ba6124c070f-1507314117476"
        ],
        "contentPackages": [
            "6f1166bc-ac2f-4e2e-9f8d-1852c704eddd"
        ],
        "categories": []
    },
    "tile": {
        "type": "StaticTile",
        "title": "Worklist",
        "subtitle": "View",
        "searchKeywords": "Worklist,View",
        "displayIconUrl": "sap-icon://approvals",
        "displayInfoText": "",
        "size": "1x1",
        "serviceURL": "",
        "refreshInterval": ""
    }
}
```

Figure 7.32 SAP Fiori Launchpad Configuration File

Important Terminology

This chapter covered the following terminology:

- **SAP Fiori launchpad**
  SAP Fiori launchpad is the entry point to all SAP Fiori apps on all devices.

- **BSP application**
  A Business Server Page (BSP) application is a functional application executed in a web browser. SAPUI5 applications are stored as BSP applications when they are deployed to the SAPUI5 ABAP repository.

- **SAPUI5 ABAP repository**
  The SAPUI5 ABAP repository is based on the BSP repository, and stores all SAP-delivered and customer-created SAPUI5 applications deployed to the SAP Gateway server.

- **Target mapping**
  Target mapping is a step in SAP Fiori launchpad configuration that defines the target application that is launched when a user clicks on a specific tile or a specific link (in application-to-application navigation).

- **Catalog**
  An SAP Fiori catalog is used to control access to SAP Fiori applications. A catalog is a set of SAP Fiori applications, which, when assigned to a role of a user, gives the user authorization to access those applications.

- **Tile**
  A tile is a container that represents an application on the SAP Fiori launchpad. It is used to access specific applications.

- **Group**
  A group is a set of applications that are displayed to users on the SAP Fiori launchpad.

- **Role**
  A role authorizes users to access a specific group or catalog of applications. Catalogs and groups are added to a role, which is then assigned to a user to allow access.

- **Portal service**
  The SAP Cloud Platform portal service enables users to create freestyle HTML or SAP Fiori launchpad-based websites.

Practice Questions

These practice questions will help you evaluate your understanding of the topics covered in this chapter. The questions shown are similar in nature to those found on the certification examination. Although none of these questions will be found on the exam itself, they will allow you to review your knowledge of the subject. Select the correct answers, and then check the completeness of your answers in the "Practice Question Answers and Explanations" section. Remember, on the exam, you must select all correct answers and only correct answers to receive credit for the question.

1. An SAP Fiori app deployed to an SAP Gateway system can be registered on an SAP Cloud Platform portal site.

   ☐   A. True

   ☐   B. False

2. Which of the following objects is *not* one of the objects that gets created upon deploying an SAP Fiori app to an SAP Gateway system?

   ☐   A. Nodes in Transaction SICF

   ☐   B. An ABAP function module

   ☐   C. A BSP application in the ABAP repository

3. By adding an SAP Fiori group to a user's role, which of the following happens?

   ☐   A. User gets authorization to all the tiles within the SAP Fiori group

   ☐   B. User gets all the tiles within the SAP Fiori group in his SAP Fiori launchpad

   ☐   D. All the tiles within the group are marked as user's favorite tiles

   ☐   E. All the tiles within the group are added to user's home group

4. What is the name of the SAP Cloud Platform service allowing you to create SAP Fiori launchpads?

   ☐   A. Launchpad

   ☐   B. Site

   ☐   C. Dashboard

   ☐   D. Portal

5.   In the on-premise SAP Fiori launchpad, where are the application's URL and component name provided?

☐   A. Tile definition

☐   B. Target mapping

☐   C. Group definition

☐   D. Project settings

6.   When an SAP Fiori app is deployed to an SAP Gateway system, it's accessible from this URL of the SAP Gateway system.

☐   A. */sap/bc/ui5/sap/<app name>*

☐   B. */sap/bc/nw/fiori/<app_name>*

☐   C. */sap/bc/ui5_ui5/sap/<app_name>*

☐   D. */sap/bc/fiori/sap/<app_name>*

7.   An SAP Fiori application in an SAP Gateway system is represented by which of the following?

☐   A. BSP application

☐   B. Module pool program

☐   C. Web Dynpro application

☐   D. Function module

8.   Consider a scenario in which you updated an SAPUI5 application which was already deployed in the ABAP repository and now redeployed it after the update. What is expected?

☐   A. Only the changed files are updated into the ABAP repository

☐   B. Changed files are deleted and recreated, others are left as-is

☐   C. All files are updated regardless of which were changed

☐   D. Automatically updated in a linked Git repository

9.   When you deploy an SAP Fiori application to SAP Cloud Platform for the first time, which of the following are true? (2 correct answers)

☐   A. The app gets registered to the default SAP Fiori app

☐   B. A new HTML5 app gets created on SAP Cloud Platform

   ☐   C. A new Git repository gets created on SAP Cloud Platform

   ☐   D. All existing members get access to the new application

Practice Answers and Explanations

1. Correct answer: **B**

   False. To register an application to SAP Fiori launchpad on SAP Cloud Platform, the application must be deployed to SAP Cloud Platform.

2. Correct answer: **B**

   An ABAP function module doesn't get created upon deploying the SAP Fiori app. Upon deploying a new SAPUI5 application, a new BSP application gets created in the SAP Gateway server to hold the SAPUI5 application. It also creates a SICF node to access this application over HTTP.

3. Correct answer: **B**

   By adding an SAP Fiori group to a user's role, corresponding tiles appear in SAP Fiori launchpad when user opens it. If a user has access to an app through the SAP Fiori catalog, but has no corresponding group assigned, then the application can be added to the SAP Fiori launchpad by personalizing the SAP Fiori launchpad.

4. Correct answer: **D**

   The portal service allows you to create multiple sites, which can be freestyle HTML sites or SAP Fiori launchpad-based sites.

5. Correct answer: **B**

   SAP Fiori app's URL and component name are provided at the target mapping part of the SAP Fiori catalog. In the tile definition, target mapping is referred so as to link the SAP Fiori tile with the SAPUI5 application.

6. Correct answer: **C**

   When an SAP Fiori app gets deployed to an SAP Gateway system, it will be accessible at */sap/bc/ui5_ui5/sap/<app_name>*.

7. Correct answer: **A**

   An SAP Fiori app will be deployed into the SAPUI5 ABAP repository, which is built on a BSP repository. So an SAP Fiori app will look like a BSP application within an SAP system.

8. Correct answer: **C**

   Whenever a deployment happens to ABAP repository, every file is overwritten regardless of whether a file was changed or not. Because of this reason, it is recommended to use a Git server for version management capabilities.

9. Correct answers: **C, D**

   A new HTML5 app gets created and can be seen under **SCP Cockpit • Applications • HTML5** applications. For version management of the app, a new Git repository also gets created on SAP Cloud Platform. It can be viewed by navigating to **SCP Cockpit • Repositories • Git Repositories**.

Take Away

An SAP Fiori application can be deployed to an SAP Gateway system. You can use catalogs, groups, and roles to control authorizations and default applications that appear on the SAP Fiori launchpad.

SAP Fiori apps can also be deployed to SAP Cloud Platform and then be registered to an SAP Fiori launchpad running on the SAP Cloud Platform. Multiple SAP Fiori launchpads can be created in SAP Cloud Platform using the portal service. Just like on-premise systems, there are catalogs, groups, and roles within the portal service to control the access and appearance of tiles.

Summary

In this chapter, you saw how to deploy an SAP Fiori app to both on-premise and cloud systems. You also saw how to organize the access and display of tiles within the SAP Fiori launchpad both in SAP Gateway and SAP Cloud Platform.

In the next chapter, we'll see how an SAPUI5 application can be mobilized using SAP Hybrid App Toolkit (HAT).

Chapter 8
SAP Hybrid App Toolkit

Techniques You'll Master:

- Mobilizing SAP Fiori apps
- Consume SAP Fiori through different channels
- Using SAP Fiori Client
- Building a custom SAP Fiori Client
- Using Hybrid App Toolkit Connector
- Using Hybrid App Toolkit Companion app

In this chapter, we'll start with discussing mobile features of SAP Fiori and exploring how SAP Fiori can be consumed over mobile devices. We'll discuss the SAP Hybrid App Toolkit (HAT) and its components. We'll also create an Apache Cordova-based hybrid app and deploy it to SAP Fiori mobile service.

Real-World Scenario

You want to develop an SAP Fiori app in the materials management space. You want your enterprise users to find and install the app from an app store. To speed up the application usage, the app user should be able to scan the material's barcode instead of manually entering an 18-digit material ID. You also want the capabilities to push the new upgrades to the app seamlessly.

In addition, you want the app to make use of single sign-on (SSO) for user authentication to make it easier for users to launch the app. You also want the users not to miss any important information and tasks relevant to their roles by sending them instant notifications. As your users are always on the move, you want to ensure that they don't lose their data when the device gets disconnected from the network, and you want to enable use of the app with limited but important features.

Objectives of This Portion of the Test

The objective of this portion of the SAP Fiori Certification Test is to test your fundamentals around mobilizing SAP Fiori apps. The certification test expects SAP Fiori developers to be knowledgeable in the following areas:

- Features of an SAP Fiori mobile service app
- Consuming SAP Fiori apps over mobile devices
- SAP Hybrid App Toolkit (HAT) and its components

Key Concepts Refresher

Let's start by understanding what it means to mobilizing an SAP Fiori application. We'll go through recommended techniques and tools provided by SAP to convert a web-based SAP Fiori app into a mobile app with the capabilities required by a business enterprise.

Features of a Mobile Application

An SAP Fiori app can be accessed on a variety of devices, including a mobile phone. But such an application can't be called as an enterprise mobile application unless it has the features discussed in the following subsections.

Native capabilities

It's common for enterprise business applications to require access to device capabilities, such as the following:

- **Barcode scanner**
  For reading and identifying materials marked with a bar code.
- **Camera**
  For taking pictures of receipts for attaching in a Travel Expense app.
- **GPS location**
  For determining the optimum route for a Delivery app used by a delivery truck.

A browser can't get access to these sensors, thus an SAP Fiori app running on a browser can't make use of these device features.

Advanced Caching and Better Performance

An SAP Fiori app contains a lot of static resources such as the SAPUI5 library and SAPUI5 application files. Loading these files every time the app is launched can slow it down. Although a browser can cache these static files, it isn't always optimum. A native app can have complete control of these static resources and can result in much better performance compared to SAP Fiori apps running on a browser.

Push Notifications

Push notifications are messages that pop in to a user's screen whenever a predefined scenario occurs. These can be very useful to alert users and provide important and time-sensitive information.

Offline Capability

For many mobile scenarios, users using an SAP Fiori app might be required to travel to places where there is patchy Internet service. In such cases, users expect the ability to work with the application at least with partial and important functionality and to sync with the server whenever the Internet connection is reestablished.

User Authentication and Single Sign-On

A native app can support multiple authentication and SSO procedures. One-time password (OTP) authentication, SAML 2.0, X.509 certificates, and SAP Logon Tickets are a few of the authentication mechanisms that a native application needs to support.

Security

As a native application, there are many additional options available such as a passcode, pattern, biometric identification, and face recognition for securing access to SAP Fiori apps. In addition, data stored by the user on the device can be secured by encryption.

SAP Fiori Client

SAP Fiori Client is a native mobile application available for Android, iOS, and Windows platforms, and it acts as a container for SAP Fiori apps. SAP Fiori Client also acts as a specialized browser that provides capabilities for consistent caching of application resources and SAPUI5 libraries. In addition, as it's a native application, it provides access to device features such as Camera, Contacts, Device Storage, GeoLocation, Bar Code Scanner, Accelerometer, and other sensors and resources.

SAP Fiori Client is built on Apache Cordova, which is an open-source mobile development framework. Apache Cordova allows you to use HTML5, JavaScript, and CSS3 to create the user interface (UI) of the mobile app, while providing plugins to access various features and resources of the device. In SAP Fiori Client, application resources are downloaded from the SAP Gateway/frontend server and cached.

Apache Cordova provides ways for developers to create custom plugins that can add more features to your mobile app. SAP has released a set of plugins called *Kapsel* to augment the features provided by Apache Cordova. Some of these additional plugins are for push notification, logging on to SAP Mobile Platform, Attachment Viewer, and Calendar.

As you see in Figure 8.1, some of the plugins like Push Notifications require SAP Mobile Platform/SAP Fiori mobile services to work, and some like Logon, can work directly with SAP Gateway server, where as some other plugins like Bar code scanner just work with the device's OS APIs without working with any servers.

An SAP Fiori Client's architecture is shown in Figure 8.1.

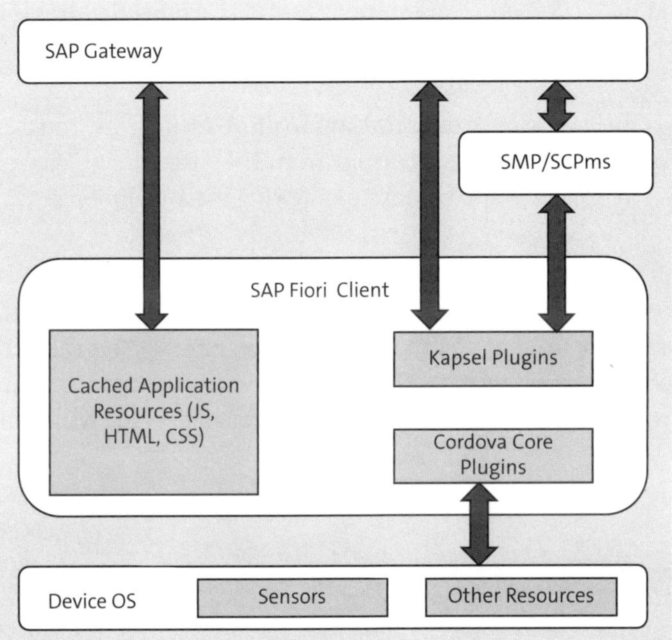

Figure 8.1 Architecture of SAP Fiori Client

Let's briefly look into various available plugins within SAP Fiori Client. All these plugins are available both in Android and iOS platforms. However, a few of these plugins aren't available on the Windows platform.

Apache Cordova Plugins

Following are some of the Apache Cordova plugins:

- **Camera**
  This plugin allows you to take a picture from an SAP Fiori app. It's usually used for attaching images to business documents.

- **Contacts**
  This plugin allows the SAP Fiori apps to access the contact list from the device. This plugin isn't available on the Windows platform.

- **Geolocation**
  This plugin allows the SAP Fiori app to access the device's location. the device can provide location details (latitude/longitude) using various sources such as the Global Positioning Systems (GPS), inferred locations from IP addresses, RFID, Wi-Fi networks, and cellular networks.

- **Printer**
  This plugin enables SAP Fiori apps to offer features to print documents. You can print the current page of the application, print from the Attachment Viewer plugin, or print directly from the app without previewing the attachment.

- **Privacy Screen**
  When there are multiple apps open on the device, app switcher allows you to choose between previously opened apps. For choosing different apps, you get to see a screenshot of the app so that you recognize the app visually. But this can be risky if your app shows sensitive data. This plugin allows you to hide the sensitive part in app switchers. However, this plugin isn't available on the Windows platform.

Kapsel Plugins

Following are some of the available Kapsel plugins:

- **Application Preferences**
  This plugin provides a native settings page for the app so that preferences can be viewed and maintained.

- **Attachment Viewer**
  This plugin uses the web view to show the attachments within the application.

- **AuthProxy**
  This plugin provides a JavaScript application programming interface (API) to make HTTPS calls. It handles basic authentication and handles the sending of client certificates on HTTPS for authenticating the client.

- **Bar Code Scanner**
  This plugin allows the SAP Fiori app to scan and decode a bar code using the device's camera. This is a fork of an open-source PhoneGap plugin called *barcodescanner*.

- **Cache Manager**
  Developers can use this plugin to improve the performance of SAP Fiori apps by caching static application resources. It's also compatible with SAP Fiori cache buster.

- **Calendar**
  This plugin is based on an open-source PhoneGap plugin also called *calendar*, and it allows the app to interact with device's calendar.

- **Encrypted Storage**
  This plugin allows the SAP Fiori app to store a large amount of data in the device securely as encrypted data. Thus, it can minimize server access for data and improve app performance.

- **Federation Provider**
  This plugin enables sharing of X.509 certificates for authentication across different applications. Using this plugin, SAP Fiori Client can federate both SAP and third-party certificates. This plugin is available only in Android and iOS platforms.

- **Logger**
  This plugin helps the app enable logging, log various pieces of information. and then upload these logs to SAP Mobile Platform for later analysis.

- **Logon**
  As the name suggests, this plugin handles user authentication and then application registration. The target can be SAP Mobile Platform, SAP Fiori mobile services, or SAP Gateway.

- **Certificate Delivery Service Provider**
  This plugin is dependent on the Logon plugin. It provides a client-side certificate to the SAP Cloud Platform Mobile Services server so that it can be used to authenticate with backend systems. This isn't available on the Microsoft platform.

- **Online Application**
  This plugin allows you to display an external URL's content within the SAP Fiori app using the app's web view. This plugin isn't available on the Microsoft platform.

- **Settings**
  This plugin is used to synchronize application-related settings between SAP Mobile Platform/SAP Fiori mobile services and SAP Fiori Client. When settings such as log level and log upload mode are updated on the server, these settings

get pushed to SAP Fiori Client. When settings such as subscribing to push notifications and other user settings are changed, they are sent to the server for corresponding changes on the server.

- **Toolbar**
  This plugin can show a native toolbar on your SAP Fiori app. You can configure buttons and actions on this toolbar.

- **Usage**
  This plugin helps you collect information on how users use the SAP Fiori apps and provide details about user's devices. This plugin requires SAP Mobile Platform or SAP Fiori mobile services. Using the Usage plugin in SAP Fiori Client requires an SAP Cloud Platform admin to enable it and the consent of the user.

- **Voice Recording**
  This plugin allows you to use voice as an input in your SAP Fiori app by using the native voice recorder feature. You can also record, encrypt, and save audio information.

- **Push Notification**
  This plugin allows you to have notifications sent from the backed to your SAP Fiori app/SAP Fiori Client. However, this functionality uses SAP Mobile Platform or SAP Fiori mobile services for configuring and pushing the notifications. This plugin isn't available in the Windows framework.

Custom SAP Fiori Client

Customers can create a custom SAP Fiori Client when they want to enhance the SAP Fiori Client with additional features. Following are a few of the reasons for creating a custom SAP Fiori Client:

- Add additional authentication mechanisms
- Add additional SAP, third-party, or open-source Apache Cordova plugins
- Change application behavior
- Add brandings such as logos and colors
- Deploy the app to third-party app stores
- Connect to other servers such as the mobile service for app and device management

There are two ways to create a custom SAP Fiori Client:

- **Using SAP Mobile Platform Software Development Kit (SDK)**
  The SAP Mobile Platform SDK contains a script file named *create_fiori_client.js*

that can be used to create a custom SAP Fiori Client in each of the Android, iOS, and Windows platforms. You can create custom branding, configure custom authentication schemes, and add custom Apache Cordova plugins for your custom SAP Fiori Client.

- **Using Visual Studio**
  The Kapsel SDK provides a template for Microsoft Visual Studio, which can be used in Android and iOS platforms but not in Windows.

SAP Fiori Client provides security features in multiple areas as discussed in the following subsections.

Communication Security

Privacy and integrity of communication between SAP Fiori Client and the server should be protected by encrypting the data. This can be achieved by using HTTPS for all communications. In addition, SAP Fiori Client confirms the identity of the server by verifying the server certificate.

Authentication

SAP Fiori Client can connect to SAP Gateway, SAP Fiori mobile services, and SAP Mobile Platform. For each of these servers, multiple authentication procedures are supported. Let's discuss all the supported authentication procedures next.

Single Sign-On with One-Time Password

SAP Fiori Client allows users to use OTP-based authentication. The OTP required for the authentication is generated by the SAP Authenticator app, which the users need to install on their mobile devices.

Note

OTP-based authentication is only available when you connect to the SAP frontend server directly without using SAP Mobile Platform or SAP Fiori mobile services.

Users can start either at the SAP Authenticator app or at the SAP Fiori Client. When starting at the SAP Authenticator app, the user will click on the predefined bookmark pointing to SAP Fiori Client. Now a passcode is generated by the SAP Authenticator app and sent to SAP Fiori Client along with the user name.

Only the first time, SAP Fiori Client asks for a password for authenticating. The next time, this is stored as a security token and supplied to the identity provider (IdP) server along with the user name and the passcode supplied by the SAP Authenticator.

The IdP server validates the input and, if successful, generates a Security Assertion Markup Language (SAML) assertion back to SAP Fiori Client. When SAP Fiori Client accesses the frontend server with this SAML assertion, it will be able to access the SAP Fiori launchpad. The entire flow is shown in Figure 8.2.

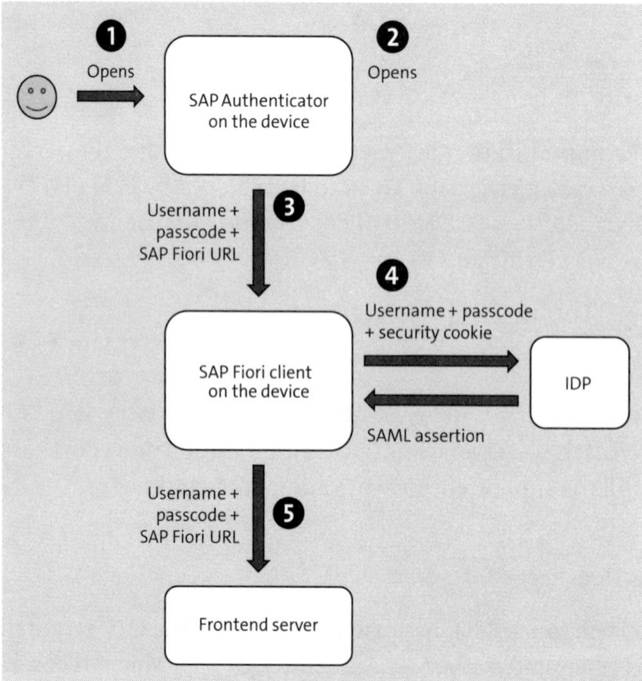

Figure 8.2 OTP-Based SSO Initiated from the SAP Authenticator

When users open SAP Fiori Client, they can click on the **Log On with SAP Authenticator** option, which will fetch the passcode from the SAP authenticator, send it to the server for verification, and request that the user enter the password. A password is required to generate the security token for the first time only. For all subsequent calls, the password won't be asked for; instead, the security token will be sent along with the user name and passcode to receive a SAML assertion, which is sent to the frontend server for a successful authentication.

This flow is shown in Figure 8.3.

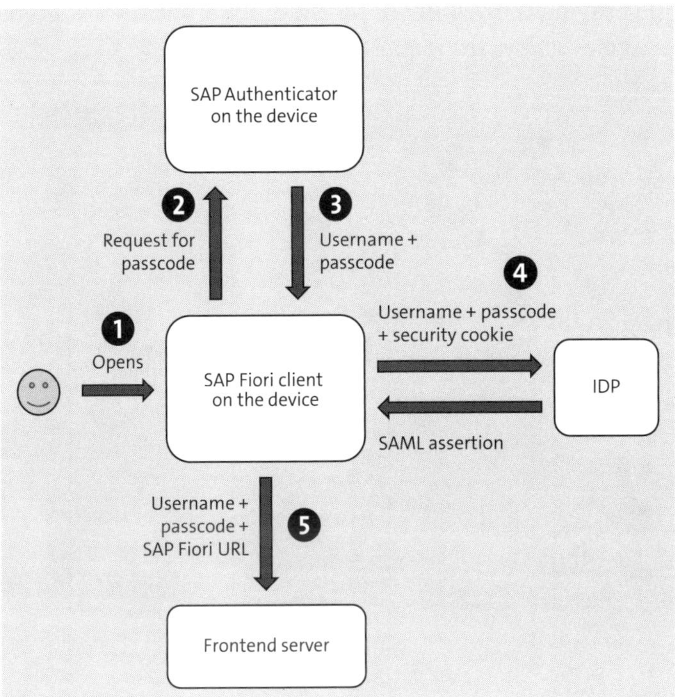

Figure 8.3 OTP-Based SSO Initiated from the SAP Fiori Client

SAML 2.0

SAML 2.0 is a version of the SAML standard that defines protocols for exchanging authorization and authentication data between a service provider (frontend server, in our case) and an IdP.

SAP Fiori Client can use SAML 2.0 by directly connecting to the frontend server or through any one of SAP Mobile Platform and SAP Fiori mobile services.

Figure 8.4 illustrates the communications in a SAML 2.0 SSO scenario.

When a user accesses SAP Fiori Client, and it subsequently makes a call to the frontend server, the frontend server sees that the request isn't authenticated, creates a SAML request, and sends it to SAP Fiori Client asking it to redirect to a trusted IdP along with the SAML request. SAP Fiori Client sends that SAML request to the IdP server. The IdP server will ask the user to authenticate using a basic authentication or a X.509 certificate. Upon successful authentication to the IdP server, it will send the SAML assertion to SAP Fiori Client asking to redirect to the frontend server. Upon verifying the validity of the SAML assertion, the frontend server will log in the user and supply the requested resources.

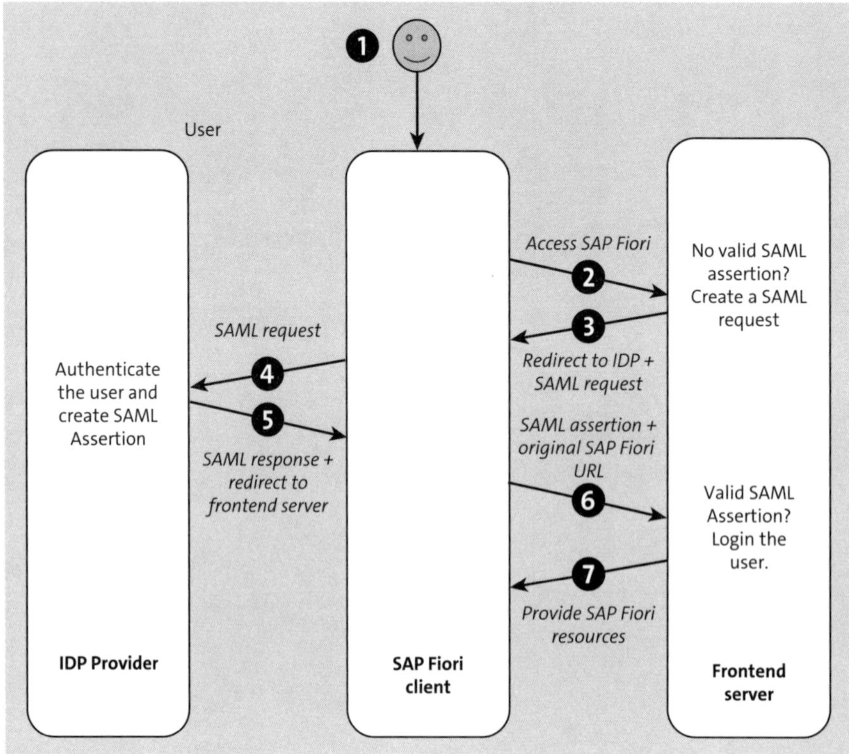

Figure 8.4 SAML SSO Flow

All further requests with the SAML assertion will be honored by the frontend server if the SAML assertion is within the validity period. Upon expiry, another round of SAML transactions kicks in.

X.509 Certificates

X.509 is a standard for the format of public key certificates. An X.509 certificate will contain a public key and an identity, which, in our case, is that of a user. It will be signed by a Certification Authority (CA) after verification. X.509 can be used for both server authentication (SSL) and client authentication. In case of SAP Fiori Client, because we want to use it for user authentication, these certificates are called client certificates. This mode of authentication is supported while directly connecting to the frontend server or through any one of SAP Mobile Platform and SAP Fiori mobile services.

For SAP Fiori Client, provisioning of X.509 certificates to user's devices need to be done using mobile service for app and device management (previously known as Afaria and SAP Mobile Secure).

SAP Logon Tickets

This is an SAP proprietary authentication mechanism. A digitally signed cookie (called MYSAPSSO2) is exchanged between the client and the server for authentication and SSO. This mode of authentication is supported while directly connecting to the frontend server or through any one of SAP Mobile Platform and SAP Fiori mobile services.

Basic Authentication

In this case, users use their user ID and password to log in to servers. This is the easiest of all the authentication methods to implement but also the least secure. When this method is used, it's important to provide a password reset functionality to the user.

Security of Data on the Device

It's common for SAP Fiori Client to download data onto the device as users use the SAP Fiori apps. This data can be sensitive attachments, cached data, or any other data stored on the device. Another security scenario involves anyone getting unauthorized access to the mobile device, opening the SAP Fiori Client, and accessing sensitive information from it.

It's important to secure the application as well as its data footprint from unauthorized access. SAP Fiori Client provides multiple ways to ensure this.

Application Passcode

Users can set an application passcode for SAP Fiori Client so that it challenges the user to enter the passcode whenever an attempt to open SAP Fiori Client is made. This is an effective method of protection from unauthorized access to the device and then to the app.

SAP Fiori Client comes with a default Passcode Policy with the following conditions for the application passcode:

- Minimum length of eight characters
- Lock timeout of five minutes
- Seven maximum unsuccessful attempts
- Enable fingerprint encryption

This default policy can be overwritten if you use SAP Mobile Platform or SAP Fiori mobile services with SAP Fiori Client. In such a case, the administrator can override the default policy defined by SAP Fiori Client.

If instead of using SAP Mobile Platform or SAP Fiori mobile services, you directly connect to a frontend server, you can have your own custom passcode policy by creating a custom SAP Fiori Client and defining the passcode policy in the application configuration file (*appconfig.js*).

The passcode screen shown in Figure 8.5 can be accessed by choosing **Settings** • **Manage Passcodes** within SAP Fiori Client.

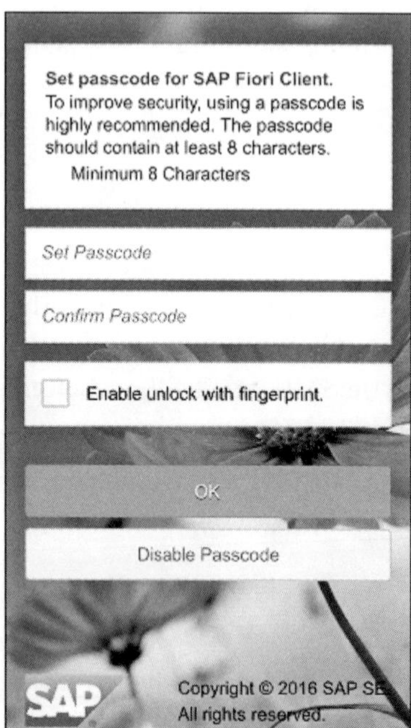

Figure 8.5 Passcode Screen in SAP Fiori Client

Warning

If SAP Mobile Platform or SAP Fiori mobile services aren't used with SAP Fiori Client, then the application passcode isn't mandatory, and the user will be able to skip this step of enabling this security feature.

Fingerprint Authentication

From version 1.8, the SAP Fiori Client application can be unlocked using your fingerprint. However, this feature is available only on iOS and Android and not available in Windows 10 mobile devices.

To support this authentication, devices should be running Android 6 or later with fingerprint recognition hardware. For iOS devices, they should be running iOS 9 or newer and must support the Touch ID feature.

Fingerprint authentication is available only if the passcode is also enabled. If the user fails to authenticate with a fingerprint, the user can use the passcode to enter. Figure 8.5 shows the passcode screen with the **Enable unlock with fingerprint** option.

Note

If there is more than one fingerprint stored in the device's system settings, fingerprint authentication is automatically disabled for SAP Fiori Client. Next time, the user needs to authenticate with a passcode, and re-enable fingerprint authentication.

Logon Plugin Data Vault

Kapsel's Logon plugin provides a data vault that is used by the application to store user names, passwords, and server connection details. The data vault is secured with the application passcode that is set for unlocking SAP Fiori Client.

If the user forgets the passcode and tries unsuccessfully for more than the maximum allowed limit, the content of the data vault is deleted automatically for security reasons.

Encrypted Storage

The Encrypted Storage plugin available in SAP Fiori Client is suitable for securely storing application data. A random encryption key is used for encrypting the data, and the encryption key will be stored in the Logon plugin's data vault.

Encrypted storage also gets destroyed whenever the user's Logon plugin data vault gets destroyed (after a maximum number of unsuccessful tries).

Attachment Viewer

Attachments usually contain sensitive data, so it's important to protect them. Each platform handles attachments differently. Let's see how attachments are protected on each of these platforms.

- In SAP Fiori Client for Android, attachments are opened either in web view or in a third-party application. For certain file types such as *.png* files, attachments won't be downloaded to the device; instead, they are directly shown in the web view. But for certain other files, such as Microsoft Word files, the file will be downloaded to the device, and SAP Fiori Client gives read access to a third-party application to display the file. However, as soon as the user clicks the **Back** button, the attachment is deleted so that no other application can access the file later.
- iOS also uses a native class to preview the attachments and provide access to third-party apps for displaying the attachment. These attachments are stored in a temporary folder. After you close the preview or the third-party display application, the temporary folder is deleted.
- Windows also has a similar behavior when it comes to displaying the attachments. However, the attachment isn't deleted when you move back to SAP Fiori Client or even if you quit SAP Fiori Client. The attachment gets deleted when you load SAP Fiori Client the next time or when SAP Fiori Client is resumed from the tombstone state (i.e., a suspended state).

Privacy Screen

App switcher is a tool that displays screenshots of apps so that you can switch between currently running apps. This can pose a security and privacy risk, as the screenshot used in these app switchers might contain sensitive data.

The Privacy Screen plugin is an open-source Apache Cordova plugin that blanks out the screenshots in app switchers so that the security risk is mitigated. This plugin is included in SAP Fiori Client and enabled by default. This plugin will also disable the screenshot and screen share feature in SAP Fiori Client. This can be also be disabled using **Settings • Screen Sharing**. Figure 8.6 shows two screens of app switcher in an Android device, one with Privacy Screen enabled and the other with Privacy Screen disabled.

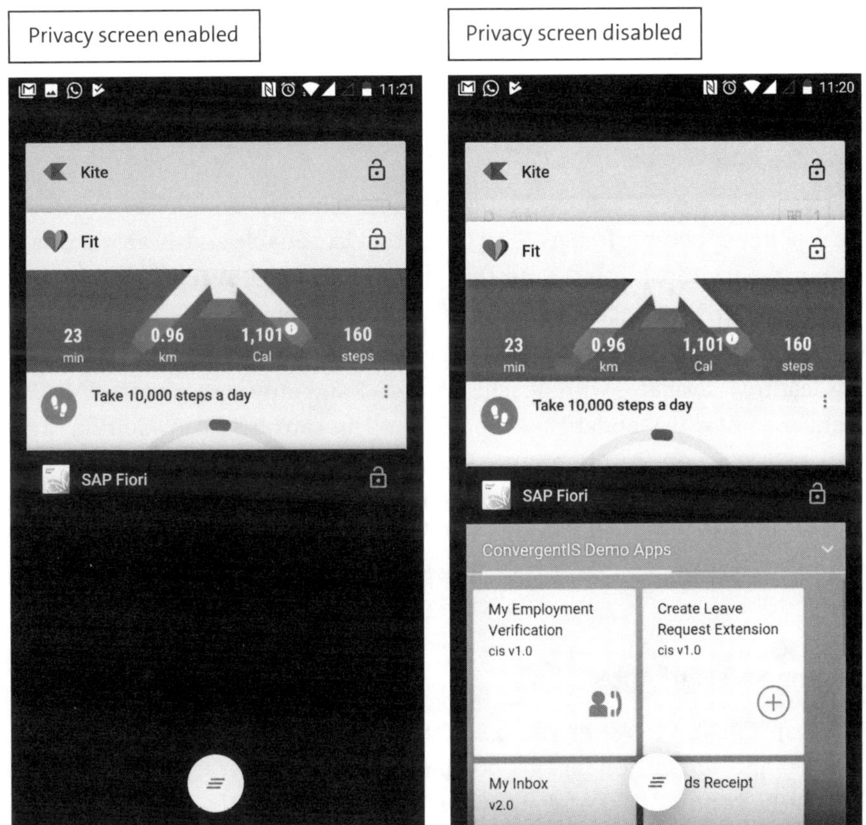

Figure 8.6 Privacy Screen in SAP Fiori Client

Securing Native Device Capabilities

Because of the Apache Cordova and Kapsel plugins within SAP Fiori Client, it has access to a wide range of device features such as camera, contacts, calendar, bar code scanner, and geolocation. When SAP Fiori Client opens any other website or web application, it can also make use of these device features. Therefore, it's important to enable only the required device capabilities within SAP Fiori Client to minimize any unauthorized accesses.

The following features can be used to secure access to device capabilities:

- **No-Bridge Enhancement**
  No-Bridge Enhancement blocks access to all the device features from the web view within Sap Fiori Client if the web view has a different host name than that of the SAP Fiori URL.

  This feature is available in SAP Fiori Client version 1.5 or newer for Android and iOS platforms. For Windows, this feature is available form version 1.6 and newer.

- **Feature Restriction**
  This feature allows SAP Mobile Platform or SAP Fiori mobile services to define a client policy applicable for SAP Fiori Client that can enable and disable access to various device capabilities. Note that this feature isn't available if SAP Fiori Client is directly connected to the SAP frontend server.

- **Apache Cordova Whitelist**
  This feature is available with Apache Cordova 5 and only with custom SAP Fiori Client and not with standard SAP Fiori Client. This can be used in addition to the Feature Restriction feature to fine-tune security. It's used to restrict access to network destinations where the web view can be navigated to by using entries in a configuration file (*config.xml*).

  This feature is obtained by adding the Apache Cordova Whitelist plugin.

Packaging SAP Fiori Apps

In SAP Fiori Client, whenever you open an SAP Fiori launchpad, all the SAPUI5 library files and application files get downloaded from the server. Although these files get cached, the initial download of the files can result in a bad user experience. In addition, if the download of any of the application resources fails, it results in poor rendering of the app. The packaging of SAP Fiori apps is used to ensure best application performance in all scenarios.

SAP provides tools to package SAP Fiori apps as self-contained apps, which means that these apps will have all the SAPUI5 library files and application files as part of the application itself. Thus, network calls are used only for fetching and updating the business data, which optimizes the time required to open the SAP Fiori apps. See Figure 8.7 for the visual representation.

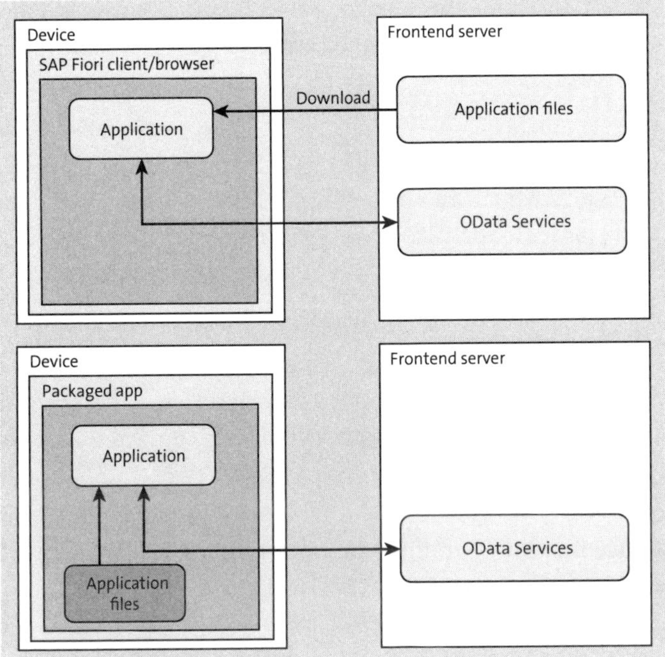

Figure 8.7 Application Files in a Packaged Application and in SAP Fiori Client/Browser

The packaging of SAP Fiori apps is required if you want to enable offline experience with SAP Fiori apps. For offline experiences, you need to connect the app with SAP Mobile Platform or SAP Fiori mobile services, which will create an offline store within the app and a local OData service for the app to communicate during offline scenarios. Upon reestablishing a connection with the network, data will synchronize with the server.

There are two options to package SAP Fiori apps for Android and iOS platforms:

- **CLI Packager**
  The CLI Packager is a *Node.js* application that is part of the SAP Mobile Platform SDK. You can choose multiple SAP Fiori apps to be packaged. This tool will download all the application files and package them into an Apache Cordova app. For opening each application, there is a local launchpad within the packaged application that will have tiles for each packaged SAP Fiori app.

- **Visual Studio packager extension**
  You can use Visual Studio with a packager extension for SAP Fiori apps for packaging SAP Fiori apps. This packager extension fetches all the application files

from the frontend server and adds them to the project. You can also add and remove Kapsel plugins required for the packaged app.

SAP Fiori Mobile Service

SAP Fiori mobile service is a fully featured mobile application platform provided as an application service on SAP Cloud Platform. SAP Fiori mobile service provides multiple tools for development and operations of SAP Fiori mobile apps.

Following are a few important features of the SAP Fiori mobile service:

- **Build in the cloud**
  An SAP Fiori hybrid application can be fully built in the cloud without installing any tools in the on-premise system. You don't even need to have a Mac for building a hybrid app for iOS.

- **Plugin management**
  SAP Fiori mobile service provides a unified interface for plugin management. Developers can use this to add plugins to the SAP Fiori apps using this UI.

- **Integration with SAP Mobile Place**
  SAP Mobile Place is SAP's enterprise app store. This makes it easy for enterprises to make the applications available to its employees and business partners.

SAP Hybrid App Toolkit

SAP Hybrid App Toolkit (HAT) is an optional plugin in SAP Web IDE that can be used to mobilize SAP Fiori apps. This has three components as shown in Figure 8.8.

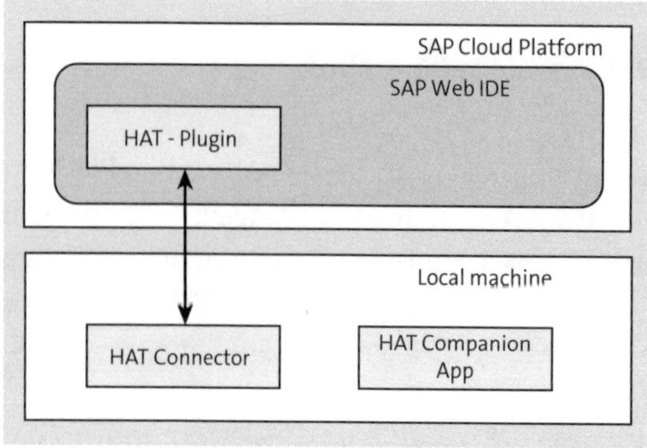

Figure 8.8 Components

SAP Web IDE Plugin

The HAT add-on is an optional SAP Web IDE plugin that provides mobile development tools from within the SAP Web IDE. It has the following features:

- Code completion for Apache Cordova and Kapsel APIs
- Hybrid app that runs on browser, Companion app, and the actual device
- Deploys to SAP Cloud Platform
- Performs device configuration

SAP Hybrid App Toolkit Companion

This is a native mobile application available for iOS and Android that runs on a mobile device or a mobile emulator. This is available on Google Play and Apple's App Store. After the app is created, it can be tested and previewed using this companion app just by scanning the barcode of the app available within the SAP Web IDE. It contains a superset of all the supported Apache Cordova and Kapsel plugins, so you can set all the native features using it.

SAP Hybrid App Toolkit Connector

The HAT Connector is available in the SAP Store for download. This is a local server process that runs on the local development system and enables connection from the SAP Web IDE to trigger a local build of the local project.

Enable HAT

In this section, we'll package an SAP Fiori app into an hybrid app using HAT. We'll use the SAP Web IDE plugin and HAT Companion app, and we'll perform a local build as well.

Enable the SAP Web IDE Plugin

To enable SAP Web IDE, go to **Tools • Preferences**, and choose **Plugins.** Click the **HAT** plugin as shown in Figure 8.9.

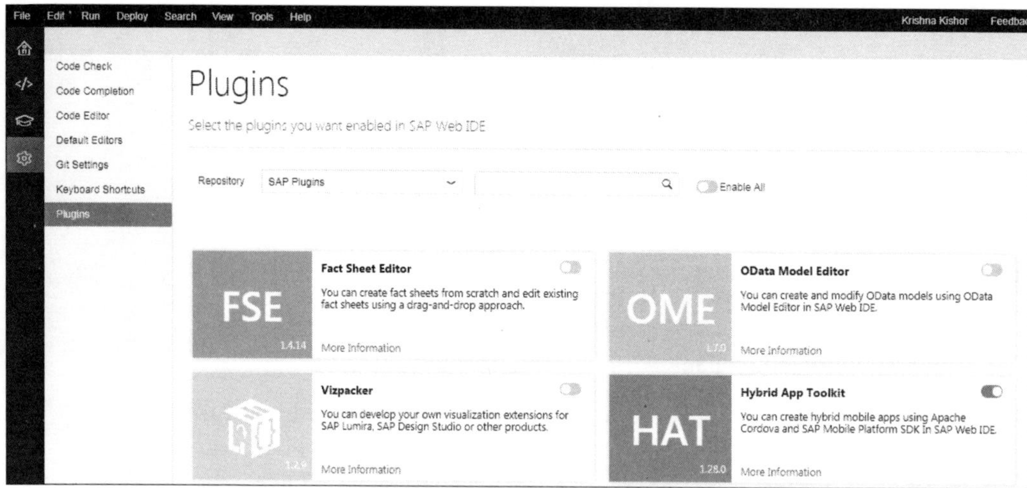

Figure 8.9 Enabling the SAP Hybrid App Toolkit

Enable SAP Fiori Mobile Services (Development and Operations)

Hybrid apps built within SAP Web IDE can be deployed to SAP Mobile Platform or SAP Fiori mobile services. To enable this, SAP Fiori mobile services development and operations needs to be enabled in SAP Cloud Platform. Go to the **SAP Cloud Platform Cockpit** screen, and choose **Services**. Locate the **Development & Operations** tile as shown in Figure 8.10.

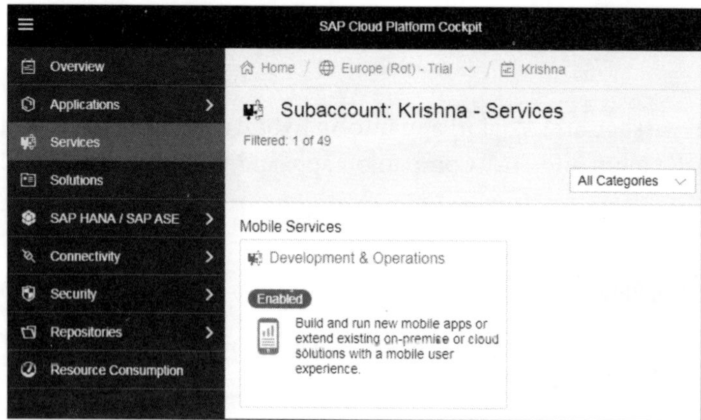

Figure 8.10 Enabling SAP Fiori Mobile Services in the SAP Cloud Platform Trial

Enable SAP Fiori Mobile Services

SAP Fiori mobile services enable developers to build hybrid apps with no setup in the developer's local environment. To enable the SAP Fiori mobile service, go to the trial **SAP Cloud Platform Cockpit** screen, and click on **Services**. Locate and click on the **Fiori Mobile Service**. Click on the **Enable** button to enable the service. Figure 8.11 shows the enabled service.

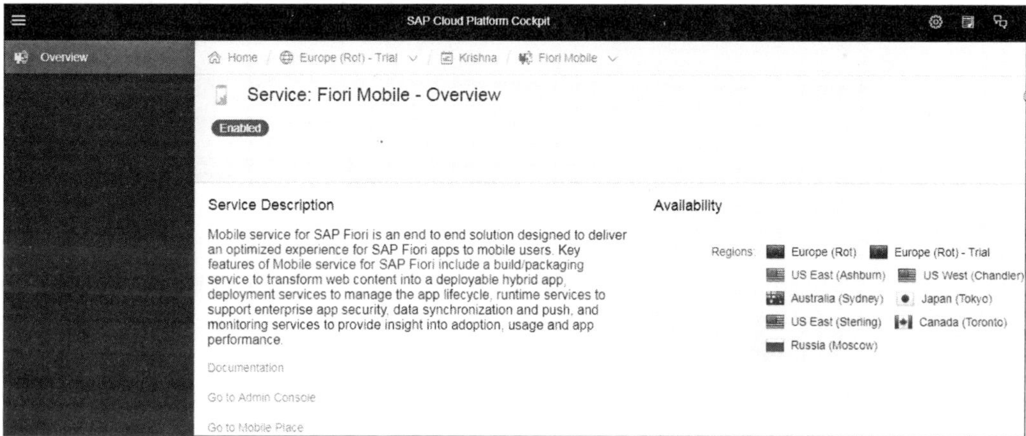

Figure 8.11 Enabled SAP Fiori Mobile Service

Connectivity Requirements

When preparing your local development system, keep the following in mind:

- If you're behind a proxy, it's important to ensure that all the development tools (*node.js*, emulators, etc.) are configured to use your network proxy.
- SAP recommends that you don't change your network configurations in-between installing all the required tools.

Prepare Apache Cordova Development Environment

If you plan to perform a local build, HAT is dependent on Apache Cordova. The Apache Cordova development environment must be set up before installing HAT-related resources. Let's go through each of these requirements in a Windows environment:

1. Install Apache Cordova 6.5 by entering the following command in your command-line tool:

```
npm install -g cordova@6.5
```

2. Set up a command-line Git client by downloading and installing it from *https://git-scm.com*.

3. Install the Apache Ant Java-based build tool for automating build processes from *http://ant.apache.org*.

4. Install Android SDK 6.0 by going to *https://developer.android.com/studio/index.html* and getting the platform-dependent version. This is required for packaging an Android app. By installing Android Studio, the Android SDK also gets installed.

Installing the SAP Mobile Platform Software Development Kit (Optional)

Some of the HAT features may require the SAP Mobile Platform SDK. You need to install the SAP Mobile Platform SDK on your local system as described next.

Licensed Version

If you have the license to SAP Mobile Platform or to SAP Fiori mobile services, you can install the licensed version from *https://launchpad.support.sap.com*. Select the **Software Downloads** tile. Then search for "SAP Mobile Platform SDK", click on **SAP Mobile Platform SDK 3.0.** and download the version according to your operating system. See Figure 8.12 for more details.

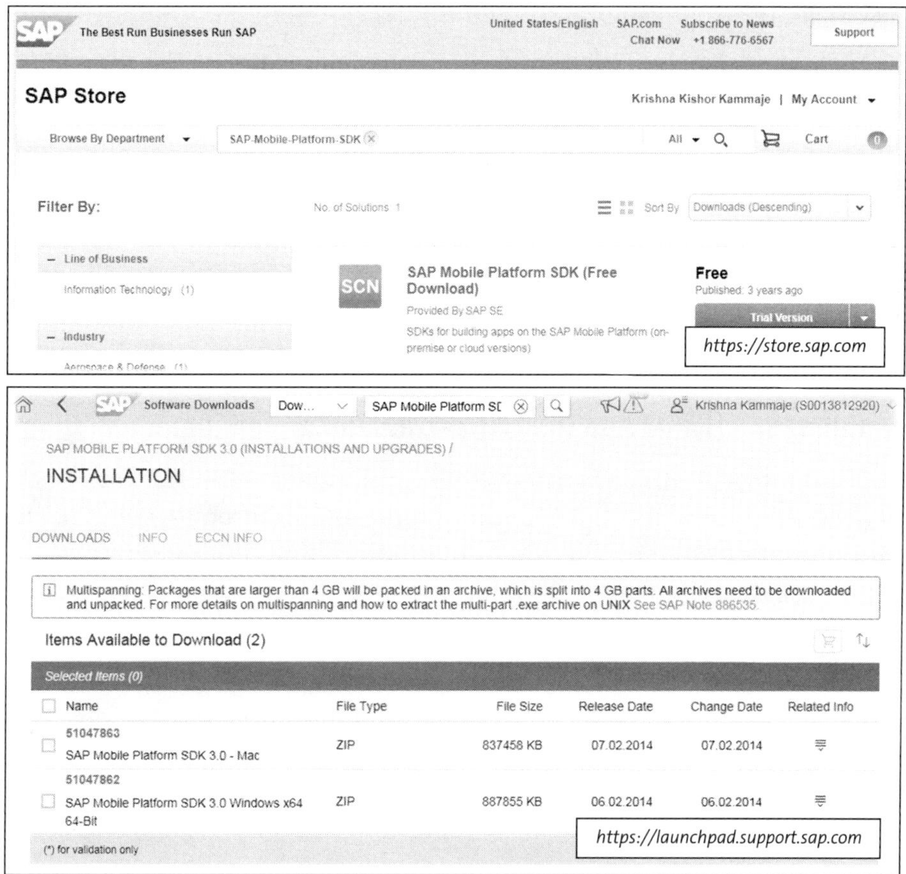

Figure 8.12 Downloading Options for SAP Mobile Platform SDK 3.0

Trial Version

If you don't have a license to SAP Mobile Platform, you can download a trial version from the SAP Store at *https://store.sap.com*. Search for "SAP Mobile Platform SDK". Click on the **Trial Version** to get an email with a link to the installation resource. See Figure 8.12 for more details.

For the trial version, after clicking on the **Trial Version** button, an email will be sent to your registered email address with a link to download the SAP Mobile Platform SDK.

To install SAP Mobile Platform, follow these steps:

1. After downloading, expand the archive, and double-click on the setup file to start the installation process for the SAP Mobile Platform. A wizard opens and takes you through the installation process.

2. If you're adding Kapsel add-ons in your hybrid app, create an environment variable called `KAPSEL_HOME` and its value as the path to the Kapsel SDK. For example: `C:\SAP\MobileSDK3\KapselSDK`.

3. Install the Kapsel command-line interface as follows:

```
npm install -g C:\SAP\MobileSDK3\KapselSDK\cli
```

Installing SAP Hybrid App Toolkit (for Local Build)

HAT needs to be installed locally on your development machine if you want to perform a local build for your hybrid application using the local Apache Cordova development environment.

Node.js needs to be installed as a prerequisite to installing HAT. Follow these steps:

1. Go to *https://nodejs.org/download/release/v5.4.1*.

2. Select the suitable installer per your platform as shown in Figure 8.13.

3. Install using the installer.

```
← → C   🔒 Secure | https://nodejs.org/download/release/v5.4.1/
```

Index of /download/release/v5.4.1/

```
../
docs/                               12-Jan-2016 21:21              -
win-x64/                            12-Jan-2016 21:11              -
win-x86/                            12-Jan-2016 21:09              -
SHASUMS256.txt                      12-Jan-2016 23:45           2480
SHASUMS256.txt.asc                  12-Jan-2016 23:45           3371
node-v5.4.1-darwin-x64.tar.gz       12-Jan-2016 21:03        9886320
node-v5.4.1-darwin-x64.tar.xz       12-Jan-2016 21:03        6976268
node-v5.4.1-headers.tar.gz          12-Jan-2016 21:26         469263
node-v5.4.1-headers.tar.xz          12-Jan-2016 21:26         340968
node-v5.4.1-linux-arm64.tar.gz      12-Jan-2016 21:00       11368463
node-v5.4.1-linux-arm64.tar.xz      12-Jan-2016 21:00        7401076
node-v5.4.1-linux-armv6l.tar.gz     12-Jan-2016 21:49       11246606
node-v5.4.1-linux-armv6l.tar.xz     12-Jan-2016 21:54        7315712
node-v5.4.1-linux-armv7l.tar.gz     12-Jan-2016 21:06       11251830
node-v5.4.1-linux-armv7l.tar.xz     12-Jan-2016 21:07        7312512
node-v5.4.1-linux-x64.tar.gz        12-Jan-2016 20:59       11932557
node-v5.4.1-linux-x64.tar.xz        12-Jan-2016 21:00        8165600
node-v5.4.1-linux-x86.tar.gz        12-Jan-2016 20:58       11467084
node-v5.4.1-linux-x86.tar.xz        12-Jan-2016 20:59        7779172
node-v5.4.1-sunos-x64.tar.gz        12-Jan-2016 21:05       12759240
node-v5.4.1-sunos-x64.tar.xz        12-Jan-2016 21:06        8364608
node-v5.4.1-sunos-x86.tar.gz        12-Jan-2016 21:01       11796150
node-v5.4.1-sunos-x86.tar.xz        12-Jan-2016 21:02        7702128
node-v5.4.1-x64.msi                 12-Jan-2016 21:11       10375168
node-v5.4.1-x86.msi                 12-Jan-2016 21:09        9449472
node-v5.4.1.pkg                     12-Jan-2016 21:21       12564658
node-v5.4.1.tar.gz                  12-Jan-2016 21:22       22559624
node-v5.4.1.tar.xz                  12-Jan-2016 21:24       12812444
```

Figure 8.13 Node.js Installers

Now, HAT needs to be installed on the local machine. SAP Store provides versions for both Windows and Mac. You can click on the **Trial Version** button, and the link to download HAT will be sent to your registered email.

To install HAT, follow these steps:

1. After the archive gets downloaded, extract it into a folder. Navigate to the setup folder, and double-click on *setup.cmd* as shown in Figure 8.14.

Name	Date modified	Type	Size
logs	7/14/2017 4:48 AM	File folder	
res	7/14/2017 4:48 AM	File folder	
scripts	7/14/2017 4:48 AM	File folder	
setup	10/16/2017 10:31 ...	File folder	
signing	7/14/2017 4:48 AM	File folder	
util	7/14/2017 4:48 AM	File folder	
views	7/14/2017 4:48 AM	File folder	
WebIdeCompanion	7/14/2017 4:48 AM	File folder	
assistmsg.json	7/14/2017 4:48 AM	JSON File	5 KB
build.json	7/14/2017 4:48 AM	JSON File	1 KB
config.json	7/14/2017 4:48 AM	JSON File	1 KB
package.json	7/14/2017 4:48 AM	JSON File	1 KB
proxy.cmd	7/14/2017 4:48 AM	Windows Comma...	1 KB
proxy.sh	7/14/2017 4:48 AM	Shell Script	1 KB
run.cmd	7/14/2017 4:48 AM	Windows Comma...	1 KB
run.sh	7/14/2017 4:48 AM	Shell Script	1 KB
setup.cmd	7/14/2017 4:48 AM	Windows Comma...	1 KB
setup.sh	7/14/2017 4:48 AM	Shell Script	1 KB

Figure 8.14 Installation Folder for HAT

This will trigger a wizard in the local system at *http://127.0.0.1:3000/index.html#/step1*.

2. Step 1 of the wizard is to verify the prerequisites for starting the hybrid development. Click on the **Check All** button as shown in Figure 8.15 to check all the prerequisites, such as Java SDK, Ant, Android SDK (for creating Android apps), Apache Cordova, and Kapsel for installing the HAT. Android SDK will check for the availability of an Android Virtual Device (AVD) for running the app on an emulator. If the AVD isn't available, you can create an AVD using Android Studio or using the command-line interface. It even performs a sample Apache Cordova build for a sample app to verify that the local build works fine.

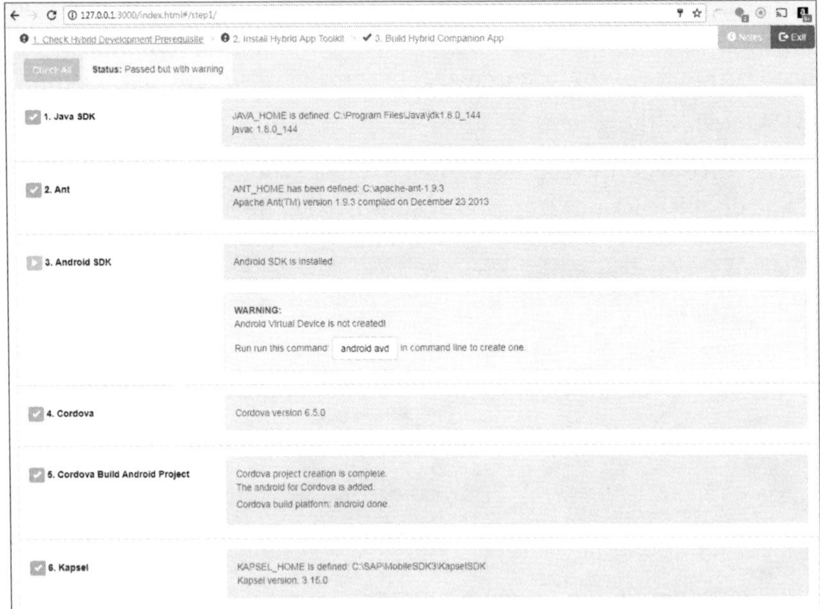

Figure 8.15 Step 1 of the HAT Installation

3. Step 2 of the wizard is **Install Hybrid App Toolkit** as shown in Figure 8.16. If you have any custom Apache Cordova plugins, they can be provided at the fifth task of this step as shown in Figure 8.16.

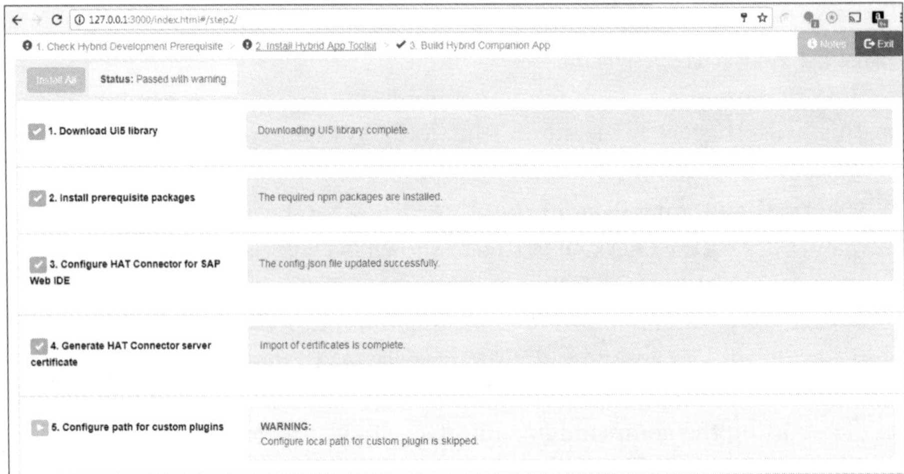

Figure 8.16 Step 2 of the HAT Installation

4. In step 3 of the HAT installation, the HAT Companion app will be built after installing the prerequisites. This should be done only once unless there is a HAT release upgrade. WebIdeCompanion.apk is the Android app that was created in the fourth task of this step, as shown in Figure 8.17.

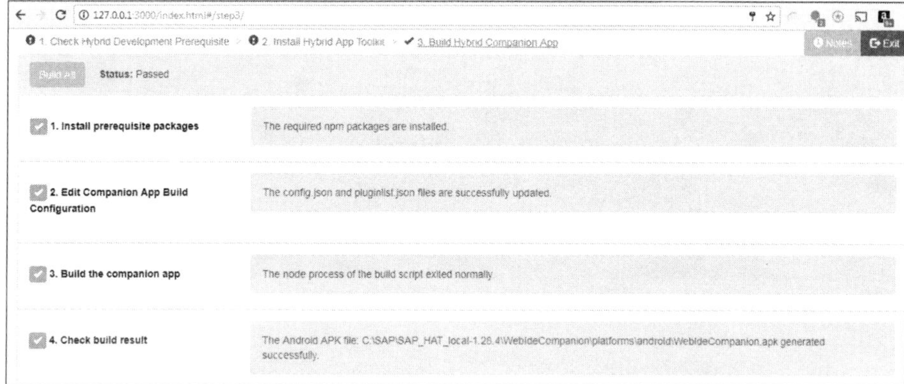

Figure 8.17 Step 3 of the HAT Installation

This step completes the HAT installation in the local system.

Warning

If SAP Web IDE and the HAT plugin version have been upgraded by SAP, you need to upgrade the locally installed components of HAT as well to be compatible.

Creating a Hybrid App

In this section, we'll create a hybrid app using the installed HAT.

Start SAP Hybrid App Toolkit Connector

The HAT Connector manages the integration of SAP Web IDE in the cloud with HAT in the local system.

To start the HAT Connector, navigate to the extracted archive of the HAT add-on as shown in Figure 8.17:

- On Windows, double-click on **run.cmd**.
- On Mac, open the terminal window and run `chmod +x *.sh`, followed by `./run.sh`.

It prompts you to enter the HAT Connector certificate password. This is the same password that you entered while installing HAT at step 2, task 4, as shown earlier in Figure 8.16. HAT Connector will start listening now for any incoming connection from the SAP Web IDE at port 9010, as shown in Figure 8.18.

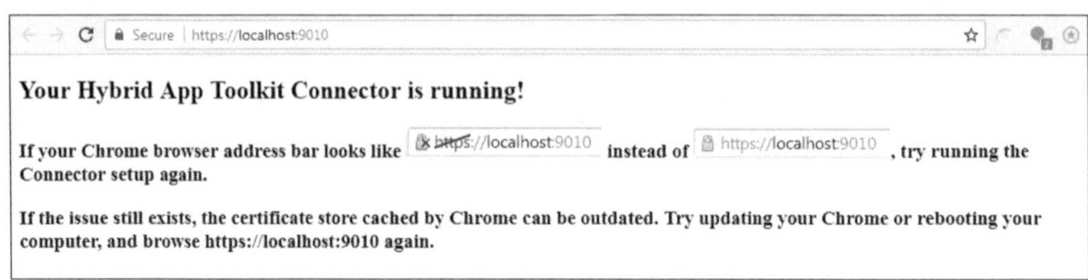

Figure 8.18 HAT Connector Listening on Default Port 9010

You can also verify this by navigating to *https://localhost:9010* and by seeing the message **Your Hybrid App Toolkit Connector is running!** (Figure 8.19).

Figure 8.19 HAT Connector Running Successfully

You need to enable cookies in your browser for the proper functioning of the HAT Connector. In addition, different browsers need different settings to allow SAP Web IDE to successfully connect to the HAT (Table 8.1).

Browser	Configuration to Enable Cookies
Chrome	Settings • Advanced • Privacy • Content settings • Cookies • Enable Allow sites to save and read cookie data

Table 8.1 Connecting SAP Web IDE to HAT with Different Browsers

Browser	Configuration to Enable Cookies
Internet Explorer	After loading the Web IDE, go to **Internet Options • Security • Trusted Sites • Sites**. By clicking on 'Add' here, you'll be adding the Web IDE URL to the Trusted sites. Click on the 'Custom Level' is the above screen and a Security Settings screen opens. Under subheading; Miscellaneous', disable 'Access data sources across domains'.
Firefox	Upon opening *https://localhost:9010*, you'll get a warning page. Choose **Advanced • Add Exception**; check the **Permanently Store this Exception** checkbox; and then click **Confirm Security Exception**. Navigate to **about:preferences#privacy**, and then choose **History • Remember History**.
Safari	Choose **Preferences • Privacy • Cookie and Website Data • Always allow**.

Table 8.1 Connecting SAP Web IDE to HAT with Different Browsers (Cont.)

Test Connection from SAP Web IDE to SAP Hybrid App Toolkit

After setting the preceding browser settings, you need to verify if the SAP Web IDE can talk to the HAT component on the local machine by following these steps:

1. Open SAP Web IDE, and go to **Tools • Preferences • Hybrid Application Toolkit**.
2. Check the **Enable Local Add-On Features** box.
3. Click on **Test Connection**.
4. If the connection to the HAT Connector is successful, you'll get a message indicating the version of the HAT, as shown in Figure 8.20. If an error occurs, follow the details provided in the error to resolve it.

API Key Security

In the preceding Figure 8.20, you can see an API key. This key has to match the API key in the *config.json* file in the HAT folder. The default API keys needs to be changed for security reasons.

Replace the current API key in both the places as shown in Figure 8.21. Ensure that the HAT Connector is restarted, so that the new API key is considered.

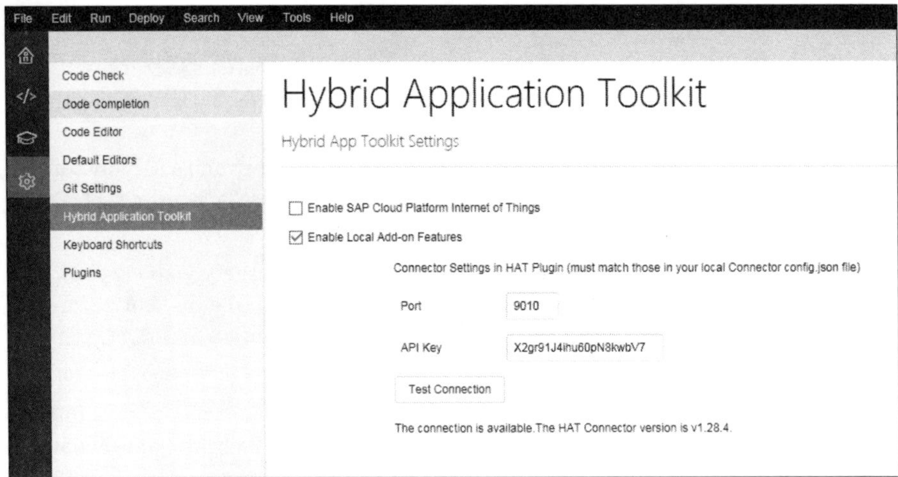

Figure 8.20 Testing the Connection to HAT

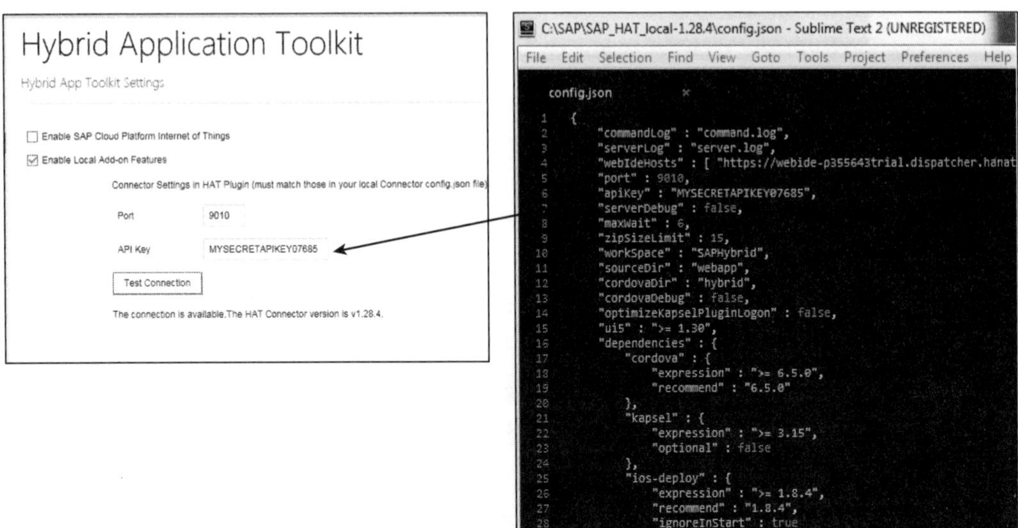

Figure 8.21 Changing the API Key

Note

If you receive an error in the preceding step indicating that default port 9010 is already in use, you can change the default port at *config.json* within the HAT folder and restart the HAT Connector.

Creating a Hybrid Application Project

You can convert any SAPUI5 project into a hybrid project. For this exercise, we'll use the FB_Worklist project, which we used in previous sections.

Configuring Device Properties

You can set various device-related properties in your SAP Web IDE project. These settings define the properties of the target device to which hybrid applications are deployed.

To open device properties, right-click on your project, and choose **Project Settings •Hybrid App Toolkit •Hybrid App Configuration**. The configuration form opens as shown in Figure 8.22.

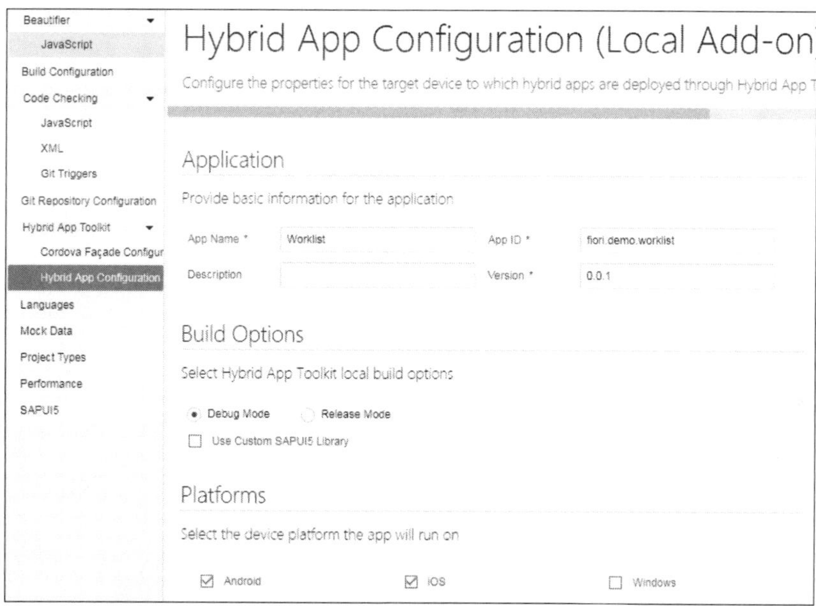

Figure 8.22 Device Configuration File

You can use Kapsel Logon Manager for logging into the app. After you select the **Logon Manager**, you can either use the SAP Cloud Platform mobile services or SAP Mobile Platform server for logging in. Under **Logon Options**, you can select the **Simplified Screen** as the login screen for the application (see Figure 8.23).

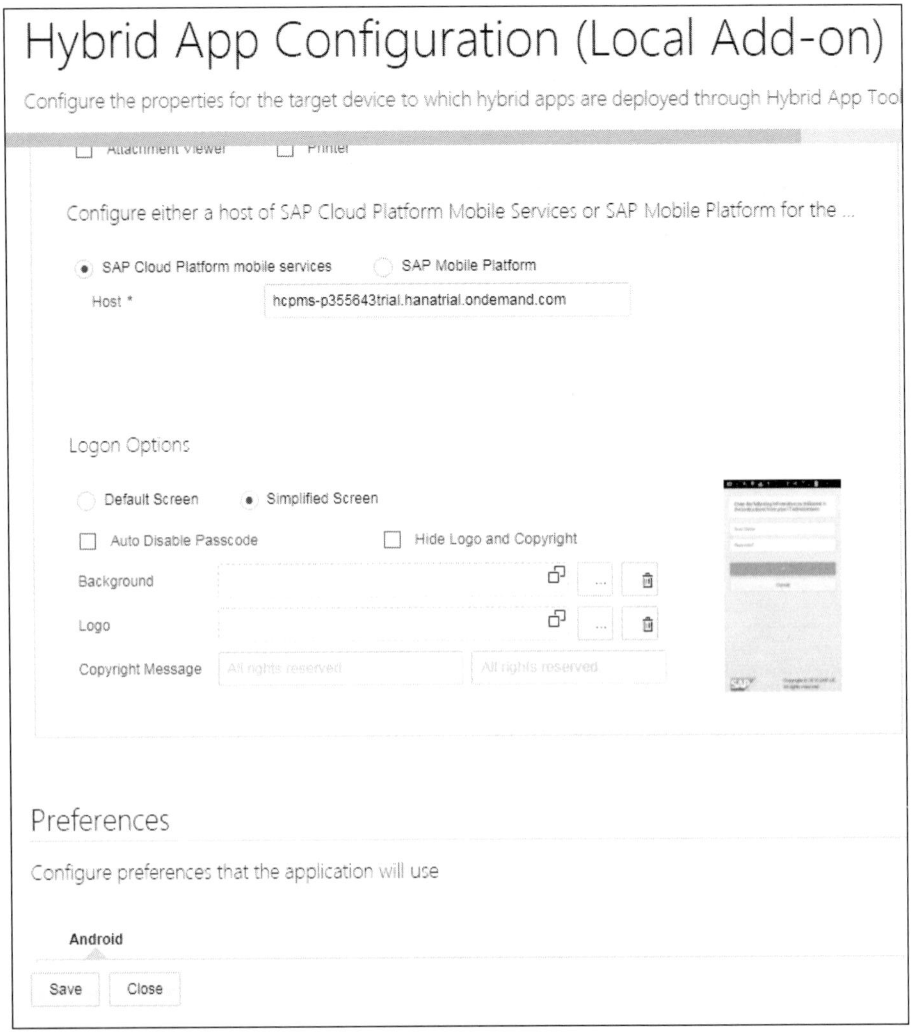

Figure 8.23 Configuring Application Logon Using Logon Manager

Following are the options in this form as shown in Figure 8.23:

- **Application**
  Under **Application**, provide an application name under **App Name**, an application ID including your namespace under **App ID**, and application's version under **Version**.

- **Build Options**
  Under **Build Options**, you have two options:

- **Debug Mode**: With this option, the app will be debuggable in Chrome and Safari browsers. On Android devices, after enabling **Debugging** mode, you can debug the app by navigating to *chrome://inspect* in the Chrome browser. In iOS devices, you can enable Web Inspector by navigating to **Settings • Safari • Advanced**. Open the Safari browser, and you can debug the app.

- **Release Mode**: With this option, the SAPUI5 build is also performed, and the app isn't debuggable on devices.

  In addition, by selecting the **Use custom UI5 library** checkbox, you can direct your app to use a custom SAPUI5 library. This custom SAPUI5 library should be available within the project as a *.zip* file with the name starting with *sapui5-*.

- **Platforms**
  Under **Platforms**, choose all the platforms the app will run on.

- **Plugins**
  Here you can select all the plugins such as core Apache Cordova plugins, Kapsel plugins, and any custom plugins.

- **Preferences**
  This section provides various configurations for the splash screen, icon, log level, orientation, and so on. There are separate configurations for Android and iOS platforms.

All of the preceding settings are stored in the *.project.json* file.

Testing

There are multiple ways to test the hybrid application to validate the business requirements of the application. We'll discuss these testings methods next.

Testing on the Browser: Preview Option

To test in the browser with the preview option, follow these steps:

1. In the hybrid app project, click on the *index.html* file.
2. Right-click on the `index.html` and choose the **Run** icon on the SAP Web IDE toolbar. This will open the application in a new tab and load the application from SAP Web IDE itself.

3. You need to enable the preview mode with frame in the **Run Configurations** screen so that you can see the viewing options while previewing the application. To do so, right-click on the project, and choose **Run · Run Configurations.** Then choose **Run Index.html** configurations as shown in Figure 8.24. If you don't see the **Run index.html** option, you can create a new configuration by clicking the **+** button.

4. Choose the **With Frame** option, and then click on **Save and Run**.

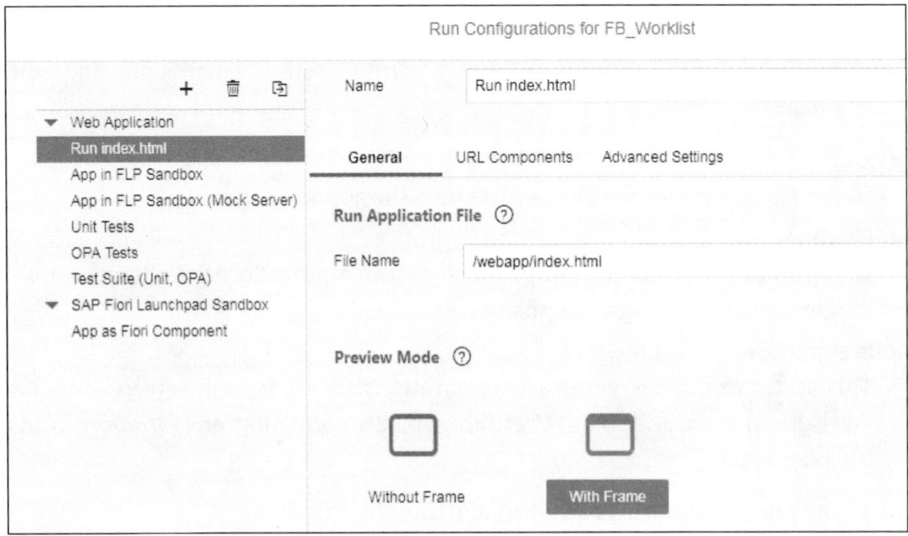

Figure 8.24 Run Configuration with the "With Frame" Option

You can check the application in different form factors and screen orientations using the toolbar on the preview page. However, you won't be able to make use of any device-specific features such as Bar Code Scanner and Camera.

Testing in the Browser with the Cordova Façade

The Cordova Façade Preview allows you to simulate the functionality of a list of device features from within the browser without using the simulator or the device. Right-click on the project, and choose **Run • Run as • Web Application**. When a Cordova Façade is available, a round, blue button appears as shown in Figure 8.25.

Supported Apache Cordova plugins are Camera, Contacts, Device Information, Dialogs, Geolocation, Device Motion, Device Orientation, Media Capture, File, and Printer.

Supported Kapsel plugins are Bar Code Scanner, Calendar, Attachment Viewer, Encrypted Storage, Voice Recording, App Update, and Offline OData.

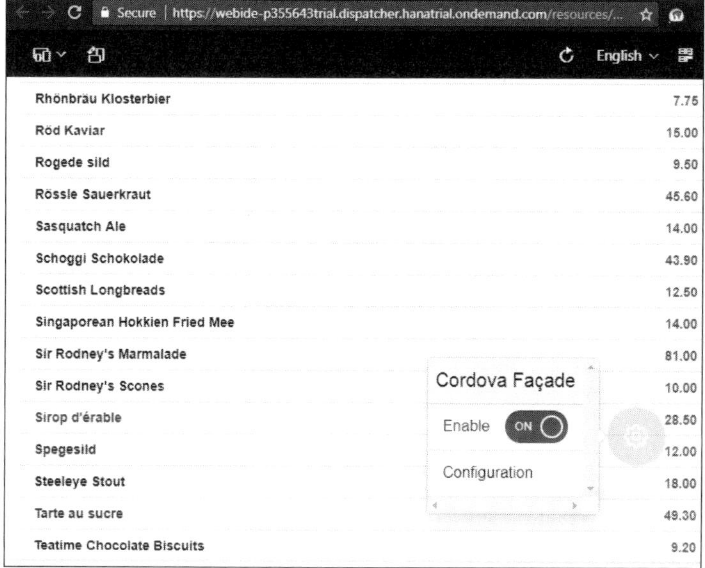

Figure 8.25 Enabling the Cordova Façade

Testing Using the Device Test Cloud Service

Device test providers provide a service on SAP Cloud Platform to test your applications on a real device. This service is provided by Perfecto and is integrated with SAP Fiori mobile services.

To use this device test provider, follow these steps:

1. Open SAP Fiori mobile services from the SAP Cloud Platform services page.
2. Click on the **Go to Admin Console**' link from within the service message to opens the SAP Fiori mobile services admin page.
3. Click on **Account • Device Test Cloud** as shown in Figure 8.26.
4. Under **Service Provider**, select **Perfecto Mobile Continuous Quality Lab**.
5. Click on **Save** to save the configuration.

Tip

Licensing and support responsibilities of this Device Test Cloud service lie with the Perfecto vendor.

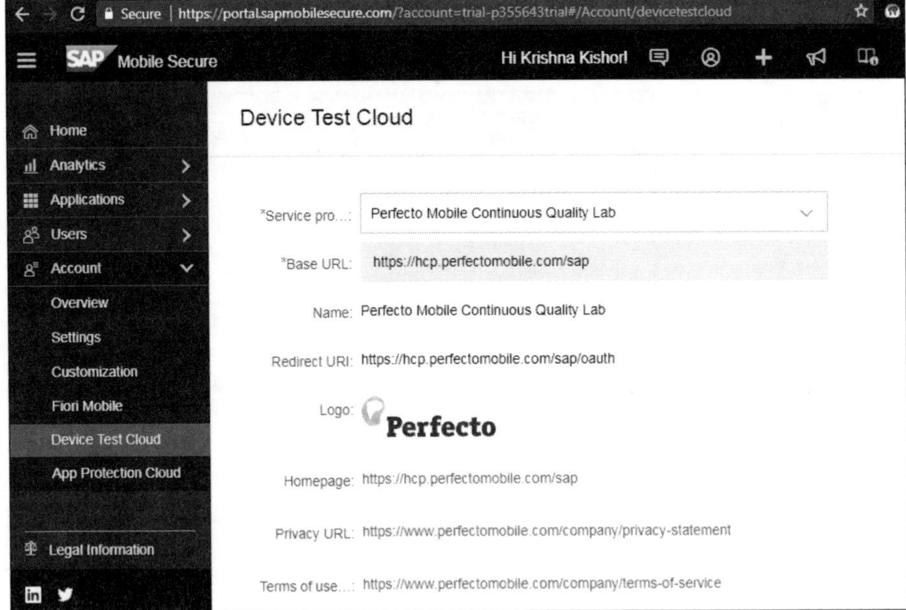

Figure 8.26 Enabling the "Device Test Cloud" Option from SAP Fiori Mobile Services

This integration adds a **Fiori Mobile • Launch on Device Cloud** option in the app context menu, as shown in Figure 8.27.

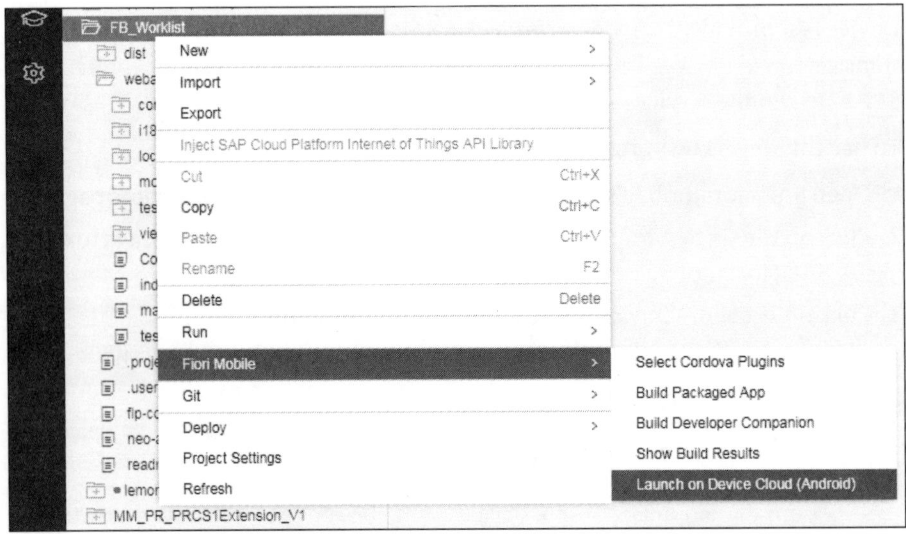

Figure 8.27 Testing the App on Device Cloud

6. This navigates to the Perfect Mobile site and provides a list of Android apps to be chosen. Select one of the apps, and click **Open**. This will install the app first and then show it (see Figure 8.28).

7. You can test the app now on a real device.

Figure 8.28 Installing the App on an Android Device

Testing Using the Companion App on an Actual Device

The HAT Companion app is used for testing the app, including the device-specific features. The HAT Companion app is built during installation of the HAT. You can test or preview the app either using the locally built HAT Companion app or an Android device that contains the HAT Companion app from the Google Play store.

To test the app using the HAT Companion app on your development system, follow these steps:

1. Right-click on the *index.html* file of the project, and choose **Run • Preview on Local Companion App • Android Emulator**. The HAT Companion app will be launched, and the app to be tested will be displayed in it.

2. Test the app with all the features supported by the app.

3. If there are any changes to the app files, test it by double-clicking on the HAT Companion app to refresh it.

4. The HAT Companion app is also available in iOS and Android app stores. This can be installed on your mobile devices, and the application can be tested in that app. To get the HAT Companion app on your device, go to the corresponding app store of your platform (Figure 8.29).

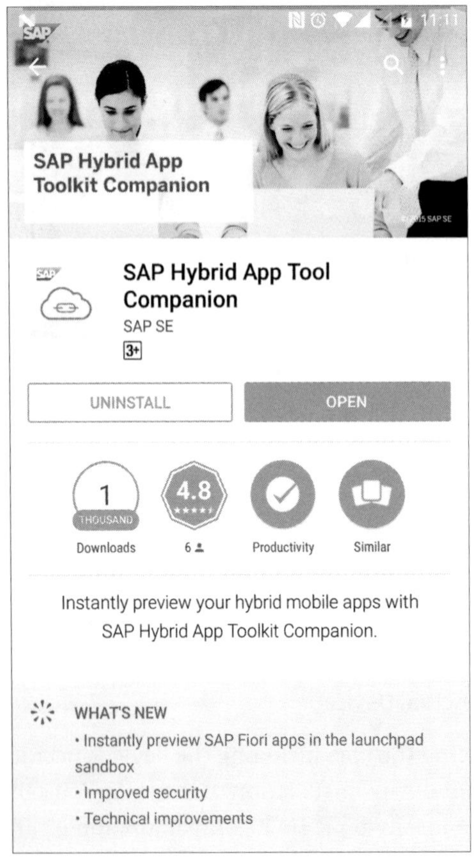

Figure 8.29 Installing the HAT Companion App on Your Device (Android)

5. To open the app on the device's HAT Companion app, right-click on the *index.html* file of the project, and select **Run • Run index.html**. This opens the app in a new tab.

   On the top right of the preview page, there is a button that opens a QR code as shown in Figure 8.30. This QR code can be scanned from the HAT Companion app to open the development project and perform testing.

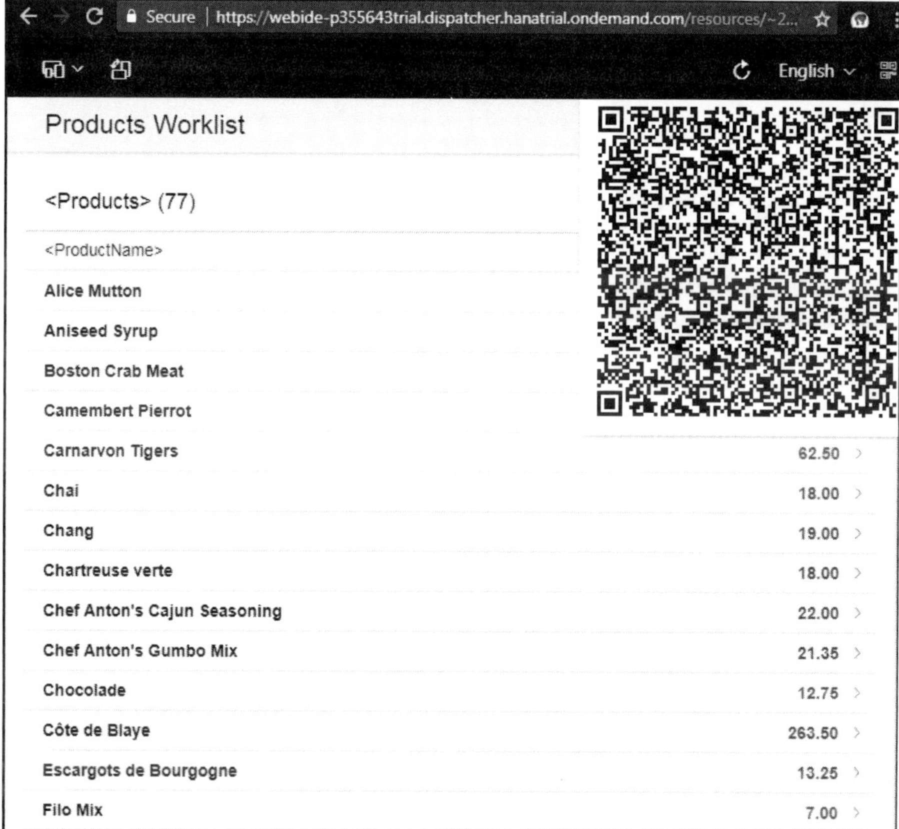

Figure 8.30 QR Code for Scanning the App into the HAT Companion App on the Device

Tip

If you want to log in to the app with a different user, you can log out of the HAT Companion app and log back in with the correct user.

Building Apps

After the successful testing process, an installable app will be created by the build-ing process. Let's explore the process involved.

Tip

The building process usually takes a long time to complete. Therefore, the Com-panion app should be used for testing.

Before the local building process begins, the app must be deployed to the local HAT.

Deploy the App to the Local HAT

The app needs to be deployed to the local HAT, so that it can be tested and built later. To do so, right-click on the project, and choose **Deploy** • **Hybrid App Toolkit (Local Add-On)** • **Prepare Hybrid Project,** as shown in Figure 8.31.

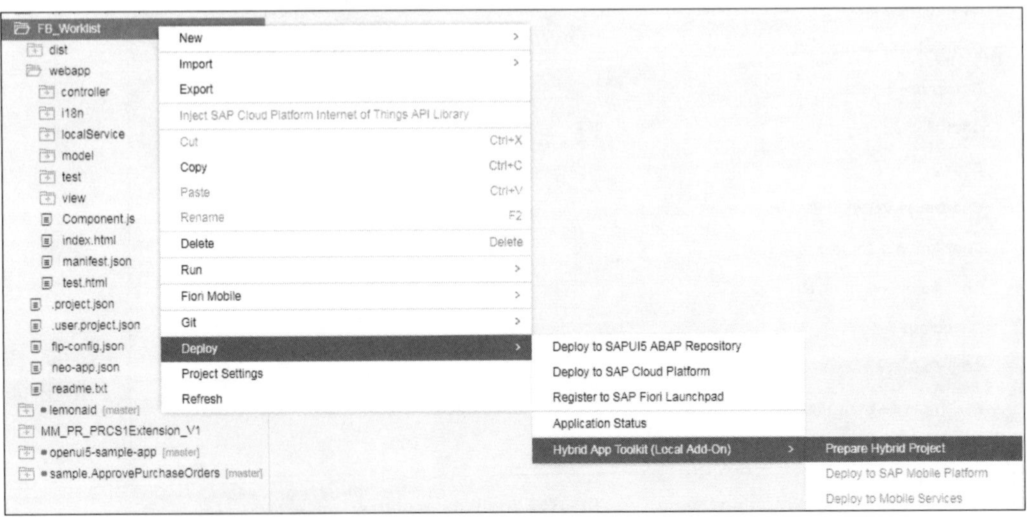

Figure 8.31 Deploying to the Local HAT

Upon completion of the deployment, you'll get a success message. The deploy-ment process creates a new folder in the user's directory with the same name as the project and with all the application resources, as shown in Figure 8.32.

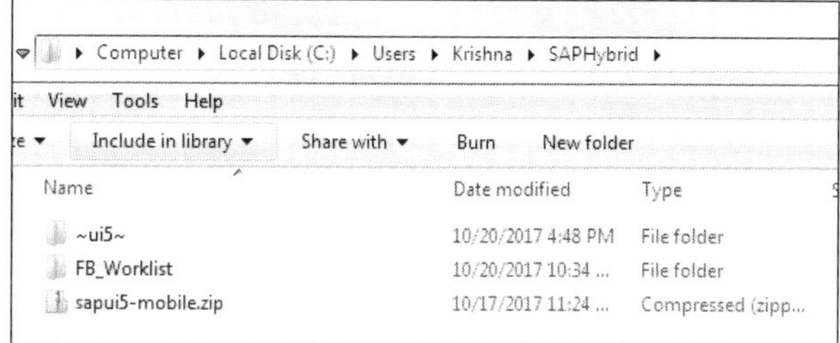

Figure 8.32 Result of Deployment

Building for Android

To build for Android devices, follow these steps:

1. In the device configuration file (**Project Settings • Device Configuration**), change the mode from **Debug Mode** to **Release Mode**.

2. Right-click on the project, and choose **Run • Run on Local Device Simulator/Emulator • Android Emulator** (see Figure 8.33).

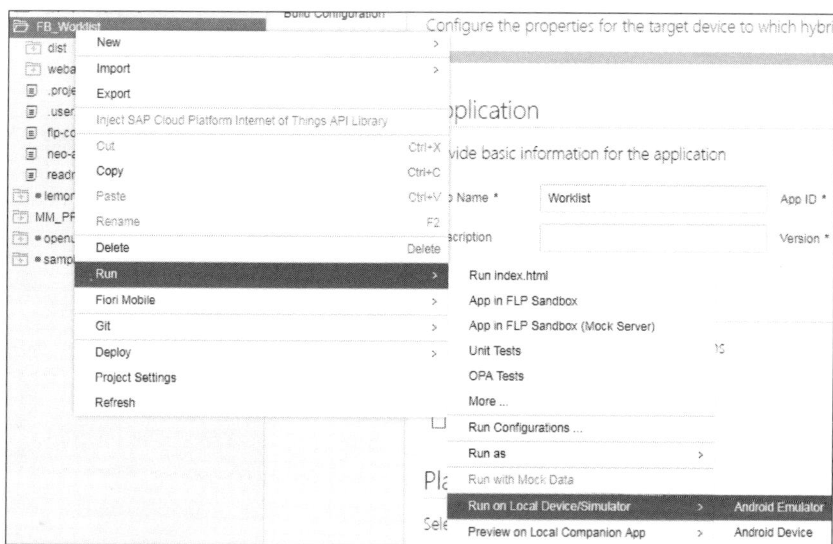

Figure 8.33 Running/Building the Hybrid Apps

3. Now the application needs to be signed by a private key that is known only to you. This is used to identify the author of the application in the Android platform. You can use a test key if you don't plan to publish the app into the app store. Otherwise, select **Custom Key**.

4. To generate a custom key, enter the following command in your command line interface (CLI):

```
keytool -genkey -v -keystore release.keystore -alias releaseKey -keyalg RSA -key-
size 2048 -validity 20000
```

5. This prompts you to enter a **Key Store Password** and basic information about yourself as shown in Figure 8.34. This will create a self-signed certificate in the current directory.

6. Enter these details into the SAP Web IDE popup, as shown in Figure 8.35, and click **OK**.

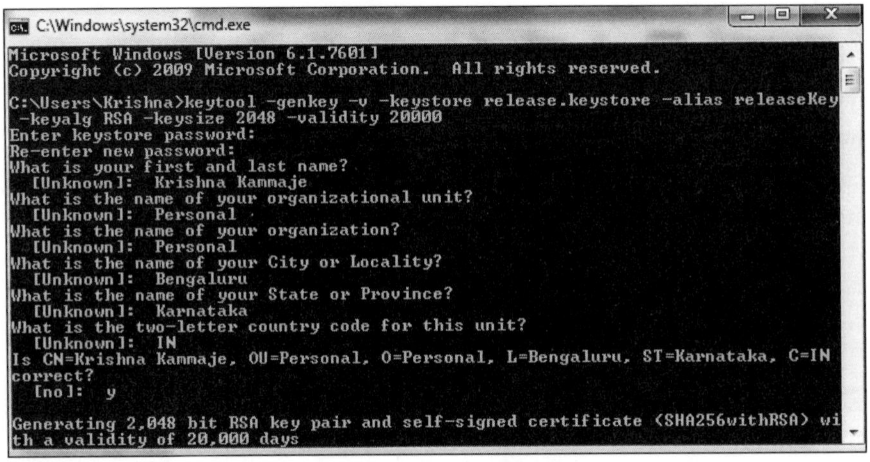

Figure 8.34 Generating a Custom Key for Signing the Android App

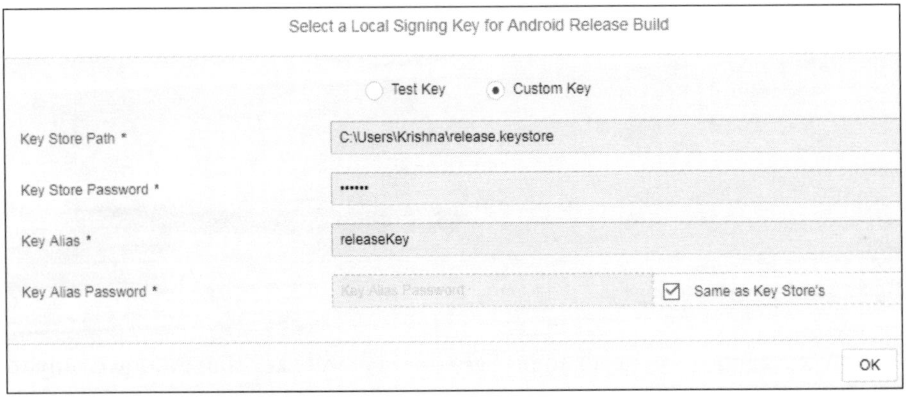

Figure 8.35 Custom Key Details

If there is more than one emulator or device, you can select the right target in a popup. The console will show the progress of the build process.

Building for iOS and Windows Devices

Building for other platforms involves similar steps as performed with the Android platform:

- For the iOS platform, right-click on the *index.html* file, and then click **Run • Run On • iOS Simulator or iOS Device**.
- For Windows apps, right-click on the *index.html* file, and then click **Run • Run On • Windows Local, Windows Phone, or Windows emulator**.

Building in the Cloud

SAP Fiori mobile services provide an option to build on the cloud so that you can save efforts in setting up the local build environment. Before building in the cloud, perform the follow prerequisites:

1. The **Fiori Mobile, Development & Operations**, and **Portal** services should be enabled. The app needs to be deployed to this SAP Fiori launchpad.
2. The appropriate roles must be assigned within all these services.
3. A published site needs to be available in the portal service and must be selected as the default site.
4. In the trial landscape, a destination of type HTTP must be available with the name **webidetesting** and pointing to *https://webidetesting-account name.dispatcher.hanatrial.ondemand.com*.
5. Signing profiles must be created for each of the platforms where the app needs to be built.

After performing these prerequisites, follow these steps:

1. Right-click on the project, and choose **Fiori Mobile • Build Packaged App**.
2. In the next screen, leave the default configurations as they are.
3. In the next screen, choose each platform where the app needs to be built, as shown in Figure 8.36.

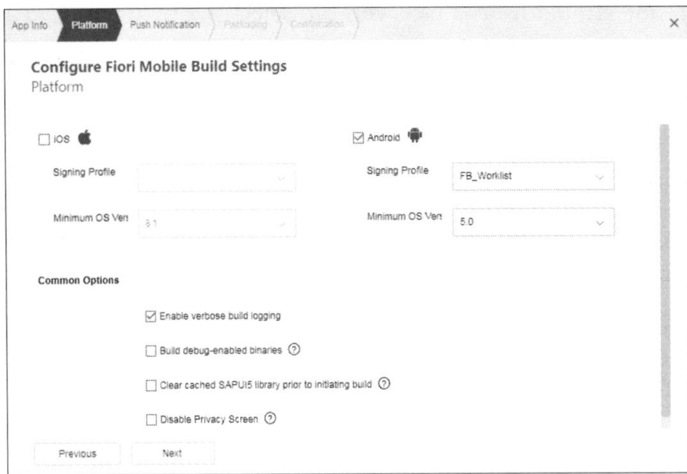

Figure 8.36 Server Build Settings

4. Continue with the default settings in the next screens, and click **Build** in the last screen.

5. The SAP Web IDE console will show the logs of the build progress and will show a confirmation popup (Figure 8.37). The Android app can be downloaded by clicking on **Worklist Demo.apk** or by scanning the QR code and installed on a device.

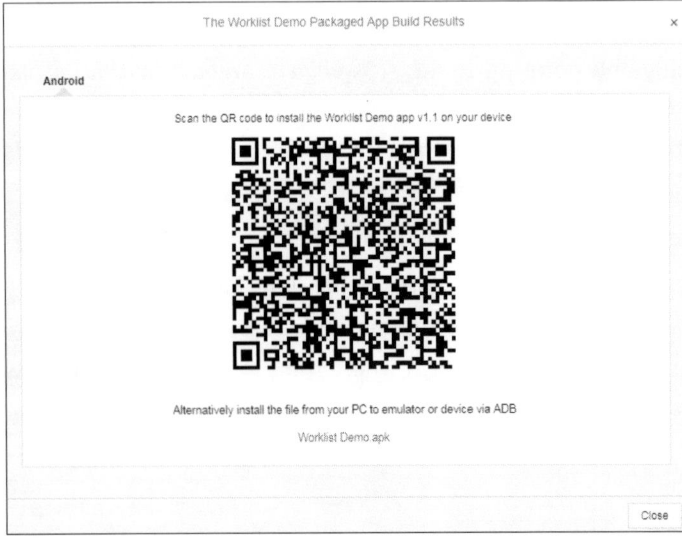

Figure 8.37 SAP Fiori Mobile Build Creating an .apk File

Deploying Apps

In this section we'll explore deploying to SAP Cloud Platform, SAP Fiori Mobile Services, SAP Mobile Platform, accessing SAP Fiori from Mobile Devices, using and creating a custom SAP Fiori Client, and using hybrid apps.

Deploying to SAP Cloud Platform

By deploying the hybrid app into SAP Cloud Platform, it can be consumed by various clients, especially SAP Fiori Client. By deploying to SAP Cloud Platform, the corresponding Git repository also gets updated and can be used for managing versions.

To deploy to SAP Cloud Platform, right-click on the project, and choose **Deploy • Deploy to SAP Cloud Platform.** You'll see a popup with details of the application, as shown in Figure 8.38. By clicking **Deploy**, the app will be deployed to SAP Cloud Platform, and you'll get a popup containing an URL to access the deployed app.

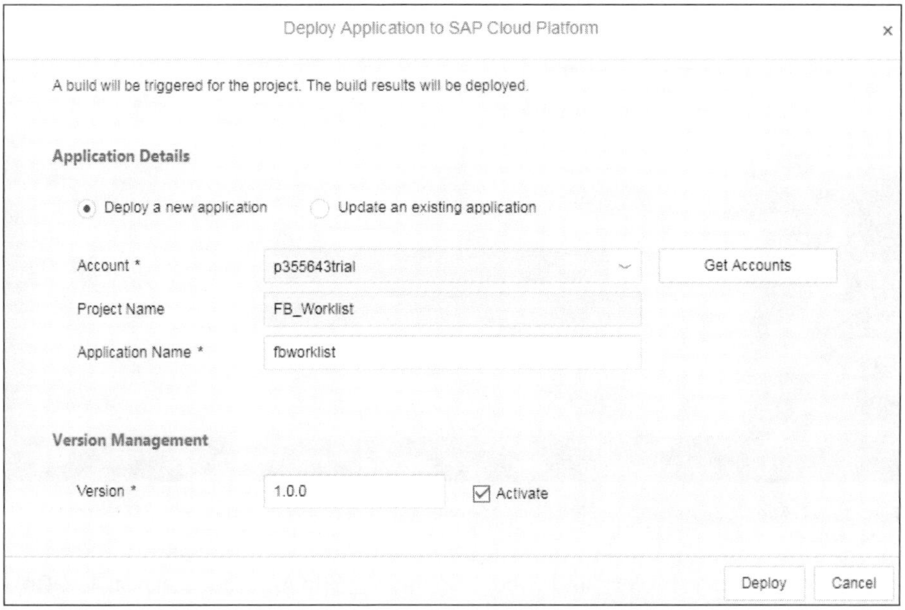

Figure 8.38 Deploying the App to SAP Cloud Platform

Deploying to SAP Fiori Mobile Services

By deploying to SAP Fiori mobile services, you can use the Kapsel plugin App Update to provide the application updates directly to the devices using SAP Mobile Place or other application stores. You can also get other features such as push notifications, secure on-device storage, app monitoring, storage reporting, and so on.

Before deploying to SAP Fiori mobile services, the app must be created in the **Mobile Services Cockpit** screen by following these steps:

1. Open the service in the **SAP Cloud Platform Cockpit** screen, and then click on **Go to Service**.

2. Click on **Create New App**.

3. In the popup that appears, enter the application details. In the **ID** field, enter "appid" from the **Project Settings** of the app, and provide a **Name** for the application, as shown in Figure 8.39.

4. Click **Save**.

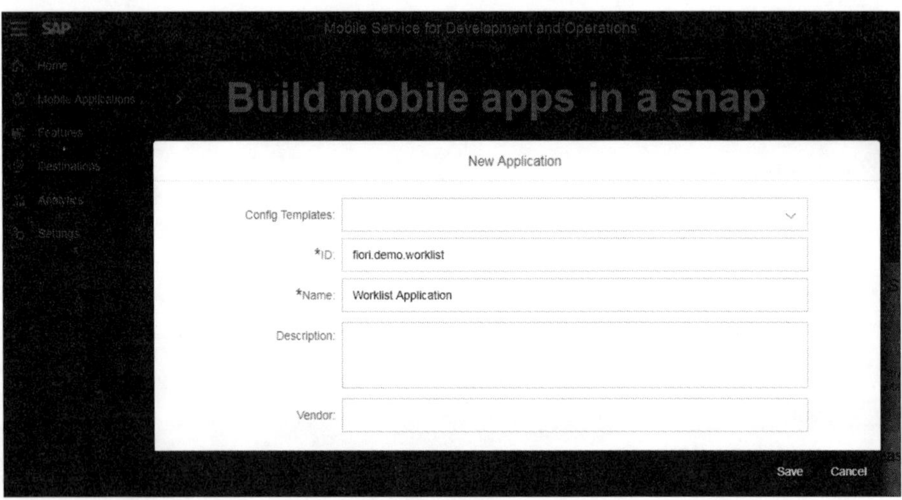

Figure 8.39 Adding an App in SAP Fiori Mobile Services

5. Right-click on the project, and choose **Deploy • Hybrid App Toolkit (Local Add-On) • Deploy to Mobile Services**.

   SAP Web IDE will look for an existing packaged hybrid app in the local *hybrid* folder within the project space at *C:\Users\Krishna\SAPHybrid\FB_Worklist*. If it finds an existing app, then it will skip packaging and just create a *ZIP* file from the packaged app. If not, the app will be packaged, and a *ZIP* file will be created.

6. After the zip file is created, a popup will be displayed as a confirmation (Figure 8.40). Click **Deploy** to deploy this app to SAP Fiori mobile services.

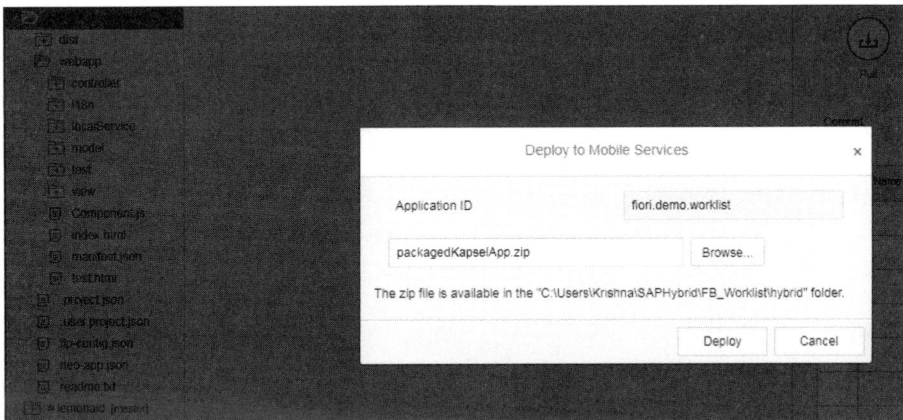

Figure 8.40 Packaged App to Be Deployed to SAP Fiori Mobile Services

You'll see a progress indicator as the deployment happens and a confirmation message after the deployment completes.

Deploying to SAP Mobile Platform

By deploying to SAP Mobile Platform, you can administer the app on premise. First, perform the following prerequisites:

1. Create an application in SAP Mobile Platform cockpit with an **App ID** that is the same as that in the project's device configuration.
2. In the device configuration, select at least the **Logon Manager** and **App Update** Kapsel plugins.
3. In the device configuration, choose **SAP Mobile Platform** as your platform, and provide its URL and port.

To deploy the app, follow these steps:

1. Right-click on the project, and choose **Deploy • Hybrid App Toolkit (Local Add-On) • SAP Mobile Platform.**
2. Enter the SAP Mobile Platform account details, and click **Deploy**. You'll see a confirmation message after the successful deployment.

All the devices that are connected to the SAP Mobile Platform and use the App Update plugin will be notified of the new update.

Accessing SAP Fiori from Mobile Devices: Summary

As you saw earlier, there are three primary ways to access the SAP Fiori apps:

- In a browser
- In SAP Fiori Client or a custom SAP Fiori Client
- In a hybrid app with Kapsel/Apache Cordova plugins

Using a Browser

When the SAP Fiori app runs on a browser, you have no extra installable software. It works well on all three types of devices and thus is a convenient method. SAP-delivered SAP Fiori apps are tested in the following three operating systems.

- iOS
- Windows Phone
- Android

Although it has advantages, there are many disadvantages to using SAP Fiori in a browser:

- **Startup performance**
  Because the browser doesn't have the required SAPUI5 libraries, it needs to download an SAPUI5 library if it isn't already cached. This significantly slows performance on a mobile device.
- **Attachment handling**
  Although attachments can be downloaded and uploaded, there are no security features regarding storing attachments.
- **Native device capability**
  Because a browser doesn't have access to device APIs, SAP Fiori app rendering within the browser can't make use of any device features.
- **Offline capability**
  For working with offline features, you need to connect with SAP Mobile Platform using Kapsel plugins, which can't be achieved with the browser.

Using SAP Fiori Client

SAP introduced SAP Fiori Client, which is a native application in Android, iOS, and Windows platforms. This was introduced mainly to improve the performance and provide a consistent performance to the end user. SAP Fiori Client is considered a specialized browser with a dedicated use for opening SAP Fiori apps, and it has the following benefits.

- Available as a native application in all three major mobile operating systems
- Designated using open-source Apache Cordova project
- No additional development required
- Consistent user experience with better cache management

Custom SAP Fiori Client

SAP Fiori Client comes with a fixed set of features that customers might need to extend. In such cases, a custom SAP Fiori Client can be built and used. With a custom SAP Fiori Client, you can do the following:

- Apply custom branding such as a company's logo.
- Add custom Apache Cordova plugins.
- Use the application with mobile service for app and device management.
- Use your own custom app store to host the new application.
- Enable custom authentication schemas.

One thing you can't do, however, is create offline applications with the SAP Fiori Client.

Using Hybrid Apps

You can convert one or more SAP Fiori apps into a mobile app. You can either use HAT or SAP Fiori mobile services for creating SAP Fiori apps. This approach has the following features and advantages:

- Hybrid apps can be created in all three platforms: iOS, Android and Windows.
- Support is provided for downloading and installing from SAP Mobile Place.
- You can test the application on browsers and on devices using the Companion app.

- Offline applications can be created using SAP Fiori mobile services/SAP Mobile Platform.
- You can use Kapsel plugins while using SAP Fiori mobile services/SAP Mobile Platform.

Important Terminology

This chapter covered the following terminology:

- **SAP Fiori Client**

  This is a native application available on Windows, Android, and iOS platforms. This acts as a container application for running SAP Fiori applications in online mode and allows the application to make use of selected device capabilities. Custom versions of this application can be built for enhancing the functionalities using SAP Mobile Platform SDK.

- **SAP Mobile Platform**

  This is an on-premise version of the product, which aims to simplify the process of mobile application development, deployment and maintenance. It provides SDKs, and services for developers to speed up the development process. It is based on open standards like HTTP, REST, OData, and HTML5.

- **SAP Fiori Mobile Service**

  This is a cloud version of SAP Mobile Platform. This is provided as a service from SAP Cloud Platform.

- **Apache Cordova**

  This is an open-source mobile application development framework. It wraps the HTML and JavaScript based web application into a native container, and thus allows the web application to access the device capabilities of the underlying platform.

- **Kapsel**

  Kapsel is a set of plugins developed by SAP for Apache Cordova to enhance its capabilities with those required for enterprises. Most of these Kapsel plugins require integration with SAP Mobile Platform (or the cloud version of it) to utilize the advanced capabilities.

- **SAP Hybrid Application Toolkit**

  SAP Hybrid Application Toolkit is a set of three tools made available by SAP to develop, build and test hybrid mobile applications. These three tools are an SAP

Web IDE plugin for assisting in developing, building and previewing, a companion app for testing on actual devices and a connector tool for connecting with the local development environment.

 Practice Questions

These practice questions will help you evaluate your understanding of the topics covered in this chapter. The questions shown are similar in nature to those found on the certification examination. Although none of these questions will be found on the exam itself, they will allow you to review your knowledge of the subject. Select the correct answers, and then check the completeness of your answers in the "Practice Question Answers and Explanations" section. Remember, on the exam, you must select all correct answers and only correct answers to receive credit for the question.

1. Which of the following is *not* true about SAP Fiori Client?

    ☐   A. Application passcode isn't mandatory for using an SAP Fiori Client.

    ☐   B. SAP Fiori Client comes with a default passcode policy.

    ☐   C. Custom SAP Fiori Client can have its own passcode policy.

    ☐   D. While using directly with the frontend server, you can override the default passcode policy.

2. Normally in SAP Fiori Client, when you navigate back from the Attachment Viewer, the attachment file is deleted. However, this does *not* happen in which of the following platforms?

    ☐   A. Windows

    ☐   B. Android

    ☐   C. iOS

3. Which of these is *not* one of the advantages of SAP Fiori Client?

    ☐   A. Native experience with iOS, Android, and Windows clients

    ☐   B. Ability to add logo to the SAP Fiori Client

    ☐   C. Consistent cache behavior, improving the performance

    ☐   D. Available in popular commercial app stores

4.   The SAP Companion app is available in the iOS app store.

☐   A. True

☐   B. False

5.   Which of the following application types is recommended option to create offline apps?

☐   A. Hybrid application

☐   B. SAP Fiori app accessed from browser

☐   C. Custom SAP Fiori Client

☐   D. SAP Fiori Client

6.   The SAP Hybrid App Toolkit does *not* have which of the following components?

☐   A. SAP Web IDE plugin

☐   B. HAT Companion app

☐   C. Apache Cordova plugins

☐   D. HAT Connector

7.   SAP Web IDE does *not* allow you to deploy to which server type?

☐   A. Java Tomcat server

☐   B. ABAP server

☐   C. SAP Mobile Platform

☐   D. SAP Cloud Platform

Practice Answers and Explanations

1.   Correct answer: **D**
For overriding the default passcode policy, you need to connect through either SAP Mobile Platform or SAP Fiori mobile services.

2.   Correct answer: **A**
In the Windows platform, the attachment gets deleted only when the SAP Fiori Client resumes from a suspended state or is relaunched.

3. Correct answer: **B**

   SAP Fiori Client doesn't allow any personalization. If you need personalization such as custom branding, you can create a custom SAP Fiori Client.

4. Correct answer: **A**

   True. The SAP Companion app is available in all of the three major operating systems (iOS, Android, Windows).

5. Correct answer: **A**

   A hybrid application with connection to SAP Mobile Platform or SAP Fiori mobile services is the official way to create an offline app.

6. Correct answer: **C**

   HAT contains an SAP Web IDE plugin, a HAT Companion app for device testing, and a HAT Connector for achieving local builds.

7. Correct answer: **A**

   SAP Web IDE doesn't have an option to deploy to a Java Tomcat server.

Take Away

In this chapter, we discussed the features of a mobile application, and then covered how SAP Fiori Client can be used to quickly mobilize SAP Fiori apps. This method has both advantages and disadvantages, but the latter can be addressed by hybrid apps.

Next, we explored HAT and its features. We used it to test the hybrid app in various ways such as via browser, device, and emulator. You also learned how a hybrid app can be built using either the HAT local build add-on or using cloud build features for SAP Fiori mobile services.

Summary

A hybrid application brings the advantages of a native application to an SAP Fiori apps. This is also how an offline SAP Fiori app should be developed. The HAT provides many tools for supporting the various lifecycle events of a hybrid app.

In the next chapter, we'll go through the various strategies to perform unit and integration testing for an SAP Fiori app.

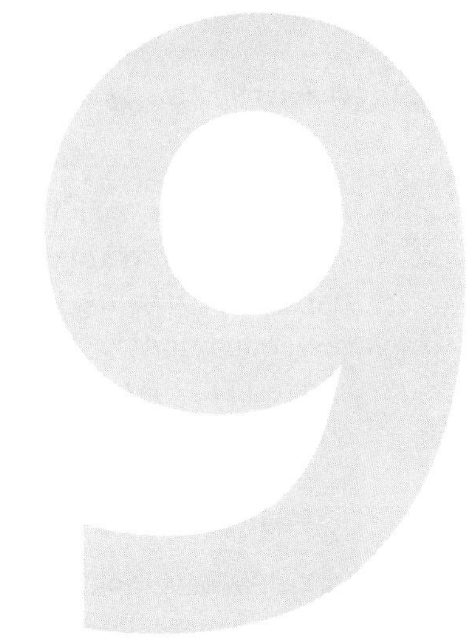

Chapter 9
Testing

Techniques You'll Master:

- Differentiate between unit tests and integration tests
- Write a unit test using QUnit
- Write an integration test using One Page Application (OPA5)
- Use a mock server to mock OData calls

In this chapter, we'll focus on how to improve the development of your SAPUI5 application by writing unit and integration tests. For unit tests, we'll use the QUnit framework, and for integration tests, we'll use OPA5. We'll also explore mock server and find out how to use it to decouple the dependency on OData services and test SAPUI5 applications.

Real-World Scenarios

You're developing an SAPUI5 application with many views and controllers. You want to determine how each controller or view works with the others by testing a specific functionality of an app. Rather than doing manual testing, which is time consuming and error prone, you want to automate these tests. OPA5 is one of the integration testing frameworks that can be used to code and run various integration test scenarios to get a report on successes and failures.

Although integration tests automate and test the functionality, they don't tell you which part of the code is broken. To get this information, the programmer needs to write unit tests, which test a smaller but independent piece of code. You can use the open-source framework QUnit for writing unit tests.

Objectives of This Portion of the Test

The objective of this portion of the SAP Fiori Certification Test is to test your understanding of the following concepts:

- Importance of writing unit tests and integration tests
- Writing unit tests using QUnit
- Writing integration tests using OPA5
- Using mock server

Key Concepts Refresher

Let's start by discussing the importance of unit and integration testing and its need in the software development. We'll discuss the difference between unit and integration testing and then use QUnit and OPA5 libraries to write sample tests in these sections.

Introduction to Testing

Various studies have established that the cost of fixing a bug increases as one moves away from the place where the bug was introduced. For example, the effort involved in identifying and fixing a bug during development of an app is much less that the effort involved when the bug is identified by the customer. This requires several people to be involved, including developers and management, thus increasing the cost of fixing the bug. Therefore, it's important to set up a testing framework for your app to identify the bugs as soon as possible and ensure that the application meets all quality standards.

The traditional way of ensuring a quality product is by performing extensive manual testing before the application is delivered to end users. However, applications require changes throughout their lifecycles such as adding new features, fixing bugs, or upgrading libraries. In such cases, applications must be retested for all the effected functionalities. Regression testing will require a huge manual effort and a lot of time. Manual testing is also prone to human errors as well. Again, the full list of impacts may not always be known and can result in either over testing or under testing. The solution is code-based automated testing.

Testing can be broken down into two types based on the scope of what is getting tested: unit tests and integration tests.

Unit Tests

Unit tests are written by developers to test a unit such as a function, method, or small piece of code for logic and code behavior. Only the piece of code is tested while assuming that the rest of the application is working correctly. This dependency decoupling is done by mocking up all the external dependencies of the piece of code under testing (Figure 9.1).

When a feature that depends on a large piece of code fails, unit tests will help you identify the unit where the bug was introduced. The effort required to build unit tests is justified by the huge savings that result from quick identification of bugs.

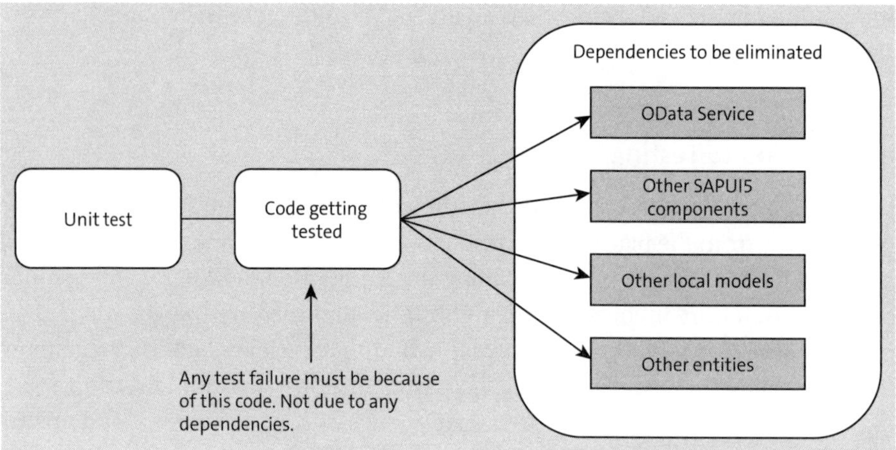

Figure 9.1 Unit Testing and Dependencies

Unit tests are directly useful only to the developers, although they indirectly lead to reduced bugs and reduced maintenance.

Each programing language usually has one or more unit testing frameworks written in the same language as the code under testing.

Integration Tests

Integration tests test two or more units (classes, methods, functions) at a time with an aim to test a feature of the application that is important to the end user. Integration tests can be written by the developer of the code, but they don't have to be.

Integration tests test the functionality and report if it works correctly; however, the tests don't indicate where the problem is. Because integration tests need to test multiple units, it requires more effort to build integration tests compared to unit tests.

Figure 9.2 compares unit tests, integration, and manual tests by the number of units involved in a test and the number of tests in an application.

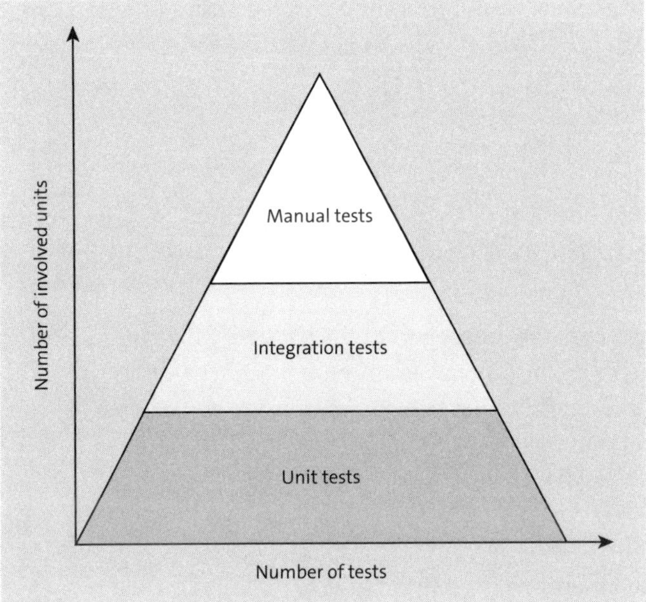

Figure 9.2 Comparing Testing Types

Unit Testing with QUnit

QUnit is a very popular open-source JavaScript library providing a framework for performing unit testing. QUnit can test any generic JavaScript applications. QUnit was originally developed by John Resign as part of jQuery. Later, it became standalone in 2009, and developers can now use it without jQuery. QUnit is one of the several open-source libraries that are part of SAPUI5, so you don't have to load it separately within the app.

Like most test frameworks, QUnit uses the Arrange Act Assert pattern. In the Arrange phase, preparation for the test is done. An example step in this phase is instantiation of a class under testing. In the Act phase, the actual action under test is performed. In the Assert phase, the result of the Act phase is compared with the expected result to determine whether the test case has passed.

QUnit Test Cases

The following listing shows a sample QUnit test. `QUnit.test` creates a QUnit test for testing a function called `Add` that adds two integers. The first parameter is a string that provides a name for the test case. The second parameter is a function where the testing happens.

```
QUnit.test("Sample Addition Test1", function(assert){
var sum = Add(1,2)
    Assert.equal(sum, 3, "1 + 2 = 3, Pass");
});
```

Within the testing function, the first statement represents the Act part of the Arrange Act Assert pattern. Here it calculates a variable called sum, which represents the sum of number 1 and 2.

The next statement represents the Assert part of the pattern, which uses an assertion named equal here. This application programming interface (API) is the Assertion part, and it checks whether the first two parameters are equal; if yes, the test is passed.

Assertions

QUnit provides multiple Assertions in addition to equal:

```
ok(parameter1, "Information to display");
```

The ok()assertion takes a parameter or an expression, which is evaluated either true or false. If it's evaluated as true, then the test is passed; otherwise, it's a fail. The second parameter is an optional string used as an information message.

In addition to true, a nonempty string is also considered as a test case pass.

Outputs such as 0, null, NaN, empty string, and undefined are considered a fail.

Stubs and Mocks

Stubs and mocks are used while unit testing and are designed for unique purposes:

- **Stubs**
  Stubs come with a predefined behavior so you can get rid of external dependencies. Stubs usually return objects that the actual execution of a function would return but without executing the actual code. For example, it can return exceptions while testing error handling.

- **Mocks**
  Mocks come with expectations of how the current code under test is treated. Expectations can be how many times an API is called, which arguments are to be passed, or what exact values of arguments are to be passed. Thus, mocks define expectations on implementation of the code under test.

Sinon.JS

Sinon.JS is an open source library to be used with any unit testing framework line QUnit. Its aim is to simplify the process of creating mocks, stubs, and spies. Sinon.JS is also part of SAPUI5, so you can use it in your unit tests to create mocks and stubs.

Following is an example of creating stubs using sinon.JS. In this code, a controller's method, `getAge`, which gets the age of the user, is stubbed. Calling this method will always return 45 as the age.

```
oStandaloneController.getAge = sinon.stub().returns(45);
```

The following code stubs the method `calculateCost` with exact arguments '3323234' and 2, and returns 330 as the return value:

```
oStandaloneController.calculateCost
= sinon.stub().withArgs(['3323234', 2]).returns(330);
```

The following mock sets the expectation that `oObj.method` gets called at least twice and at most five times. Only then are the expectations verified as fine. Failing these expectations will fail the test itself.

```
sinon.mock(oObj).expects("method").atLeast(2).atMost(5);
```

The following mock expects that `oObj.method` is called with exact arguments 3 and 4, respectively:

```
sinon.mock(oObj).expects("method").withArgs(3, 4);
```

Creating a Unit Test

In this section, let's consider a simple SAPUI5 application and write unit tests for its functionality. We'll also discuss the important QUnit APIs and understand their usage. Then, we'll also explore how to measure the test coverage to ensure that all the important parts of our code have been tested.

Application under Test

This application for which we are going to write a unit test is a simple calculator with the ability to perform addition, subtraction, multiplication, and division. After each operation, it also displays a word representation of the calculation performed.

Figure 9.3 shows the project hierarchy, and Figure 9.4 shows the functionality of the application. The application has multiple methods in *View1.controller.js*, which needs to be unit tested.

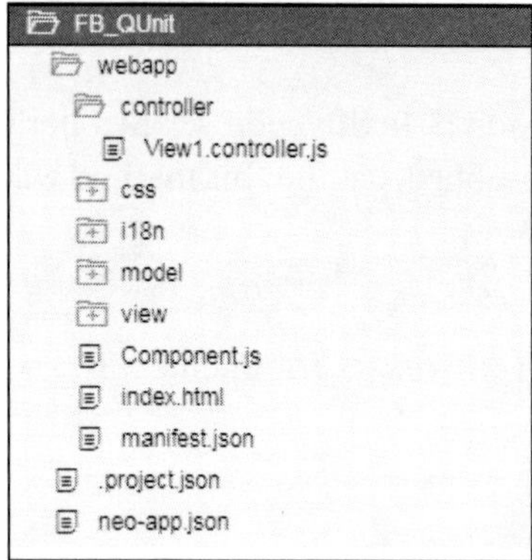

Figure 9.3 Project Hierarchy of the Application under Unit Test

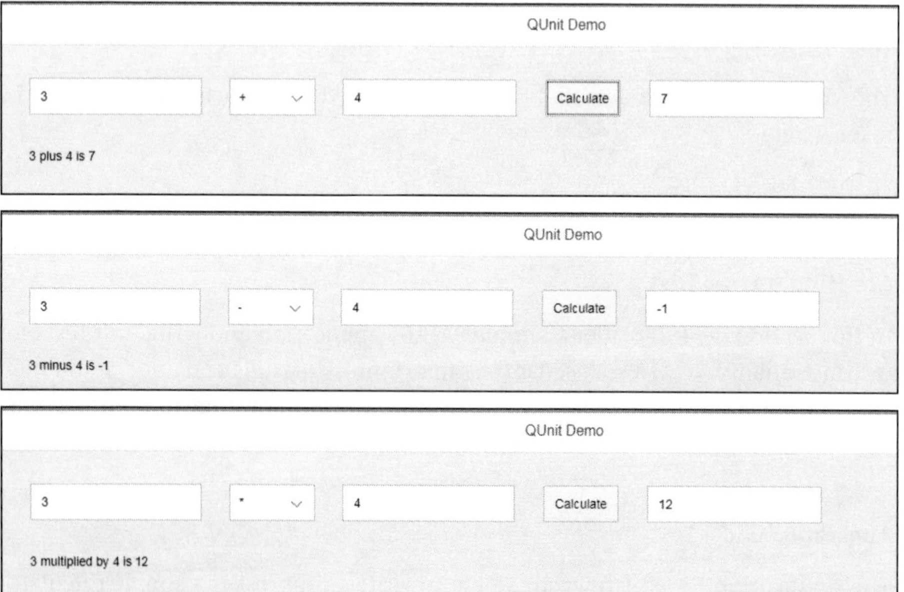

Figure 9.4 Functionality of the App under Unit Test

As you can see, there are two main pieces of logic here. One is the calculator functionality, and the other is writing the calculation in words. We'll write tests to test both these functionalities without external dependencies. Figure 9.5 shows the controller code that displays two methods for each of the preceding functionalities.

```javascript
View1.controller.js  ×

 1▾ sap.ui.define([
 2       "sap/ui/core/mvc/Controller"
 3▾ ], function(Controller) {
 4       "use strict";
 5▾     return Controller.extend("fb.QUnit.controller.View1", {
 6▾         getModel: function(sModelName){
 7               return this.getView().getModel(sModelName);
 8           },
 9▾         runCalculator: function() {
10               var par1 = this.getView().byId("par1").getValue();
11               var operation = this.getView().byId("operation").getSelectedKey();
12               var par2 = this.getView().byId("par2").getValue();
13               //Calculate result
14               this.result = this.calculate(par1, par2, operation);
15               //Update the result
16               this.getView().byId("answer").setValue(this.result);
17               //Update the operation in words
18               this.getView().byId("inWords").setText(this.inWords(par1, par2, operation));
19           },
20▾         calculate: function(par1, par2, operation) {
21               var result;
22▾             if (operation === "+") {
23                   result = (par1 * 1) + (par2 * 1);
24▾             } else if (operation === "-") {
25                   result = (par1 * 1) - (par2 * 1);
26▾             } else if (operation === "*") {
27                   result = (par1 * 1) * (par2 * 1);
28▾             } else if (operation === "/") {
29                   result = (par1 * 1) / (par2 * 1);
30               }
31               return result;
32           },
33▾         inWords: function(par1, par2, operation){
34               var words;
35               var oResourceBundle = this.getModel("i18n").getResourceBundle();
36▾             if (operation === "+") {
37                   words = par1 + " " + oResourceBundle.getText("add") + " " + par2
38                   + " " + oResourceBundle.getText("is") + " " + this.calculate(par1, par2, operation);
39▾             } else if (operation === "-") {
40                   words = par1 + " " + oResourceBundle.getText("substract") + " " + par2 + " "
41                   + oResourceBundle.getText("is") + " " + this.calculate(par1, par2, operation);
42▾             } else if (operation === "*") {
43                   words = par1 + " " + oResourceBundle.getText("into") + " " + par2 + " "
44                   + oResourceBundle.getText("is") + " " + this.calculate(par1, par2, operation);
45▾             } else if (operation === "/") {
46                   words = par1 + " " + oResourceBundle.getText("divide") + " " + par2 + " "
47                   + oResourceBundle.getText("is") + " " + this.calculate(par1, par2, operation);
48               }
49               return words;
50           }
51       });
52   });
```

Figure 9.5 Code under Test: Calculate and Writing Calculations in Words Functions

Project Hierarchy

As testing code is useful only during development and maintenance of the application, it's usually not sent while distributing it to the customer. Therefore, it's important to organize all the testing code together so that you can remove it before distribution.

We've created a new folder called *test* under the *webapp* folder to contain all the unit test code. Inside the *test* folder, we'll create another folder called *unit*, which will contain only the test cases. In the future, it can contain other folders for integration tests, for example.

Folder and files inside the *unit* folder will reflect the structure of the application inside the *webapp* folder. Now let's create a controller folder under the *unit* folder and create a file with the same name as the controller name as shown in Figure 9.6.

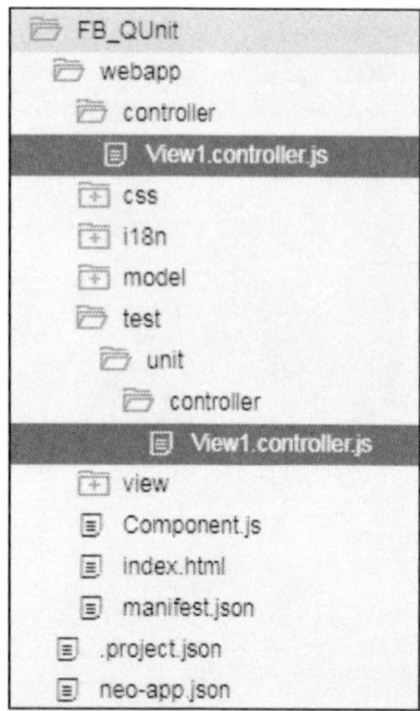

Figure 9.6 Conventions for Folder Structure and File Names for Unit Tests

The `calculate` method shown earlier in Figure 9.5 contains the logic for calculations. Let's start writing unit tests for this. Figure 9.7 shows a unit test case for this method that tests the addition functionality. At line 2, we load the original controller, which contains the code under test.

```
View1.controller.js  ×      View1.controller.js  ×

 1 ▾ sap.ui.require([
 2       "fb/QUnit/controller/View1.controller"
 3 ▾ ], function(View1Controller) {
 4       "use strict";
 5 ▾     QUnit.module("addition", {
 6 ▾         beforeEach: function() {
 7               this.oView1Controller = new View1Controller();
 8           },
 9 ▾         afterEach: function() {
10               this.oView1Controller.destroy();
11           }
12       });
13 ▾     QUnit.test("add 1 and 2", function(assert) {
14           //Act
15           var result = this.oView1Controller.calculate(1, 2, "+");
16           //Asert
17           assert.strictEqual(result, 3, "text computed OK");
18       });
19   });
```

Figure 9.7 Unit Test Case along with the Module

QUnit APIs

`QUnit.module` defines a module that can contain one or more test cases. A QUnit module has hooks `beforeEach` and `afterEach` that run before and after each test case, respectively. We've used these hooks to create and destroy instance of the controller, respectively.

`QUnit.test` is used to define a test case. The first parameter is a string that will be shown in the QUnit results page. Next, we have a function that contains the test case code. In line 15, we call the `calculate` method with a parameter and operator and get the results of the calculation.

In line 17, the `assert.strictEqual` API compares the expected output with the calculation result and, if successful, shows the string, which is the third parameter that gets shown on the QUnit results at the test case level.

Now we need to create an infrastructure through which we can run this test. Inside the folder unit, create two files called *allTests.js* and *unitTests.qunit.html*, which will help us run the unit tests. See Figure 9.8 for the code list of `unitTests.qunit.html`.

```
View1.controller.js ×    View1.controller.js ×    unitTests.qunit.html ×    allTests.js ×
 1   <!DOCTYPE html>
 2 ▾ <html>
 3 ▾     <head>
 4           <title>Unit tests Demo</title>
 5           <meta http-equiv='X-UA-Compatible' content='IE=edge'/>
 6           <meta charset="UTF-8">
 7 ▾         <script id="sap-ui-bootstrap"
 8               src="../../../../resources/sap-ui-core.js"
 9               data-sap-ui-resourceroots='{
10                   "fb.QUnit": "../../",
11                   "test.unit": "./"
12               }'>
13           </script>
14 ▾         <script>
15               jQuery.sap.require("sap.ui.qunit.qunit-css");
16               jQuery.sap.require("sap.ui.thirdparty.qunit");
17               jQuery.sap.require("sap.ui.qunit.qunit-junit");
18               jQuery.sap.require("sap.ui.qunit.qunit-coverage");
19               QUnit.config.autostart = false;
20               sap.ui.require(
21                   ["test/unit/allTests"],
22 ▾                     function () {
23                           QUnit.start();
24                       }
25                   );
26           </script>
27       </head>
28 ▾     <body>
29           <div id="qunit"></div>
30           <div id="qunit-fixture"></div>
31       </body>
32   </html>
```

Figure 9.8 HTML Page That Launches All Unit Tests

The code for this page usually remains the same. As you can see, it loads the
SAPUI5 library for running the unit tests, and then from line 15 to 18, it loads various QUnit-related files. At line 20, it loads *allTests.js*, which inside it loads all the
test files (we have only one so far) as shown in Figure 9.9.

```
View1.controller.js ×    View1.controller.js ×    unitTests.qunit.html ×    allTests.js ×
1 ▾ sap.ui.define([
2           "test/unit/controller/View1.controller"
3 ▾     ], function() {
4           "use strict";
5       }
6   );
```

Figure 9.9 Calling All Test Cases of the App

Figure 9.10 summarizes the testing infrastructure that we've built so far. `unit-
Tests.qunit.html` includes `allTest.js`, which in turn includes all the test cases writ-
ten for various functionalities. `unitTests.qunit.html` triggers the unit testing using
`QUnit.start();`.

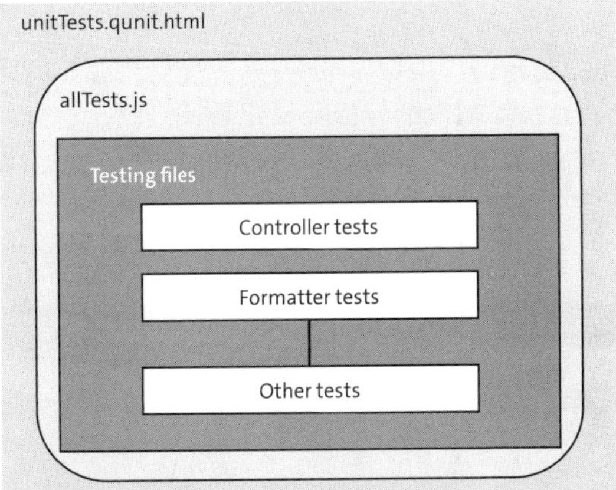

Figure 9.10 QUnit Testing Infrastructure Conventions

To run the test case, right-click on unitTests.qunit.html, and then choose **Run • Run As • Web Application**. Figure 9.11 shows the results of the QUnit test and how it relates to the unit test case that we wrote.

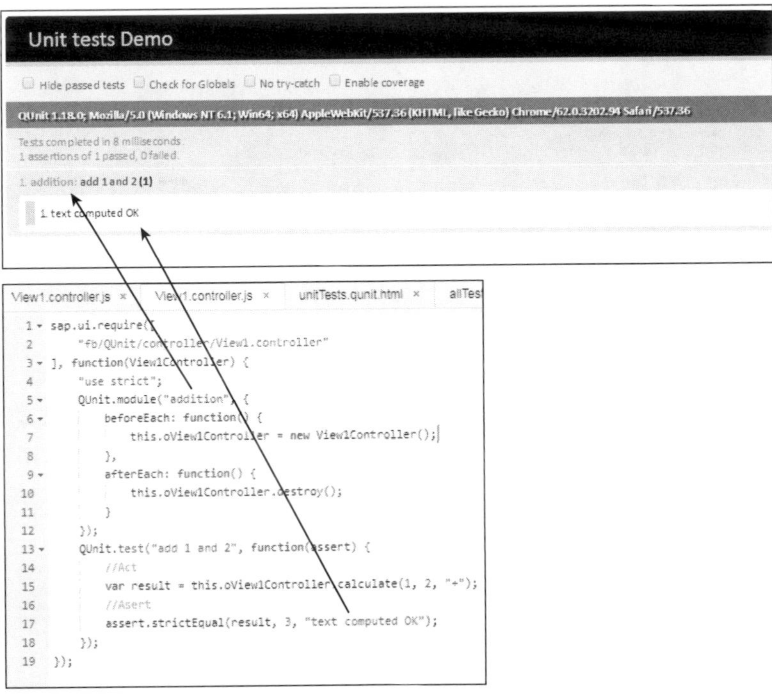


```
1 ▾ sap.ui.require([
2       "fb/QUnit/controller/View1.controller"
3 ▾ ], function(View1Controller) {
4       "use strict";
5 ▾    QUnit.module("addition", {
6 ▾        beforeEach: function() {
7               this.oView1Controller = new View1Controller();
8           },
9 ▾        afterEach: function() {
10              this.oView1Controller.destroy();
11          }
12      });
13 ▾    QUnit.test("add 1 and 2", function(assert) {
14          //Act
15          var result = this.oView1Controller.calculate(1, 2, "+");
16          //Asert
17          assert.strictEqual(result, 3, "text computed OK");
18      });
19  });
```

Figure 9.11 Result of Unit Tests

Test Coverage

You can also see the test coverage to see how much of the code has been tested so far. Click on **Enable Coverage** on the screen, which will show all the JavaScript files in the app and corresponding coverages. Click on the controller file of the app, and it will show all the uncovered code in red. Because we've just tested the addition operation, we'll see a significant part of our code in red as shown in Figure 9.12.

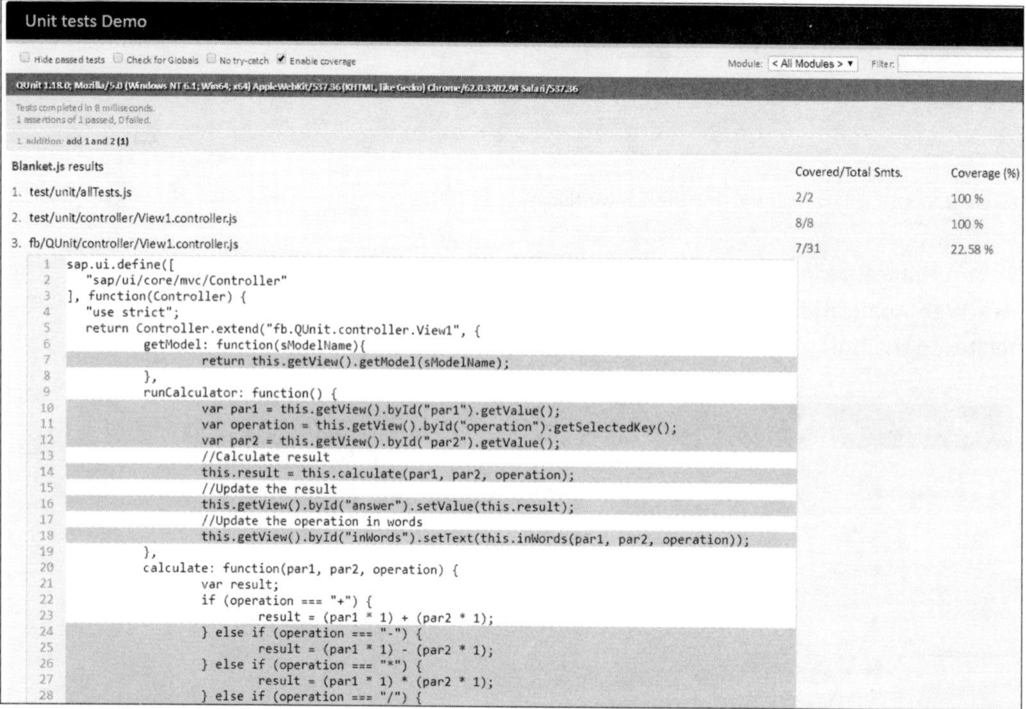

Figure 9.12 QUnit Test Coverage

Now let's write more test cases to improve the coverage. We'll test all four operations coded in the `calculate` method. Figure 9.13 shows all four test cases, the test results after this, and the test coverage showing that the complete method has tested okay.

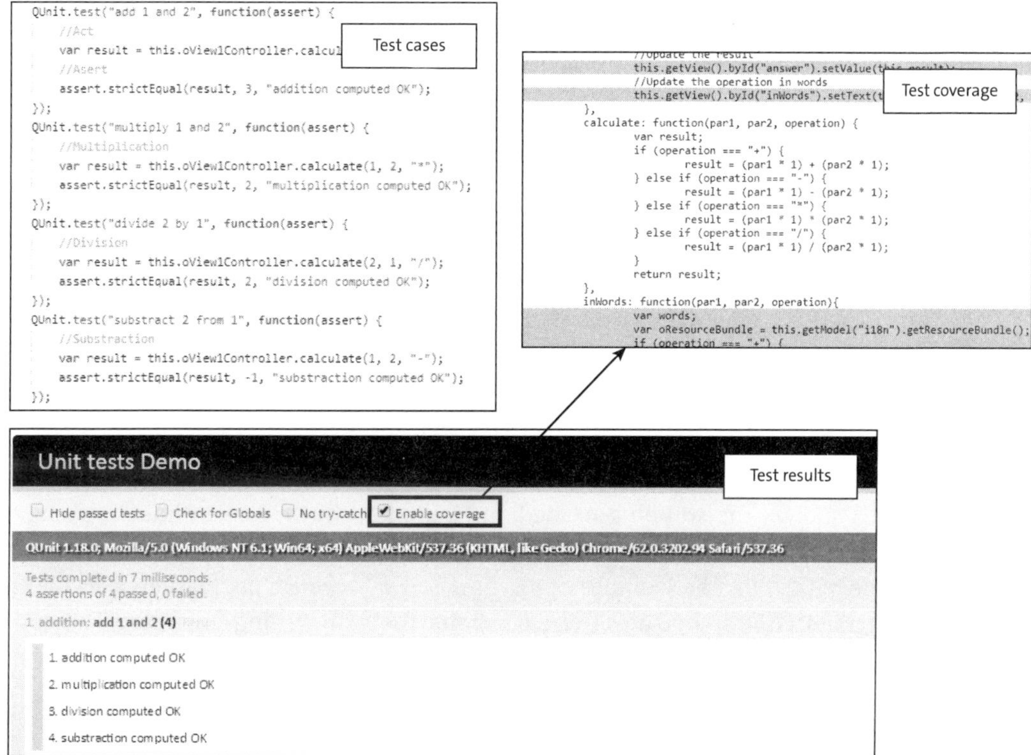

Figure 9.13 Test Cases, Test Results, and Test Coverage

Stubbing

This section covers stubbing by creating stubs for unit tests without external dependencies. In Figure 9.5, shown earlier, you saw function `inWords`, which computes the string to be shown on the screen. Let's write a unit test for this function. Unlike the `calculate` function, this function has a couple of dependencies. The first dependency is with the i18n model, which the function uses to fetch several texts. The second dependency is the `calculate` method itself, which we tested earlier.

To stub the i18n resource bundle, a fake i18n model can be created as shown in Figure 9.14. `test.unit.helper.FakeI18nModel` takes a JavaScript Object Notation (JSON) object of ID and text pairs of text strings. This file will be created under the *helper* folder inside the *unit* folder.

```
1 ▾ sap.ui.define([
2       "sap/ui/model/Model"
3 ▾ ], function(Model) {
4       "use strict";
5 ▾     return Model.extend("test.unit.helper.FakeI18nModel", {
6 ▾         constructor: function(mTexts) {
7               this.mTexts = mTexts || {};
8           },
9 ▾         getResourceBundle: function() {
10 ▾            return {
11 ▾                getText: function(sTextName) {
12                      return this.mTexts[sTextName];
13                  }.bind(this)
14              };
15          }
16      });
17  });
```

Figure 9.14 Fake i18n Model

Let's analyze the stubbing needed. In Figure 9.5, shown earlier, line 35, we have `this.getModel("i18n").getResourceBundle();`, which can be stubbed by the following code. `FakeI18n` is the instance of `FakeI18nModel` that we created earlier. It has been supplied with three strings that we're going to use in writing a test case. This code suits to be put inside the `beforeEach` function of the QUnit module, so that this model can be reused by other tests that we write in future for other operations.

```
this.oView1Controller.getModel
= sinon.stub().withArgs("i18n").returns(
    new FakeI18n({
            divide: "divided by",
            add: "plus",
            is: "is"
        })
);
```

We need to write a stub for the `calculate` method as well, but this needs to return different outputs each time. This stub is better written as part of the Arrange step within each test case, so that expected output can be arranged. The following code ensures that the `calculate` function will return 3 as the answer:

```
this.oView1Controller.calculate = sinon.stub().returns(3);
```

Figure 9.15 shows the QUnit module and a test case for the addition operation. Lines 4 and 5 ensure that the sinon.js-related library is imported, so that it can be used in stubbing.

```
View1.controller.js  ×     View1.controller.js  ×     View1.controller.js  ×     FakeI18nModel.js  ×

  1 ▾ sap.ui.require([
  2        "fb/QUnit/controller/View1.controller",
  3        "test/unit/helper/FakeI18nModel",
  4        "sap/ui/thirdparty/sinon",
  5        "sap/ui/thirdparty/sinon-qunit"
  6 ▾ ], function(View1Controller, FakeI18n) {
  7        "use strict";
  8 ▾     QUnit.module("addition", {
  9 ▾         beforeEach: function() {
 10                this.oView1Controller = new View1Controller();
 11            },
 12 ▾         afterEach: function() {
 13                this.oView1Controller.destroy();
 14            }
 15        });
 16 ▸     QUnit.test("add 1 and 2", function(assert) {⟱});
 22 ▸     QUnit.test("multiply 1 and 2", function(assert) {⟱});
 27 ▸     QUnit.test("divide 2 by 1", function(assert) {⟱});
 32 ▸     QUnit.test("substract 2 from 1", function(assert) {⟱});
 37 ▾     QUnit.module("Text computing", {
 38 ▾         beforeEach: function() {
 39                this.oView1Controller = new View1Controller();
 40                this.oView1Controller.getModel = sinon.stub().withArgs("i18n")
 41 ▾                 .returns(new FakeI18n({
 42                        divide: "divided by",
 43                        add: "plus",
 44                        is: "is"
 45                    }));
 46            },
 47 ▾         afterEach: function() {
 48                this.oView1Controller.destroy();
 49            }
 50        });
 51 ▾     QUnit.test("add 1 and 2", function(assert) {
 52            //Arrange
 53            this.oView1Controller.calculate = sinon.stub().returns(3);
 54            //Act
 55            var result = this.oView1Controller.inWords(1, 2, "+");
 56            //Asert
 57            assert.strictEqual(result, "1 plus 2 is 3", "1+2=3 ; calculated OK");
 58        });
 59 });
```

Figure 9.15 New QUnit Module with Stubs

At line 37, there is a test case for addition. At line 39, we stub and ensure that the `calculate` method always returns 3. Next, we're going to call the code under test, that is, `inWords` function, with parameters 1, 2, and +. In line 43, we assert that the output is as the expected string. Let's run the `unitTests.qunit.html` for running this test.

Figure 9.16 shows the result of the run and the test coverage.

```
20          calculate: function(par1, par2, operation) {
21                  var result;
22                  if (operation === "+") {
23                          result = (par1 * 1) + (par2 * 1);
24                  } else if (operation === "-") {
25                          result = (par1 * 1) - (par2 * 1);
26                  } else if (operation === "*") {
27                          result = (par1 * 1) * (par2 * 1);
28                  } else if (operation === "/") {
29                          result = (par1 * 1) / (par2 * 1);
30                  }
31                  return result;
32          },
33          inWords: function(par1, par2, operation){
34                  var words;
35                  var oResourceBundle = this.getModel("i18n").getResourceBundle();
36                  if (operation === "+") {
37                          words = par1 + " " + oResourceBundle.getText("add") + " " + par2
38                                  + " " + oResourceBundle.getText("is") + " " + this.calculate(par1, par2, operation);
39                  } else if (operation === "-") {
40                          words = par1 + " " + oResourceBundle.getText("substract") + " " + par2 + " "
41                                  + oResourceBundle.getText("is") + " " + this.calculate(par1, par2, operation);
42                  } else if (operation === "*") {
43                          words = par1 +." " + oResourceBundle.getText("into") + " " + par2 + " "
44                                  + oResourceBundle.getText("is") + " " + this.calculate(par1, par2, operation);
45                  } else if (operation === "/") {
46                          words = par1 + " " + oResourceBundle.getText("divide") + " " + par2 + " "
47                                  + oResourceBundle.getText("is") + " " + this.calculate(par1, par2, operation);
48                  }
49                  return words;
50          }
51  });
```

Figure 9.16 Running with Stubs

Integration Testing with OPA5

OPA5 is a testing framework developed specifically as an integration testing tool for SAPUI5. OPA5 tests are part of SAPUI5 based on QUnit, and you don't need to install any external tools to create unit tests. Integration tests are usually tough to develop because of an application's asynchronous nature. For example, you might have to wait for the user to click on a button or wait for the result from an OData service. Like QUnit, OPA5 also follows the Arrange Act Assert pattern or the Given When Then pattern, so that OPA5 tests score high on readability.

Components of OPA5

In this section, let's discuss various OPA5 artifacts that we'll make while creating an integration test.

Figure 9.17 shows a typical project hierarchy with OPA5 tests. *integration* is the top-level folder that contains all the integration tests.

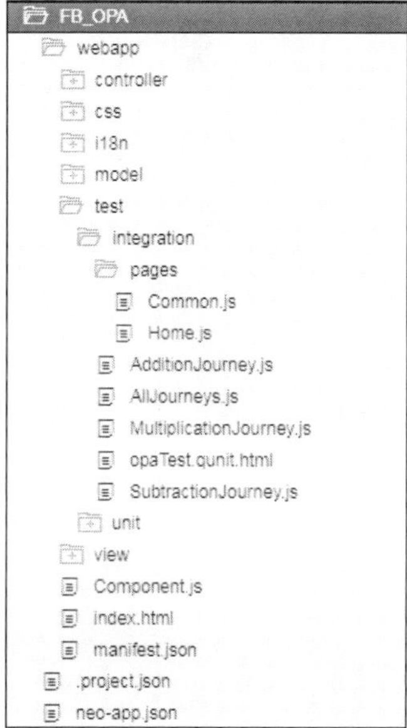

Figure 9.17 Common Hierarchy of an SAPUI5 App with OPA5 Integration Tests

OPA Page

An OPA page is a JavaScript file that is created in the *pages* folder and it contains tests for each page in the application. A page can be roughly pointing to an SAPUI5 view, and page has actions and assertions for the controls within that SAPUI5 view. These actions and assertions are written as functions with a name that is easily readable. SAP Web IDE provides a wizard for creating an OPA page, which can speed up the test-writing process.

To create an OPA page, right-click on the project, and choose **New • OPA Page ❶**, as shown in Figure 9.18. Provide a name for the page ❷, and it's recommended to provide the same as the SAPUI5 view to associate the page with the view. The wizard also proposes to create a container (if not present already) with the name *AllJourneys.js* and include the new page within that container as shown in Figure 9.18.

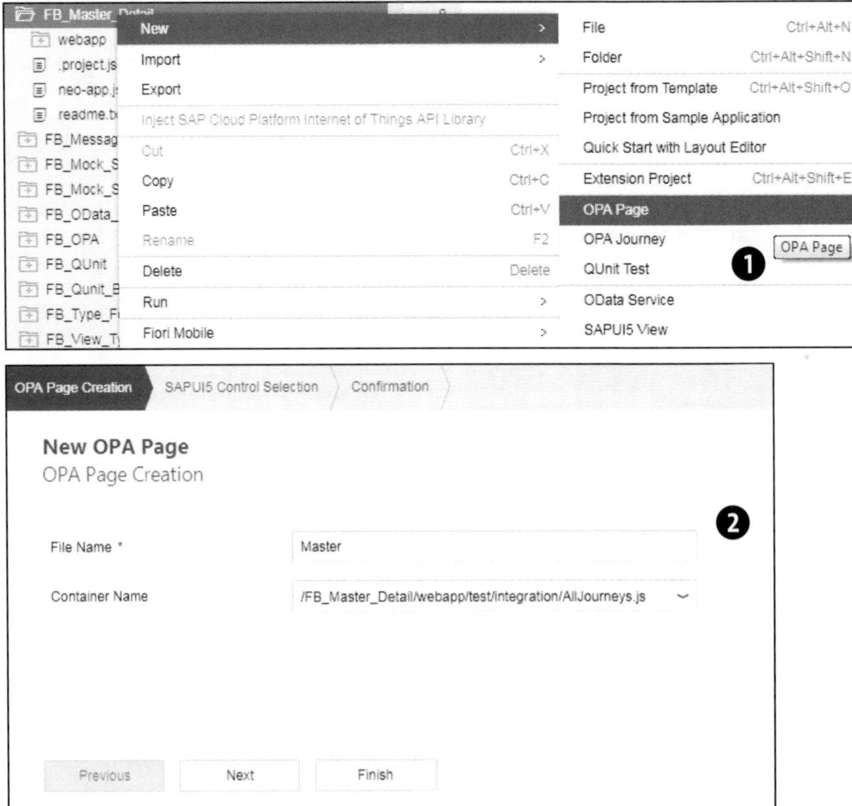

Figure 9.18 Launching the OPA Page Wizard

Upon clicking **Next**, you can choose the SAPUI5 view for which you're creating the view ❸. Choosing a view will populate the controls inside the view as a list, so that you can choose which controls are used to perform actions and assertions. Choose the required controls, and click **Next** (Figure 9.19). This will show a confirmation screen ❹, and when you click **Finish**, *Master.js* is created along with the hierarchy you saw earlier in Figure 9.17.

The generated code is shown in Figure 9.20. This code provides most of the required code based on the involved controls. As you see in the code, there are definitions of several functions with self-explanatory names. These functions will be used while writing OPA5 tests.

Figure 9.19 Selecting View and Controls inside the View for Testing

The *pages* folder will usually have a special purpose utility file called *Common.js*, which will contain definition or arrangement functions required for running tests.

Under the *pages* folder, you can also create a file (not shown in the preceding project hierarchy) for defining commonly reused functions that logically don't belong to any views. Some other example functions that can go into this file are the following:

- Check if the control exists.
- Check if the control has any specific text/label on it.
- Check if the control is visible/editable.

```javascript
sap.ui.define([
    "sap/ui/test/Opa5",
    "sap/ui/test/actions/Press",
    "sap/ui/test/actions/EnterText"
], function(Opa5, Press, EnterText) {
    "use strict";

    Opa5.createPageObjects({
        onMyPageUnderTest: {
            actions: {
                iPressSearchField_searchField: function() {
                    return this.waitFor({
                        id: "searchField",
                        viewName: "Master",
                        actions: new Press(),
                        errorMessage: "Was not able to find the control with the id searchField"
                    });
                },
                iEnterTextSearchField_searchField: function() {
                    return this.waitFor({
                        id: "searchField",
                        viewName: "Master",
                        actions: new EnterText({
                            text: "Text to enter in the control"
                        }),
                        errorMessage: "Was not able to find the control with the id searchField"
                    });
                },
                iPressList_list: function() {
                    return this.waitFor({
                        id: "list",
                        viewName: "Master",
                        actions: new Press(),
                        errorMessage: "Was not able to find the control with the id list"
                    });
                }
            },
            assertions: {
                iDoMyAssertion: function() {
                    return this.waitFor({
                        id: "ControlId",
                        viewName: "Master",
                        success: function() {
                            Opa5.assert.ok(false, "Implement me");
                        },
                        errorMessage: "Was not able to find the control with the id ControlId"
```

Figure 9.20 Generated Code from OPA Page Wizard

OPA Journey

A journey is a group of integration test definitions defined in an order. When these integration tests are run in a sequence, they complete a logical flow within the app. As a journey gets executed, navigation between SAPUI5 views happen by running integration tests, which will further call the functions (actions and assertions) defined in pages and other standard functions.

Journeys are stored directly under the *integration* folder. Just like a page, a journey can also be created from a wizard. To launch this wizard, you can right-click on the project, and choose **New • OPA Journey**. You can provide a name and click **Finish**, which will create a JavaScript file with some template coding for creating an OPA5 integration test.

Along with journeys, there is a special-purpose file called *AllJourneys.js* that includes all journeys and all pages written as part of the integration test. After loading all the required files, it triggers execution on OPA5 tests by calling `QUnit.start();`. Because OPA5 is based on QUnit, this API is the same as that used for triggering unit tests. We'll see more of this file when we write a simple integration test in subsequent sections.

HTML Page Running Tests

As in the QUnit tests, we need an HTML page that can run all the OPA5 tests. This test file, which is usually named *opaTests.qunit.html* (generated by the OPA5 page wizard), includes *AllJourneys.js*; thus, in effect, it includes all pages, journeys and OPA5 tests and triggers the execution of integration tests. It also has QUnit specific `divs`, which will show the test results.

Components of an OPA Test

Let's understand how to write an OPA5 test. As we discussed earlier, integration tests are written inside a journey. Consider a simple test in Listing 9.1 within a master journey.

```
sap.ui.define(["sap/ui/test/opaQunit"],
function (opaTest) {
  "use strict";
  QUnit.module("Master List");
  opaTest("Should see the master list with all entries",
function (Given, When, Then) {
        // Arrangements
        Given.iStartTheApp();

        //Actions
        When.onTheMasterPage.iLookAtTheScreen();

        // Assertions
        Then.onTheMasterPage.iShouldSeeTheList().
```

```
                    and.theListShouldHaveAllEntries().
                    and.theHeaderShouldDisplayAllEntries().
                        and.theListShouldContainFormattedUnitNumbers();
            });
    }
);
```

Listing 9.1 An Example Journey

As shown in Listing 9.1, the only required class here is `sap.ui.test.opaUnit`. Next, we define a module here as we did in a QUnit test using `QUnit.module()`. Next, we use the loaded class `opaTest` and define an integration test. The first parameter is a string describing the test. The second parameter is a function with three parameters: `Given`, `When`, and `Then`. These objects are filled by the OPA5 infrastructure, and they contain the arrangements, actions, and assertions functions defined in the test infrastructure so far.

- Given

  `Given` will call the functions that are arrangements for the test to start. Examples can be setting initial status to controls or starting the app. As you see in the preceding test case, the app is started as part of this step. This is an optional step; a test case need not always have a `Given` part.

- When

  `When` functions are called that simulate the user's actions, which are directly related to the test case. Example simulated actions are entering a search term, pressing ⌊Enter⌋, pressing a button, and so on. OPA5 provide standard actions for pressing a button and entering a text, but you can write custom actions by writing an inline function.

- Then

  `Then`, also called the Assertion step, test case checks if the expected results have happened. These functions will throw errors if expectations aren't met, which will be shown in test results.

Test Functions

Test functions are defined inside pages, as arrangements, actions, and assertions. As you can see in these pages, these functions extend the class `sap.ui.test.Opa5`. In all the pages, as shown earlier in Figure 9.20, API `createPageObjects` is used to define objects and functions inside them. You can also extend `sap.ui.test.Opa5` and add functions to it. This is how arrangement functions are usually defined.

Let's discuss how to define a function. Listing 9.2 shows a sample action. Note the self-explanatory name of the function `iPressSubmitButton`.

```
iPressSubmitButton: function(){
      return this.waitFor({
        id: "submitBtn",
        viewName: "EditView",
        action: new Press(),
        errorMessage: "could not find submit button"
      });
    }
```

Listing 9.2 A Function Defining an Action

waitFor

This API is responsible for the asynchronous nature of OPA5, which is one of its biggest advantages. In Listing 9.2, this will wait for a button with ID `submitBtn` in SAPUI5 view `EditView` to render. Upon rendering, it will trigger a press button on it. If it can't find the button within the predefined time, it will show the error message specified by property `errorMessage`.

matchers

`matchers` are used for selecting a control to perform an action. In Listing 9.2, it was easy to select a control using its ID. However, all controls need not have an explicit ID.

Another scenario is that you need to wait for the rows in a table to be filled so that you can click on one of the items. In such cases, you can use the `matchers` classes with namespace `sap.ui.test.matchers`. You can use multiple attributes of a control to search and select a control. This functionality can be compared with jQuery's $ API.

Listing 9.3 waits for a button with label of Submit to render.

```
iPressSubmitButton: function(){
      return this.waitFor({
        viewName: "EditView",
      matchers: new sap.ui.test.matchers.PropertyStrictEquals({
                            name : "text",
                            value: "Submit"
                  }),
        action: new Press(),
        errorMessage: "could not find submit button"
      });
    }
```

Listing 9.3 Matcher Example

Some example `matchers` classes are available for the following:

- Search based on binding path
- Search on multiple properties
- Search on aggregation content
- Search on parent control

After the controls are selected, they might be used for triggering actions on them or asserting their status.

Actions

In the `When` part of the test case, you need to perform some actions so that you can assert on the results. As we saw in the previous examples, `new Press()` is an OPA5-provided action that will trigger a press event on the selected control. Similarly, `new EnterText({text: "sample text"})` will enter a text "sample text" into the selected control. But if you need any other action, such as selecting an item in a combo box, you can write custom actions by writing inline functions as shown in Listing 9.4.

```
iPressSubmitButton: function(){
      return this.waitFor({
        viewName: "EditView",
        matchers: new sap.ui.test.matchers.PropertyStrictEquals({
                              name : "text",
                              value: "Submit"
               }),
          action: function(oControl){
             ........ code to perform custom action..........
          },
          errorMessage: "could not find submit button"
      });
    }
```

Listing 9.4 Writing Custom Actions

OPA5 Configurations

You can use `sap.ui.test.Opa5.extendConfig` to extend and overwrite default values of OPA5 configurations. Following are the global configurations available for OPA5:

- `arrangements`
  This instantiates a class, which contains arrangement methods for OPA5 tests.

In the below code, we instantiate the common object as shown. It contains the arrangement method `iStartMyApp` as we've seen before.

- `actions/assertions`

  We've already defined actions and arrangements at pages. We did this to easily identify the context as these functions are view specific. If there are any generic actions and assertions, you can create classes for them and instantiate here.

- `viewNamespace`

  This specifies the namespace for every `waitFor` call within the OPA5 tests. Consider a case where we used `viewName` as `View1` in `waitFor` calls. In the configuration, if we provide `viewNamespace` as `fb.OPA.view.`, views with name `fb.OPA.view.View1` will be considered.

- `timeOut`

  This is the time in seconds until which OPA5 will wait during a `waitFor` call. The default value is 15 seconds.

- `pollingInterval`

  This is time in milliseconds for the frequency with which the OPA5 framework looks for the control during a `waitFor` call. The default is 400 milliseconds.

- `debugTimeout`

  This is time in milliseconds. Consider a case where you're debugging a test case. You don't want OPA5 to timeout and show an error message while you're debugging. 0 is the default value, which means infinite timeout.

- `executionDelay`

  This is time in milliseconds. This time will delay the execution of every `waitFor` call by the specified milliseconds. You can use this parameter to slow down the running of integration tests, so that you can view those tests getting executed on screen.

Creating a Simple Integration Test

Now that you understand the concepts of OPA5, let's write a simple integration test for the Calculator application that we used in the section "Creating a Unit Test."

Application

We'll use the calculator application as explained in Figure 9.3 and Figure 9.4. We'll write an integration test for the various operations from the user interface (UI) of the app.

Pages

The first step is to create a page for the view we have. Because we have only one view in the app, let's name the page *Home.js*. You may create this manually or use the OPA5 page wizard to create this file along with the test infrastructure hierarchy.

In this page, we need to define functions that are used for triggering actions on the view's controls or assert the expected results. Actions on this view are as follows:

- Enter the first parameter.
- Choose an operation (+, -, /, *).
- Enter a second parameter.
- Press the calculate button.

Finally, you need to assert that the right result was calculated.

Listing 9.5 lists the code for Home.js. All the preceding actions are implemented here. EnterText() was used to enter parameters, and Press() was used for pressing the calculate button. For selecting an operation, an inline action has been used.

In the assertion part, a matcher is used to wait till the result calculated and expected result was available.

```
sap.ui.define([
    "sap/ui/test/Opa5",
    "sap/ui/test/actions/Press",
    "sap/ui/test/actions/EnterText",
    "sap/ui/test/matchers/PropertyStrictEquals"
], function(Opa5, Press, EnterText, PropertyStrictEquals) {
    "use strict";

    Opa5.createPageObjects({
        onView1: {
        actions: {
        iPressCalculateButton: function() {
            return this.waitFor({
                id: "calculateButton",
                viewName: "View1",
                actions: new Press(),
                errorMessage: "could not find the button"
            });
        },
        iEnterFirstParameter: function(val) {
            return this.waitFor({
                id: "par1",
                viewName: "View1",
                actions: new EnterText({ text: val }),
```

```
                errorMessage: "could not find par1"
            });
        },
        iEnterSecondParameter: function(val) {
            return this.waitFor({
                id: "par2",
                viewName: "View1",
                actions: new EnterText({ text: val }),
                errorMessage: "could not find par 2"
            });
        },
        iEnterOperation: function(operation) {
            return this.waitFor({
                id: "operation",
                viewName: "View1",
                actions: function(oControl){
                            oControl.setSelectedKey(operation);
                },
                errorMessage: "could not find the operation"
            });
        }
        },
        assertions: {
         theResultFieldShouldShowThisValue: function(val){
            return this.waitFor({
                id: "answer",
                viewName: "View1",
                matchers: new PropertyStrictEquals({
                    name: "value",
                    value: val.toString()
                }),
                success: function(oResultControl){
Opa5.assert.strictEqual(oResultControl.getValue(), val.toString(), "Right result
calculated");
                }
            });
        }
        }
    }
    });
});
```

Listing 9.5 Home.js Containing Action Implementations

Let's also create *Common.js*, as shown in Listing 9.6, which contains all the arrangement functions in the application, such as the one to start the application (iStart-MyApp).

```
sap.ui.define([
    "sap/ui/core/routing/HashChanger",
```

```
    "sap/ui/test/Opa5"
], function(HashChanger, Opa5) {

    "use strict";

    var Common = Opa5.extend("test.opa5.pages.Common", {
        *//
Start the app via Component.js for best performance and easier debugging.
        iStartMyApp: function(sFunctionHash) {
            var sNewHash = String(sFunctionHash || "");
            if (jQuery(".sapUiOpaComponent").length !== 0) {
                this.iTeardownMyUIComponent();
            }

            HashChanger.getInstance().replaceHash(sNewHash);
            return this.iStartMyUIComponent({
                componentConfig: {
                    name: "fb.OPA"
                },
                hash: sNewHash
            });
        }
    });
    return Common;
});
```

Listing 9.6 Common.js Containing Arrangements

The `iStartMyApp` function uses OPA5's `iStartMyUIComponent` function to instantiate the component. This function is going to be the same across all SAPUI5 applications. You need to ensure that you mention the right component name while instantiating the component.

Journeys

Now that we have all the required functions, we can write a journey for the addition functionality. We'll write two test cases: one for adding two positive numbers and another for adding one positive and one negative number.

Let's create a new file called *AdditionJourney.js* under the *integration* folder. You may also use the OPA5 journey wizard to create this file with some sample coding.

In the beginning, let's create a QUnit module called "`Addition`". In the `Arrangements` section of the first test, let's start the app using `iStartMyApp()`, which we had created in *Common.js*. In this test case, we'll use functions that we created in the page *Home.js* to enter two parameters, select an operation, and press the calculate button. Next in the `Assertion` section, we'll use another function to assert the expected output number. Similarly, let's create another test case for adding a positive number and a negative number. The code is shown in Listing 9.7.

```
sap.ui.define(["sap/ui/test/opaQunit"], function(opaTest) {
    "use strict";
    QUnit.module("Addition");

    opaTest("Adding two +ve numbers", function(Given, When, Then) {
        // Arrangements
        Given.iStartMyApp();
        //Actions
        //Enter parameters and actions
        When.onView1.iEnterFirstParameter(3);
        When.onView1.iEnterSecondParameter(2);
        When.onView1.iEnterOperation("+");
        When.onView1.iPressCalculateButton();
        //Assertion
        Then.onView1.theResultFieldShouldShowThisValue(5);
    });

    opaTest("Adding +ve & -ve nos", function(Given, When, Then) {
        //Actions
        When.onView1.iEnterFirstParameter(3);
        When.onView1.iEnterSecondParameter(-2);
        When.onView1.iEnterOperation("+");
        When.onView1.iPressCalculateButton();
        //Assertion
        Then.onView1.theResultFieldShouldShowThisValue(1);

    });
});
```

Listing 9.7 Examples of Journeys

Now, let's create *AllJourneys.js* in which we'll include all pages and journeys and trigger running the integration texts. At the first level, you see that all the pages are included in addition to OPA5 classes. Next, we use `Opa5.extendConfig` to define OPA5 configurations. Next, we include all the journeys in our tests. Because we have only one journey so far, we include that here. At last, we trigger the execution of integration tests by calling `QUnit.start();` (Listing 9.8).

```
jQuery.sap.require("sap.ui.qunit.qunit-css");
jQuery.sap.require("sap.ui.thirdparty.qunit");
jQuery.sap.require("sap.ui.qunit.qunit-junit");
QUnit.config.autostart = false;

//Include all pages
sap.ui.require([
        "sap/ui/test/Opa5",
```

```
            "test/opa5/pages/Common",
            "sap/ui/test/opaQunit",
            "test/opa5/pages/Home"
    ], function (Opa5, Common) {
    "use strict";
    Opa5.extendConfig({
            arrangements: new Common(),
            viewNamespace: "fb.OPA.view."
    });

    //Include all journeys
    sap.ui.require([
            "test/opa5/AdditionJourney"
    ], function () {

            //Start running all OPA tests.
            //This is similar to starting QUnit tests as OPA5 is based on QUnit
            QUnit.start();
    });
});
```

Listing 9.8 AllJourneys.js

Now that we have all the integration tests, we need to run and see results. We'll create an HTML page as we did for running the QUnit tests.

Let's create `opaTests.qunit.html` with the content in Listing 9.9.

```
<!DOCTYPE html>
<html>
    <head>
        <title>Opa tests for Manage Products</title>
        <meta http-equiv='X-UA-Compatible' content='IE=edge' />
        <meta charset="UTF-8">

        <script id="sap-ui-bootstrap"
            src="../../../resources/sap-ui-core.js"
            data-sap-ui-resourceroots='{
                "fb.OPA": "../../",
                "test.opa5" : "./"
            }'>
        </script>

        <script>
            jQuery.sap.require("test.opa5.AllJourneys");
        </script>

    </head>
```

```
    <body>
        <div id="content"></div>
        <h1 id="qunit-header">Opa5 test demo</h1>
        <h2 id="qunit-banner"></h2>
        <h2 id="qunit-userAgent"></h2>
        <ol id="qunit-tests"></ol>
    </body>
</html>
```

Listing 9.9 opaTests.qunit.html

Initially, we're loading the SAPUI5 library along with `data-sap-ui-resourceroots`, which details where to find the application files (namespace `fb.OPA`) as well as the test files (namespace `test.opa5`).

Next, we just need to load *AllJourneys.js* because it includes all the files and starts running the OPA5 tests. We also have standard `div`s to show the results of the OPA5 results.

Now that we've created all the required test artifacts, let's run `opaTests.qunit.html` by right-clicking on the file and choosing **Run • Run AS • Web Application**.

Figure 9.21 shows the output of OPA5 results and describes various feature.

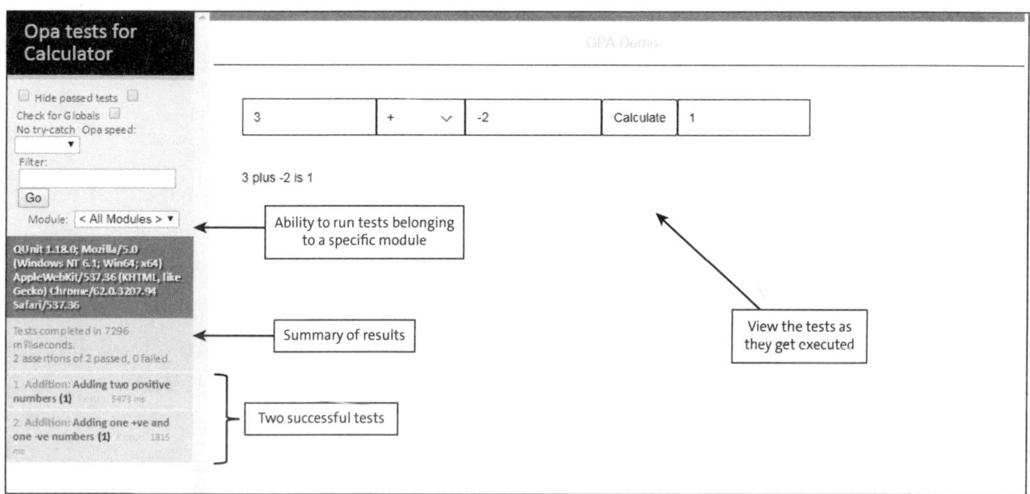

Figure 9.21 OPA5 Test Results

Figure 9.22 shows a summary of the OPA5 infrastructure that we built so far.

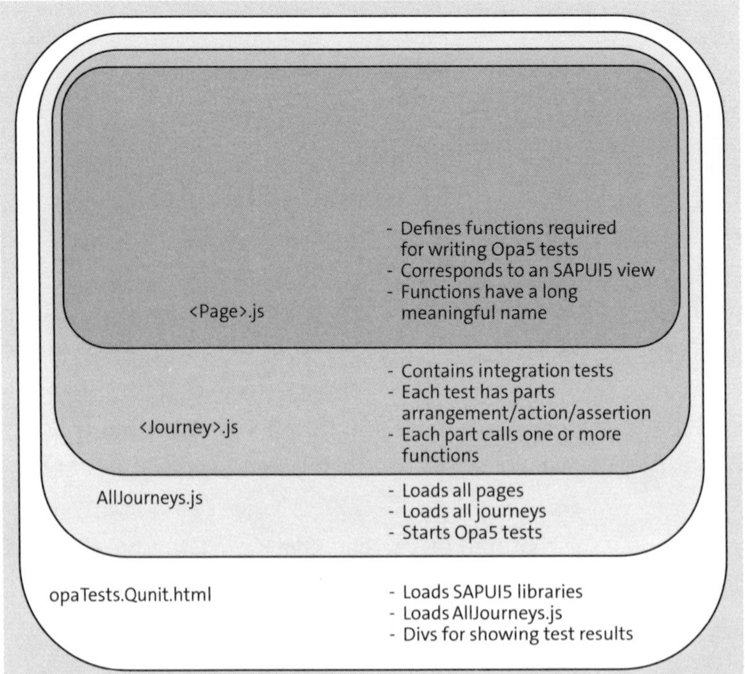

Figure 9.22 OPA5 Test Infrastructure

Using a Mock Server

SAPUI5 provides an important feature called a mock server, which can speed up the SAPUI5 development by removing its dependency on an actual OData service for testing.

Another important advantage of the mock server is to work on UI development, even without a network connection. A mock server serves data from local files but simulates an OData service. It even supports data updates in addition to data fetches. It intercepts the calls to the OData server and provides output from the mock server and static files containing test data.

Configuration Mock Data

Let's consider a simple application getting data from the server and then make changes to make this app use mock data source. Along the way, we'll describe all the required components and concepts around the mock server.

The demo application in Figure 9.23 shows a list of customers from the Northwind service using a simple SAPUI5 view.

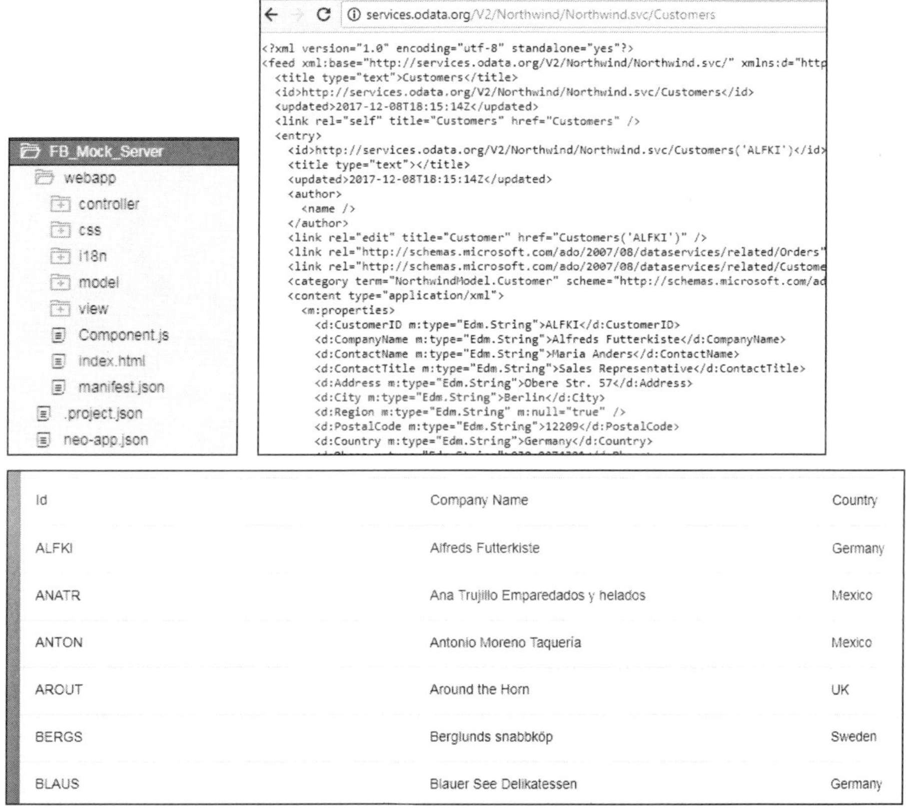

Figure 9.23 Sample Application without Mock Data, and Fetching Data from the Server

Now, let's add mock server configuration to this app.

Step 1: Add the localService Folder

Create a new folder named *localService* under *webapp*. Add the OData service's metadata into this folder. You can get the metadata from the service itself. For example, for the Northwind service, you can get the metadata from the following URL:

http://services.odata.org/V2/Northwind/Northwind.svc/$metadata

After the metadata loads on the server, you can right-click on the metadata and use the **Save As** option to save the metadata as a *metadata.xml* file on your local machine. Next, you can import this file into the recently created *localService* folder. The app's folder structure now looks as shown in Figure 9.24.

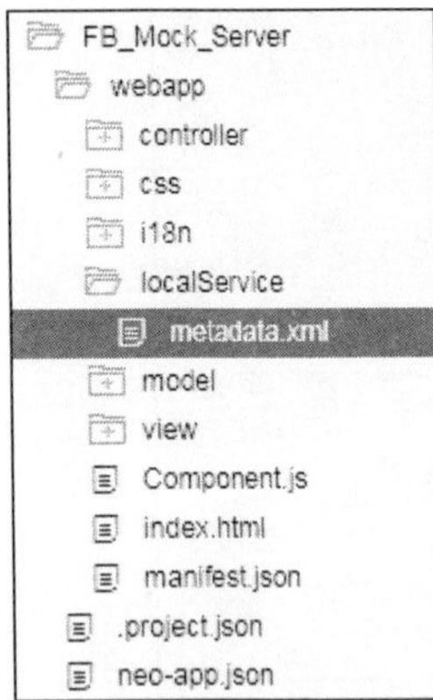

Figure 9.24 New localService folder with the Metadata.xml File of the OData Service

Step 2: Create the Mock Data

After the metadata file is in *localService*, the next step is to create or generate mock data required by the mock service. Right-click on the *metadata.xml* file, and select **Edit Mock Data**.

A popup window opens, listing all the entities of the service on the left-hand side (by scanning the *metadata.xml* file) and corresponding data on the right-hand side as shown in Figure 9.25. You can create new rows of data by clicking on **Add Row**, edit existing data by directly clicking on the table's cell, or delete a row by selecting it and clicking on **Delete Row**. It can become tedious to create mock data for every entity in the service. In such cases, you can choose to generate random data by clicking on **Generate Random Data**. You might use it for value helps, for example, or you can generate random data and then edit important properties to make it more realistic. Based on the data type (e.g., integer, string, date) of each property inside the entity, random data will be generated. Figure 9.25 shows the manually created mock data as well as the generated random data.

Edit Mock Data

Entity Sets | Mock Data

Add Row   Delete Row   Generate Random Data

	CustomerID (String)	CompanyName (String)	ContactName (String)	ContactTitle (String)	Address (String)
	ALFKI	Alfreds Futterkiste	Maria Anders	Sales Representative	Obere Str. 57
	ANATR	Ana Trujillo Emparedados y l	Ana Trujillo	Owner	Avda. de la Constitución
	ANTON	Antonio Moreno Taquería	Antonio Moreno	Owner	Mataderos 2312
	AROUT	Around the Horn	Thomas Hardy	Sales Representative	120 Hanover Sq.

Entity Sets: Categories, CustomerDemogra.., Customers, Employees, Order_Details, Orders, Products, Regions, Shippers, Suppliers, Territories

Manually entered mock data

Edit Mock Data

Entity Sets | Mock Data

Add Row   Delete Row   Generate Random Data

	EmployeeID (Int32)	LastName (String)	FirstName (String)	Title (String)	TitleOfCourtesy (String)
	2267	LastName 1	FirstName 1	Title 1	TitleOfCourtesy 1
	9116	LastName 2	FirstName 2	Title 2	TitleOfCourtesy 2
	2553	LastName 3	FirstName 3	Title 3	TitleOfCourtesy 3
	2001	LastName 4	FirstName 4	Title 4	TitleOfCourtesy 4
	5521	LastName 5	FirstName 5	Title 5	TitleOfCourtesy 5
	2373	LastName 6	FirstName 6	Title 6	TitleOfCourtesy 6
	2730	LastName 7	FirstName 7	Title 7	TitleOfCourtesy 7
	741	LastName 8	FirstName 8	Title 8	TitleOfCourtesy 8
	7877	LastName 9	FirstName 9	Ti	
	926	LastName 10	FirstName 10	Ti	

Entity Sets: Categories, CustomerDemogra.., Customers, Employees, Order_Details, Orders, Products, Regions, Shippers, Suppliers, Territories

Generated random data

Figure 9.25 Creating Mock Data for the Service

Note

By creating the metadata of the OData service as the first step of development, UI development can be decoupled from the dependency of the live OData service.

Step 3: Create mockServer.js

We need to create a mock server now. SAPUI5 provides a class `sap.ui.core.util.Mock-Server`, which has various APIs to set up, configure, and simulate the OData service. The process of instantiating the mock server and configuring it is done in a separate JavaScript file called *mockServer.js*. Create a new folder called *test* under *webapp*. Inside the *test* folder, create a file named *mockServer.js*.

Listing 9.10 shows the code inside *mockServer.js*.

```javascript
sap.ui.define([
  "sap/ui/core/util/MockServer"
], function (MockServer) {
  "use strict";
  return {
    init: function () {
      // create
      var oMockServer = new MockServer({
          rootUri: "/V2/Northwind/Northwind.svc/"
      });
      // configure
      MockServer.config({
          autoRespond: true
      });
      // simulate
      var sPath = jQuery.sap.getModulePath("FB_Mock_Server.localService");
      oMockServer.simulate(sPath + "/metadata.xml", sPath + "/mockdata");
      // start
      oMockServer.start();
      }
    };
});
```

Listing 9.10 mockServer.js

As you can see in , in the `init` method of this server file, the first step is to initialize the mock server by specifying the `rootUri`. It indicates to the mock server that any call starting with this URI is an OData call, so intercept it and instead supply data from the mock data JSON files.

In the next step, we call the configuration API, where we can pass mock server configurations as an object. For now, we just send `autoRespond: true` to direct the mock server to respond to requests automatically.

In the next step, we call the `simulate` API of the mock server to supply it the locations of service metadata file, mock JSON files, and other settings. Mock data for each entity should be in a separate JSON file. If the mock data's base URL of the simulate API isn't provided, then the mock server will generate mock data using the metadata file.

Finally, we call the `start` API to start the mock server.

Step 4: Set Up an HTML File for Running with Mock Data

Next, we should set up a new HTML page that will be used exclusively for running the application with mock data. The new HTML page will be similar to *index.html* of the application but has additional code for initiating the mock data server that we wrote in the previous step.

Let's create a new file under the *test* folder called *mockServerIndex.html*. To start with, you can copy the code from the *index.html* file. The final HTML file looks like that shown in Figure 9.26.

```html
1   <!DOCTYPE HTML>
2   <html>
3       <head>
4           <meta http-equiv="X-UA-Compatible" content="IE=edge" />
5           <meta charset="UTF-8">
6           <title>Running with Mock Data</title>
7
8           <script id="sap-ui-bootstrap"
9               src="../../resources/sap-ui-core.js"
10              data-sap-ui-libs="sap.m"
11              data-sap-ui-theme="sap_bluecrystal"
12              data-sap-ui-compatVersion="edge"
13              data-sap-ui-resourceroots='{"FB_Mock_Server": "../"}'>
14          </script>
15          <link rel="stylesheet" type="text/css" href="css/style.css">
16
17          <script>
18              sap.ui.getCore().attachInit(function() {
19                  sap.ui.require(["FB_Mock_Server/test/mockserver",
20                      "sap/m/Shell",
21                      "sap/ui/core/ComponentContainer"],
22                      function(mockserver, Shell, ComponentContainer){
23                          //Initialize mock data server as the first step
24                          mockserver.init();
25
26                          new Shell({
27                          app: new ComponentContainer({
28                              height : "100%",
29                              name : "FB_Mock_Server"
30                          })
31                      }).placeAt("content");
32                  });
33              });
34          </script>
35      </head>
36      <body class="sapUiBody" id="content">
37      </body>
38  </html>
39
40
```

Figure 9.26 Index File to Run the App with Mock Data

The only difference we see here when compared with a regular *index.html* of an SAP Fiori app is this statement:

```
mockserver.init();
```

`mockserver` here is the object that we created earlier in Step 3. We call its `init` method to call all the initialization, configurations, and starting of the mock server.

Step 5: Run mockIndex.html

We've completed the required configurations now. To run the application with mock data, right-click on **mockServerIndex.html**, and then choose **Run • Run As • Web Application**. This will open the application with mock data as shown in Figure 9.27.

Edit Mock Data					
Entity Sets	**Mock Data**				
	Add Row Delete Row				Generate Random Data
Categories	☐ CustomerID (String)	CompanyName (String)	ContactName (String)	ContactTitle (String)	Address (Strin
CustomerDemog...	☐ ABCD	Alfreds Futterkiste	Maria Anders	Sales Representative	Obere Str. 57
Customers	☐ PQRS	Ana Trujillo Emparedados y l	Ana Trujillo	Owner	Avda. de la Cc
Employees	☐ KLMN	Antonio Moreno Taquería	Antonio Moreno	Owner	Mataderos 23
Order_Details	☐ UIOP	Around the Horn	Thomas Hardy	Sales Representative	120 Hanover S
Orders					

Running with Mock Data		
Id	Company Name	Country
ABCD	Alfreds Futterkiste	Germany
PQRS	Ana Trujillo Emparedados y helados	Mexico
KLMN	Antonio Moreno Taquería	Mexico
UIOP	Around the Horn	UK

Figure 9.27 App Showing Mock Data

Tip

If the application is loaded with the server data instead of mock data, check the console (F12 – Developer Tools) for the following tips:

- The wrong `rootUri` is used while initializing the `MockServer`.
- In the `simulate` API on `MockServer`, metadata URL or the mock data-based URL are incorrect.

Mock Server Event Handlers

Mock server provides events both after and before a request gets executed, so that you can manipulate the request and corresponding response data.

attachAfter

The `attachAfter` event fires after the request processing of the mock server. This can be useful if you want to edit the fetched mock data before it gets delivered to the OData model.

`attachAfter(event, fnCallback, sEntitySet)` event is the name of the HTTP method involved, for example, `GET`, `POST`, `PUT`, and so on.

`fnCallback` is the handler function that gets called after the request is processed. This function has parameters such as the request parameters, keys of requested records, list of records about to be returned, and so on.

`sEntitySet` is a string containing the name of the entity set. The `fnCallback` will be called only if the request is for this particular entity set. A sample use case might be to get rid of fetched mock data records based on a property value.

attachBefore

As the name indicates, this event gets fired before the processing of the request by the mock server:

`attachBefore(event, fnCallback, sEntitySet)` event is the name of the HTTP method involved, for example, `GET`, `POST`, `PUT`, and so on.

`fnCallback` is the handler function that gets called before the request is processed. This function has parameters such as the request parameters, keys of requested records, and so on.

`sEntitySet` is a string containing the name of the entity set. The `fnCallback` will be called only if the request is for this entity set. A sample use case might be to add the OData parameters such as `$top` to limit the maximum number of records fetched.

Handling Function Imports

Although mock servers support CRUD requests automatically, service operations or function imports aren't supported out of the box. You need to extend your mock server to write explicit code to support each function import. This is basically because, unlike CRUD operations, the functionality of a function import can't be implied by the mock server.

Here are the steps involved in simulating a function import using a mock server. These will be performed in the `init` method of the *mockServer.js*:

1. Get all the internal requests of the mock server as follows to give an array of request:

   ```
   aRequests = oMockServer.getRequests();
   ```

2. Append this array with a new request for the specific function import. Let the name of the function import be `CalculateCost`. The request object is a JSON object with three parameters. `method` and `path` ensure that the right function import is intercepted. The `response` parameter defines a function that calculates or fakes the output of a function import and sets the response object to be returned as the output of the function import. This function receives two parameters. An `xhr` parameter (`oXhr` in Listing 9.11) is used to set the response. `sOperationParams` contains the function import's parameters.

   ```
   aRequests.push({
           method: "GET",
       //Ensure that the call is for this specific Function import
           path: new RegExp("CalculateCost(.*)"),
           response: function(oXhr, parmeter1, sOperationParams) {
             //Calculate or Simulate the response object here
             ................ oResponse Calculation Code............
           //Set the response as the function import's response
       oXhr.respondJSON(200, {}, JSON.stringify(oResponse.data));
             return true;
           }
   });
   ```

Listing 9.11 Testing Function Imports

Tip

You can issue a synchronous call using `jQuery.sap.sjax` to the OData service within the response function to fetch data from other entities. This call will be intercepted by the mock server, and mock data will be returned.

3. Update the new set of requests back to the mock server:

   ```
   oMockServer.setRequests(aRequests);
   ```

   This will ensure that the mock server intercepts this function import going forward.

Important Terminology

This chapter covered the following terminology:

- **QUnit**

  QUnit is a popular JavaScript-based unit testing framework and is part of SAPUI5. It's an open source, easy-to-use framework that can be used to test any generic JavaScript code.

- **Sinon.js**

  This is an open-source tool to create stubs and mocks when you write a unit test. It's primarily used to fake external dependencies such as AJAX calls, external functions, timers, and so on.

- **OPA5**

  OPA5 is a QUnit-based JavaScript library that was developed to create integration tests for SAPUI5 projects. It can simulate user interactions, navigations, and bindings.

- **Mock server**

  Mock server is one of the important features of SAPUI5 that allows you to mock a real server serving data. You can have your own data in JSON files and get it served to SAPUI5 projects. This can speed up the SAPUI5 development by removing the dependency on a real server and allowing for testing the app.

 ## Practice Questions

These practice questions will help you evaluate your understanding of the topics covered in this chapter. The questions shown are similar in nature to those found on the certification examination. Although none of these questions will be found on the exam itself, they will allow you to review your knowledge of the subject. Select the correct answers, and then check the completeness of your answers in the "Practice Question Answers and Explanations" section. Remember, on the exam, you must select all correct answers and only correct answers to receive credit for the question.

1. Which of the following is *not* true about unit tests?

    ☐   A. Easy to write

    ☐   B. Helps to identify the location of bugs

    ☐   C. Tests the interaction of multiple code components

    ☐   D. Developer writes it

2. While testing, where should the least amount of efforts be invested?

    ☐   A. Unit testing

    ☐   B. Integration testing

    ☐   C. Manual testing

3. When will the following assertion pass?

    ```
    assert.ok( status, "Success" );
    ```

    ☐   A. When variable status has value integer `0`

    ☐   B. Only when the value in variable status is equal to string "`Success`"

    ☐   C. When status evaluates to Boolean `true`

    ☐   D. Only when the variable status has a value string '`OK`'

4. Which of the following is true about an OPA page? (2 correct answers)

    ☐   A. It contains function definitions that are used in integration tests.

    ☐   B. It contains integration tests for a specific SAPUI5 view.

    ☐   C. It's directly added to the HTML page running the integration tests.

    ☐   D. It's usually created directly under the *integration* folder.

5. Which OPA5 configuration parameter can be used to slow down the execution
    of integration tests for comfortable viewing?

    ☐   A. `delay`

    ☐   B. `timeOut`

    ☐   C. `executionDelay`

    ☐   D. `slow`

Practice Answers and Explanations

These practice questions will help you evaluate your understanding of the topics covered in this chapter. The questions shown are similar in nature to those found on the certification examination. Although none of these questions will be found on the exam itself, they will allow you to review your knowledge of the subject. Select the correct answers, and then check the completeness of your answers in the "Practice Question Answers and Explanations" section. Remember, on the exam, you must select all correct answers and only correct answers to receive credit for the question.

1. Correct answer: **C**

   Unit tests don't test the interaction between code components. Rather, they test a single component of code for logic and correctness with all the dependencies stubbed.

2. Correct answer: **C**

   The least amount of effort should be spent on manual testing because it's error prone and least effective. The most effort should be spent on unit testing, which will improve the robustness of the application.

3. Correct answer: **C**

   `assert.ok(status, "Success")` will pass only when the variable status evaluates to `true`. The assertion will be successful even if the variable status has the value "`Success`"; however, any other nonempty string will also pass the assertion.

4. Correct answers: **A, B**

   An OPA page corresponds to an SAPUI5 view and contains definitions of functions used in integration tests.

5. Correct answer: **C**

   `executionDelay` can be used to slow down the execution of each integration test. It adds this delay before the execution of the next test so that you can view the result of each test.

Take Away

In this chapter, you've learned the importance of writing unit and integration tests to your application. We've discussed how it can make your code robust and reduce maintenance costs.

We discussed QUnit and its principles, as well as how to write and execute a unit test. You also learned about OPA5 and how it helps to write easy integration tests. We explored the components of an OPA5 test by writing a simple integration test.

Summary

Unit and integration tests, which are created by developers using QUnit and OPA5, respectively, are great ways to improve the robustness of your SAPUI5 application. They are part of the SAPUI5 library as well, thus making it easy to use those tools. Although they require additional efforts to develop them, they provide huge value and savings in maintenance costs.

The Author

 **Krishna Kishor Kammaje** is a consultant working at Convergent Information Systems, an SAP Fiori consulting company. He was recognized as an SAP Community top contributor for SAP Fiori and SAP Gateway for a number of years, and was named an SAP mentor in March 2017.

Index

A

D

Data binding 146, 231, 261
   by model type 147
   modes 146, 147
   types 149, 151
Data model formatting
   custom 160
   formatter functions 161
   in controller 161
Data provider class 236
Data query 89
Data visualization 171
   responsive design 172
   responsive layouts 173
   responsive tables 175
Database 82
Decomposition 43, 44, 71
Deep linking 231, 273
Deployment 333
Descriptor 178
Design Services 32
Design stencils
   Axure RP 54
   Microsoft PowerPoint 54
Design Thinking 32, 35, 39, 69, 73
   exercises 40
   tasks 40, 42
   workshops 40
Development environment
   Cloud Foundry 188
   Neo 188
Dialogs 279
Document Object Model (DOM) 139
DPC 237–239, 241
Draft document 68
Draft documents 71
   handling 68
Draft handling 90

E

Element binding 156
Embedded deployment 118
Enterprise Procurement Model (EPM) 210
Entity 233
ES5 210

Event handler 268, 277
Event handlers 139
Expression binding 162
Extensibility 221
Extensibility in SAPUI5 .... 287, 289
Extensibility pane 296
   controller hooks 314
   extension points 301
   hiding controls 297
   view replacement 309
Extensibility wizard 328
   controller replacement 317
   extension points 305, 307
Extension points 299, 327, 328
   complex implementation 304
   creating 305
   default content 300
   examples 300
   extensibility pane 301, 302
   extensibility wizard 305
   extension project 305
   finding 299
   generated default code 303
   implementation results 304
   implementing 300
   People Profile app 301
Extension projects 327
   component configuration 294
   component.js file 294
   creating 291
   deploying 326
   manifest.json file 294
   SAP Cloud Platform 292
   SAP Gateway system 292
   SAP Web IDE 293
Extension types 290
External access point 119

F

Facet filter
   content 264
   control 231
   controller coding 268
   events 267
   light 263
   SAPUI5 266

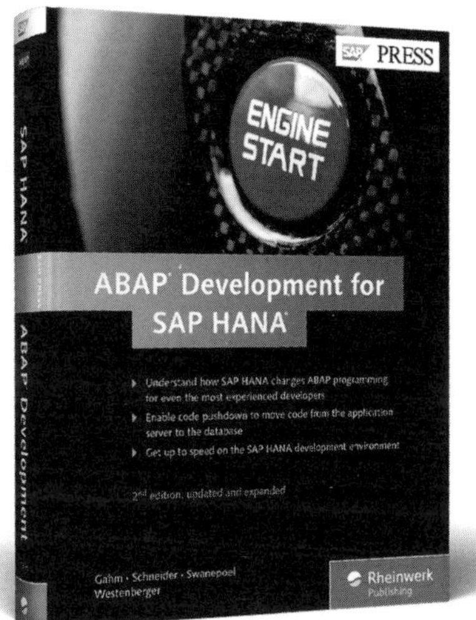

- Understand how SAP HANA changes ABAP programming for even the most experienced developers

- Enable code pushdown to move code from the application server to the database

- Get up to speed on the SAP HANA development environment

Gahm, Schneider, Swanepoel, Westenberger

ABAP Development for SAP HANA

See how SAP HANA has changed ABAP, and learn how to bring your skills up to par. This comprehensive guide uses detailed programming examples to help you design simple and advanced applications with ABAP. Learn to enable code pushdown, use Open SQL enhancements and CDS views, integrate native SAP HANA objects, and more. You'll be programming for SAP HANA in no time!

641 pages, 2nd edition, pub. 04/2016
E-Book: $69.99 | **Print:** $79.95 | **Bundle:** $89.99

www.sap-press.com/3973

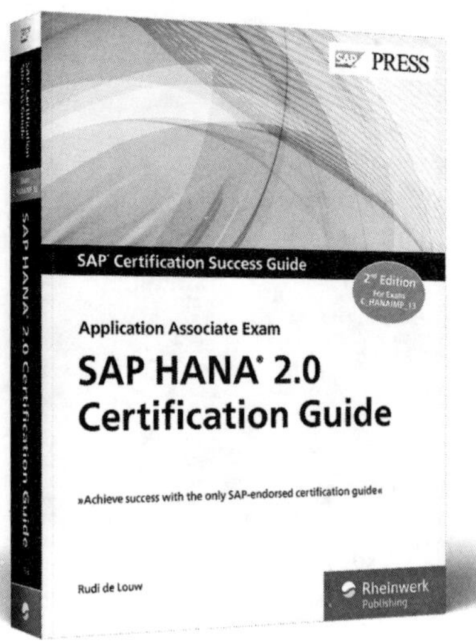

- Learn about the SAP HANA certification test structure and how to prepare
- Review the key topics covered in each portion of the exam
- Test your knowledge with practice questions and answers

Rudi de Louw

SAP HANA 2.0 Certification Guide

Application Associate Exam

Need to get certified in SAP HANA 2.0? With this guide, you'll get everything you need to pass the SAP Certified Application Associate test for SAP HANA (C_HANAIMP_13)! Understand the structure of the exam and review the key concepts you'll be tested on, from SAP HANA XSA to CDS views. Quiz yourself with hundreds of practice questions and detailed answers so you can walk in feeling confident on exam day!

540 pages, 2nd edition, pub. 12/2017
E-Book: $69.99 | **Print:** $79.95 | **Bundle:** $89.99

www.sap-press.com/4567